Terrestrial Ecosystem Ecology

Human activities impact the environment and modify the cycles of important elements such as carbon and nitrogen from local to global scales. In order to maintain long-term and sustainable use of the world's natural resources it is important that we understand how and why ecosystems respond to such changes.

This book explains the structure and functioning of terrestrial ecosystems, using examples ranging from the arctic to the tropics to demonstrate how they vary under different conditions. This knowledge is developed into a set of principles that can be used as starting points for analysing questions about ecosystem behaviour. Ecosystem dynamics are also considered, illustrating how ecosystems develop and change over a range of temporal and spatial scales, and how they react to perturbations, whether natural or man-made. Throughout the book, descriptive studies are merged with simple mathematical models to reinforce the concepts discussed and aid the development of predictive tools.

GÖRAN I. ÅGREN is Professor of Systems Ecology at the Swedish University of Agricultural Sciences and has been teaching ecosystem ecology and the use of mathematical models in ecology for more than 30 years. His research focuses on carbon and nitrogen cycles in terrestrial ecosystems and how these processes can be most efficiently expressed in mathematical terms.

FOLKE O. ANDERSSON is Emeritus Professor of Ecosystem Ecology at the Swedish University of Agricultural Sciences. He has been active in ecosystem research and teaching since the 1960s. His research includes areas such as descriptive plant ecology and applied issues such as the effects of air pollution and management on forests, including field experiments with acidification, fertilisation and liming.

Terrestrial Ecosystem Ecology

Principles and Applications

Göran I. Ågren

Swedish University of Agricultural Sciences

Folke O. Andersson

Swedish University of Agricultural Sciences

CAMBRIDGE
UNIVERSITY PRESS

CAMBRIDGE UNIVERSITY PRESS
Cambridge, New York, Melbourne, Madrid, Cape Town,
Singapore, São Paulo, Delhi, Tokyo, Mexico City

Cambridge University Press
The Edinburgh Building, Cambridge CB2 8RU, UK

Published in the United States of America by Cambridge University Press, New York

www.cambridge.org
Information on this title: www.cambridge.org/9781107011076

First published 2012

Printed in the United Kingdom at the University Press, Cambridge

A catalogue record for this publication is available from the British Library

Library of Congress Cataloging-in-Publication Data
Ågren, Göran I.
  Terrestrial ecosystem ecology : principles and applications / Göran I. Ågren,
Folke O. Andersson.
    p.   cm.
  ISBN 978-1-107-01107-6 (Hardback) – ISBN 978-1-107-64825-8 (Paperback)
1. Ecology.   2. Climatic changes–Environmental aspects.   3. Global
environmental change.   4. Biological systems.   5. Ecophysiology.
I. Andersson, Folke, 1933–   II. Title.
  QH541.A326 2011
  577–dc23

                                                                    2011019454

ISBN 978-1-107-01107-6 Hardback
ISBN 978-1-107-64825-8 Paperback

"We must not forget that when radium was discovered no one knew that it would prove useful in hospitals. The work was one of pure science. And this is a proof that scientific work must not be considered from the point of view of the direct usefulness of it. It must be done for itself, for the beauty of science, and then there is always the chance that a scientific discovery may become like the radium a benefit for humanity."

Marie Curie (1867–1934),
Lecture at Vassar College,
May 14, 1921

Contents

Colour plate section is found between pp. 174 and 175.

Boxes

Preface

There are three major reasons behind this textbook *Terrestrial Ecosystem Ecology* – a fast-growing science. The first one is that the discipline provides us with basic facts on how Nature functions. New knowledge has accumulated. A wealth of information and data on ecosystems and their processes are now available. Development in measuring techniques, computers and other technologies are major reasons behind these achievements. This allows us today to better formulate principles and hypotheses for ecosystems and their function. The intention with our book is to identify and strengthen the base of ecosystem ecology in order to provide a platform on which to build future, solid scientific development. Although there are obvious links between aquatic and terrestrial environments we have chosen to focus on terrestrial ecosystems.

A second reason is that Man's activities lead to a number of direct and indirect effects on ecosystems, which are a threat to long-term and sustainable use of the natural resources for our survival. We need to understand how Nature and ecosystems function in order to interpret the effects of various degrees of utilisation. We need also broad, basic knowledge in order to give advice for utilisation, management and mitigation of detrimental effects. It is also important to have a holistic view and understand how atmosphere, water, biota and soils interact under the influence of Man.

The third reason is an ambition to bring together classical, often descriptive, knowledge on ecosystems with mathematically based, mechanistic thinking. This provides us with opportunities for increased understanding, development of predictive tools and derivations of principles.

We address the book to both undergraduate and graduate students. Basic knowledge of plants, animals and soils is assumed. Elementary textbooks in botany, zoology, earth sciences and mathematics, as well as ecology, provide this.

The book also exemplifies methods of how to study terrestrial ecosystems and their processes, although the emphasis is on concepts rather than exhaustively covering all methodologies. Another ambition is that the examples and results used to illustrate the different methods and processes will mainly be chosen from Nordic and European investigations. Examples are also taken from outside Europe. Many of the examples represent objects which the authors directly or indirectly have been involved with. In this way the book will hopefully be a complement to existing trans-Atlantic textbooks.

This textbook is organised in four sections and has 15 chapters, together with a prologue and an epilogue (Figure Pre.1). The ecological and ecosystem terminology follows conventional sources (e.g. Odum & Barrett 2005). The different sections, as well as the chapters, are linked.

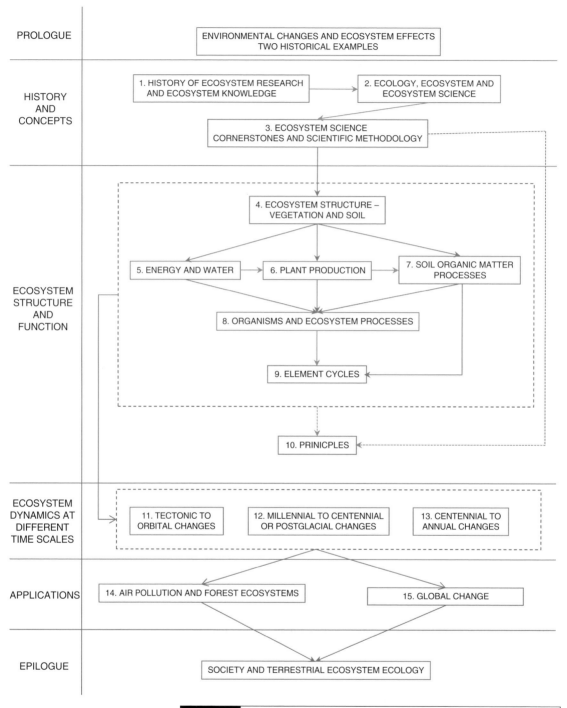

Figure Pre.1 The structure of the textbook *Terrestrial Ecosystem Ecology*. The different sections and chapters are connected by arrows indicating the linking of the different chapters and the flow of the text. Feedbacks between chapters/processes exist, but these are dealt with in the individual chapters.

The Prologue describes, with two examples, the nature of ecosystem ecology. The first section gives history and concepts (Chapters 1 and 2) as a background to present-day ecosystem ecology (Chapter 3). In the latter chapter some fundamental cornerstones based on general biological and chemical knowledge are presented, which are meant to serve as a scientific base or backbone for the further elaboration of insights into how ecosystem processes and ecosystems operate, leading to principles.

The second section is on ecosystem structure and function and contains seven chapters. Chapter 4 describes ecosystem structure in terms of vegetation and soils as dominating features of terrestrial ecosystems essential for the processes, which will be dealt with in more detail. Chapters 5–6 discuss energy and water, and plant production. Chapter 7 is about soil organic matter processes and Chapter 8 deals with organisms and ecosystem processes. Mineral cycling, Chapter 9, represents a major functional characteristic of terrestrial ecosystems. The section ends with a chapter on principles derived from findings in the previous chapters (Chapter 10). We see here also a link to the introductory fundamental cornerstones in Chapter 3.

The third section is devoted to ecosystem dynamics and deals with changes at different temporal and spatial scales, from tectonic to millennial, centennial and annual changes (Chapters 11–13). The dynamics are often seen as functional characteristics. Interesting questions are how ecosystems react to natural as well as man-made perturbations. These are dealt with in the fourth, applied section: air pollution (Chapter 14) and climate change (Chapter 15). The final part of the book is an epilogue dealing with the relation between society and ecosystem ecology.

The book is strongly influenced by the achievements in recent years in our closest research environment. We will name this the SWECON inheritance! SWECON – the 'Swedish Coniferous Forest Project' – was an integrated ecosystem project operating from 1972–1981 on the initiative of the Swedish Natural Science Research Council. This project led to the establishment of the discipline 'terrestrial ecosystem ecology' at the Swedish University of Agricultural Sciences in 1979. We depend, to a great extent, on the research efforts and knowledge of our predecessors!

In the process of writing this textbook contacts have been made with several known and unknown colleges for advice, clarification and support. We are grateful for the positive responses and assistance. We would like to acknowledge the following people: Ghasem Alavi, Uppsala, SE; Todd Anderson, Groningen, NL; Johan Bergholm, Uppsala, SE; Åsa Böker, Kronau, DE; Lage Bringmark, Uppsala, SE; Michael Bredemayer, Göttingen, DE; Jiquan Chen, Toledo, Ohio, US; Torben Christensen, Lund, SE; Kevin deLaplante, Ames, Iowa, US; Ted Farrell, Dublin, IR; Peringe Grennfelt, Gothenburg, SE; Heljä-Sisko Helmisaari, Vantaa, FI; Rafael Herrera, Valencia, ES; Hans Hultberg, Gothenburg, SE; Håkan Hytteborn, Trondheim, NO; Per-Erik Jansson, Stockholm; SE, Björn Lindahl, Uppsala, SE; Sune Linder, Alnarp, SE;

Anders Lindroth, Lund, SE; Carl Jordan, Athens, Georgia, US; Nils Malmer, Lund, SE; Ernesto Medina, Caracas, VE; Bengt Nihlgård, Lund, SE; Per Nilsson, Umeå, SE; Oskar Olsson, Uppsala, SE; Hans Persson, Uppsala, SE; Mats Sonesson, Lund, SE; Richard H. Waring, Corvallis, Oregon, US; Sofia Wikman, Uppsala, SE. Special thanks goes to John Pastor, Duluth, Minnesota, US and Tryggve Persson, Uppsala, SE for reading and commenting on the manuscript, or parts thereof, and giving valuable suggestions. We greatly appreciate the copy-editing, including linguistic as well as technical improvements, made by Jo Tyszka, Hartlepool, UK.

Emma Ågren (cover photo), Uppsala, SE

Prologue

Environmental changes and ecosystem effects: two historical examples

The prologue provides an introduction to terrestrial ecosystem ecology. Two historical examples describe the nature and scope of the discipline. These examples also show the close link between ecosystem ecology and applications to environmental problems.

Acid rain

At the UN conference on the 'Human Environment' in 1972, in Stockholm, a Swedish case study on transport of air pollutants over national boundaries was presented. Its political and scientific message led to immediate consequences for legislation and research (Anonymous 1972, 1982). The large-scale effects of combustion of fossil fuels containing sulfur and nitrogen, as well as roasting of sulfide ore containing copper and other metals, were now acknowledged as harmful to organisms and ecosystems. The small-scale effects of mining operations have, on the other hand, been well known for hundreds of years. Linnaeus' (1734) experience from the copper mine in Falun, in the province of Dalecarlia, central Sweden (Box Pro.1), is one example. Here the production of copper from ore with high levels of sulfur led to emissions of sulfur dioxide that had direct toxic effects on trees and other vegetation. The soils in the surroundings were acidified and heavy metals accumulated, with consequences for soil biological processes. Nearby lakes were also acidified (Ek *et al.* 2001).

The understanding of the causes of 'acid rain' rests upon a long history of observations and research (Cowling 1980). As early as during the seventeenth century it was apparent that emissions from industry were harmful to plants and humans. The English chemist *Robert Angus Smith* noted in 1852 that the rain became more acid the closer one came to the city of Manchester. Later he realised that pollutants could travel as great a distance as between England and France. In 1872 he published the foundation of chemical meteorology in his book *Air and Rain*, where the term 'acid rain' was used for the first time (Smith 1872).

The Swedish case study mentioned introduced the 'modern issue of acid rain' (Box Pro. 2). A regional and temporal pattern over Europe

Acid rain is an old environmental problem

Box Pro.1 | Linnaeus in Falun

'From this mine a steady smoke came . . . learning us to understand, that the description of the entire hell given by theologians, to impress the mind of the wise Man, is taken from this and similar mines. Never has any Poet been able to describe Styx, Regnum subterraneum and Plutonis, nor any theologus hell as gruesome as we can see it here. For outside a poisonous, acrid sulphurous smoke rises and poisons the air far and wide so that one cannot without pain go there. The smoke corrodes the Earth so that no plants can grow around.'

Figure Pro.1 Area devastated by sulfur dioxide from roasting of ore is seen in the upper part of the photo. In the seventeenth century this smoke encapsulated the town of Falun. Photo from 1905. With kind permission from the Archive of the Dalecarlia Museum, Falun, Sweden.

of increasing acidity and decreasing pH of rain, which correlated with the combustion of sulfur-containing coal and oil, was observed. From this case study a number of predictions about possible future effects on organisms and ecosystems were made. Besides direct effects on leaves and photosynthesis of plants, a chain of indirect effects were hypothesised. The acid deposition would acidify the soil by increasing the leaching of base cations. Hence, the decreasing availability of mineral nutrients, in spite of increased weathering, could lead to decreased tree growth. There could also be negative effects on the soil biology leading to decreased availability of nitrogen, the element usually limiting plant growth in boreal and temperate ecosystems. Partial compensation could occur through increased deposition of nitrogen. Changes in the vegetation cover were also anticipated.

The chemical changes in the soil also had consequences for water courses and lakes. Acidification of lakes could be anticipated, with ultimately a change in the fish fauna – even death of fish populations. Such an acidification of lakes with accompanying death of fish was also found in 1972, in south-west Sweden. The acidification of soils caused by the increased deposition of sulfur could be demonstrated during the 1980s. However, it was more difficult to identify a decreased rate of forest growth. We will return to these problems in the coming chapters.

The issue of 'acid rain', as well as the Falun pollution history illustrates the nature of ecosystem ecology. Pollution, a man-made perturbation, affects the atmosphere, the organisms, the soil, the ground water and even the aquatic systems. A number of processes responsible for the metabolism of the ecosystem or turnover and movement of mineral elements are modified, often with negative consequences for the ecosystems and Man. We need a scientific, mechanistic understanding of the changes occurring in order to determine acceptable loads of pollution, a prerequisite for a healthy environment.

Box Pro. 2 | 'Acid rain' and identification of environmental problems

The ways in which environmental problems are found and develop into scientific issues are not easily foreseen. The 'acid rain' problem is such an example. There was an awareness of air pollution, but the importance of transport of pollutants over national borders was not recognised. How, then, was it discovered?

A Swedish agricultural soil chemist, Hans Egnér (1896–1989), with an interest in phosphorus and grain crops, realised that what was found in the crop and what was removed from the soil did not balance. From this he drew the conclusion that there must be an additional source – the rain. Egnér is claimed to have said: 'It is a part of the missing phosphorus budget and then one ought to know about it.' He therefore initiated measurements of the chemical composition of rain and found what he was looking for.

Egnér´s finding attracted interest from other Scandinavian and European colleges. Egnér organised a European network, which in 1956 became the 'European Air Chemistry Network' hosted by the International Meteorological Institute in Stockholm. Erik Eriksson and Carl Gustav Rossby, a well-known soil scientist and a well-known meteorologist, respectively, were convinced by the data from Egnér's network that transport of pollutants over national boundaries took place.

Later, Svante Odén interpreted 20 years of data from Egnér, as well as those from the European network, and presented his findings in 1967 in a daily newspaper, *Dagens Nyheter*, as follows (Figure Pro. 3):

- Acid precipitation is a large-scale regional phenomena with well-defined source and sink regions
- Rain and lakes are becoming increasingly acidic
- Air pollution containing sulfur and nitrogen is transported by winds over distances of 100 to 2000 km across several nations in Europe
- The probable consequences will be changes in the chemistry of lakes, decreased fish populations, leaching of toxic metals from soils to lakes and streams, decreased forest growth, increased plant diseases and accelerated damage to materials.

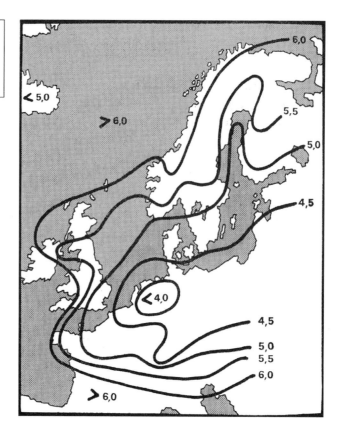

Figure Pro. 3 The distribution of pH in precipitation over Europe in 1962. From Odén (1967). With kind permission from the Svante Odén family.

Global warming

As early as 1827 it was suggested by the French physicist *Jean Baptiste Joseph Fourier* that carbon dioxide in the air was important because it trapped heat like a pane of glass. The Swedish chemist *Svante Arrhenius* (1896a,b) developed the idea later, in order to see if a variation in atmospheric carbon dioxide concentration could explain the ice ages. The calculations led him to state, 'If the present quantity of carbonic acid [water vapour and carbon dioxide, our note] is put equal to unity, the average value of the temperature change will be as follows: if the carbonic acid content sinks to 2/3, − 3.2 °C, if it rises to 1.5, +3.4 °C, if it rises to 2, +5.7 °C, if it rises to 2.5, +7.4 °C, and finally if it rises to 3, +8.4 °C' (Arrhenius 1896a). His calculations are remarkably close to current predictions using much more sophisticated models.

Although it was already clear at the time of Arrhenius that combustion of fossil fuels, coal at that time, added carbon dioxide to the atmosphere, it did not cause much concern. It was believed that oceans could rapidly absorb most of the emissions and rates of emissions were also much lower than today. Observations in the 1950s by *Roger Revelle* and *Hans E. Suess* that the $^{12}C/^{14}C$ in atmospheric carbon dioxide was decreasing showed that the capacity of the oceans to

Global warming is an ongoing environmental problem, although the greenhouse effect has been understood for 200 years

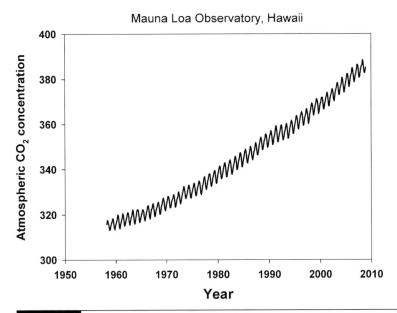

Mauna Loa Observatory, Hawaii

Figure Pro. 2 Time series of atmospheric carbon dioxide concentration measured at Mauna Loa, Hawaii. From Keeling *et al.* 2009. The first published time series by Pales & Keeling (1965) only extended between 1958 and 1963.

absorb carbon dioxide was much lower than previously thought. This led *Charles David Keeling* to initiate a measurement series of atmospheric carbon dioxide at Mauna Loa, Hawaii in 1958; a site chosen far from local pollution sources. Although the first published data set from this measurement series (Pales & Keeling 1965) was met with scepticism, the record up to today (Figure Pro. 2) stands out as the epitome of the most important driver behind global warming. Today we recognise these measurements as a cornerstone in illustrating how Mankind is modifying the environment on a global scale, but the measurements at Mauna Loa were close to being terminated after the first publication as a result of lack of funding.

Approaches to solutions

The examples of acid rain and global warming – the global carbon budget – show that the discovery of environmental problems and their causes, as well as how they interfere with the natural ecosystems, quite often is not a result of a direct search for such problems; rather they are discovered more or less accidentally during research on fundamental scientific questions. Acid rain was 'discovered' when agronomists tried to balance sulfur budgets for crops, and global warming was actually a result of the search for the causes of ice ages and understanding of the distribution of carbon isotopes in the atmosphere.

The lesson to be learnt is that the search for a deeper understanding of how Nature functions can reveal unexpected phenomena. If we want to prepare ourselves for future unpleasant surprises in our environment we need to understand how Nature works. In this way we may be able to discover early when processes deviate from the expected and avoid surprises.

These stories tell us that environmental problems can be discovered unintentionally when other questions are investigated. Keeling's measurement of atmospheric carbon dioxide concentrations at Mauna Loa is another example. The importance of individual research efforts should never be underestimated. Thus, one problem leads to the discovery of another!

Environmental problems do not appear suddenly. They are found through the devoted work of individuals representing many disciplines. Governments and research bodies giving priority to research areas need to be sensitive and respect individual research efforts. Funding priorities do not always have the potential to lead to unexpected findings.

FURTHER READING

Bolin, B. 2007. *A History of the Science and Politics of Climate Change: The Role of the Intergovernmental Panel on Climate Change.* Cambridge: Cambridge University Press.

Section I

History and concepts

Understanding the environment has always been important for mankind. In this section we briefly trace how this has led to the development of modern ecology. We will also define the scientific arena of ecology and in particular that of ecosystem ecology and how it relates to other scientific disciplines. Ecosystem ecology relies on some fundamental cornerstones: mass balance, limiting nutrients, optimality and steady state. These concepts are explained and used to demonstrate our philosophical attitude towards the discipline.

Chapter 1

History of ecology

Understanding the present requires insights into the past. We will therefore briefly describe the development of ecology and ecosystem knowledge. In particular, we will follow how terrestrial ecosystem ecology has grown from early primitive ideas about Nature and how a natural science perspective gradually has become the foundation for investigating Nature and its function. From early ecology there has been a steady development, eventually leading to the introduction of the ecosystem concept. This development towards an independent discipline is, however, dependent on a number of basic disciplines. We see a number of ecological directions dealing with basic understanding, as well as applied questions, such as worldwide production of food and maintaining the ecosystems in a sustainable way. Major actors or profiles and their impact on the discipline are presented.

Protoecology

Mankind has always depended, and will always depend, on what Nature gives. We can read in historical documents how we have used plants and animals as the basis for our existence. In the Bible we meet the first professions of farming and cattle breeding. Medical plants are mentioned by *Hippocrates* (460–377 BC), as well as ideas about plant and animal life.

A scientific discipline develops from mythology to observation and description to gradual understanding supported by experiments

Aristotle (384–322 BC) introduced a speculative understanding of plants, which eventually became the base of today's natural sciences. From direct observations with his senses and 'experiments', such as boiling and combustion, he draw a number of conclusions and stated that 'all living is nourishing from what it consists, and that all living is nourishing from many things; also those who seems to nourish only on one single source, as plants of water, nourish from several – as the soil is mixed with water'. His understanding of how it happened was vague. The 'force of the heat' was essential for transformations of the substances in the soil from which plants were built. The plants were dependent on soil, water and heat. In modern language we call them *site factors*.

The search for relationships between plant and site factors was more clearly expressed in the work by *Theophrastus* (371–286 BC), who considered site factors such as precipitation, temperature, light, soil, water, salts, insects etc. The need to derive practical information for agriculture and horticulture motivated his investigations.

The ideas of Aristotle and Theophrastus prevailed for almost 2000 years. *Linnaeus* followed Aristotle and said in his *Philosophia Botanica* (1751) that the soil is the stomach of the plants (*'plantarum ventriculus est terra'*). Linnaeus was of the opinion that trees were taking up 'mull' through their roots – the *'humus theory'*. He interpreted this as an interaction between organisms and their environment, which he denoted 'the economy of Nature' – an expression close to the present day 'ecology'. Still, at this time opinions were not founded on observations and experiments. Natural sciences were therefore full of magic and mysticism.

During the seventeenth century the Europeans learnt the distillation technique from the Arabs. *Robert Boyle* (1627–1691) was then able to confirm the findings of Aristotle concerning the composition of plants. How different components were formed was still an unsolved mystery and their uptake was thought to happen analogously to the processes in the human body. The physician, philosopher and botanist *Andrea Cesalpino* (1519–1603) had already described how nutrients were formed and taken up in this way.

Gradually the understanding of the importance of water, soil, humus and mineral nutrients for plant growth increased. In 1804 *Nicolas-Théodore de Saussure* (1767–1845) finally showed that water was bound in plants. This was also confirmed by, among others, *Justus von Liebig* (1840). de Saussure (1804) and von Liebig (1802–1873) both contributed to the 'death' of the humus theory and demonstrated the importance of mineral nutrients for plant growth. The weathering process in mineral soil was introduced in order to understand the origin of the minerals used for plant growth. Water and mineral nutrients became included among the important site factors. We will later on (Chapter 7) come back to von Liebig and his 'law of the minimum', which states that the mineral in shortest supply will determine the growth of plants.

Early ecology

There are several definitions of *ecology*, some focussing on the organisms, others on the ecosystem. These definitions were created at different times and represent the historical development of ecology. The term ecology (from the Greek *oikos*, meaning house or household, and *logos*, meaning science) was first used by a German ecologist *Ernst Heinrich Haeckel* in 1866 (1834–1919). His concept was focussed on the organisms in relation to the environment. He was a prominent proponent of Darwinism. Haeckel was also an early advocate of scientific rigour and emphasised that observed phenomena should be interpreted in terms of evolution.

Since Haeckel, modern ecology has developed from plant and animal ecology. Early European plant ecologists observed that

A synthetic discipline becomes established

similar climates had similar vegetation forms, although the species differed. Important representatives of this time are the German botanists *Carl Ludwig Willdenow (1765–1812)* and *Alexander von Humboldt (1769–1859)*. The latter conducted extensive studies in South America and noted that plant communities were related to the physical aspects of the environment. He also introduced the concept of 'association' for distinct plant communities. The Danish botanist *Johannes Warming (1841–1924)* made similar observations in Brazil. Another Danish botanist, *Christen Raunkier (1860–1938)* developed a scheme of life forms relating plants to their way of survival. He also developed quantitative methods for descriptions of vegetation allowing statistical treatments. Gradually the discipline *phytosociology* developed for dealing with characteristics, classification, relationships and distribution of plant communities. Different schools of phytosociology developed in Central Europe (*Josias Braun-Blanquet 1884–1980*) and Nordic countries (*Einar du Rietz 1895–1967*). Scientific developments in different ecological sub-disciplines also converged, e.g. phytosociology and forestry. Thus a scheme of forest types, identified by the Finnish botanist *Aimo Kaarlo Cajander* (1909, 1930), made it possible to correlate vegetation with site factors.

Important early European works in animal ecology came from *Karl Möbius (1825–1908)*, who studied oyster beds and used the term 'biocoenosis', and also developed the idea of equilibrium of communities.

Ecology gradually emerged as a recognised science in the 1890s and early 1900s, as a mix of oceanography and limnology, and, in addition, the branch of plant and animal ecology. It originated from descriptive field studies and later from laboratory studies of physiology and genetics to be followed by investigations under field conditions. Plant and animal ecology has been important by providing experimental standards in laboratory and field.

In the USA *Stephan A. Forbs (1844–1930)* initiated studies of lakes and streams in the 1880s in the Midwest. In the 1890s *Edward A. Birge (1851–1950)* pioneered lake studies at the University of Wisconsin. *Frederic E. Clements (1874–1945)* initiated vegetation studies at the University of Nebraska and formulated ideas of ecological communities that dominated American ecology for 50 years. In the same decade *Henry C. Cowles (1869–1939)* at the University of Michigan studied the vegetation of sand dunes at Lake Michigan. Clements and Cowles, with advanced academic degrees in ecology, followed the changes in plant species, populations, communities and environment over time. The communities were considered to be superorganisms and the idea was that the development (*succession)* of the communities was towards a fairly stable status, the *climax*. Simultaneously, ecology became institutionalised, with the foundations of the British and American Ecological Societies in 1913 and 1915, respectively.

The ecosystem concept

For some time the focus in ecological studies was on the organisms, often disregarding their dynamic interaction with the environment. To break this trend *Sir Arthur Tansley* (1871–1955) introduced the *ecosystem* concept (Tansley 1935). The ecosystem is an integrated system of living organisms (biotic part) and an inorganic, non-living environment (abiotic part). As ecology developed it became evident that Man's actions needed be considered within the ecosystem concept in order to understand the dynamics of populations, communities and environment. A similar concept, *biogeocoenosis*, was introduced in the 1940s by the Russian *Vladimir Nikolayevich Sukachev* (1880–1967) (Sukachev 1959).

From animal ecology an important contribution came with *Charles Elton* (1900–1991), who in his textbook integrated earlier ideas on population and community ecology through the concepts of food chains and food cycles (in today's terminology a *food web*) or *trophic structure*, the sequence of food from plants to herbivores to predators (Elton 1927). He also introduced the *niche* concept and the *pyramid of numbers*. The latter is used to illustrate how many small animals are needed to support fewer, larger organisms.

During the 1920s and 1930s the early development of quantitative ecology and mathematical theory took place. The number of quantitative field observations of populations and communities with measurements of the physical environment increased. *Alfred Lotka* (1880–1949), a physicist, developed theoretical, mathematical population models. The principles of physical chemistry were applied to ecology by *Vito Volterra* (1860–1940) with the use of differential equations to describe the growth of populations over time. Their set of differential equations, the Lotka–Volterra equations, is nowadays a standard starting point for many models of population interactions (Volterra 1926).

Prominent theoretical work was published during the 1950s by *George Evelyn Hutchinson* (1903–1991) and *Robert Helmer MacArthur* (1930–1972), in which the niche theory for animal communities and the emphasis on competition between species were the key elements. Simultaneously the community concept by *Henry Allan Gleason* (1882–1975) was revitalised, pointing out that organisms were responding individualistically to environmental factors as an alternative to Clements' super-organism. The importance of historical and chance events were also emphasised in the development of ecological theories.

Hutchinson also bridged the epoch from Darwin, being friends with his son, to the time of *Raymond Laurel Lindeman* (1916–1942) and the publication of the famous paper in 1942 on 'The trophic-dynamic aspect of ecology'. The publication has become famous as it was refused for publication by opponents to the research of Hutchinson. However, the paper was finally published and the editor added a note saying: 'Time is a greater sifter of these matters and it alone will judge

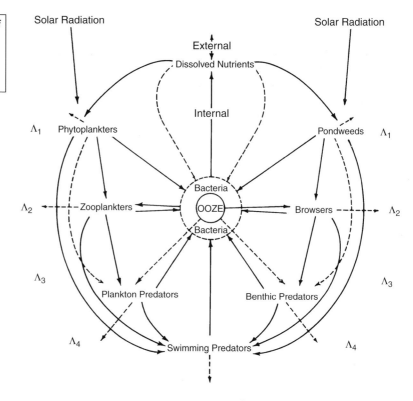

Figure 1.1 The first description of energy fluxes in a lake ecosystem. From Lindeman (1942) with kind permission from the Ecological Society of America.

the question.' Hutchinson has become famous for both his limnological work and his work on mineral nutrients and *biogeochemistry*, an interest he gained from relationships with the Norwegian geochemist *Victor Moritz Goldsmith* (1888–1947) and the Russian *Vladimir Ivanovich Vernadsky* (1863–1945). The latter is considered to have introduced the terms geochemistry and biogeochemistry.

Lindeman's paper (1942) is by many considered to mark the foundation of *ecosystem ecology* proper (Figure 1.1), when he expanded the food web concept to couple fluxes of energy with those of nutrients. It also includes a loop through detritus (OOZE).

Modern ecology

Among the most outstanding ecologists of the second half of the twentieth century we recognise the American brothers *Eugene Pleasants Odum* (1913–2002) and *Howard Thomas Odum* (1924–2002). The former's textbooks *Fundamentals of Ecology* (1953, 1959, 1971), Odum & Barrett (2005), *Basic Ecology*, Odum (1983), as well as the latter's *Systems Ecology: An Introduction* (1983) have had a huge impact on the development of ecology and ecosystem ecology. The brothers were influenced by their father, who was a professor of sociology and had adopted the concept of *holism*. Eugene trained in animal physiology at the University of Illinois, where he was exposed to contemporary ecology and vegetation science. It became natural for Eugene to apply physiological thinking to the ecosystem. Howard was a pupil of Hutchinson. He had trained in physics, which led him to look at the ecosystem from a physical and mechanistic point of view. He was also inspired by Alfred Lotka and his textbook *Elements of Physical Biology* (1925).

Eugene Odum, to a great extent, based his textbook on his own research and presented a view on the ecosystem, its structure, function and dynamics, which has been widely accepted and has had a profound impact on ecosystem research. In particular, the idea that ecosystems are regulated by a tendency to resist change and to remain at equilibrium – *homeostasis* – has inspired discussions and research. Eugene developed Clements' views to include cells, organisms and populations, each having self-regulatory properties striving towards equilibrium, when working together in a system. Howard stressed the importance of natural selection, which favoured systems that maximised power output in terms of growth, reproduction and maintenance. A summary of expected major trends in the development of ecosystems (Odum 1971; Table 13.3) has challenged thoughts and research. Many of the assumed trends have been under debate and sometimes found to be incorrect. In spite of this, the importance of hypotheses and principles to stimulate thoughts cannot be underestimated.

Biome ecology

During the 1960s concern for the biological basis of human welfare became a world issue. Several threats to the production of food were seen, indicating a need to increase our knowledge of the biological basis of food production or, more generally, knowledge of the functioning of the world's natural ecosystems – the *biomes*. This resulted in the International Biological Programme (IBP). Large-scale research efforts were organised around deserts, forests, grasslands and tundra ecosystems; initially in North America, but Europe and other continents followed. Considerable funds were suddenly available for ecosystem research. This happened at a time when 'big science' was in fashion, inspired by the development of 'space research'. The idea was that even complex natural systems such as ecosystems could be modelled if only we had sufficient data. With such models one hoped to increase understanding and make forecasts of assumed future changes. Measurements and computer techniques now allowed detailed measurements and treatment of data. Methods for estimation of plant growth and production developed rapidly. The insights into ecosystem structure and processes increased. Promoters of European ecosystem research were, among others, *Paul Duvigneaud* (1913–1991) (1980), *Heinz Ellenberg* (1913–1997) (Ellenberg *et al.* 1986) and *John D. Ovington* (1925–) (1962). Well-known biome projects in the USA (Mitchell *et al.* 1976, Loucks 1986) were the desert, grassland

(Breymeyer & Van Dyne 1980), coniferous (Edmonds 1982) and deciduous forest projects (Reichle 1981). Scandinavian efforts within IBP have been summarised by Vik (1975).

Alternative biome ecology: the Hubbard Brook project

The value of the biome ecology projects was questioned. Some consider that no major scientific breakthroughs were achieved. Others advocate that the development of methods and systematic analyses of the ecosystem were essential, in particular the development of methods and identification of gaps in knowledge.

Simultaneously with the IBP projects, a more individualistic ecosystem research project was going on in the USA – the *Hubbard Brook* project initiated mainly by *Herbert Fredrick Bormann* (1922–), *Robert Stanley Pierce* (1925–1993) and *Gene Elden Likens* (1935–). Their approach was experimental. Seven small watersheds were manipulated by herbicide and clear-cutting treatments, and the effects on structure and function were followed. Various research efforts were added depending on the interest of individual scientists, in contrast to the biome projects where efforts were centrally determined. Many small, in contrast to the complex biome, models have been developed with the aid of or relied upon Hubbard Brook data. One example is the JABOVA forest growth model (Botkin *et al.* 1972). In a synthesis in 1979 Bormann & Likens concluded that diversity and ecosystem stability were not as closely related and that the relation between photosynthesis and respiration was more complicated than Eugene Odum had suggested. They emphasised the important role of chance fluctuations and local disturbances in determining ecosystem structure and function. The steady state was not a stereotypical Clementian climax, rather a 'shifting mosaic steady state made up of irregular patches of vegetation of various ages'.

Postbiome ecosystem research

In Sweden an integrated forest ecosystem project was started after the IBP programme in 1972 and continued until 1981 – the SWECON project (Persson 1980), with a focus on the boreal coniferous forests. The project was built upon the experiences gained in national and international IBP projects, as well as the research tradition in the country. Besides observations of forest ecosystem structure and processes it had also an experimental approach and a modelling component. The experimental part was built on experiences from old and new field experiments with fertilisation (Andersson & Lundkvist 1989) and new hypotheses about nutrition and growth of trees as fluxes of matter (Ingestad *et al.* 1981). Modelling initially followed the paradigm of the North American IBP projects, but the models, e.g. of tree growth, tended to be too complicated. As a result, a modelling philosophy, where simplicity was sought, emerged and main objectives became to find new variables that represented emerging properties of the ecosystem. One such example is how the amount of leaf mass and its nitrogen content act as a driving variable for tree growth. Major achievements of the project first materialised after the official end of the project (Ågren & Bosatta 1996, 1998). Another important gain from the project was that a new generation of ecosystem scientists was trained for the Swedish academic world. A detailed account of the development of Swedish ecology in the period 1895–1975 is found in Söderqvist (1986).

The SWECON experimental field approach has been followed by new fertilisation and irrigation experiments, not only in Sweden (e.g. Bergh *et al.* 2005, Eliasson *et al.* 2005, Ward *et al.* 2008), but also in other countries (Benson *et al.* 1992).

Later ecosystem research

A number of ecosystem projects have been running since 1980. Many of these have their origin in applied questions such as the effects of air pollution, climate change and introduction of new species. They have been initiated by individual countries with national (Andersson & Olsson 1985, Staaf & Tyler 1995, Johnson & Lindberg 1992, Olson *et al.* 1992) or international funding. Field experiments in forestry as well as the IBP projects have been a solid base from which new applied problems have been approached.

In common, these later experiments have good statistical design, and coordinated methodology, measurement and sampling programmes. There is also good interaction between different disciplines. Their ultimate aim is to produce knowledge and information which can be used to address environmental policy problems, legislation and mitigation of problems. Well-known air pollution projects addressing problems of soil acidification and nitrogen have been the European 'Whole Ecosystem Experiments of NITREX and EXMAN' (Hultberg & Skeffington 1997, Wright & Rasmussen 1998). In these experiments the loads of acids and nitrogen, as well as water, have been manipulated by using roofs, under which different acidification and nitrogen regimes have been maintained. Other field experiments have been used to address issues related to how a changed climate will affect the dynamics of carbon and nitrogen of forests in Europe (Schulze 2000). Additional examples are the AmeriFlux network (www.ornl.gov), where the focus is on understanding the dynamics of greenhouse gases, as well as networks for the dynamics of carbon (www.bgc-jena.mpg.de) and nitrogen (www.nitroeurope.eu).

Applied questions and demand for predictions drives ecosystem ecology forward

Ecosystem research requires long-term observations and aspects

A lesson from the biome projects is the importance of long-term observations of well-controlled areas, such as the biome sites. In the USA a programme has been started on this basis – the Long-Term Ecosystem Research Network – LTER (www.lternet.edu/sites). This is developing into an international network ILTER (www.ilternet.edu) with representation in China, South America and many European countries.

Considerable effort is today devoted towards making the data from long-term research efforts available for use. An example is the databases available at Oak Ridge National Laboratory, Tennessee, USA (www.public.ornl.gov).

Landscape ecology

Alternative ecosystem research philosophies and directions develop

Landscape ecology is a sub-discipline of ecology and geography (Troll 1939). It addresses the importance of spatial variation, or heterogeneity, in the landscape and how this affects ecosystem processes such as spatial flows of energy, material and individuals. It has grown in importance with the availability of new techniques, such as aerial photography, GPS, and powerful computer and soft-wares. The main difference from classical ecosystem studies, which mostly assume spatial homogeneity, is the explicit consideration of spatial patterns (Turner & Gardner 1991, Forman 1995, Sanderson & Harris 2000).

Gaia and non-equilibrium ecology

During the 1980s the Gaia hypothesis (Lovelock 1979, 1988) inspired new thinking and research. It also had an impact on the political scene. The Gaia hypothesis states that the biosphere is supposed to be a self-regulating machine controlled by living organisms, with micro-organisms as the most important agents for biogeochemical cycling. The Gaia hypothesis, with its sometimes religious overtones, is highly controversial in ecology as it can seem incompatible with evolution, which only occurs at the level of individuals. As a reaction to this idea of constancy, non-equilibrium ecology has developed, favouring inde-terminism, instability and constant change. Ecosystems may always be out of balance (Pickett & White 1985, Kolasa & Pickett 1991, Reynolds 2001). These ideas have been formalised in the concept of *adaptive cycles* in which ecosystems move between four phases: growth, conservation, release and reorganisation (Holling 1992). The growth phase is dominated by *r*-selected species and the conservation phase by *K*-selected species (see also Table 13.3).

Sustainability and biodiversity

Encouraged by the Gaia hypothesis, the need to manage and utilise natural resources in a sustainable way became a priority issue at the UN Rio conference in 1992. The topics of sustainability and biodiversity rapidly became worldwide issues. Countries established agendas, environmental goals, for how they should reach sustainable use of the resources. These ideas have also had an impact on research agendas. Since 1992 there has been constant development of the concept of sustainability, recently expressed in the Millennium Ecosystem Assessment (2005) coupling the changes in ecosystems with the wellbeing of humans.

FURTHER READING

Coleman, D.C. 2010. *Big Ecology – The Emergence of Ecosystem Science*. Berkley, CA: University of California Press.

Golley, F.B. 1993. *History of the Ecosystem Concept in Ecology. More than the Sum of the Parts*. New Haven, CT: Yale University Press.

Hagen, J.B. 1992. *An Entangled Bank: The Origin of Ecosystem Ecology*. New Brunswick, NJ: Rutgers University Press.

Chapter 2

Ecology, ecosystem and ecosystem science

Ecology and ecosystems have many faces or directions. We explain the relations between different sub-disciplines. The scientific field dealing with structure, functions and dynamics of ecosystems is ecosystem ecology. The recent development of the field suggests that it should be considered as a discipline in its own right. A definition is given and its relation to other disciplines is discussed.

Ecology

Ecology and its sub-disciplines

In the historical account on the development of ecology we learnt about the early origins of ecology and defined it as the mutual relationships between organisms and their physical environment. The discipline is complex and builds upon an integration of components from different disciplines, all depending on the focus of the problem to be investigated (Figure 2.1). The focus can shift from the organisms, *biotic* focus, to the physical environment, *abiotic* focus. The relations to other disciplines will then at the same time shift from biological to physical and chemical.

Along this axis of different foci we can also identify a number directions or sub-disciplines. Ecology concentrating on species and populations are usually called *autecology*. Ecology where communities

Figure 2.1 The discipline of ecology. Investigations can have an abiotic or a biotic focus. Basic disciplines for both these fields are given, as well as a number of ecological sub-disciplines covering different biological organisation levels or specific ecosystem functions. From Likens (1992) with kind permission from the Institute of Ecology.

BIOTIC FOCUS

ECOLOGY

ABIOTIC FOCUS

METEOROLOGY
GEOLOGY
HYDROLOGY

BIOGEOCHEMISTRY
ECOSYSTEM ECOLOGY
LANDSCAPE ECOLOGY
CHEMICAL ECOLOGY
COMMUNITY ECOLOGY
PHYSIOLOGICAL ECOLOGY
POPULATION ECOLOGY
BEHAVIOURAL ECOLOGY
EVOLUTIONARY ECOLOGY

SYSTEMATICS
GENETICS
PHYSIOLOGY

and ecosystems are considered is called *synecology*. Of course we can also break up ecology with respect to biological groups, e.g. plant, animal or microbial ecology. Ecology can also be classified according to different media, such as water and land, giving names to limnology (fresh water) and marine ecology, as well as terrestrial ecology. Ecology can be basic or applied. In this book we will be particularly interested in biogeochemistry and ecosystem ecology (Figure 2.1 left side).

The spatial scale at the disposal of an organism is important and leads to different biological organisation levels. Organisms or *species* form *populations*. Populations combine to *communities*. Communities together with their abiotic environment form *ecosystems* and similar ecosystems occurring over wider geographic areas are called *biomes (formations)*. The spatial scales for species, populations, communities, ecosystems and biomes can be seen as follows:

Biological organisation level	Spatial scale
Organism, species	Site
Population(s)	Site, local habitat
Community	Site, local habitat
Ecosystem	Site
Complex of ecosystems	Catchment/watershed
Complexes of ecosystems	Landscape
Biome (Formation)	Regional or global

During the development of ecology there has been tension between different approaches or schools. In the beginning research in different branches, like plant and animal ecology, developed without close contact, each developing according to their own praxis. Later the battleground was occupied by population and evolutionary ecology fighting against ecosystem-orientated research or a reductionistic or holistic approach. Today most of this tension has disappeared as an understanding of the value of different approaches in ecology has developed.

In order to stimulate and to bridge barriers, ecology needs to be defined in a manner that favours common thoughts and collaboration. We endorse a definition that has been expressed by a group of ecologists at the Institute of Ecosystem Studies, Millbrook, New York (Likens 1992):

> Ecology is the scientific study of the processes influencing the distribution and abundance of organisms, the interactions among organisms, and the interactions between organisms and the transformation and flux of energy and matter.

The purpose of this definition is to bring different fields of ecology together as a scientific discipline, organism as well as ecosystem orientated. The characteristic of ecology is its encompassing and synthetic view, not fragmented!

Ecosystem

What is an ecosystem?

The central concept of this book is the ecosystem, which is an integrated system of living organisms (biotic part) and its non-living environment (abiotic part). An ecosystem consists of a community of plants and other organisms, as well as their non-living environment. Within an ecosystem there are continuous fluxes of matter and energy, but there are also exchanges across the boundaries of the ecosystem. However, to be a useful construct the exchanges within the ecosystem should dominate over those across its boundaries. The delimitation of an ecosystem depends usually on the purpose of the study or investigation, but should refer to some unit, homogeneous at the spatial and temporal scale of investigation. A typical terrestrial ecosystem can be a forest, meadow, bog or even a stump or a stone rising over the water surface with its vegetation of lichens and mosses. The ecosystem concept can also be applied to larger objects, such as a watershed, or even have a global context in which we want to apply ecosystem principles (Figure 2.2).

Sometimes criticism has been raised when the delimitation of an ecosystem is considered vague and can lead to ambiguities. However, the ecosystem is *the* basic unit of study, independent of scale. Confusion can arise because the ecosystem concept can have multiple

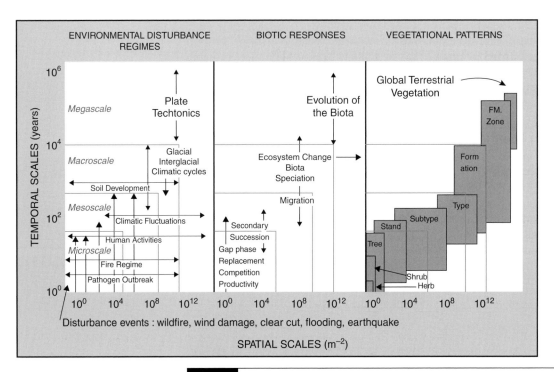

Figure 2.2 Spatial and temporal scales of disturbances and their responses on biota and vegetation/ecosystems. From Farcy & Tabush (2005).

meanings (deLaplante, 2005; Pickett & Cadenasso, 2002). We use it in the meaning of object of study, but it can also have the meaning of ecosystem theory such as flow of energy – *'ecological energetics'*, flow of matter as carbon, mineral nutrients, water etc. – *'biogeochemical cycling'* or more narrowly when balances and ratios of chemical elements in an ecosystem is analysed – *'ecological stoichiometry'*. A third meaning can be ecosystem as method. This means that ecosystem principles will be used in the handling of a problem or as a style or philosophy of research.

Conventionally an ecosystem is defined by structure, function and dynamics. The *structure* can be described from the trophic (nutritional) point of view where there is a building-up, *autotrophic*, part, where green plants or the vegetation fix light energy and simple inorganic substances (CO_2, water, minerals and nutrients) to form complex organic substances. These are then used by a breaking-down, *heterotrophic*, part, which again converts the complex organic substances to the original simple inorganic constituents. The green plants, the *primary producers*, produce energy-rich material for the heterotrophic organisms, mainly animals, called macroconsumers (phagotrophs) and microconsumers or decomposers (saprotrophs and osmotrophs). The latter are mainly bacteria and fungi feeding on dead organic matter and as a result convert it back to the original simple components. The structure also includes the physical climate, as well as the soil.

The *function* is characterised by processes. The building-up processes are photosynthesis and growth of green plants. The main breaking-down process is respiration. Seen in an ecosystem context the function results in flows of energy, as well as organic and inorganic matter. Energy flow is unidirectional, whereas matter is cyclical. In Figure 2.3 we illustrate how the ecosystem carbon cycle can be described, combined with nutrient and water dynamics. The following chapters will describe these processes more in detail. The function of an ecosystem also needs to include the diversity of organisms in time and space, including food webs. This latter aspect will, however, only be treated to a limited extent in this book, but we will later discuss the importance of organisms in relation to processes responsible for the turnover of organic matter and mineral nutrients.

The *dynamics*, which describe the changes with time of the different components of the ecosystem, and the controls of these changes, are at the heart of ecosystem ecology and are also a base for managing ecosystems.

Ecosystem science or ecosystem ecology?

When the study object is ecosystems and their structure, function and dynamics, we talk about *ecosystem ecology*. It is a discipline investigating the flows of energy and matters in the environment and how man-made factors affect ecosystems. It is an advancing discipline where the theoretical background and fundament are improving, as well as

Ecosystem ecology has developed into a discipline in its own right

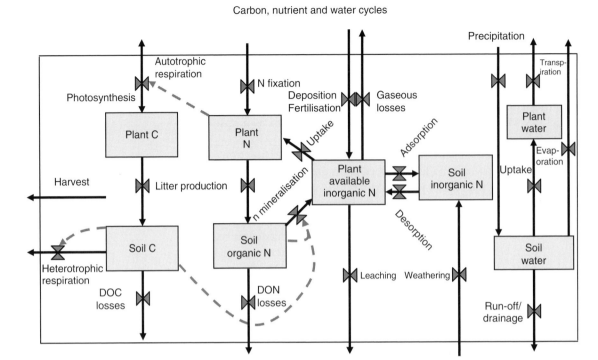

Figure 2.3 An outline of carbon (C), nutrient (n) and water cycles in a terrestrial ecosystem. Some of the most important processes that will be dealt with in detail are shown. Solid lines show fluxes and broken lines important controls. Water influences almost all processes, either as a medium for transport of other substances, or as a medium in which reactions occur.

its importance for applied questions. Five recent textbooks on the subject bear evidence of this fact (Aber & Melillo 2001, Chapin *et al.* 2002, Odum & Barrett 2005, Pastor 2008, Raffaelli & Frid 2010). The existence of a specialised journal, *Ecosystems*, is another indication (Carpenter & Turner 1998).

We dedicate this book to ecosystem ecology. Considering how this field of research has developed its own language and methods, it can now be considered a discipline in its own right – *ecosystem science*. Ecosystem ecology and ecosystem science are essentially synonymous; the choice of term is a matter of convention and ease of use. Independent of which word we use it must be stressed that the nature of the discipline is holistic and builds upon an integration of knowledge from other disciplines (Figure 2.4).

A debated issue is how Man should be looked upon within the ecosystem context (Figure 2.5). Undoubtedly human activities have a large influence on virtually all ecosystems and are dependent upon the functions of virtually all ecosystems. But does this necessarily mean that Man must be treated as an integral part of ecosystems or can Man be considered as an external force? The answer to that question will partly depend upon the temporal and spatial scale of

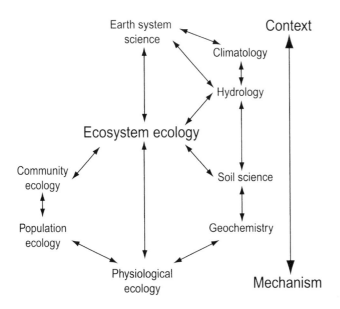

Figure 2.4 Ecosystem ecology and its relation to other disciplines. Ecosystem ecology integrates principles and mechanisms from biological, physical and chemical sciences and provides the basis for Earth system science and several applied sciences. From Chapin *et al.* (2002) with kind permission from Springer Science + Business Media.

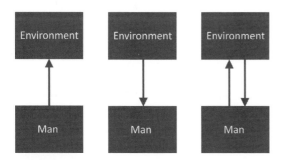

Figure 2.5 Alternative views of the relations between Man and the environment. To the left, Man is acting without feedback from the environment. In the middle, Man's living conditions are determined by the environment in which he lives. To the right, Man and his environment are seen as an interacting system where each component affects the other. In control systems theory the two systems to the left are described as open-loop systems, and the system to the right as a closed-loop system. All three views have their advantages and disadvantages. The open-loop systems are simpler to study, but do not provide the complete picture.

the question. At small spatial scales and short temporal scales the feedback from changing ecosystem functions will not be strong enough to modify human behaviour and it will mostly be convenient to leave Man outside the ecosystem. At the global scale and over longer time scales, changes in ecosystem functions will necessarily modify human behaviour. To integrate the natural science of ecology with social sciences is, however, a challenge. We will in this book restrict ourselves to the more modest task of just looking at the functioning of ecosystems, but remembering that Man is a forceful external factor that cannot be overlooked. We prefer also to use the term ecosystem ecology in the more restricted sense, where human activities are exogenous actors; other authors prefer to include Man as an integral part of the ecosystems (e.g. Raffaelli & Frid 2010).

We will conclude with our definition of ecosystem ecology, which is a reformulation of the definition of ecology given previously in this chapter:

> Ecosystem ecology is the scientific discipline, which investigates the processes influencing the distribution and fluxes of energy and matter as well as their interactions and transformations.

FURTHER READING

Aber, J.D. & Melillo, J.M. 2001. *Terrestrial Ecosystems*. Philadelphia, PA: Saunders College Publishing.

Chapin III, F.S., Matson, P.A. & Mooney, H.A. 2002. *Principles of Terrestrial Ecosystem Ecology*. New York: Springer.

Landsberg, J. & Sands, P. 2011. *Physiological Ecology of Forest Production – Principles, Processes and Models*. Oxford: Elsevier.

Chapter 3

Ecosystem ecology: cornerstones and scientific methodology

Ecosystem ecology is to a great extent about mass balances of elements and their interactions. The fluxes of elements are strongly coupled to each other, and often one limiting element regulates the fluxes of the others. This chapter gives an introduction to the most important elements and to some key concepts or cornerstones: mass balance, limiting nutrients, optimality and steady state.

A note on terminology

When we talk about ecosystems we need to define the quantities of which they are made. We will refer to concrete, measured or calculated quantities, as *stocks* of elements. When we talk about these quantities in more abstract terms we use the terms *pools* or *compartments*. The movements of matter between pools will interchangeably be called *flows* or *fluxes*. The transfer of energy between compartments was previously a key study area in ecology. Today we stress movements of individual elements, in particular carbon, as this approach provides insights into more aspects of ecosystems functionality. Amounts of elements can be expressed either by mass or by number of moles. We will follow the convention in terrestrial ecosystem ecology and use mass units, unless otherwise stated, rather than the molar units that are common in aquatic ecology. The typical units are kg m^{-2} and Mg ha^{-1} (1 kg m^{-2} = 10 Mg ha^{-1}) for stocks, and flows are per year or per day. Mass can also be expressed as dry weight (dw), when all water has been removed, or fresh weight (fw), when the sample is at its ambient water content. Dry weight is often replaced by its carbon content; if no measurements are available a carbon content of 50% can be assumed.

Understanding processes

The elements in an ecosystem move between different compartments, which can be both within an organism, between organisms or between an organism and its environment. Following these

Ecosystem ecology – a matter of elements and their movements in nature

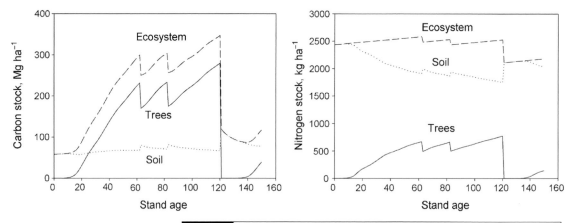

Figure 3.1 Typical developments of carbon and nitrogen stocks in a managed forest ecosystem, starting with planting of tree seedlings and ending with a clear-cut harvest and planting of new seedlings. During the development of the stand two harvests of biomass take place, which remove carbon and nitrogen from the stand, but also transfer some residues from trees to soil. The carbon cycle is open with large variations in the ecosystem carbon store, whereas the nitrogen cycle is essentially closed, with mostly redistribution between vegetation and soil such that the ecosystem store of nitrogen (vegetation + soil) remains virtually constant; although the harvests remove carbon-rich, but nitrogen-poor tree components more nitrogen may be lost than deposition and fixation can balance. At the clear-cut harvest, residues increase both soil carbon and soil nitrogen stocks.

movements and understanding their causes and the regulating factors is what this book is about. As a typical example we take a rotation period of a forest, where, as a result of natural causes, such as fire, storms or harvesting by Man, new trees start to grow in a space previously occupied by the removed trees. These new trees will, however, develop on the soil resources (nutrient stock) left from the previous stand and during their growth part of the nutrient stock will move from the soil to the trees (Figure 3.1). The rate at which this occurs depends both on soil processes making the nutrients available to the trees and tree processes utilising the nutrients and other resources.

All living organisms base their lives on a few atomic species, and in mostly similar proportions, in sharp contrast to the availability in the environment (Table 3.1). Except for the ubiquitous carbon, hydrogen and oxygen, the other elements are concentrated in a few well-defined classes of biologically active compounds (Table 3.2). It should be noted that a large proportion of the oxygen used in plants and animals is actually oxygen bound in water molecules. Lack of access to a certain element sets restrictions on the performance of organisms; restrictions that can be related to specific functions. Moreover, the acquisition of a given element from the organism's environment can require the availability of another element; e.g. plants fixing carbon from the atmosphere require nitrogen for this function. The element cycles are therefore strongly coupled. One way to understand ecosystems is therefore to focus on how different elements circulate in the ecosystem and which factors control this circulation.

Table 3.1 Distribution of elements in the Earth's crust, a plant (alfalfa) and an animal (Man) in percentage by weight (Ågren & Bosatta 1998)

Element	Earth's crust	Plant	Animal
O	47.0	78.0	65.0
Si	28.0	0.009	0.004
Al	8.0	0.003	0.0
Fe	5.0	0.003	0.005
Ca	3.6	0.6	2.0
Na	2.8	0.03	0.1
K	2.6	0.2	0.2
Mg	2.1	0.08	0.04
H	0.14	9.0	10.0
P	0.12	0.7	1.0
S	0.052	0.1	0.6
C	0.032	11.0	18.0
N	0.0046	0.8	3.0

Table 3.2 Functions of elements in living organisms. From Sterner & Elser (2002) with kind permission from Princeton University Press

Function	Elements	Chemical form	Examples
Major constituents of organic matter	H, O, C, N, P, S	Mostly covalently bound	Carbohydrates, proteins, fats, nucleic acids
Structural (polymers and support material)	P, Si, B, F, Ca, (Mg), (Zn)	Mostly in chemical compounds, sparingly in soluble inorganic form	Tissues, skeleton, shells, teeth
Electrochemical	H, Na, K, Cl, HPO_4^{2-}, (Mg), (Ca)	Free ions	Message transmission in nerves; cellular signalling; energy metabolism; establishing osmotic potential
Mechanical	Ca, HPO_4^{2-}, (Mg),	Free ions exchanging with bound ions	Muscle contraction
Catalytic (acid-base)	Zn, (Ni), (Fe), (Mn)	Complexed with enzymes	
Catalytic (redox), electron transport	Fe, Cu, Mn, Mo, Se, (Co), (Ni), (V)	Complexed with enzymes, chelated	Reactions with O_2 (Fe, Cu); nitrogen fixation (Mo); reduction of nucleotides (Co)

Figure 3.2 Some element fluxes into or out of an ecosystem are controlled by factors inside the ecosystem, whereas other fluxes occur independently of the state of the ecosystem. The same reasoning can also be applied in a hierarchical way to fluxes between components inside the ecosystem; e.g. within a plant or inside a cell.

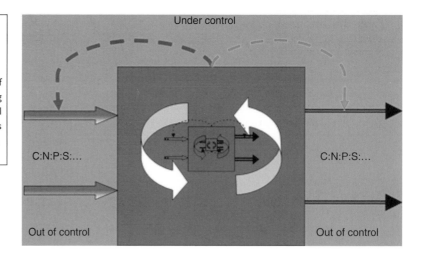

Fluxes through an ecosystem can be broadly categorised in two classes: those over which control is exerted from inside the ecosystem and those which passively pass through the ecosystem (Figure 3.2). Control over fluxes through a system can occur at the influx side, the outflux side or both. For most of the biologically active elements the state of the ecosystem exerts a strong control on both in- and out-fluxes. Carbon is a prominent element of this class. Uptake of carbon through photosynthesis is entirely controlled by the state of the ecosystem and similarly with losses of carbon through respiration. The influx through precipitation of water, which in our context can be treated similarly to elements, is basically outside the control of an ecosystem, but the partitioning of losses into transpiration, evaporation and run-off is strongly dependent on ecosystem proper-ties. The influx of many mostly biologically inert elements even depends to some extent on the state of the ecosystem because ecosys-tems with tall canopies can more effectively scavenge particles from passing air than low-statured ones. However, since organisms will not actively take up such elements, they will be passively lost. To the extent that they are lost with water seepage to the groundwater there will be ecosystem control on the outflow, but this is totally incidental. The origin of an element (Table 3.3) is therefore a major determinant of the availability and the extent to which control of its availability is in the realm of ecosystem processes.

Ecosystem ecology – a matter of plant–soil interactions

To be more concrete, our basic view of a terrestrial ecosystem is the structure already shown in Figure 2.3. The major components of the ecosystem are plants and organic matter in the soil and the fluxes between them. Of course, carbon dioxide in the atmosphere is an important part of the cycle for carbon, but from the perspective of a specific ecosystem this pool of carbon can be seen as a static compon-ent. With this view of an ecosystem the most important controls on the cycles are the ones that plant nutrient availability exerts on plant carbon uptake and the release of carbon from soil organic matter. The latter process is also strongly linked to the release of nutrients in

Table 3.3 Macro- and micronutrient utilised in plant growth and their major origin

Macronutrients >0.1% of dry plant tissue		Micronutrients <0.1% of dry plant tissue
Mostly from air and water	Mostly from soil solids	From soil solids
Carbon (CO_2) Hydrogen (H_2O) Oxygen (O_2, H_2O)	*Cations* Calcium (Ca^{2+}) Magnesium (Mg^{2+}) Nitrogen (NH_4^{+}) Potassium (K^+)	*Cations* Copper (Cu^{2+}) Cobolt (Co^{2+}) Iron (Fe^{2+}) Manganese (Mn^{2+}) Sodium (Na^+) Zinc (Zn^{2+})
	Anions Nitrogen (NO_3^{-}) Phosphorus ($H_2PO_4^{-}$, HPO_4^{2-}) Sulfur (SO_4^{2-}) Silicon ($H_4SiO_4^{-}$, $H_3SiO_4^{-}$)	*Anions* Boron (H_3Bo^{3-}) Chlorine (Cl^-)

forms available to plants from soil organic matter. The nutrient that we will emphasise is nitrogen, but phosphorus and other nutrients will also be included. For some nutrients, like sulfur, there can be considerable pools in inorganic forms bound to soil mineral and organic complexes that buffer the availability of the nutrient to the plant. Higher animals are mostly left out of this picture. In certain ecosystems they can be important by increasing the flux of elements from plants to soil and also by modifying the form in which the elements are transferred. However, in most ecosystems these effects are minor. Soil animals, on the other hand, are important, but they are included in the processes releasing soil organic carbon and nutrients and will be dealt with in that context.

Basic principles and scientific methodology

Every science has its *principles* or *theories*. Here we understand a principle to be a broad generalisation that can be used to describe various specific situations. In physics and chemistry there are a number of solid principles that have been thoroughly tested and on which the practising scientist can rely. Conservation laws (e.g. mass, charge, momentum) form one group. Principles expressed as equations (Newton's laws, the Schrödinger equation and Maxwell's equations) form another group.

Science is based on experiments and theories

Principles have different origins and also validity. True principles, such as those in physics, are rare in ecology. However, the first law of thermodynamics is such a law, stating that energy entering an organism, population or ecosystem can be transformed, but not lost, and the second law determines the direction of transformation. Further, no ecosystem is completely efficient. So, in ecosystem ecology conservation of mass is fundamental and conservation of charge can sometimes be important. In contrast, there is no correspondence to the equations used in physics. The nearest one comes is the theory of evolution, but it is not as forcefully applicable because it cannot be given a general mathematical formulation.

Other principles are more or less empirical generalisations, which satisfy some scientists, as they have been shown to withstand certain scientific tests in the form of experiments. With time these principles can become a basic principle. Other less-proven principles should be considered *hypotheses*.

In science there is therefore a demand to test hypotheses. Different assumptions are made, which are the bases for different forms of testing a hypothesis. Classically there are experiments in the field or in the laboratory. The results of these give certain facts or relations, which can lead to a principle – an inductive finding. We can also use mathematics to trace relations – a deductive method. Mathematical modelling is today a frequently used method to synthesise knowledge and to test various management scenarios. An example can be the development of forest production assuming different management scenarios. Finally, hypotheses can be tested by comparing the development of various properties and processes over time.

We will in the coming chapters show how a number of processes and structures can be expressed in mathematical terms in order to better understand their content; some formulations even approach the generality of physics. In Chapter 10 the results will be summarised in a number of principles.

Cornerstones

In the following, four cornerstones, which can be seen as principles, will be presented and serve as a foundation for this book: *mass balance*, *steady state*, *limiting nutrients* and *optimality*.

Mass balance

The masses of all elements are always conserved

The most fundamental cornerstone for all areas of ecosystem science is mass balance. Since ecosystem ecology to a large extent is about distribution and transformation of matter, mass balance is the natural starting point. However, in ecosystem ecology we can go even further than just applying simple total mass balances; i.e. just making sure that we can account for all mass in all processes. We can apply mass balances for each and every element that is involved in life. Indeed, we can sometimes even look at mass balances for individual isotopes (Fry 2006). Since we have given up the alchemists' ideas of transmutation of elements through chemical methods, the conservation of elements sets a powerful constraint on what may happen in Nature. An atom of an element that appears somewhere has been elsewhere before, and an atom that disappears from one place has to appear in another; radioactive decay is the exception to this rule of course and can be a problem with the use of certain isotopes, but in other cases leads to useful tools. The existence of only one stable phosphorus isotope, with the rest having short half-lives, is a serious restriction on the possibilities of following phosphorus movements in ecosystems. The slow, relative to most ecological process, decay of ^{14}C, on the other hand, has given rise to many interesting ecological studies. Because there are only a handful of elements that are necessary for living organisms (Table 3.2) and several of these are in most instances not limiting, an understanding of the abundances and movements of elements can give us most of the insights into the functioning of the world around us that we need. Which elements we need to consider can, however, vary, and in some cases knowing whether the element is present or absent can be enough.

A 'back-of-the-envelope' calculation can demonstrate the utility of mass balances. In some popular texts you may read that we need to conserve the Amazon rain forest as 'the lung of the Earth' that restores the oxygen to the atmosphere. Can this be true? The atmosphere today contains about 20% O_2 and 0.04% CO_2. All terrestrial vegetation contains somewhat less carbon than the atmosphere (Figure 9.21). So, if we were to burn all the carbon in the vegetation, the CO_2 concentration would go up to approximately 0.08%; there would be twice as much carbon in the atmosphere. Because each mole of carbon added through combustion requires one mole of O_2, the oxygen concentration would drop to 19.96%. Thus, there is actually plenty of oxygen in the atmosphere already. Of course, we should not burn all the vegetation on Earth, but this extreme example illustrates how simple mass balance calculations can identify which statements are reasonable and which are not.

Steady state

In terrestrial ecosystems the distribution of the elements is almost always changing over time (Figure 3.1). This can make it difficult to compare ecosystems and identify key features. An important exception is when the ecosystem is at *steady state*. By this we mean that all fluxes between different compartments of the ecosystem and over the ecosystem boundary balance such that there are no net changes in the amounts of the elements. In mathematical terms, all derivates with respect to time are zero. This does not mean that nothing happens; just that processes are exactly balanced. For example, plants take up carbon through photosynthesis, but this uptake is precisely balanced by equal losses of carbon through respiration and litter production; the plant biomasses do not change, in spite of a large flux of carbon through the plants. Steady state should not be confused with

Steady state is an idealised condition, which permits easy comparisons of systems equilibrium, which not only requires that all variables remain the same, but also that there are no fluxes in the system. Compare this to you in the bathtub with the tap open fully, but the outlet also slightly open (steady state) and when both the faucet and outlet are closed (equilibrium); in both cases the level of water in the bathtub will be constant. Although ecosystems may never be at steady state in reality, it is theoretically well defined concept and permits comparison of ecosystem properties under conditions that are well defined. Many properties of ecosystems can also be derived from their properties at steady state.

Limiting nutrients

Plants are always short of some element

The stoichiometry, the proportions of elements, of living organisms is constrained and different from that of the environment. As a consequence the availability of elements in an environment will rarely be in the proportions required by the organisms living there. It will, therefore, in almost all circumstances be possible to identify one element as, in relative terms, being in shortest supply. This *limiting* element will determine the potential for the development of the organism. Although nitrogen and phosphorus are in most cases the limiting elements, other elements may also be limiting. Which element is limiting will depend on factors like age of the site, underlying bedrock, site history and so forth. Different elements may be limiting for different organisms living at the same site; this is particularly relevant for food chains where *autotrophs*/detritus at the bottom of the chain are rich in carbon and low in other elements compared to *heterotrophs* living there. In part this is compensated by carbon compounds serving as an energy source for the heterotrophs and therefore being required in proportionally larger quantities.

In absolute amounts, the requirements of elements differ greatly. For this reason nutrients are conventionally categorised as *macronutrients* and *micronutrients* (Box 3.1 and Table 3.3). The macronutrients are N, P, K, S, Ca and Mg. Sometimes carbon, hydrogen and oxygen are also included. Sodium and Si can for certain species also appear as macronutrients. The most important micronutrients are Fe, Mn, B, Zn, Cu, Mo, Cl and Ni. The concentrations of macronutrients in plants are approximately 1/10 or more than that of nitrogen whereas micronutrient concentrations are less than 1/100 of nitrogen (Table 6.4).

Optimality

Organisms must handle several simultaneous constraints from the environment

The theory of evolution tells us that the fittest individuals will reproduce most efficiently and their genes will eventually dominate the population. As a consequence, in a given environment it should be possible to derive the properties of organisms that give them maximal reproduction. Since organisms are facing an environment that constrains them in different aspects, the organisms must balance their use of resources to meet all these constraints; an organism must solve an optimality problem. A typical case is how a plant should allocate between aboveground vs.

Box 3.1	The periodic table, excluding the lanthanide series and transuranium elements. Important isotopes for ecological work are given in parenthesis; numbers in italic indicate radioactive isotopes

1	2	3	4	5	6	7	8	9	10	11	12	13	14	15	16	17	18
1 **H** 1.00 (1,2,3)																	2 **He** 4.00
3 **Li** 6.94	4 **Be** 9.01											5 **B** 10.81	6 **C** 12.01 (12,13,14)	7 **N** 14.01 (14,15)	8 **O** 16.00 (16,18)	9 **F** 19.00	10 **Ne** 20.18
11 **Na** 22.99	12 **Mg** 24.3											13 **Al** 26.98	14 **Si** 28.09	15 **P** 30.97 (31,32)	16 **S** 32.07 (32,34)	17 **Cl** 35.45	18 **Ar** 39.95
19 **K** 39.10	20 **Ca** 40.08	21 **Sc** 44.96	22 **Ti** 47.87	23 **V** 50.94	24 **Cr** 52.00	25 **Mn** 54.94	26 **Fe** 55.85	27 **Co** 58.93	28 **Ni** 58.69	29 **Cu** 63.45	30 **Zn** 65.41	31 **Ga** 69.72	32 **Ge** 72.64	33 **As** 74.92	34 **Se** 78.96	35 **Br** 79.90	36 **Kr** 83.80
37 **Rb** 85.47	38 **Sr** 87.62	39 **Y** 88.91	40 **Zr** 91.22	41 **Nb** 92.91	42 **Mo** 95.94	43 **Tc** 98	44 **Ru** 101.07	45 **Rh** 102.91	46 **Pd** 106.42	47 **Ag** 107.87	48 **Cd** 112.41	49 **In** 114.82	50 **Sn** 118.71	51 **Sb** 121.76	52 **Te** 127.60	53 **I** 126.94	54 **Xe** 131.29
55 **Cs** 132.91	56 **Ba** 137.23	57 **La** 138.91	72 **Hf** 178.49	73 **Ta** 180.95	74 **W** 183.84	75 **Re** 186.21	76 **Os** 190.23	77 **Ir** 192.22	78 **Pt** 195.08	79 **Au** 196.97	80 **Hg** 200.59	81 **Tl** 204.38	82 **Pb** 207.2	83 **Bi** 208.98	84 **Po** 210	85 **At** 210	86 **Rn** 220
87 **Fr** 223	88 **Ra** 226	89 **Ac** 227	90 **Th** 232.04	91 **Pa** 231.04	92 **U** 238.03												

Legend: Macroelements | Microelements | Elements that might be essential for some organisms belowground production. Resources invested aboveground are needed for photosynthesis (light and carbon dioxide capture), whereas belowground resources are needed for acquisition of water and mineral nutrients. Plants growing in a nutrient-rich environment can obtain the nutrients they need with relatively little investment in roots and hence spend more on aboveground growth. We expect, therefore, to observe increasing above- to belowground biomass ratios as nutrient availability increases. This is also the case when nitrogen or phosphorus limits growth, but not with magnesium limitation (Chapter 7).

Although identifying what should be an optimal behaviour of an organism is valuable for understanding its functioning, using the results of the optimisation must be used with caution. A major obstacle is that fitness is expressed in terms of reproduction, but we often have to use proximate variables such as plant size as the target for the optimisation and such proximate targets may fail to identify the fittest individual. For example, a tall tree gains an advantage from shading its neighbours, but by protruding above the protection of the canopy it also exposes itself to wind. Evolution can also be slow relative to changes in the environment, which is particularly relevant for plants that can have life spans of thousands of years; e.g. some plants that mainly reproduce vegetatively. Under such circumstances it is difficult to know which environment the plant is adapting to. One should also remember that many organisms modify their own environment, which means that the optimisation is aiming for a moving target. Finally, organisms do not have infinite flexibility; they carry a heritage of biochemistry that only allows certain changes, at least over shorter time spans. It is actually this that makes ecological stoichiometry meaningful; organisms have to behave in a constrained manner.

One equation says more than a thousand words

In general, we are more interested in the dynamic properties of ecosystems, how they change in time (Figure 3.1), than in their static properties. We are also interested in the causes of these changes and how different components in the ecosystem interact. For example, we know that the rate of photosynthesis depends on the amount of nitrogen in the leaves. The amount of nitrogen in the leaves in its turn depends on how efficient a plant can acquire mineral nitrogen from the soil. This efficiency will in part depend on how much carbon the plant can invest in root growth, and hence on the rate of photosynthesis. We therefore end up with a feedback loop, in this case a positive one where more photosynthesis produces more roots that can take up more nitrogen that increases photosynthesis still more.

Mathematics is the language of deductive reasoning

Feedback loops are notoriously difficult to analyse in conventional language. When several feedback loops interact and some of them are positive and some of them are negative it becomes impossible to predict the outcome by just using words. Fortunately we have a language, mathematics, which is ideally suited for questions of this kind (Ågren & Bosatta 1990, Pastor 2008). Not only will a mathematical formulation of a problem more or less by default provide a quantitative analysis, but it will also be economic in the sense that an equation with a few symbols can express precisely what otherwise might require paragraphs to describe loosely. For these reasons we will extensively use differential equations to express relations, where we differentiate variables representing stocks with respect to time in order to capture the system dynamics.

As an example, consider Equation (3.1, also 6.12), which describes the rate of change in canopy biomass (W_L) as a function of its content of a limiting element (n_L) in an equation with parameters a, b and μ_L.

$$\frac{dW_L}{dt} = (a - bW_L)n_L - \mu_L W_L \qquad (3.1)$$

If we were to try to describe in words what this equation contains, we might say something like:

> The change in canopy biomass over an infinitesimally short time span equals the newly produced biomass minus losses, which are proportional to the biomass. The amount of newly produced biomass is proportional to the amount of the limiting nutrient in the canopy. The proportionally factor is a linearly decreasing function of canopy biomass.

This description in words is not only more difficult to penetrate (given comparable knowledge of English and the mathematical language), but its consequences are still harder to realise. Who can, for example, from the formulation in the English language conclude how the stationary canopy biomass is related to canopy mortality and canopy nutrient concentration? In mathematical language the answer is obtained almost immediately, Equation (6.13). Moving to more complex relations, e.g. the Farquhar–von Caemmerer model of photosynthesis (Box 6.1), is entirely out of the question in ordinary language.

Understanding the cornerstones

To illustrate the *cornerstones* and to introduce the main ideas of the book we will use a simple ecosystem model. One major theme in this book is the cycling of elements between the vegetation and the soil, and the transformations involved in these cycles. Another major theme is how the cycles of elements interact. The simplest possible description including these two themes is a model consisting of a vegetation component and a soil component, each of these consisting of two elements. We choose carbon and nitrogen as these two dominate (Figure 3.3; this is a simplified version of Figure 2.3).

The model is an example of *mass balance*. The uptake of carbon in the vegetation (plant growth) is directly proportional to the amount of nitrogen in the vegetation (nitrogen productivity, concept *of limiting element* – Chapter 6). The loss of carbon from the vegetation (litter production) is proportional to the amount of vegetation. Uptake of

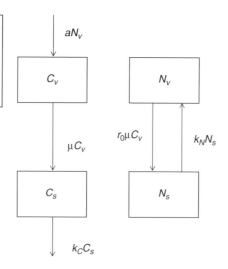

Figure 3.3 A simple ecosystem model consisting of vegetation carbon (C_v), soil carbon (C_s), vegetation nitrogen (N_v) and soil nitrogen (N_s). The functions describing the fluxes are shown.

nitrogen from the soil to the vegetation depends on the rate at which nitrogen in the soil becomes available. We assume here that this rate is simply proportional to the amount of soil nitrogen; a more detailed description in Chapter 7 couples this rate to the rate of release of soil carbon ($k_C C_s$). With the loss of carbon from the vegetation, nitrogen also follows at a fixed concentration. Full descriptions and explanations of the fluxes of the elements are given later in the book. Since no nitrogen is lost or added to the ecosystem the total amount of nitrogen ($N_T = N_v + N_s$) remains constant. We can then write down four dynamic equations that describe the carbon and nitrogen in the ecosystem

$$\frac{dC_v}{dt} = aN_v - \mu C_v$$
$$\frac{dN_v}{dt} = k_N N_s - r_0 \mu C_v$$
$$\frac{dC_s}{dt} = \mu C_v - k_C C_s$$
$$\frac{dN_s}{dt} = r_0 \mu C_v - k_N N_s$$

(3.2)

Since the soil carbon does not affect any other variable we will not consider it any further. The two equations for N_v and N_s are identical, except for the sign. We need, therefore, only one of them, together with the equation for the total ecosystem nitrogen, leaving us with only two equations for the vegetation carbon and nitrogen

$$\frac{dC_v}{dt} = aN_v - \mu C_v$$
$$\frac{dN_v}{dt} = k_N (N_T - N_v) - r_0 \mu C_v$$

(3.3)

Before we solve these equations to see what they can tell us about the ecosystem, we note that many plant properties are correlated (Chapter 7) such that:

- Nitrogen productivity (a) and turnover (μ) increase together, $a = c_1 \mu$
- Easily decomposable plant litter is produced by plants with high turnover, $k_N = c_2 \mu$

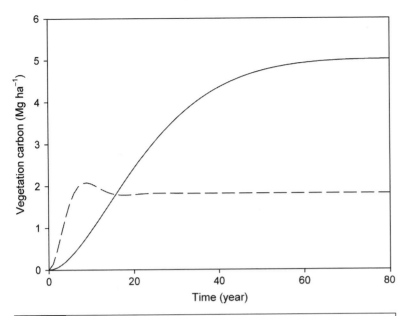

Figure 3.4 Development over time of carbon in long-lived (solid line) and short-lived (broken line) plants in ecosystems with the same amount of nitrogen and starting from almost bare ground. Parameter values are chosen to correspond to approximately savannas/grassland (see Figures 4.6 and 4.8).

- High nitrogen concentration is found in litter from plants with high turnover, $r_0 = c_3\mu$.

This leaves us with only two properties to describe all ecosystems; the total amount of nitrogen and the life span of the plants. First of all we calculate the *steady-state* plant carbon (C_{vss}, subscript ss denotes steady state)

$$C_{vss} = \frac{N_T}{\frac{\mu}{a} + \frac{\mu r_0}{k_N}} = \frac{N_T}{\frac{1}{c_1} + \frac{c_2}{c_3}\mu} \tag{3.4}$$

The plant steady-state carbon is thus proportional to the amount of nitrogen in the ecosystem, but decreases with the turnover rate of the plant. In the long run, ecosystems with long-lived plants will contain more plant carbon (and soil carbon, as follows from Equation 3.2). But what happens over short periods of time? Figure 3.4 shows the development of plant vegetation in two ecosystems with the same total nitrogen, but one short-lived plant and one long-lived plant when we start from almost bare ground.

When we compare ecosystems at steady state we can conclude that the more long-lived the plants are, the more plant carbon the ecosystem will contain. There is no ambiguity to this conclusion and this is what makes analyses of steady-state properties so useful. In contrast, when we compare the two ecosystems at other times, any of the two ecosystems can have the highest plant carbon; it is just a matter of choosing the appropriate time. One might then conclude that long-lived plants

Box 3.2 | Advanced analysis of the simple ecosystem model (Figure 3.4)

We see in Figure 3.4 that slow-growing plants reach their steady-state value monotonously, whereas the slow-growing plants oscillate in biomass during the approach to steady state. Are these properties that can be anticipated and explained? To examine this we rewrite Equation (3.3) in matrix form

$$\frac{d}{dt}\begin{pmatrix} C_v \\ N_v \end{pmatrix} = \begin{pmatrix} -\mu & a \\ -\mu r_0 & -k_N \end{pmatrix}\begin{pmatrix} C_v \\ N_v \end{pmatrix} + \begin{pmatrix} 0 \\ k_N N_T \end{pmatrix} \quad (3.5)$$

The eigenvalues to the matrix

$$\lambda_{1,2} = -\frac{\mu + k_N}{2} \pm \sqrt{\left(\frac{\mu + k_N}{2}\right)^2 - a r_0 \mu} \quad (3.6)$$

give us the characteristic time constants for the system. Equation (3.6) shows that the real parts of the eigenvalues are always negative such that any perturbation always is damped out; this is also expected as the fixed amount of nitrogen bounds the system. However, the term $a r_0 \mu$ is, under the assumptions made above, proportional to μ^3 and will therefore increase faster than the term $(\mu + k_N)^2$. When μ increases, we can therefore come to a point where the term under the radical becomes negative and we get oscillations. It is a common result that systems with rapid turnover tend to become unstable. Although this is a powerful technique for analysing system behaviours we will not pursue it further in this book (see, however, Pastor (2008)).

should dominate all ecosystems, but many ecosystems experience more or less regular disturbances such that steady states are never attained. Under such circumstances plants with rapid growth (r-selected) will be at an advantage compared to the more slow-growing (K-selected), although the latter can reach larger biomasses. The *optimal* properties of the plants will therefore depend on the time scale of perturbations relative to the time scale for growth of the plants.

The model in Figure 3.3 also illustrates another important theme in this book: open and closed element cycles (Chapter 9). Carbon is here depicted as an entirely open cycle; there is no limit to the amount of carbon that the ecosystem can acquire. In contrast, nitrogen is a completely closed cycle; no nitrogen is lost to the environment and no new nitrogen is added to the ecosystem.

FURTHER READING

Fraústo da Silva, J.J.R. & Williams, R.J.P. 2001. *The Biological Chemistry of the Elements – The Inorganic Chemistry of Life*. Oxford: Oxford University Press.
Pastor, J. 2008. *Mathematical Ecology of Populations and Ecosystems*. Chichester: Wiley-Blackwell.
Sterner, R.W. & Elser J.J. 2002. *Ecological Stoichiometry – The Biology of Elements from Molecules to the Biosphere*. Princeton, NJ: Princeton University Press.

Section II

Ecosystem structure and function

This is the major section of the book. We describe how the structure of an ecosystem can be seen as an interaction between two mutually dependent sub-systems: vegetation and soil. The vegetation is a purely biological system, but it is embedded in an abiotic environment and, therefore, we need to understand the micrometeorological environment for the aboveground components, and soil physical and chemical conditions for the roots. Hence, energy and water balances are part of ecosystem ecology. These factors also determine soil biological processes.

We will analyse the functioning of the vegetation from ecophysiological knowledge, with an emphasis on interactions between carbon, as the structural component, and other elements, including water, as regulating factors. Similarly, the differential need and use of carbon versus other elements is the basis upon which we build our description of soil organic matter processes. For both sub-systems we use simple models to guide us when we identify the most important aspects of the systems.

We take a different look at ecosystems when we integrate the vegetation and soil into complete cycles of the elements, both at the ecosystem and the global scale. This allows us to further investigate the processes regulating the behaviour of elements in ecosystems.

In the end we summarise our understanding in 17 principles, which should be useful points of departure when addressing ecological questions.

The variations and similarities in structure and function are illustrated with information from nine ecosystem types representing climatically very different conditions, from the arctic to the tropics.

Chapter 4

Ecosystem structure: site factors, soil and vegetation

Terrestrial ecosystems are characterised by their structure. The environmental factors – site factors – shape the vegetation and soil. In this chapter we will describe the coarse features of vegetation and soils. The interactions between vegetation, climate and soil material lead to the formation of biomes and soil types on global and regional scales. This chapter includes also some basic soil physics and chemistry.

Terrestrial ecosystems and site factors

Terrestrial ecosystems are shaped and governed by a number of interacting factors – site factors. These can be summarised in the following expression (Jenny 1941, Amundson & Jenny 1997):

$$E = f(c, o, r, p, t \ldots) \tag{4.1}$$

where E = ecosystem; c = climate; o = organisms; r = topography; p = parent material or bedrock, which gradually changes into soil and t = time.

Site factors shape land ecosystems

This expression and Figure 4.1 show in a simplified way how these major factors affect a terrestrial ecosystem and resulting effects. We have grouped the factors according to their way of working. Of prime importance for the organisms and the ecosystem is the climate, in terms of its physical and chemical components. Light as a component of the physical climate is necessary for organisms, in particular plants. Further, the energy coming from light and expressed in temperature or heat is fundamental as a rate regulator of all biological activities (Chapters 5–7). A part of the physical climate is also water, with its double importance through its physiological action and its function as a carrier of substances in the plants, as well as in the whole ecosystem (Chapter 5). There is also a chemical dimension to the climate. The air contains not only gases such as oxygen, carbon dioxide and nitrogen, but also acids such as carbonic and sulfuric acid. The soil contains mineral or nutrient elements essential to the organisms. Over time there are also changes as a consequence of Man's actions or from natural causes (Chapters 9, 11, 12, 14 and 15). The topography or slope determines the incoming radiation to the ecosystems and also affects the ways water passes through the ecosystem. In addition, there are mechanical factors acting in and

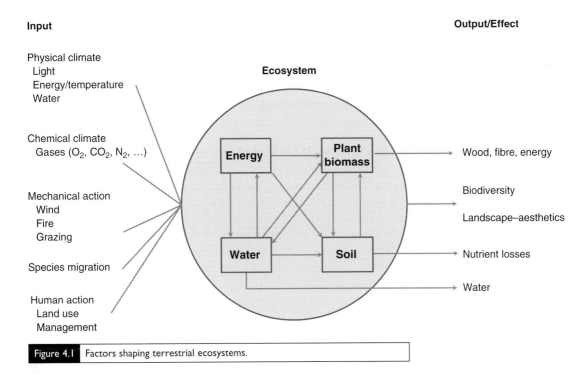

Input

Physical climate
  Light
  Energy/temperature
  Water

Chemical climate
  Gases (O_2, CO_2, N_2, ...)

Mechanical action
  Wind
  Fire
  Grazing

Species migration

Human action
  Land use
  Management

Ecosystem

Energy

Plant biomass

Water

Soil

Output/Effect

Wood, fibre, energy

Biodiversity

Landscape–aesthetics

Nutrient losses

Water

Figure 4.1 Factors shaping terrestrial ecosystems.

on the ecosystem: wind, fire, grazing and Man's activities, such as harvesting in fields and forests (Chapter 13). Finally, time is an essential factor, sometimes forgotten. It is always a question of the time perspective in which different factors should be considered – short term vs. long term.

The soil has a key role in terrestrial ecosystems as its properties determine the type of species and ecosystem that can and will develop under specific climatic regimes. To understand what shapes the structure of terrestrial ecosystems we need some insight into and understanding of basic soil properties and processes.

Soil physics and chemistry

The soil in an ecosystem context

The word soil is ambiguous as it used in many meanings. We use *soil* or *the soil*, *soils* and *soil type* with the following understanding:

What is soil?

> *soil* and *the soil* – refers to the material itself; its organic and inorganic composition

> *soil* or *soils* – refer to a natural body with a specific composition such as sandy clay

> *soil type* – refers to a soil, such as a spodosol, produced by a specific set of soil-forming factors.

A prime function of the soil is to support growth of higher plants. It is the medium for plant roots, offering physical support, transporting air, gases and water, buffering against extreme temperatures and other extreme weather conditions, providing protection from toxins and last but not least delivering mineral nutrients.

Plant roots need energy, which is gained through respiration and requires oxygen, which for most plants is taken up by the roots from the soil environment, and yields carbon dioxide. The soil must thus be ventilated or aerated in order to let oxygen enter and carbon dioxide escape. This requires a system or network of pores in the soil. The pore system is also essential for infiltration of water to the soil as plants and soil organisms more or less continuously need water for their life processes, such as photosynthesis, cell turgor, nutrient transport and heat balance. The capacity of a soil to hold water is important for the plants to withstand periods without precipitation (Chapter 5). Water, with its high specific heat and the high latent heat of fusion of ice, is also important for the thermal properties of the soil.

The soil is also a habitat for soil organisms, everything from soil-dwelling higher fauna to insects, fungi and microbes. The soils provide a huge variation in chemical and physical environment from basic to acid, from well aerated to anoxic. This explains the high diversity of organisms found in soils. The organisms act as consumers and decomposers and are responsible for the recycling of nutrients. Seen in a landscape perspective the soil also regulates, not only quantity, but also quality of groundwater with contributions to larger water bodies. The physically and biologically functioning soil can protect plant roots from harmful substances such as gases by good ventilation, and decompose or adsorb organic compounds, as well as suppress the formation of toxins; finally the soil provides plants with essential mineral nutrients originating from weathered bedrock or recycled from the organic matter formed in the ecosystem. The soil has a major role in the gas exchange between the ecosystem and the atmosphere. Some gases are released, such as carbon dioxide and nitrogen oxides, others are absorbed, such as oxygen, and some, like methane, can, depending upon specific conditions, be either released or absorbed.

We will now consider in some detail the physical and chemical properties of soils and their importance in ecosystem functioning; the biological part of the soil is dealt with in later chapters (Chapters 7–9).

Soil physical properties

A soil is a three-dimensional system composed of minerals, organic matter, air, water and organisms (Figure 4.2)

There are two major types of soil depending on the material: *mineral soil* and *organic soil*. The mineral soils originate from bedrocks of different chemical compositions and are composed of different fractions, such as rock fragments, stones, gravel, sand, silt and clay. The smaller the particles are, the more important they are for the ecological properties of the soil (Table 4.1). The organic soils consist of

Table 4.1 | General properties of sand, silt and clay

Property	Sand	Silt	Clay
Diameter (mm)	2.0–0.05	0.05–0.002	< 0.002
Means of observation	Naked eye	Microscope	Electron microscope
Dominant minerals	Primary	Primary and secondary	Secondary
Attraction of particles for each other	Low	Medium	High
Attraction of particles for water	Low	Medium	High
Ability to hold chemicals and nutrients in plant-available form	Very low	Low	High
Water-holding capacity	Low	Medium to high	High
Aeration	Good	Medium	Poor
Soil organic matter level	Low	Medium to high	Medium to high
Decomposition of organic matter	Rapid	Medium	Slow
Warm-up in spring	Rapid	Medium	Slow
Pollutant leaching potential	High	Medium	Low/High
Resistance to pH change	Low	Medium	High

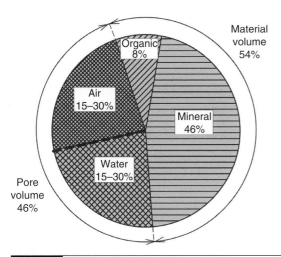

Figure 4.2 The composition of a soil from a deciduous forest: material and pore volume in volume %. The average composition of a soil favouring plant growth usually has 50% occupied by soil solids and 50% by air/gases and water. The latter fluctuates with weather conditions. Data from Andersson (1970a).

less decomposed plant material and more decomposed material – *humus*. The distinction between mineral and organic soils is not always clear, as mineral soils contain varying amounts of organic matter and minerals are mixed into organic soils.

The distribution of particle sizes in the mineral soil – the *texture* – as well as the content of organic matter determine many soil properties. The conventional classification of particles into size classes is: sand, silt and clay (Table 4.1). A gradual change in the mineral

More fine particles – better structure, more nutrients and water in the soil but less oxygen particles occurs through *physical* and *chemical weathering* processes, where *primary minerals* are changed into *secondary minerals*. The latter are of a colloidal size, < 0.001 mm. The distribution of particle sizes is important because the surface area per unit mass increases rapidly as the proportion of small particles increases. The surfaces of the colloids (both mineral and organic – clay–humus complexes) are electrically charged and therefore attract ions, positively or negatively charged, depending upon the type of mineral and pH of the soil, as well as water content. This fine fraction plays a key role for most soil chemical and physical processes.

Soil structure is another important physical property of the soil. The structure of the soil consists of a system of pores of different sizes and determines the volume of pores in the soil or the *porosity* (Box 4.1). This is the available volume for air and water. It determines the behaviour of gases and water in the soil and influences that of the plant roots. The soil structure depends on the ability of the soil to form aggregates, as well as their size and form. The aggregates can take different forms: spheroidal (granular, crumb), platelike, blocklike (angular, sub-angular) and prismalike (columnar, prismatic). The form

---

Box 4.1 | Soil texture, soil structure and water content

The *soil texture* or particle size composition can be crudely determined in field tests by 'feeling' in the hand. Different fractions such as sand, silt and clay have different characteristics. More detailed analyses are done on soil samples where the organic matter has been removed by oxidation. Coarse fractions are first sieved away. Finer fractions can then be determined in a water suspension because large particles fall faster than small ones (Stoke's law). Using the percentages of clay, silt and sand in a triangular diagram the (mineral) soil is then assigned to a texture class (Figure 4.3).

The *soil structure* is visible to the eye. The distribution of pore sizes is determined on volume-based samples saturated with water subjected to different pressures or suctions. The rate at which water is extracted can then be related to pore size.

Determination of pore volume. A soil sample with known volume is taken. We then calculate:

$$\text{Pore volume in \%} = \left(1 - \frac{\text{Bulk density}}{\text{Particle density}}\right) 100 \tag{4.2}$$

where

$$\text{Bulk density} = \frac{\text{Dry weight of sample at } 105°C}{\text{Volume of sample}} \tag{4.3}$$

and particle density is the density of the mineral particles, typically 2.65 Mg m^{-3}.

The *water content* of a soil is determined by collecting soil samples from different levels of a soil profile. The fresh/wet weight as well as dry weight after drying at 105 °C to constant weight is determined. The volume % of water can now be calculated as well as the total amount of water. Water considered as non-available for organisms is determined as what remains after suction, usually at 15 atm.

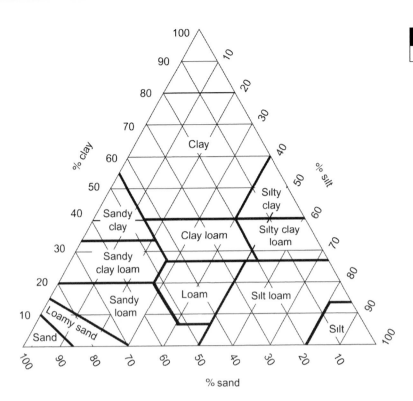

Figure 4.3 Triangle diagram for determination of texture classes.

is determined by the forces active in the soil and depends on processes such as freeze–thaw, wet–dry, shrink–swell, penetration of roots and burrowing soil animals like earthworms, as well as activity of other organisms such as fungi and bacteria.

Soil air

The soil air is essential for the biological and chemical processes in the soil. The distribution of root systems, root respiration and nutrient uptake, as well as the presence of soil organisms, are directly related to the amount and composition of the soil air. The composition of the soil air is mainly determined by the activity of soil organisms and the intensity of the exchange between soil air and atmosphere. Because the soil processes consume oxygen and yield carbon dioxide the quotient CO_2/O_2 is therefore higher in the soil air than in the atmosphere; the soil air can have more than 10 times higher concentrations of CO_2 than the atmosphere. The exchange between soil and atmosphere takes place by gaseous diffusion. As a result of the distribution of the biological activity and the diffusion process, the CO_2 concentrations will generally have its maximum at 20–30 cm depth, but with considerable variability between ecosystem and season. If the soil air falls below 10 volume %, root functioning begins to be disturbed. There are, however, plants which have special morphological adaptations to these situations.

Soil water

Availability of water determines the level of productivity of plants and is a function of climate. If there is a surplus of water, i.e. precipitation is higher than evapotranspiration, there is a downward water movement, when the opposite prevails there is an upward water movement. This is fundamental to the formation of soil types.

The soil water contains dissolved organic and inorganic constituents. It is a *soil solution* or a nutrient solution where the plant roots can take up plant nutrients such as calcium, potassium, nitrogen and phosphorus. The soil solution is also in balance with elements or nutrients adsorbed to surfaces of soil particles – clay–humus complexes. There is a constant exchange of cations and anions between the soil solution and particles. Because of this exchange the soil solution has the ability to withstand changes. It buffers in particular its contents of acid (H^+) and basic (OH^-) components.

Soil chemical properties, mineral nutrients and plants

Plant nutrients originate from the bedrock

The chemical properties of the material from which minerals essential to plant and soil reactions are derived depend on the underlying bedrock. There are three basic types of rocks: igneous, metamorphic and sedimentary. Igneous rock is a result of volcanic activity. Metamorphic bedrock consists of igneous rocks which have been transformed. From igneous and metamorphic bedrock, weathered material is transported to deep valleys and set under pressure, which leads to the formation of sedimentary bedrock. A rule of thumb is that dark-coloured igneous and metamorphic bedrocks have a more basic composition than light-coloured ones. Sedimentary bedrock is often more soft and light-coloured than igneous and metamorphic bedrock and contains generally more basic elements.

The bedrock changes gradually through physical and chemical processes – weathering. The physical processes lead to disintegration of the rock into primary minerals. The rate depends on the property of the minerals, resistant or less resistant. The main forces behind the physical weathering are changes in temperature and the rate of abrasion by water, ice and wind. In addition, roots, with their mycorrhiza, and animals may also have a physical impact. The primary minerals in the bedrock can be categorised into five classes depending on their ability to be weathered (Table 4.2). Class 1 is easily weathered and class 5 is the most resistant.

Chemical weathering is a biogeochemical process. It is more intensive in areas with warm and wet conditions. Presence of water and oxygen enhances the weathering rate as well as the activity of soil organisms, in particular fungi and other microorganisms. These organisms can accelerate the weathering process by exuding organic acids. Depending upon the substrate and the environmental conditions there are different processes acting in chemical weathering: hydration,

Table 4.2 | Weathering classes of minerals

Weathering class	Primary mineral	Contains
1	Carbonate of lime, dolomite, gypsum	Ca, Mg, C, O, S
2	Apatite	Ca, P, O
3	Dark mica (biotite), hornblende, pyroxene, plagioclase	Ca, K, Fe, Mg, Al, Si, O, H
4	Light mica (muscovite), plagioclase, feldspar	Ca, K, Na, Fe, Al, Si, O
5	Quartz, kaoline	Si, O

hydrolysis, dissolution, acid reaction, oxidation–reduction and complexation (see Glossary).

Soil reactions and availability of mineral nutrients

Mineral nutrients come in a range of availabilities to plants. The primary minerals and organic matter provide very low availability. The clay–humus complexes offer low availability and the adsorbed fractions on the colloidal surfaces give moderate availability. Finally, the dissolved fraction in ionic form in the soil solution is freely available for uptake by plant roots. The roots can actively penetrate the soil – *root interception* – and find the mineral nutrients, whereas *diffusion* and *mass flow* are mechanisms transporting the nutrients to the roots (see Chapter 6). Roots can respond to concentration differences in the soil such that root growth is directed towards regions of high nutrient availability. Uptake of nutrients creates in itself a nutrient gradient that sustains the flow of nutrients to the roots. When the mass flow caused by transpiration is higher than the uptake capacity of the roots, there can be a build-up of nutrients around the roots and the concentration gradient will be away from the root.

The *acid–base status* of the soil affects almost all chemical and biological processes in the soil, as well as the availability of mineral elements to plants (Figure 4.4). A pH between 5.5 and 7 is most favourable for nutrient availability and thus also production, which is why farmlands are kept in this pH range. Going up or down from this pH range will increase the availability of some elements, but decrease others making it difficult to maintain the nutrient balance required by plants (Chapter 6). However, functioning natural, less human-influenced ecosystems exist well outside this range. For northern conditions with acid soils the pH values are commonly lower.

The acid–base status (Box 4.2) is commonly used to describe the chemical properties of the soil. The acid–base status is fundamental to the activity of biological processes in the ecosystem. Low acid–base status corresponds to low productivity and vice versa. Several processes contribute to the acid–base status by producing and consuming hydrogen ions (Table 4.3). It should be noted that the form in which nitrogen is taken up (NO_3^- or NH_4^+) affects the acid–base status of the soil.

> Uptake mechanism are: root interception, diffusion and mass flow

> Soil pH regulates intensity of soil processes and availability of plant nutrients

| Figure 4.4 | Soil pH and availability of some important nutrients to plants, as well as some ecological and pedological processes. In the pH interval 5–7 the availability of all essential nutrients is good. |

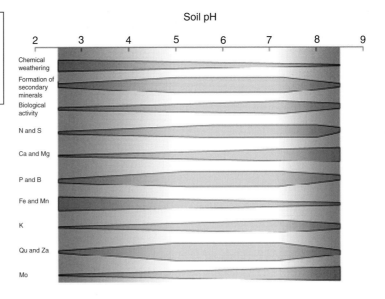

Box 4.2 | Acid–base status of a soil

Two different expressions describe the acid–base status of a soil: pH and degree of base saturation, or just base saturation (BS).

They are determined as follows:

pH

A soil sample, fresh or dry, is put in suspension with distilled water, shaken and left for sedimentation. The relation between soil and water by volume is standardised, usually 1:2. The pH is measured in the suspension.

Solutions of neutral salts such as $CaCl_2$ or KCl are also used for the suspension; $CaCl_2$ with a concentration of 0.01 M and KCl with a concentration of 0.2 or 1 M. The cations replace hydrogen ions on the surfaces of the mineral and humus colloids. As a result the measured pH is lower than in the water extracts, usually 0.5–1 pH units. pH determined from dry samples gives 0.1–0.2 pH unit lower values than from fresh samples. Fresh samples are therefore preferred.

Base saturation

Base saturation (BS) is defined as the percentage of exchangeable base cations (EBC) in total cation exchange capacity (CEC), the sum of EBC and exchangeable acidity (EA) or exchangeable acid cations (EAC):

$$EBC = Na^+ + K^+ + Mg^{2+} + Ca^{2+} \tag{4.4}$$

$$EA = \text{titratable acidity} \tag{4.5}$$

$$EAC = Al^{3+} + H^+ + Fe^{2+} + Mn^{2+} \tag{4.6}$$

$$CEC = EBC + EA \tag{4.7}$$

A soil sample (fresh or dry) is extracted with 0.01 M $BaCl_2$. One fraction of the extract is titrated with NaOH to pH 7.8 and the EA is calculated. The acidity can also be calculated by measuring Al^{3+}, H^+, Fe^{2+} and Mn^{2+} in the extract and calculating the sum of the acid cations. Another fraction of the extract is determined on its content of base cations (Na^+, K^+, Mg^{2+} and Ca^{2+}). The EBC is calculated as the sum of the base cations.

Table 4.3 | Processes producing and consuming hydrogen ions (H^+) in soils

Acidifying processes	Alkalinising processess
Deposition of acid sulfur and nitrogen compounds	Deposition of basic compounds, e.g. $CaCO_3$
Accumulation of cations by plants	Accumulation of anions by plants
Accumulation of cations in litter and humus	Decomposition and mineralisation of organic material
Leaching of metallic cations	Leaching of H^+ and Al^{3+} ions
Oxidation of nitrogen and sulfur	Reduction of nitrogen and sulfur
Desorption of sulfur compounds in the soil	Adsorption of sulfur compounds in the soil
Acid reaction of weak acids	Weathering of minerals

Soil types

Climate is the major force behind the formation of soil types through weathering of the bedrock. An example of silicate weathering is the fate of the primary mineral potassium feldspar or orthoclase ($KAlO_2\ (SiO_2)_3$). In cold, humid areas the weathering is slow and the following happens:

> Soil type – an interaction between climate, soil and vegetation

$$\text{feldspar} + \text{water} \rightarrow$$
$$\text{potassium ions} + \text{silicic acid} + \text{kaolinite (clay mineral)} \tag{4.8}$$

Potassium ions are released, together with silicic acid (a family of compounds with the generic formula $[SiO_x(OH)_{4-2x}]_n$, quartz) and aluminium hydroxide. Some silicic acid and aluminium hydroxide join and form a clay mineral (kaolinite $Si_4Al_4O_{10}(OH)_8$. This, often together with iron compounds, is then transported downwards, meets higher pH and is precipitated. Left is silicic acid, which forms a white horizon (the bleached or ash layer), while the aluminium and iron oxides form a reddish-coloured horizon below the bleached layer. In this way a *spodosol* is formed.

Water movements together with weathering lead to four major soil type-forming processes:

Podsolisation: Podsolisation is typical for cool, moist and acid areas. Iron, aluminium and organic matter are leached and quartz is left in the A horizon. The formation of secondary clay minerals is low. The B horizon is rich in accumulated aluminium and iron oxides. This is a typical *spodosol* (also named *podsol*). The O horizon is well developed. Productivity is low.

Laterisation: In hot and moist areas the silicic acid is weathered rapidly and leached out from the soil. Iron and aluminium oxides are precipitated in the B horizon, leading to a typical red tropical and sub-tropical soil type – *oxisol* – known as *laterite*. High productivity and rapid turnover of organic matter are associated with this

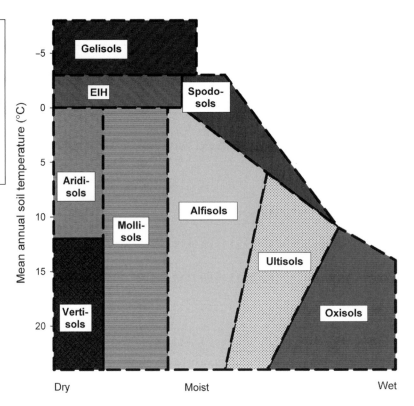

Figure 4.5 Main soil orders according to the US system in relation to soil temperature and soil moisture. EIH represents the soil orders of entisols, inceptisols and histosols. Andisols are not restricted to any particular climate. Global maps of the distribution of soil orders can be found at www.usda. gov. Modified from Brady & Weil (2007).

soil type. One form of laterisation is deposits of bauxite, which is used as a source for production of aluminium.

Lessivage and *Melanisation*: In temperate areas with fine, well-textured mineral soil and less acidic conditions the clay fraction tends to move to the B horizon – lessivage. In the A horizon humus material and mineral soil are well mixed due the activity of soil organisms. The A horizon is dark-coloured from humus material – melanisation.

Calcification and *Salinisation*: In arid areas where there is upward water movement, soluble compounds such as calcium carbonate or lime, sodium chloride and other salts remain in the soil. The upper part of the soil column may be leached to some extent during episodes of precipitation.

These processes lead to characteristic soil types. For larger regions they are grouped into soil orders (US Soil Taxonomy 1999); in addition to this US classification system the FAO/UNESCO system is often used (FAO 1998). The relations between temperature and precipitation, and soil orders are shown in Figure 4.5. Major characteristics of soil orders and their typical occurrence are seen in Table 4.4. There are also European soil systems, e.g. a German system which influences the terminology in other countries.

Table 4.4 | Names of the soil orders in the US soil taxonomy and their characteristics and typical location. The soil orders go from no development to highly developed. From Chapin *et al.* (2002) with kind permission from Springer Media + Business

Soil order	Area (% of ice-free land)	Major characteristics	Typical occurrence
Entisols	16.3	No well-developed horizons	Sand deposits, ploughed fields
Inceptisols	9.9	Weakly developed soil	Young or eroded soils
Histosols	1.2	Highly organic, low oxygen	Peatlands, bogs
Gelisols	8.6	Presence of permafrost	Tundra, boreal forests
Andisols	0.7	From volcanic ejecta, moderately developed horizons	Recent volcanic areas
Aridisols	12.1	Dry soils with little leaching	Arid areas
Mollisols	6.9	Deep dark-coloured A horizon with >50% base saturation	Grasslands, some deciduous forests
Vertisols	2.4	High content (>30%) of swelling clays, crack deeply when dry	Grasslands with distinct wet and dry seasons
Alfisols	9.7	Sufficient precipitation to leach clays into a B horizon, >50% base saturation	Humid forests, shrublands
Spodosols	2.6	Sandy leached (E) horizon, acidic B horizon, surface organic accumulation	Cold, wet climates, usually beneath conifer forests
Ultisols	8.5	Clay-rich B horizon, low base saturation	Wet tropical or sub-tropical climate, forest or savanna
Oxisols	7.6	Highly leached horizon with low clay, highly weathered on old landforms	Hot, humid tropics beneath forests
Rock and sand	14.1		

Ecosystem layering

Although an ecosystem should be homogeneous with respect to site factors, some of them will still vary within the ecosystem. A characteristic feature of the forces exerted by site factors is that layers are formed in the vegetation as well as the soil, here exemplified by a boreal forest (Figure 4.6). The aboveground layering of the vegetation is to a great extent a result of the distribution of light, which means that different species have different light conditions, and even the same species or individual can have a great variation in light as well as temperature conditions (see also Figure 6.6). The most complicated vegetation layering is found in forests, in particular tropical rain forests, with up to five tree layers, a shrub layer, a field layer with grasses and herbs, and a bottom or ground layer with mosses and lichens.

In the soil the interactions between climate (water movements), roots and other soil organisms cause stratification with often clearly visible soil horizons (or layers). The following horizons are found in many soils:

> O – Accumulation of litter and partially decomposed plant parts on top of the mineral soil. Often sub-divided into litter (S or L and F) and humus (H) horizons. This horizon consists mostly

Ecosystems have characteristic layers in vegetation and soil

Figure 4.6 A boreal forest ecosystem with characteristic layering in vegetation and soil. From Sjörs (1967) with kind permission from the Hugo Sjörs family.

of organic matter. In forest soils, this horizon is often called forest floor.

A – Eluviation (leaching) horizon. Mineral soil horizon mixed with organic matter at different stages of decomposition (A_h) and a white-coloured or bleached horizon (A_e). Mineral soil horizon with intensive weathering and from which mineral elements and dissolved humus are leached.

B – Illuvial (accumulation) horizon. Mineral soil horizon mixed with accumulation of organic and some inorganic (Al and Fe) material leached from the A horizon.

C – Mineral horizon largely unaffected by soil development.

R – Bedrock.

Sometimes these horizons are further sub-divided. Alternative labelling is also used.

Figure 4.6 illustrates such layering in a boreal forest.

(1) Tree layer of Norway spruce (*Picea abies*), Scots pine (*Pinus sylvestris*) and birch (*Betula*).
(2) Shrub layer of willow (*Salix caprea*) and young Norway spruce.
(3) Field layer of *Vaccinium myrtillus, V. vitis-idaea, Deschampsia flexuosa, Luzula pilosa, Trientalis europaea, Maianthemum bifolium* and *Melampyrum pratense*.
(4) Bottom layer with the mosses *Pleurozium schreberi, Hylocomium splendens* and *Dicranum scoparium*.

O horizon with:

S – S layer of litter and living material from plants

F – F layer with partly decomposed plant material.

H – H layer with partly decomposed and humified material. Densely rooted.

A – A horizon. Often a bleached layer overlaying humus mixed with inorganic material. Intensive weathering. Roots.

B – B horizon. Reddish of accumulated iron and aluminium compounds. Traces of humus.

C – C horizon beneath B. Mostly unweathered soil material and not affected by soil formation. Not shown in the figure.

Plants have their roots predominantly in the O and A horizons, where most of the available nutrients are found, but some roots extend down to the B horizon. The layering in the soil is also coupled to the gradual change in the proportions of organic and inorganic material.

Information on vegetation as species, biomass and production as well as chemical and physical properties of the soil and water is required for the analysis of the structure and function of the ecosystem – an ecosystem analysis (Box 4.3).

Box 4.3 | Steps in an ecosystem analysis

An ecosystem analysis is a representative investigation of vegetation and soil in order to determine stocks in a number of compartments and movements of elements between the compartments. There are three stages of the work: data collection, calculation and analyses or synthesis (Figure 4.7). A schematic illustration of an ecosystem analysis of a forest follows:

Data collection

Trees and shrubs
From a combination of non-destructive and destructive measurements a number of biomass fractions or compartments can be calculated. The standard non-destructive measurements are diameter and height. These data are collected from replicated sample areas of a given size, often at time intervals of 5 or 10 years. On the basis

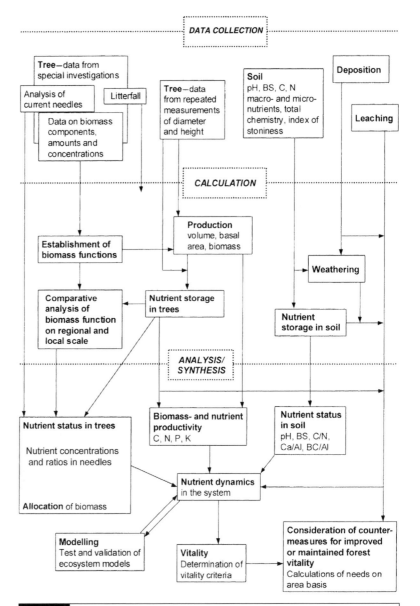

Figure 4.7 Illustration of the steps in an ecosystem analysis of a forest. Modified from Andersson *et al.* (2000) with kind permission from Elsevier.

of diameter and height distributions representative individuals are selected for destructive measurements, typically separated into stem with and without bark, branches, twigs, leaves, fruits, stump and roots in different diameter classes. *Fresh* and *dry weights* are determined. For further description of methods see, for example, Andersson (1970b) and Attiwill & Leeper (1987).

Soil

Replicated soil samples are taken for identified soil horizons. A correction for stoniness may be necessary (Viro 1952). Fresh and dry weights are determined. Chemical analyses of exchangeable and total elements are done in the laboratory.

Calculations

The stem volume of trees is calculated from diameter and height data. Volume production can be obtained as a difference between repeated measurements. The data from destructive measurements of samples are used to establish biomass as well as biomass production regressions for the different fractions by combining them with the non-destructive measurements. For this purpose *allometric* regressions are often used:

$$Y = aX^b \qquad (4.9)$$

where Y is biomass and X a variable or combination of variables such as diameter and height. These regressions are mostly calculated from the logarithmic form

$$\ln(Y) = \ln(a) + b\ln(X) \qquad (4.10)$$

Nutrient storage in trees, other vegetation and soils are calculated from measured nutrient concentrations.

Synthesis

With the data obtained, a number of ecosystem properties can now be analysed, such as nutrient status of trees and soils. From a functional point of view biomass and nutrient productivities can be calculated and analysed. By combining these data with input data for atmospheric deposition and litter, as well as output data for losses through leaching and harvesting, it is possible to investigate the element dynamics of the ecosystem. The results will be used for understanding and predicting changes as consequences of different forms of utilisation of and environmental impact on the ecosystem.

Terrestrial biomes

Seen in a global perspective, the climate, through temperature and precipitation, is the most important site factor governing the development and distribution of vegetation and soils. In areas with similar climate and parent material, similar vegetation and soil types develop – *biomes*. The distribution of different biomes can be coupled to mean annual precipitation and mean annual temperature (Figure 4.8). A key feature is the extent to which precipitation exceeds evaporation and transpiration (evapotranspiration) in an area. Evapotranspiration is described by the *potential evapotranspiration* (PET), which is the water loss from a free water surface, and the *actual evapotranspiration* (AET), which is the actual loss of water to the atmosphere and where resistances to water transport through vegetation and soil are included (see further, Chapter 5). Areas where precipitation exceeds evapotranspiration have a humid climate and a downward water movement in the soils. When the opposite is prevailing the climate is arid and there will at times be an upward movement of water.

Biomes are the result of the interaction between temperature and precipitation

Vegetation

The broad classification of biomes on a world basis (Figure 4.6) can on the local level be taken further because plant species group together

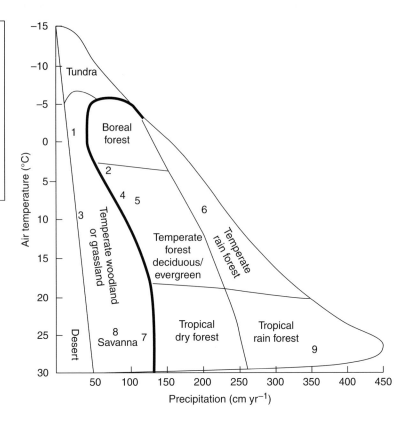

Figure 4.8 Approximate distribution of biomes as a function of temperature and precipitation. Some selected ecosystems indicated by numbers are described in detail in Figure 4.10. Note that forest ecosystems, separated by the thick line, require a certain threshold of precipitation. Modified from Whittaker (1975) with kind permission from Pearson Education, Inc.

in typical associations. The ecosystems can be identified by their dominating life forms and grouped along two gradients: acid–base (or nutrient poor–nutrient rich) and dry–wet gradients. In Norway and Sweden, which are dominated by boreal and temperate forests along with some tundra, the ecosystems fall into four series: heath, steppe, meadow and mire series (Figure 4.9). The heath series is dominated by dwarf shrubs, narrow-leafed grasses and a few herbs, as well as mosses. The steppe series has more herbs (different to the heath series) and other mosses and lichens. The meadow series is dominated by taller herbs and grasses. It is also more productive. The mire series is dominated by dwarf shrubs and graminoids as well as peat-mosses such as *Sphagnum*. The series can be represented by ground vegetation only, or with the tree layer included. The scheme can also be extended to a fifth series – the lake series, with oligotrophic and eutrophic lakes. The degree of human influence on the development of ecosystems also needs to be taken into consideration by grouping into natural and semi-natural ecosystems. (Figure 4.9a and b).

Features of terrestrial biomes and ecosystems

The broad distribution of terrestrial biomes is governed by climate – precipitation and temperature (Figures 4.8 and 4.11). Their extent,

(a) **NATURAL ECOSYSTEMS**

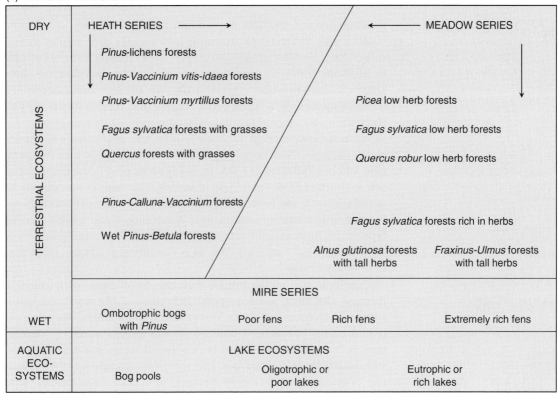

(b) **SEMI-NATURAL ECOSYSTEMS**

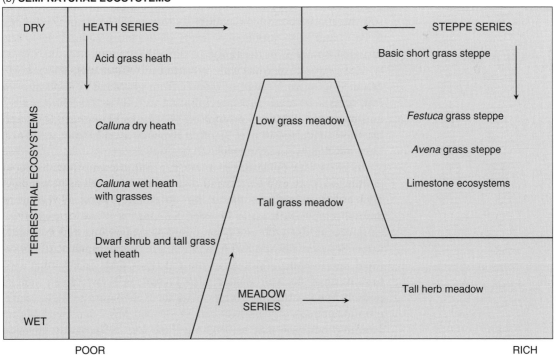

Figure 4.9 Vegetation or ecosystem types under (a) natural and (b) semi-natural conditions in south Sweden. Modified from Trass & Malmer (1973).

productivity and biomass are summarised in Table 4.5; other later studies with different partitioning into biomes give similar global values (e.g. Saugier *et al.* 2001). We have chosen nine examples to illustrate different ecosystems and in broad terms describe their structure and function (Figure 4.10). We present them according to the major climate types: arctic, boreal and temperate, as well as tropical.

In *arctic* areas and at high elevations, the *tundra*, which usually lacks tree vegetation, occurs (Stordalen – Figure 4.10 part 1). Temperature and precipitation are low. In many areas peat is the dominating soil material and the soil type is *histosol*. The vegetation consists of dwarf shrubs, a few herb species, grasses, sedges, mosses and lichens. Permanently frozen ground or peat is common – pals – with the soil type *gelisol*. Biomass (dry matter) (0.5–15 Mg C ha^{-1}) and production (0.05–2 Mg C ha^{-1} yr^{-1}) are low, as is the nitrogen uptake, reflecting slow process rates.

South of the arctic tundra lies the *boreal zone*, with conifers forming the *taiga*, a circumpolar belt around the northern hemisphere (Hytteborn *et al.* 2005, Weber & van Cleve 2005). Mean annual temperatures between −3 and +6 °C and precipitation of 300–600 mm yr^{-1} are common. There is downward water movement in the soil, which leads to leaching. The soils are strongly weathered and the dominating soil type is *spodosol*, with mor as a humus type (Jädraås – Figure 4.10 part 2). There is a well-developed O horizon. In areas with stagnating water, the humus layer may develop into peat. Peatlands, mires, within forests are common. For forests on mineral soil the aboveground biomass (dry matter) is in the range 30–200 Mg C ha^{-1} and with production levels of 2–10 Mg C ha^{-1} yr^{-1}. The nitrogen uptake is in the range 10–30 kg ha^{-1} yr^{-1}.

The *temperate zone* has wide variation in temperature and precipitation leading to a range of biomes from grassland to forests, even rain forests. In areas with precipitation as low as 250–350 mm yr^{-1} and mean temperatures around +7 °C *grasslands* (*prairies*) are found (Pawnee – Figure 4.10 part 3), often depending on human influence. They develop normally on *mollisols* or *aridisols*.

In areas with moderate temperature and precipitation, *deciduous* (Solling – Figure 4.10 part 4) and *coniferous evergreen forests* (Skogaby – Figure 4.10 part 5) are found, the latter often planted. The mean annual temperature varies between +5 and +8 °C and a yearly precipitation of 600–1200 mm is common. As evapotranspiration usually varies between 400 and 800 mm yr^{-1} there is downward water movement and leaching resulting in the soil types *alfisol* and *spodosol* with humus types mull or moder (also known as brown forest soil or podsol). The weathering degree varies from moderate to high. Aboveground biomass (dry matter) can be 30–300 Mg C ha^{-1} and aboveground production may be 3–13 Mg C ha^{-1} yr^{-1}. The yearly nitrogen demand varies in relation to the production; 40–100 kg ha^{-1} is common.

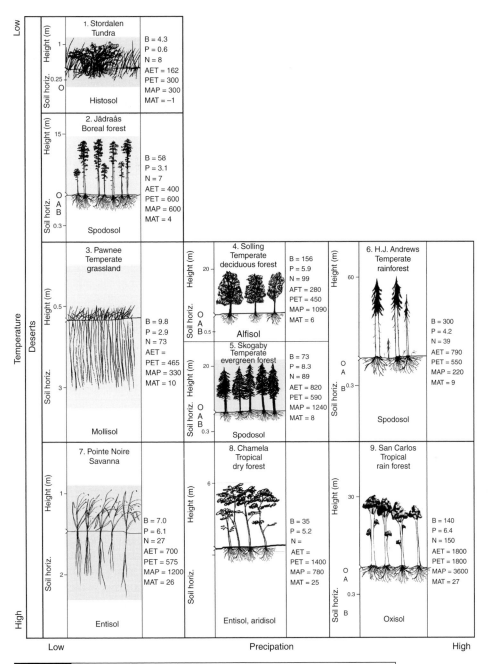

Low

Temperature

High

Deserts

Precipitation

Low   High

1. Stordalen Tundra
B = 4.3
P = 0.6
N = 8
AET = 162
PET = 300
MAP = 300
MAT = −1
Histosol

2. Jädraås Boreal forest
B = 58
P = 3.1
N = 7
AET = 400
PET = 600
MAP = 600
MAT = 4
Spodosol

3. Pawnee Temperate grassland
B = 9.8
P = 2.9
N = 73
AET =
PET = 465
MAP = 330
MAT = 10
Mollisol

4. Solling Temperate deciduous forest
B = 156
P = 5.9
N = 99
AFT = 280
PET = 450
MAP = 1090
MAT = 6
Alfisol

5. Skogaby Temperate evergreen forest
B = 73
P = 8.3
N = 89
AET = 820
PET = 590
MAP = 1240
MAT = 8
Spodosol

6. H.J. Andrews Temperate rainforest
B = 300
P = 4.2
N = 39
AET = 790
PET = 550
MAP = 220
MAT = 9
Spodosol

7. Pointe Noire Savanna
B = 7.0
P = 6.1
N = 27
AET = 700
PET = 575
MAP = 1200
MAT = 26
Entisol

8. Chamela Tropical dry forest
B = 35
P = 5.2
N =
AET =
PET = 1400
MAP = 780
MAT = 25
Entisol, aridisol

9. San Carlos Tropical rain forest
B = 140
P = 6.4
N = 150
AET = 1800
PET = 1800
MAP = 3600
MAT = 27
Oxisol

Figure 4.10 Idealised diagrams of biomes in relation to precipitation and temperature and their structure and function. Original idea from Aber & Melillo (2001) applied to selected ecosystems and biomes used in this book. Note that the vertical scales for above- and belowground are different in forest ecosystems. Photographic illustrations of the biomes can be found in the colour plate section and additional data on the ecosystems are given in Appendix 4.

B = total (aboveground + belowground) biomass in Mg C ha^{-1}; P = total (aboveground + belowground) production in Mg C ha^{-1} yr^{-1}; N = total nitrogen uptake (aboveground + belowground) by plants in kg ha^{-1} yr^{-1}; AET = actual evapotranspiration mm yr^{-1}; PET = potential evapotranspiration mm yr^{-1}; MAP = mean annual precipitation mm yr^{-1}; MAT = mean annual temperature in °C.

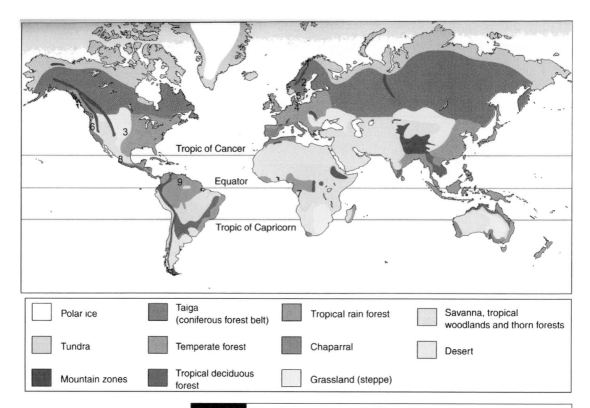

	Polar ice		Taiga (coniferous forest belt)		Tropical rain forest		Savanna, tropical woodlands and thorn forests
	Tundra		Temperate forest		Chaparral		Desert
	Mountain zones		Tropical deciduous forest		Grassland (steppe)		

Figure 4.11 Map of biomes of the world. Numbers show the locations of the biomes in Figure 4.10. From Solomon & Berg (1995) with kind permission from Cengage learning. See also colour plate section.

In areas with high precipitation and moderate temperature *rain forests*, mostly conifers, are found (H.J. Andrews – Figure 4.10 part 6). The distribution is limited for climatic reasons. The most famous ones are found on the west coast of North America with tree heights up to 90 m (Powers *et al.* 2005). Precipitation commonly amounts to 1500–2000 mm yr^{-1} and mean annual temperatures are around +10 °C. Evapotranspiration may be in the order of 700 mm, which leads to downward water movement. Podsolisation is common and the soil type is then a *spodosol*, with an accumulation of litter and humus in an O horizon. The biomass aboveground (dry matter) is typically 30–1000 Mg C ha^{-1} and above ground production 3–13 Mg C ha^{-1} yr^{-1}, respectively. The high production leads to a high demand for nutrients. A yearly nitrogen uptake of 90–120 kg ha^{-1} is common. Roots are concentrated in the upper parts of the soil, with anchoring roots found further down in the soil.

In the *tropical zone* we find a variation similar to the one in the temperate zone with *grasslands* (*savannas*), *shrublands*, *dry* or *seasonal forests* and *rain forests*. In areas with an evapotranspiration of 400–800 mm yr^{-1}

Table 4.5 | Net primary production and plant biomass for the Earth. Amounts expressed as dry matter (carbon approximately 50% of dry matter). From Whittaker (1975) with kind permission from Pearson Education, Inc.

Biome or ecosystem type	Area (10^6 km^2)	Net primary productivity (Mg ha^{-1}yr^{-1}) Range	Mean	World net primary production (Pg yr^{-1})	Biomass (Mg ha^{-1}) Range	Mean	World (Pg)
Tropical rain forest	17.0	10–35	22	37.4	60–800	450	765
Tropical dry forest	7.5	10–25	16	12.0	60–600	350	260
Temperate evergreen forest	5.0	6–25	13	6.5	60–2000	350	175
Temperate deciduous forest	7.0	6–25	12	8.4	60–600	300	210
Boreal forest	12.0	4–20	8	9.6	60–400	200	240
Woodland and shrubland	8.5	2.5–12	7	6.0	20–200	60	50
Savanna	15.0	2–20	9	13.5	2–150	40	60
Temperate grassland	9.0	20–15	6	5.4	2–50	16	14
Tundra and alpine	8.0	0.1–4	1.4	1.1	1–30	6	5
Desert and semi-desert scrub	18.0	0.1–2.5	0.9	1.6	1–40	7	13
Extreme desert, rock, sand and ice	24.0	0–0.1	0.03	0.07	0–2	0.2	0.5
Cultivated land	14.0	1–35	6.5	9.1	4–120	10	14
Swamp and marsh	2.0	8–35	20	4.0	30–500	150	30
Lake and stream	2.0	1–15	2.5	0.5	0–1	0.2	0.05
Total continental	149		7.7	115		123	1837
Open ocean	332.0	0.02–4	1.2	41.5	0.005	0.03	1.0
Upwelling zones	0.4	4–10	5	0.2	0.05–1	0.2	0.008
Continental shelf	26.6	2–6	3.6	9.6	0.001–0.4	0.1	0.27
Algal beds and reefs	0.6	5–40	25	2.1	0.1–60	10	1.4
Estuaries	1.4	2–35	15	2.1	0.1–60	10	1.4
Total marine	361		1.5	55.0		0.1	3.9
Total global	510		3.3	170		36	1841

and often with fine-textured soils, grasslands may dominate (Pointe Noire – Figure 4.10 part 7). Biomass (dry matter) and production is low, in the case of Pointe Noire and Serengeti 1–2 Mg C ha^{-1} and 1–7 Mg C ha^{-1}yr^{-1}, respectively. The soil type varies from *entisol* to *mollisol* with roots deeply and evenly distributed. The soil colour is dark – melanisation. With distinct dry and wet seasons, clay-rich soils under grasslands can form *vertisols*, which can swell or crack in response to water content. In areas with dry periods tropical seasonal forests (Chamela – Figure 4.10 part 8) exist. Here the biomass is low, as well as the production. Moving to still drier areas, the forest is replaced by thornforests and shrublands. Here the potential evapotranspiration can be 800–1400 mm yr^{-1} and exceeds incoming precipitation. This results in upward water movement during the dry season and as a consequence calcification and salinisation occur. The soil type is *aridisol*.

The tropical rain forest (San Carlos – Figure 4.10 part 9) has a complex structure. It is multilayered with a broad spectrum of life forms: trees, shrubs, lianas, ferns, herbs, mosses and epiphytes. Rain forests are also old. They have an intriguing species richness or biodiversity. The tree heights reach 40–60 m. The temperature is high and the climate is even, with a growing season the year around. The precipitation is also high. In our example the annual mean temperature is +27 °C and annual precipitation 3500 mm. The evapotranspiration is also high, in the example 1800 mm, which means that there is downward water movement leading to leaching. The biomass (dry matter) above ground can vary between 30 and 400 Mg C ha^{-1} with annual production of 5–17 Mg C ha^{-1} yr^{-1}. The soil type is extremely weathered, *oxisol*. Laterisation is common, with a typical red horizon of aluminium and iron – bauxite. The litter layer is sparse as decomposition is rapid. The production requires an ample supply of nitrogen; often 140–160 kg ha^{-1} yr^{-1}. Mineral nutrients are taken up and stored in the biomass. Fine roots are common in the litter layer, absorbing the nutrients and minimising leaching.

In addition to the soil types discussed above there are three additional soil types that are not associated with any particular vegetation type: *entisols* in which little soil formation has taken place because the soil is young or climatic conditions slows down processes; *inceptisols* which are just beginning to show profile development; and *andisols* which are formed on recent volcanic ashes.

FURTHER READING

Brady, C.B. & Weil, R.R. 2007. *The Nature and Properties of Soils*. 14th edn. Upper Saddle River, NJ: Pearson, Prentice Hall.

Fry, B. 2006. *Stable Isotope Ecology*. New York: Springer.

ICP Forestry UN-ECE 2003–2007. Manuals for sampling and analyses of soils (2006), soil solution (2003), leaves and needles (2007), tree growth and yield (2004), litterfall (2004). www.ICP.Forest-manual.com.

Klute, A. (ed.) 2006. *Methods of Soil Analysis. part 1. Physical and Mineralogical Methods*. American Society of Agronomy and Soil Science Society of America Book Series No. 5. Madison, WI: American Society of Agronomy and Soil Science Society of America.

Sparks, D.L. (ed.) 2005. *Methods of Soil Analysis. part 3. Chemical Methods*. American Society of Agronomy and Soil Science Society of America Book Series No. 5. Madison, WI: American Society of Agronomy and Soil Science Society of America.

Chapter 5

Energy and water

Solar energy powers all plant physiological and physical processes and sets up large-scale climatic conditions and patterns. Almost all of the incoming solar energy is either reflected or drives the global circulation of air masses and the hydrological cycle. It is only a small fraction of the total incoming solar radiation that is converted to chemical energy. This chapter deals with the physical effects of solar energy on terrestrial ecosystems. A large part of the solar energy goes to driving the hydrological cycle. Water is also an important component in ecosystem functioning. The physics of water in ecosystems is also described.

Solar energy

The Sun can with high accuracy be described as a black body emitting energy at 5800 K (5530 °C) with a maximum at a wavelength of 0.5 μm (Box 5.1). Averaged over the year and all surfaces of the Earth this amounts to 342 W m^{-2}. As this shortwave radiation hits the Earth's atmosphere, 77 W m^{-2} (23%) is directly reflected back into space, 67 W m^{-2} (20%) is absorbed by molecules in the atmosphere, heating it. The remaining part is partly reflected (30 W m^{-2} or 9%) and partly absorbed (168 W m^{-2} or 49%) by the Earth's surface (Figure 5.1). The total annual energy flux from the Sun that is absorbed by the surface of the Earth is, therefore, $168 \times 365 \times 24 \times 3600 \times 4 \times \pi \times (6371 \times 10^3)^2 = 2.7 \times 10^{24}$ J.

Only a small fraction of the solar energy is used in biological reactions

The gross photosynthesis on Earth is 220 Pg (C) yr^{-1} (Figure 9.22). The heat of combustion of 1 g in the form of glucose (C) is 38.9 kJ and the gross photosynthesis corresponds to 7.84×10^{21} J. The solar energy trapped in photosynthesis is thus a negligible component (3‰) in the Earth's energy budget.

Shortwave radiation in – longwave radiation out

The energy radiating from Earth consists of 107 W m^{-2} of directly reflected shortwave radiation. The remaining $342 - 107 = 235$ W m^{-2} that must be lost to maintain the energy balance of the Earth is eventually lost as longwave radiation. The temperature of a black body radiating this amount of energy is 254 K (−19 °C), which is approximately the temperature at an altitude of 5000 m. The higher average surface temperature of the Earth of +14 °C occurs because the longwave radiation from the surface of the Earth is absorbed by the atmosphere and radiated back to the surface, thus heating it. However, not all the longwave radiation from the surface of the Earth is absorbed by the atmosphere; there is a small window of wavelengths

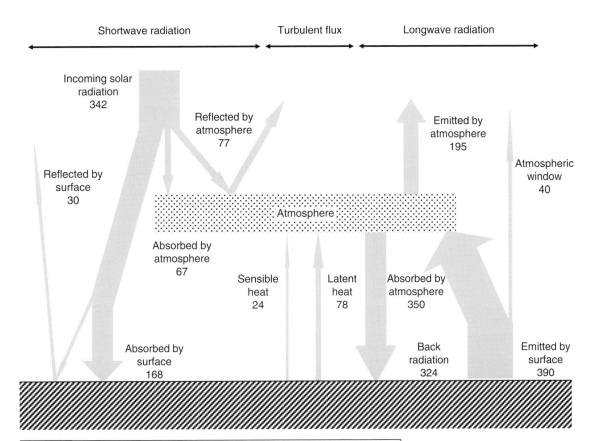

Figure 5.1 The annual global energy budget of the Earth. Shortwave radiation has a wavelength between 0.25 and 3.0 μm and longwave radiation has a wavelength between 5 and 60 μm. Turbulent energy fluxes refer to energy carried by molecules in the atmosphere. Increasing atmospheric concentrations of greenhouse gases will diminish the atmospheric window. Other air pollutants can change the reflective properties of the atmosphere. All values in W m^{-2}. Modified from Kiehl & Trenberth (1997).

where there is little absorption by water vapour (Figure 5.2). With increasing concentrations of greenhouse gases other than water vapour this window will close and the extent to which it closes can be expressed as a *radiative forcing* (W m^{-2}). This is a direct physical effect that can be calculated rather accurately from the physical properties of the greenhouse gases. Any change in this mechanism for loss of energy must be compensated by additional longwave emission from the atmosphere. The consequences of such a change in radiative forcing for the temperature at the surface of the Earth are more difficult to calculate because of several feedback mechanisms in the energy-balance system. One should also note that changes in the reflective properties (*albedo*, fraction of incoming radiation that is reflected, Table 5.1) of the Earth's surface, such as those occurring when tropical forest is replaced by agricultural land, or ice-covered surfaces change into water and bare land, can also be expressed as

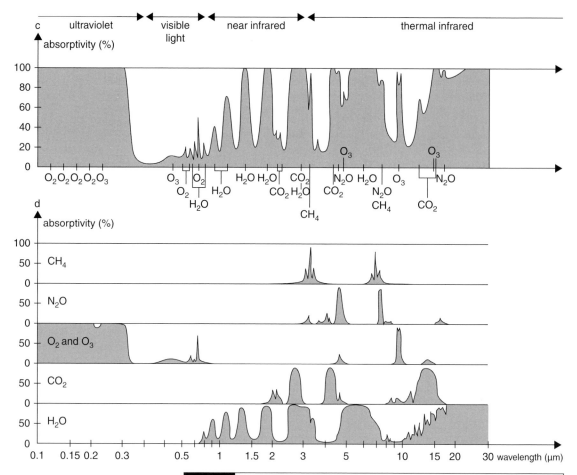

Figure 5.2 Absorption spectra of important gases in the Earth's atmosphere. The incoming radiation has its maximum around 0.6 μm. The shortest wavelengths (UV) are efficiently blocked by atmospheric ozone. The outgoing longwave radiation (> 5 μm) is absorbed by the gases indicated and then reradiated. The importance of CO_2, N_2O and CH_4 as greenhouse gases in the region of the atmospheric window around 10 μm, where absorption by water vapour is low, is clear. From Jansen (1999) with kind permission from Springer Science + Business Media.

a radiative forcing leading to a change in the components of the energy budget.

Several time scales for radiation

Solar radiation varies on several time scales. On the longest time scale there is a variation in the Earth's position relative to the Sun, which acts as a trigger for ice ages (Chapter 11). There is also a slow steady increase in solar activity. For the time scales of interest in our context, these changes are too slow to be of importance. The annual cycle is, however, a main driver for ecosystem processes because it sets up the annual climatic cycles, with their typical temperature and precipitation patterns. Similarly, the regular within-day variability in radiation is important because most ecological processes respond non-linearly, directly or indirectly, to changes in irradiance. Hence, it

Table 5.1 | Albedo of different surfaces. From Chapin *et al.* (2002) with kind permission from Springer Science + Business Media

Surface type		Albedo
Oceans and lakes		0.03–0.10[a]
Sea ice		0.30–0.45
Snow		
	Fresh	0.75–0.90
	Old	0.40–0.70
Arctic tundra		0.15–0.20
Conifer forest		0.09–0.15
Broadleaf forest		0.15–0.20
Agricultural crops		0.18–0.25
Savanna		0.16–0.26
Desert		0.20–0.45
Bare soil		
	Wet, dark	0.05
	Dry, dark	0.13
	Dry, light	0.40

[a] Albedo of water increases greatly (from 0.1 to 1.0) at solar angles <30°.

is not always possible to just operate with the daily total incoming radiation or the daily mean air temperature. On an even shorter time scale, incoming radiation can vary as a result of passages of clouds or movements of vegetation elements, causing sunflecks.

The incoming radiation is not equally distributed over the surface of the Earth (Figure 5.3). However, one should notice that at the time scale of a year, the maximum daily potential irradiance differs little between latitudes. However, an important difference is that at the equator the radiation load is distributed over only 12 hours and as one moves polewards it is distributed over longer and longer times until one crosses the polar circles where the radiation load can be distributed over 24 hours. Thus, although the total incoming irradiation can be equal, the maximum intensity of irradiation can be up to twice as large at the equator as at the poles. Another important latitudinal difference is that at the equator the solar radiation varies very little during the year, whereas closer to the poles there are extended periods with low, or even no, radiation with a consequent shortening of growing seasons. What restricts potential plant growth is, therefore, not so much the level of solar radiation during the growing season as other factors setting limits to the extent of the growing season. However, available light is not all. Even at one and the same latitude, ecological conditions differ considerably as a result of altitude (air temperature decreases approximately with 1 K or 1°C/ 100 m, the *adiabatic lapse rate*) and continentality (precipitation decreases with distance to oceans). The climatic (temperature and precipitation) variability is shown in Figure 5.4 with our nine type ecosystems as examples.

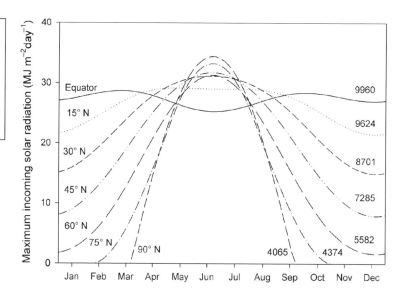

Figure 5.3 Variation in maximum incoming solar radiation over a year at different northern latitudes. The curves should be shifted by six months for the southern hemisphere. The values to the right give the annual solar radiation (MJ m^{-2}).

Soil temperature varies less than air temperature

The incoming solar radiation heats not only the air, but also the soil, with consequences for the recycling of elements, to be discussed in Chapter 7. At the top of the soil the temperature tracks closely the air temperature, but with increasing depth the soil temperature lags behind and the amplitude of both daily and annual temperature variations are attenuated (Figure 5.5). However, there is also a considerable variation within a day, as well as between days (Figure 5.6). Again the variation is largest at the surface and dampens out with depth. Also at this time scale there is a lag in temperature variation with depth, although it is less important than at the time scale of the day.

For the purpose of energy and water balances, and effects on temperature it is enough to consider the total energy, irrespective of wavelength (see Table 5.2). Of the energy emitted by the Sun most of the radiation with the shortest wavelengths is absorbed by ozone in the stratosphere, whereas for wavelengths above the visible, water vapour and oxygen absorbs considerable amounts of the radiation (Figure 5.2).

Energy or number of photons?

Light also drives photosynthesis and then it is only the radiation in the range 400 (sometimes 370 nm is used) to 700 nm that counts. This wavelength interval of visible light is called *photosynthetically active radiation* (PAR) because it is only photons in this wavelength interval that contribute to photosynthesis. Moreover, it is not the energy of the photons that matter, but their number, because each photon can only cause one photochemical reaction. For this reason plant physiologists prefer to express irradiance in units of μmol (quanta) m^{-2} s^{-1} or μE m^{-2} s^{-1}. A reasonably good approximation of the relation between energy and number of quanta in solar radiation is 1 W m^{-2} = 2.2 μE m^{-2} s^{-1}. An example of the variation in PAR during the day and over a year is given in Figure 5.7. Close to the equator, maximum PAR during the day is around 1800 μE m^{-2} s^{-1}. The excess

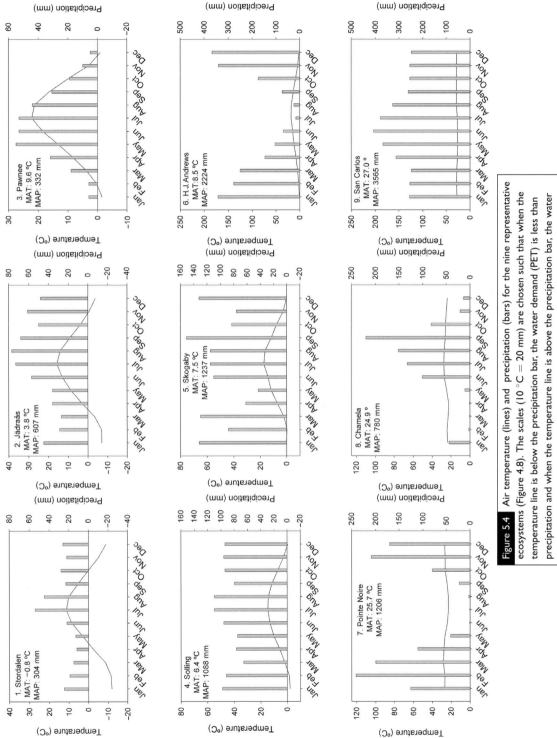

Figure 5.4 Air temperature (lines) and precipitation (bars) for the nine representative ecosystems (Figure 4.8). The scales (10 °C = 20 mm) are chosen such that when the temperature line is below the precipitation bar, the water demand (PET) is less than precipitation and when the temperature line is above the precipitation bar, the water demand exceeds precipitation.

Table 5.2 | Distribution of energy in the spectrum of the radiation emitted by the Sun

Waveband (nm)	Energy (%)
0–300	1.2
300–400 (ultraviolet)	7.8
400–700 (visible/PAR)	39.8
700–1500 (near infrared)	38.8
1500–∞	12.4
	100.0

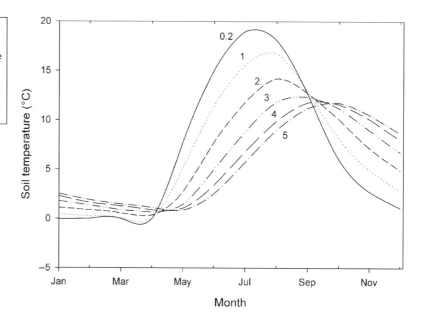

Figure 5.5 Variation in mean monthly soil temperature with depth (m) during the year. Data are from the SWECON research site Jädraås, also our site 2 (60°49′N/16°30′E). Redrawn from Halldin et al. (1980).

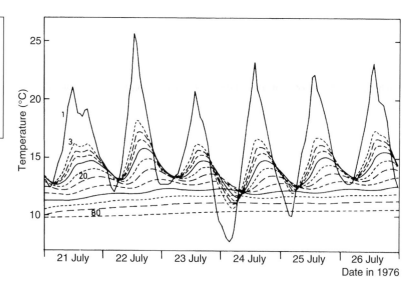

Figure 5.6 Variation in soil temperature with depth (1, 3, 5, 7, 10, 15, 20, 28, 38, 50, 63 and 80 cm) during summer days at the SWECON research site Jädraås, also our site 2 (60°49'N/16°30'E). From Halldin et al. (1980) with kind permission from Orhos.

energy in the photons of shortest wavelength of PAR is converted to heat in the plant. Of the total incoming radiation only about half is useful as PAR for the plant. The additional incoming energy represents an energy load that the plant must handle, to a large extent by transpiring water.

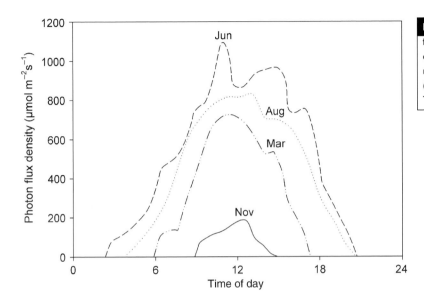

Figure 5.7 Variation in photon flux density during the day and during the year at the SWECON research site Jädraås, also our site 2 (60°49'N/16°30'E). Modified from Troeng & Linder (1982).

Box 5.1 | Black-body radiation

All physical bodies absorb and emit electromagnetic radiation. A black body is a physical body that absorbs all incoming energy and is an idealisation. Real bodies are characterised by an emissivity, which often is close to 1 (the black body) for vegetative surfaces and expresses the deviation from the ideal body. Max Planck showed, based on quantum mechanics, that the contribution to the emitted energy at a wavelength λ, $E(\lambda)$, was

$$E(\lambda) = \frac{2\pi c^2 h}{\lambda^5} \frac{1}{e^{hc/\lambda kT} - 1} \tag{5.1}$$

where c is speed of light in vacuum, h is Planck's constant, k is Boltzmann's constant and T is absolute temperature (K). The total energy (W m^{-2}) emitted by a black body is then

$$E = \frac{2\pi^5 k^4}{15 h^3 c^2} T^4 = \sigma T^4 \tag{5.2}$$

where $\sigma = 5.67 \times 10^{-8}$ W m^{-2} K^{-4} is the Stefan–Boltzmann constant.

The dependence on the fourth power of the absolute temperature makes the amount of energy emitted highly sensitive to the temperature. For example, the Sun, with a temperature approximately 20 times that of Earth, emits $20^4 = 160\,000$ times more energy per unit surface. Increasing the temperature of a leaf from 10 to 20 °C increases its longwave radiation by 15%.

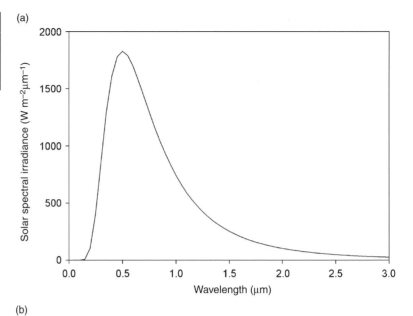

(a)

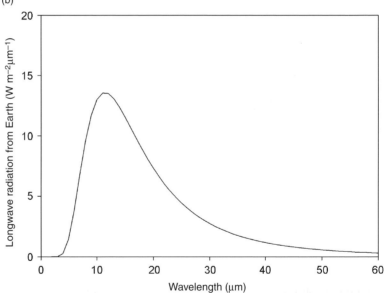

(b)

| Figure 5.8 | The spectral dependence of (a) incoming solar irradiance and (b) outgoing longwave radiation. Note the different scales on both axes.

Water balance

The water balance of a terrestrial ecosystem consists of several components (Figure 5.9). The total annual precipitation and evaporation on Earth is estimated to be 496 100 km³. Over land falls 111 100 km³, of which 71 400 km³ or 2/3 is returned to the atmosphere through evaporation and 39 700 km³ (1/3) is surface run-off and deep drainage (Baumgartner & Reichel 1975). Note that the energy expenditure for global evaporation is 1.2×10^{24} J, which corresponds to the estimated latent heat flow ($78/168 \times 2.7 \times 10^{24}$ J) in Figure 5.1. These crude numbers hide considerable variation in both the precipitation

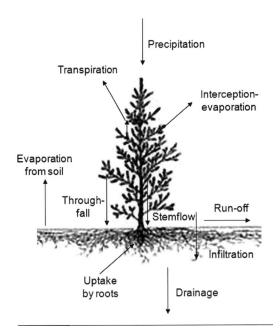

Precipitation

Transpiration

Interception-
evaporation

Evaporation
from soil

Through-
fall

Stemflow

Run-off

Infiltration

Uptake
by roots

Drainage

Figure 5.9 The main components of the water balance of an ecosystem.
Note that transpiration is shown as a two-step process with the first step from
the interior of the leaves to the interior of the canopy and the second step to the
atmosphere.

and the contributions of the components of outflows from an ecosystem. While precipitation is mainly determined by large-scale geographical features, the properties of the vegetation and the physical structure of the soil alter the pathways of water losses.

Part of the precipitation is intercepted by the canopies of the vegetation and is evaporated from there without reaching the ground, or reaches the ground by flowing along branches and stems (stemflow). The throughfall is that part of the precipitation that reaches the ground directly through gaps in the canopies or drips from leaves and branches. There are several factors that control the efficiency with which a canopy can intercept precipitation. First of all, the amount and physical characteristics of foliage plays a large role (Figure 5.10). Before water drips from the foliage (becomes throughfall as crown drip) or flows out on branches and becomes stemflow the foliage has to be more or less completely wetted. During the time it takes to wet the foliage, part of the intercepted precipitation has also evaporated. This illustrates another important factor, the intensity and duration of the precipitation event. If there is only a small amount of a precipitation, most of it will be intercepted and only a small part will reach the ground. At high enough intensity and duration of a precipitation event the canopy will become saturated and the canopy cannot intercept additional precipitation (Figure 5.11). When the precipitation comes in the form of snow, canopies can intercept a larger quantity of the precipitation.

Throughfall and stemflow becomes available water in the soil

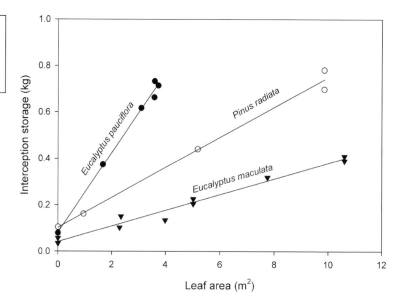

Figure 5.10 Interception storage of rain by small trees as a function of leaf area for three different species. Simplified from Aston (1979).

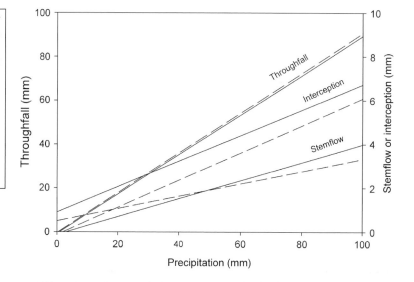

Figure 5.11 Throughfall, stemflow and interception of precipitation as a function of the amount of water during a rainfall event in hardwood forests of eastern United States. Solid lines are summer values and broken lines winter values (no leaves). During low precipitation events there is no throughfall, whereas with large precipitation events throughfall dominates. From Helvey & Patric (1965).

Although the fraction of precipitation reaching the ground through crown drip and stemflow can be small, it is important because it causes heterogeneity in the soil and transports elements from the canopy to the soil. Stemflow concentrates water to close to the stems. For highly water soluble elements and substances, such as K^+, the losses from the canopy in the form of stemflow and crown drip can be larger than the losses through litterfall.

Once the precipitation, when it is in the form of liquid water, reaches the ground, it can either infiltrate the soil or run off on the surface. Surface run-off occurs only when the infiltration rate of the soil is exceeded. Infiltration rates vary greatly, from less than 0.25 mm h^{-1} to greater than 250 mm h^{-1}. Some of the factors determining the infiltration rates are:

Soil texture. Sandy soils have higher infiltration rates than clayey soils. Cracks or holes (e.g. caused by burrowing earthworms) can greatly increase infiltration.

Water content of the soil. A dry soil has a higher infiltration rate than a wet one because of unfilled macropores. A consequence is that infiltration rates will decrease with time during a precipitation event. Such a change can occur within a few minutes after the start of the rain.

The slope of the terrain. Increasing slope of the terrain will decrease the infiltration.

Presence/absence of vegetation and litter. A vegetation cover or litter on the ground will slow down the horizontal movement of water and increase the probability that it becomes infiltrated. A major reason for no-till management of agricultural soils is to increase the infiltration rate of rain in arid climates.

The infiltrated water can then either be taken up by the vegetation and lost as transpiration, or filter down to the groundwater and flow out that way. A small part of the water reaching the groundwater may again become available for the vegetation through capillary rise.

Evapotranspiration

The partitioning of water losses from an ecosystem is mainly determined by how much is lost through transpiration and evaporation. These two processes are strongly linked to the vegetation structure. We will now look in some detail at the mechanisms of transpiration and evaporation, and how they can be calculated. The evaporative losses from an ecosystem are driven by radiation and microclimate. The net absorption of radiation in a stand is balanced by turbulent fluxes of energy: latent heat (λE, where $\lambda = 2.454$ MJ kg^{-1} at 20 °C is the latent heat of vaporisation and E the rate of water loss – evapotranspiration) and sensible heat (H). The latent heat is the energy used to evaporate water from the stand, which can be direct evaporation from free water surfaces or transpiration from vegetation. Since the two can be difficult to separate they are usually combined as evapotranspiration. This flux is therefore strongly coupled to vegetation properties and in its turn strongly affects the vegetation. The sensible heat is the energy carried by air movements and heat diffused by the temperature gradient from the surfaces in the stand to the free atmosphere outside the stand.

Evapotranspiration requires energy

The sources of water for evapotranspiration are several. Evaporation from the soil contributes to the evapotranspiration, but is generally a small component, except in open vegetation. Most

Table 5.3 | Maximum leaf stomatal conductances and canopy conductances for unstressed and well-lit leaves. From Bonan (2002) with kind permission from Cambridge University Press

Plant group	Leaf (mm s^{-1})	Canopy (mm s^{-1})
Woody plants	5.5	19.7
Natural herbaceous plants	8.0	17.0
Agricultural crops	11.6	31.6

important are the vapour-saturated interiors of leaves (transpiration) and evaporation from open wet surfaces after precipitation events, but water in other vegetation elements also contributes. Calculations of transpiration proceed in two steps. The rate of transpiration to some reference point inside a canopy is determined by the gradient in water-vapour density and the canopy conductance (g_c)

$$E = (e_{sat}(T) - e_0)g_c \tag{5.3}$$

where e_{sat} and e_0 are the saturated and reference-point vapour densities (kg m^{-3}), respectively; e_{sat} varies strongly with temperature and can be obtained from standard tables. The canopy conductance g_c includes resistance to transport from all vegetation elements and evaporation from the soil. It also includes the stomatal conductance and therefore provides a coupling to photosynthesis (see further, Chapter 6). Some typical values for stomatal and canopy conductances are given in Table 5.3.

From the interior of the canopy to the atmosphere the water flux is driven by the gradient in water-vapour density

$$E = (e_0 - e_{atm})g_a \tag{5.4}$$

where e_{atm} is the water-vapour density in the atmosphere and g_a is the conductivity from the interior of the canopy to the atmosphere (the boundary-layer conductance).

The major force determining the boundary-layer conductance is the mixing of air in the atmosphere near the vegetation surface. The efficiency of mixing is determined by the wind speed (increases with wind speed) and the structure of the vegetation. The wind speed above a canopy is well described by a logarithmic function of height (z)

$$u(z) = \frac{u_*}{\kappa} \ln\left(\frac{z + z_m - d}{z_m}\right) \tag{5.5}$$

The parameter u_*, the friction velocity, is related to the momentum transfer to the canopy and d, the *zero plane displacement*, is the apparent sink of momentum with $u(d) = 0$. The *aerodynamic roughness length*, z_m, is a measure of the momentum-absorbing capacity of the canopy, which depends, among other things, on the physical structure of the canopy (Figure 5.12). von Karman's constant, κ, is an empirical constant with a value of 0.4. It has been established

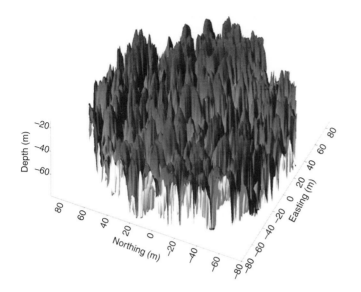

Figure 5.12 Topography of the outer surface of an old-growth *Pseudotsuga-Tsuga* canopy. From Parker *et al.* (2004) with kind permission from Springer Science + Business Media.

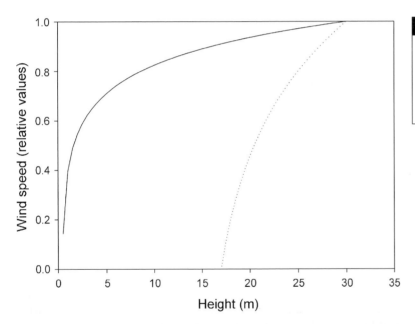

Figure 5.13 Wind speed at different heights over canopies representing a forest ($h = 20$ m, $z_m = 2$ m, $d = 15$ m) and a grassland ($h = 0.5$ m, $z_m = 0.05$ m, $d = 0.375$ m). The wind speeds are scaled to be equal at 30 m above ground.

empirically that $d \approx 0.64h$ and $z_m \approx 0.13h$, where h is the height of the canopy. Examples of wind profiles over a forest and over grassland, respectively, are shown in Figure 5.13. Note that at any height the wind speed will be higher over grassland than over a forest. Equation (5.5) should only be applied for homogeneous areas. The distance of homogeneous area that the wind has passed is named *fetch* and Equation (5.5) applies approximately up to height $\approx$ fetch/ 100. As a consequence, wind profiles over tall canopies such as forests require very long fetches to reach equilibrium. Strong heating and cooling gradients in a canopy can also cause density gradients that add to the vertical transport of air.

Equations similar to (5.5) can be derived for the vertical profiles of water vapour and temperature. When they are combined with Equation (5.5) to eliminate u_*, an expression for the canopy conductance is obtained

$$g_a = \frac{\kappa u_*}{\ln[(Z + z_v - d)/z_v]} = \frac{\kappa^2 u(Z)}{\ln[(Z + z_m - d)/z_m]\ln[(Z + z_v - d)/z_v]} \quad (5.6)$$

where Z is some reference height for wind speed and z_v is the roughness length for water vapour (or temperature); $z_v \approx 0.026h$.

An expression, the Penman–Monteith equation, can now be derived (see standard textbooks on environmental physics) for the evapotranspiration from an ecosystem in terms of the canopy and boundary conductances

$$E = \frac{sI + \gamma\lambda g_a \Delta e}{\lambda[s + \gamma(1 + g_a/g_c)]} = \frac{sI}{\lambda[s + \gamma(1 + g_a/g_c)]} + \frac{\gamma g_a \Delta e}{s + \gamma(1 + g_a/g_c)} \quad (5.7)$$

where $s = de_{sat}/dT$, $\gamma = \rho c_p/\lambda$, c_p is the specific heat of air at constant pressure (1.01 kJ kg^{-1} K^{-1}) and $\Delta e = e(Z) - e_{sat}(T(Z))$, i.e. the vapour-density deficit at the reference level. The partitioning of E into two parts in Equation (5.7) shows how the evaporation is driven on the one hand by the energy load and on the other by the diffusion of water vapour (Figure 5.14). The response of evapotranspiration to changes in environmental conditions is not simple. While increases in the driving variables, irradiance and vapour density, always increase evapotranspiration, an increase in boundary-layer conductance can both decrease and increase evapotranspiration. The reason is that increasing the boundary layer conductance facilitates both latent heat and sensible heat transport, but the total energy loss is constant. Changes in boundary-layer conductance can therefore only change the partitioning between these two fluxes and such a change in partitioning can go both ways, depending on the specific circumstances. The Penman–Monteith equation can appear in other forms when resistances rather than conductances are employed, parameters are introduced in different ways or the vapour-pressure deficit is expressed in other variables.

The ratio between sensible and latent heat losses ($H/\lambda E$), the Bowen ratio, is a useful characteristic of an environment and shows how the energy losses are partitioned between these two mechanisms. In moist areas, latent heat losses dominate and the Bowen ratio is small, whereas in dry environments it becomes large (Table 5.4). Large leaf-area indices will also lead to a larger Bowen ratio, which explains why coniferous forests typically have larger Bowen ratios than deciduous forests.

> The vegetation type determines if energy is lost as heat or water vapour

Potential and actual evapotranspiration

A useful characteristic of a land area is the potential evapotranspiration (PET), which is the rate of water loss from a free water surface under given weather conditions. This is the

(a)

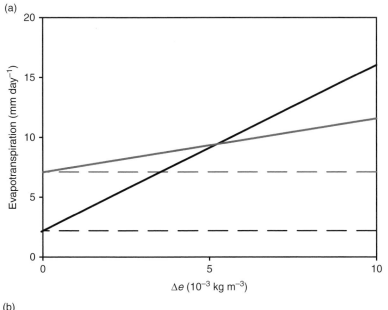

(b)

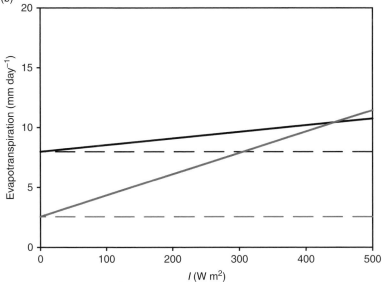

Figure 5.14 The changes in evapotranspiration as a function of (a) water vapour density deficit (Δe) and (b) irradiance (I). The solid lines show the total evapotranspiration and the broken lines the contributions from energy (a) and vapour diffusion (b). The difference between the solid and the broken line is the contribution from the change in the driving variable. The calculations are with values representative of a forest in summer ($T = 20°C$, $I = 400$ W m^{-2} (a) and $\Delta e = 6.1 \times 10^{-3}$ kg m^{-3} corresponding to a relative humidity of 65%). Other parameters: $s = 1.01 \times 10^{-3}$ kg m^{-3} K^{-1}, $\gamma = 0.495 \times 10^{-3}$ kg m^{-3} K^{-1}, $I = 2.45 \times 10^6$ J kg^{-1}, $g_a = 200 \times 10^{-3}$ m s^{-1} (thick lines), $g_a = 20 \times 10^{-3}$ m s^{-1} (thin lines), $g_c = 20 \times 10^{-3}$ m s^{-1}). The range for Δe in (a) corresponds to a range in relative humidity from 100% to 40%.

maximal rate at which water can be lost from the land and has to be supplied either as precipitation or drawn from storage. The water losses are always less in practice because water evaporates, not from free water surfaces, but from the interior of leaves or the soil, giving rise to the actual evapotranspiration (AET). There are several methods of estimating PET, depending on time scale and availability of climatic information, but one expression can be derived from the Penman–Monteith equation. In the limit of infinite canopy conductance, $g_c \rightarrow \infty$; the equation describes evaporation from free water surfaces

Table 5.4 | Ranges of Bowen ratios in various ecosystems. Data from Eugster *et al.* (2000)

Ecosystem type	Bowen ratio
Tropical oceans	0.1
Tropical wet jungles	0.1–0.3
Agricultural crops	0.1–1.0
Deciduous forests (full-leaf)	0.2–0.7
Wetlands (arctic and boreal)	0.2–0.7
Temperate forests and grassland	0.4–0.8
Arctic tundra	0.3–2.5
Forest tundra	0.4–1.7
Coniferous forest	0.6–3.8
Semi-arid areas	2.0–6.0

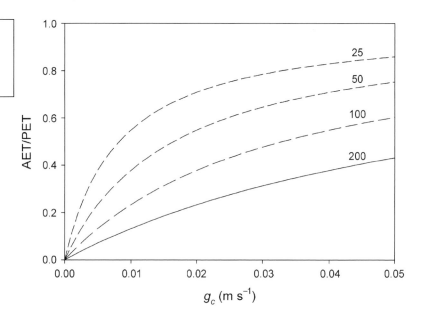

Figure 5.15 The ratio AET/PET as a function of canopy conductance, g_c, for different boundary-layer conductances, g_a(mm s^{-1}).

$$PET = \frac{sI + \gamma\lambda g_a \Delta e}{\lambda(s + \gamma)} \qquad (5.8)$$

The reduction of PET to AET as a function of canopy and boundary-layer conductance is shown in Figure 5.15. The low boundary-layer conductance values are representative of agricultural crops and other low vegetation, whereas the higher values represent forests. An increasing boundary-layer conductance increases both PET and AET, but AET is also limited by the canopy conductance and its relative increase will therefore be lower; the AET/PET ratio decreases with increasing boundary-layer conductance. Forests, with their higher boundary-layer conductances, will therefore have AETs that are lower than the PETs, whereas for agricultural crops the two can approach each other.

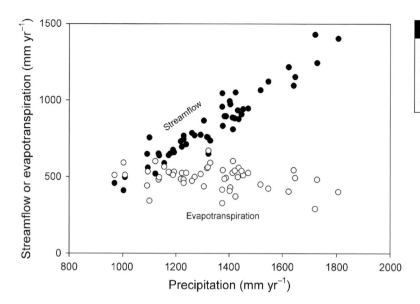

Figure 5.16 Partitioning of precipitation between streamflow and evapotranspiration from Watershed 1 at Hubbard Brook between 1956 and 2006. Updated from Bailey *et al.* (2003).

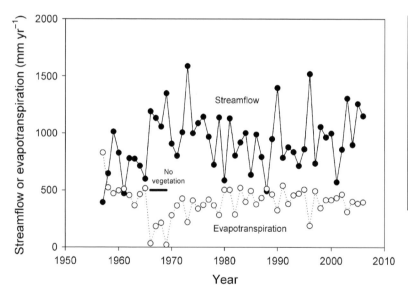

Figure 5.17 Partitioning of precipitation between streamflow (•) and evapotranspiration (○) from Watershed 2 at Hubbard Brook between 1957 and 2006. All vegetation in the watershed was cut in December 1965, indicated by the horizontal bar. The watershed was then maintained vegetation free with herbicides until regrowth was allowed in 1969. Updated from Bailey *et al.* (2003).

Over short periods of time the variability in weather will cause large variations in all the components of the Penman–Monteith equation. Over longer periods of time, such as a whole year, the short-term variability in climatic conditions will average out and the variability will be less, such that variations in precipitation between years will be taken up mostly by variation in drainage and run-off (Figure 5.16). However, drastic changes in the vegetation, such as those occurring with a clear-cut of a forest will be reflected in the partitioning of the water balance (Figure 5.17). Estimates of PET can be done with reasonable accuracy using the Penman–Monteith equation or some other similar type of function because they are only based on the physical characteristics of a site. Estimates of AET are, on the other hand, much more difficult because they involve vegetation properties that are less easily estimated. Accurate estimates of AET are best done when it can be estimated as the difference in a water budget. This requires run-off and drainage to be measured, which is best done on entire watersheds.

SPAC: The soil–plant–atmosphere continuum

The water transpired from vegetation takes the path soil–plant–atmosphere. For the flux to function properly there must be a continuous connection to water, hence the idea of the *soil–plant–atmosphere continuum* (SPAC). The previous parts have examined the plant–atmosphere relationship. Now it is time to look at the soil–plant relationship. Whereas the previous discussion has been in terms of energy load and vapour-density deficit, the soil–plant relation and its extension to the atmosphere will be considered in terms of water potentials.

The water potential is in this context defined as the potential energy of water relative to free water at the soil surface. Various units can be used to express the water potential, but mm can be a convenient unit and corresponds to the height of a water column. Alternatively, the potential is expressed in Pa and 1 mm $= 9.8$ Pa. There are four components in the water potential:

$$\Psi = \Psi_m + \Psi_s + \Psi_g + \Psi_p \tag{5.9}$$

Ψ_m the matric potential, which results from the binding of water molecules to surfaces. In soils or cells, a large fraction of the water can be close to surfaces of different kinds, but often with charges that attract the dipole in water molecules.

Ψ_s the osmotic potential, which is produced by solutes in the water.

Ψ_g the gravitational potential. This potential can be considerable for tall trees and also prevents water from rising towards the soil surface although in dry soils there can be capillary action.

Ψ_p the pressure potential, which results from external pressures. It is normally negligible in soils, but is important in cells where the elasticity of cell walls exerts an external pressure.

The matric potential is coupled to the volumetric water content of the soil (θ, cm^3 cm^{-3}), which can be calculated from the mass of water (m_w), mass of soil (m_s), density of water (ρ_w) and bulk density of soil (ρ_w)

$$\theta = \frac{m_w/\rho_w}{m_s/\rho_s} \tag{5.10}$$

With this formulation of water content, multiplying by the thickness of a soil horizon gives the amount of water in the horizon. The amount of water that can be held in a soil depends on the composition of the soil. Coarse sandy soils consist of large, but few, pores,

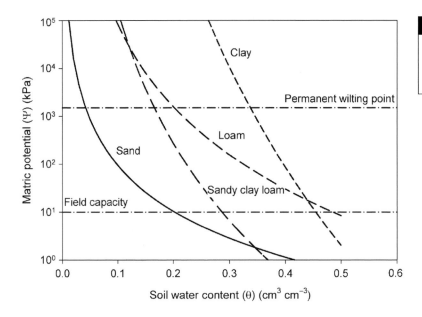

Figure 5.18 Relationships between matric potential and soil water content for some soils with different textures. From Williams et al. (1983).

which leads to a small pore volume, typically around 30% of the soil volume. At the same time the water in the pores becomes distant from surfaces, and forces between water molecules and soil surfaces become weak. At the other end of the scale, clay soils consist of many fine pores leading to a large pore volume, typically around 50% of the soil volume, and the distances between the water molecules and soil surfaces are shorter, leading to stronger interactions and lower matric potentials. Therefore, the relation between soil water potential and soil water content (soil water *retention curve*) varies greatly between soils. The following relationship has been found to work well for many soils (*a* and *b* are empirical parameters)

$$\Psi = a\theta^{-b} \tag{5.11}$$

Some examples are shown in Figure 5.18.

The *field capacity* of a soil is defined as the amount of water it can hold when it has been well drained and the matric potential balances the gravitational force. This will typically occur at matric potentials around −10 to −30 kPa. At the other end, when the water potential in the soil has reached around −1500 kPa (the *permanent wilting point*) most plant species are no longer able to extract soil water and they will wilt.

A consequence of Equation (5.11) and the differences in parameters for different soils is that the storage capacity of plant-available water varies between soils of different textures (Figure 5.19). Sandy soil will always have a low water content and also a small range of available water. Clay soil, on the other hand, will always have a high water content, but because of their steep retention curve much of that water is too tightly bound to be plant available. Soils with intermediate textures are therefore those with the greatest capacity to store plant-available water.

Loamy soils have most plant-available water

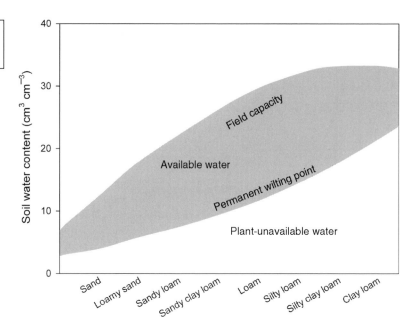

Figure 5.19 Plant-available water as a function of soil texture. From Kramer & Boyer (1995).

The (vertical, z-direction) flux of water through the soil (F, mm s^{-1}) is driven by differences in the water potential such that water will move from high potentials to lower ones. This is expressed in Darcy's law

$$F = -k \frac{\partial \Psi}{\partial z} \qquad (5.12)$$

where k is the hydraulic conductivity (mm s^{-1}). The change in water content as a result of drainage is given by Richard's equation

$$\frac{\partial \theta}{\partial t} = \frac{\partial}{\partial z}\left(k\frac{\partial \Psi}{\partial z}\right) = \frac{\partial}{\partial z}\left(k\frac{\partial \theta}{\partial \Psi}\frac{\partial \Psi}{\partial \theta}\right) \qquad (5.13)$$

Box 5.2 | Global warming potential: GWP

In order to simplify the comparison between the radiative forcing of different greenhouse gases the concept of global warming potential (GWP) was introduced. The GWP is defined as the time-integrated radiative forcing from the instantaneous release of 1 kg of a trace substance (x) relative to that of a reference substance (r) (IPCC 2001)

$$\text{GWP}_{TH} = \frac{\int_0^{TH} a_x x(t) dt}{\int_0^{TH} a_r r(t) dt} \qquad (5.14)$$

where a is the radiative efficiency due to a unit increase in the atmospheric abundance of the substance in question (i.e. W m^{-2} kg^{-1}) and x and r are the time-dependent decays in the abundance of the instantaneous release of the

Table 5.5 | Properties of some important greenhouse gases. For full details the reader is referred to IPCC (2001), Table 4.1

Chemical species	Formula	Abundance		Annual emission	Lifetime[a]	100-yr GWP
		1750	1998	late 90s	(yr)	
Carbon dioxide	CO_2 (ppm)	280	366	6.3	_[b]	1
Methane	CH_4 (ppb)	700	1745	600 Tg	8.4	23
Nitrous oxide	N_2O (ppb)	270	314	16.4 Tg N	120	296
Perflouromethane	CF_4 (ppt)	40	80	~15 Gg	>50 000	5700
Perflouroethane	C_2F_6 (ppt)	0	3.9	~3 Gg	10 000	11 900
Sulfur hexafluoride	SF_6 (ppt)	0	4.2	~6 Gg	3200	22 200
HFC-134a	CF_3CH_2F (ppt)	0	7.5	~25 Gg	13.8	1300

[a] The time taken for half of an added unit of the gas to disappear from the atmosphere, assuming an exponential loss

[b] The disappearance of additional carbon dioxide follows a more complex pattern than a single exponential loss. 50% has disappeared after 30 years but 21.7% remains indefinitely (IPCC 2007)

substances x and r, respectively. By convention, carbon dioxide is used as the reference substance. The GWP and some other properties of important greenhouse gases are summarised in Table 5.5.

There are at least three factors that one should keep in mind when using GWP to compare the effects of different substances on climate. First of all, the often used 100-yr time horizon is arbitrarily chosen and choices of other time horizons can drastically change the GWP of a substance. Figure 5.20 illustrates this. When the time horizon is 100 yr, the GWP of CH_4 and CF_4 are the ratios of the vertically hatched areas in the graphs for CH_4 and CF_4 to that of CO_2, respectively. If we change the time horizon to 250 yr, the GWP's are the corresponding ratios of the sum of the vertically and horizontally hatched areas. In the case of CH_4, the horizontally hatched area is almost zero and the numerator in the expression for GWP changes hardly at all, while the denominator increases. As a result, the GWP for CH_4, which has a short lifetime in the atmosphere, is considerably smaller for a time horizon of 250 yr than for a time horizon of 100 yr. On the other hand, for a substance like CF_4, which has a longer lifetime than CO_2 in the atmosphere, the opposite occurs and its GWP increases with the length of the time horizon.

A second factor to consider is that the radiative efficiency of a substance may not increase linearly with its abundance because of saturation of absorption. This is particularly relevant for the most important and abundant greenhouse gases, CO_2, CH_4 and N_2O. Since the concentration of these gases changes over time, GWP will also depend upon the time period for which the calculation is done.

Third, there are uncertainties in how substances will disappear from the atmosphere. This applies in particular to carbon dioxide, which depends on interactions between oceans and the biosphere. For this reason, the numerator in GWP is not calculated from any model of disappearance of CO_2 from the atmosphere, but is assigned an estimated value.

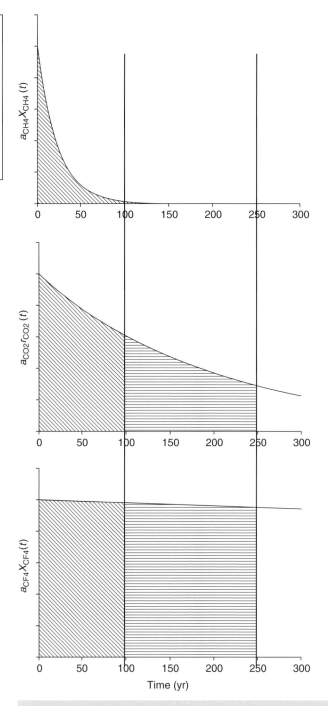

Figure 5.20 The temporal development of the radiative forcing of three different greenhouse gases (CH_4, CO_2 and CF_4). A lifetime of 200 yr has been assumed for CO_2 in this example. The different hatchings indicate the areas that contribute to the integrals in the calculation of GWP for time horizons of 100 and 250 yr, respectively.

The discussion above pertains to what is called the direct GWP of a substance. There is also an indirect GWP resulting from the presence of one substance changing the lifetime of another substance. For example, CO, which has a small GWP in itself, can consume OH radicals that otherwise would have oxidised CH_4 and as a result the lifetime of CH_4 is prolonged.

This equation can be complicated to solve because k varies strongly as a function of the soil water potential. The soil texture also varies with depth, which adds an additional variability to both k and the retention curve. A complete description of soil water changes also requires removal of water through vegetation uptake. This uptake will depend on the presence of roots at different depths (see Chapter 6).

FURTHER READING

Bonan, G. 2002. *Ecological Climatology – Concepts and Applications*. Cambridge: Cambridge University Press.

Campbell, G.S. 1977. *An Introduction to Environmental Biophysics*. New York: Springer-Verlag.

Kramer, P.J. & Boyer, J.S. 1995. *Water Relations of Plants and Soils*. San Diego, CA: Academic Press.

Monteith, J.L. & Unsworth, M.H. 1990. *Principles of Environmental Physics*. London: Edward Arnold.

Chapter 6

Plant production

Plant production is the basis for almost all processes in terrestrial ecosystems. Photosynthesis is the only process that introduces energy in a chemical form that can be used to drive biochemical processes, be these within the ecosystem or in organisms living on consumed, harvested or exported products. Other processes within plants convert the primary result of photosynthesis, glucose, into a variety of other compounds, which may be useful or harmful to other organisms. Many aspects of plant production have therefore been studied in great detail. However, we focus on processes and structures at the whole-plant level, although excursions into plant biochemistry are inevitable to establish the basis for functioning at the ecosystem level.

Carbon is the major element, but the limiting constraints from other elements are apparent. Therefore, interactions between carbon, nutrients (or more precisely mineral nutrients), water and light are key topics of this chapter. These interactions also determine the type of plants that will dominate under given conditions and which properties those plants will have.

Photosynthesis at leaf level

Rubisco, the most common enzyme in the world, is the centre for photosynthesis

The beginning of plant production is *photosynthesis*. Photosynthesis is one of the most studied plant processes. In 2009 more than 6000 scientific papers that in some way referred to photosynthesis were published. Our understanding of photosynthesis, from details of its biochemistry to the controls at leaf level, is therefore well advanced. The principles behind photosynthesis are simple. Light converts ADP (adenosine diphosphate) to ATP (adenosine triphosphate), thus providing the energy necessary to reduce carbon dioxide to glucose. Carbon dioxide diffuses/is transported from outside the leaf to reaction sites inside the leaf. The reaction sites in the leaf are enzymes (*Rubisco* = **Ru**bulose **bis**phosphate **c**arboxylase/**o**xygenase). The double ending in Rubisco alludes to the double functioning of Rubisco; both carbon dioxide and oxygen molecules can be bound to the enzyme, with the consequence that this enzyme can drive both carbon fixation and respiration, depending upon which molecule binds the strongest.

Net photosynthesis = gross photosynthesis – dark respiration

Photosynthesis can be described as *gross photosynthesis* (A_g) or as *net photosynthesis* (A_n). Gross photosynthesis is the rate at which carbon dioxide is fixed by Rubisco. However, any photosynthesising leaf also has simultaneously ongoing respiratory processes. This rate of *respiration* is usually estimated by placing the leaf in dark-ness and is therefore called *dark respiration*, R_d, and is mostly a function of leaf nitrogen content and temperature (see section on plant respiration). The net gain of carbon and the carbon which can be used in other processes is net photosynthesis. From an ecosystem perspective it is therefore net photosynthesis that is of interest, but for a mechanistic understanding it can be useful to consider gross photosynthesis and respiration separately. Almost all measurements are done on A_n and gross photosynthesis is then obtained from

$$A_g = A_n + R_d \tag{6.1}$$

The rate of net leaf photosynthesis depends on the difference between the carbon dioxide concentration inside the leaf (c_i) and outside the leaf (ambient) (c_a) (Figure 6.1). This difference in concentration determines the rate, A_n, at which carbon dioxide can diffuse through stomata into the leaf

$$A_n = g_s(c_a - c_i) \tag{6.2}$$

where g_s is the *stomatal conductance*. This produces a *supply curve* with no carbon dioxide uptake when the internal and external carbon dioxide concentrations are equal. When the internal carbon dioxide concentration is lower, supply is possible and the rate is determined by the stomatal conductance, which is regulated by plant water status, but also by feedback from c_i

$$g_s = g_s(H_2O, c_i) \tag{6.3}$$

Inside the leaf the biochemical processes determine the rate at which carbon dioxide can be processed, the *demand curve*. A common description of this curve is the Farquhar–von Caemmerer model (Box 6.1) where photosynthesis is determined by leaf nitrogen status and temperature. Actual photosynthesis occurs at the intersection between the supply and demand curves. At low internal carbon dioxide concentrations photosynthesis is limited by carbon dioxide, but as the internal carbon dioxide concentration increases there is a smooth transition to limitation by biochemical reactions. The internal carbon dioxide concentration at which gross photosynthesis just balances dark respiration is called the *carbon dioxide compensation point.*

From the above the major controls of photosynthesis are obvious: light, carbon dioxide, nitrogen to produce enzymes and temperature as an overall rate regulating factor. The water status of a leaf is also a key factor. Increasing light modifies the demand curve by shifting it upwards. Increasing the ambient carbon dioxide concentration will initially move the supply curve to the right without changing its slope. Increasing leaf nitrogen concentration increases the capacity of the biochemical machinery in the leaf and the supply is, in general, shifted upwards. However, dark respiration will also increase,

Light, CO_2, N, H_2O and temperature determine the rate of photosynthesis

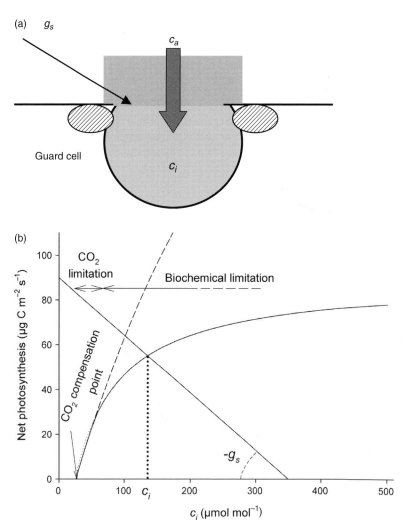

Figure 6.1 (a) Carbon dioxide diffuses from outside a leaf (concentration c_a) to the inside (concentration c_i) (a). To enter the leaf the carbon dioxide molecules have to pass the stomata, which has a conductance g_s. This produces the supply curves for leaf net photosynthesis as a function of internal CO_2 concentration (broken line) (b). The stomatal conductance is controlled by the guard cells, which respond to the water status of the leaf and c_i. When c_i increases, the guard cells close the stomata; this closes the stomata during the night when there is no light available for photosynthetic reactions and thereby prevents unnecessary water losses; see however CAM species below. The demand curve is a result of the biochemical properties of the leaf. The intersection between the supply and demand curves defines the actual internal carbon dioxide concentration. When conditions are such that c_i is low it is the concentration of carbon dioxide at the reaction sites of Rubisco that limits the rate of photosynthesis. When c_i is high, the reaction sites of Rubisco are saturated and it is the amount of Rubisco and the reaction rates that limit the rate of photosynthesis.

drawing the demand curve down and towards lower internal carbon dioxide concentration; the balance between these two factors can go in either direction. Limited increases in temperature will act in the

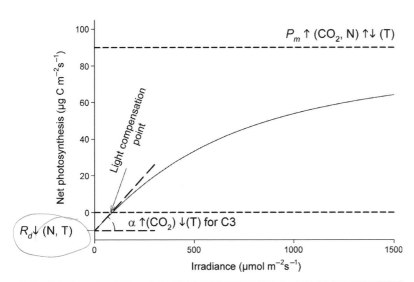

P_m = maximal rate of photosynthesis

Figure 6.2 Light response curve of net photosynthesis. Directions of changes in parameters describing the response curve to environmental factors are indicated.

same way as increases in nitrogen concentration. Any changes in demand and supply curves that shift the intersection between the curves to higher or lower internal carbon dioxide concentration will be modified by the negative feedback on stomatal conductance. The stomatal conductance responds to the internal carbon dioxide concentration and decreases when the internal carbon dioxide concentration increases; this feedback will therefore stabilise the internal carbon dioxide concentration. This response also causes the stomata to close during the night when there is no utilisation of carbon dioxide and the internal carbon dioxide concentration becomes equal to the external one. In this way plants restrict water losses through transpiration.

Since light is one of the key factors in photosynthesis and varies in a regular manner within plant canopies, the response of net photosynthesis to light is important (Figure 6.2). The light response of net photosynthesis is characterised by three biologically interpretable parameters. First there is a maximal rate, P_m

$$P_m = P_m(CO_2, T, N, H_2O, plant\ species) \qquad (6.4)$$

P_m

The initial slope of the response of photosynthesis to light, the quantum yield (α) is a second characteristic parameter. The quantum yield is a measure of the maximal efficiency with which light quanta can be utilised for fixation of carbon and is as such a parameter that does not vary as much as others between species. Third, dark respiration, R_d, has to be accounted for.

There are several possibilities for describing the light response curve for photosynthesis, but a non-rectangular hyperbola is a commonly used function for gross photosynthesis, which in addition to P_m

and α, uses a shape parameter θ to better fit to experimental data (e.g. Cannell & Thornley 1998)

[handwritten: Gross photosynthesis]

$$A_g = \frac{\alpha I + P_m - \sqrt{(\alpha I + P_m)^2 - 4\theta \alpha I P_m}}{2\theta} \xrightarrow[\theta \to 0]{} \frac{\alpha I P_m}{\alpha I + P_m} \tag{6.5}$$

The parameter θ ($0 \leq \theta \leq 1$) accounts in an empirical way for the structural organisation within leaves. In the limit of $\theta = 1$, Equation (6.5) becomes two straight lines, the Blackman response curve, one passing through the origin, the other horizontal at P_m.

C3, C4 and CAM photosynthesis

Although the previous section gives a general description of leaf photosynthesis, the current rapid change in climate and atmospheric carbon dioxide concentration makes it important to distinguish between three different modes of photosynthesis:

> CO_2 transport in C3 plants is by diffusion

[handwritten: $C_3 \to 3PGA \ (3C)$]

(1) *C3* derives its name from the first organic compound in the photosynthetic process, namely the three-carbon chain, 3-phosphoglyceric acid (PGA). The transport of carbon dioxide to the chloroplasts, where the carbon dioxide is converted to organic carbon, in C3 plants is simple diffusion. The scheme below shows the first steps in the *Calvin cycle*, which eventually results in the formation of glucose and the release of oxygen. Trees and plants originating from high latitudes are typical C3 plants. A key step in C3 photosynthesis is:

RuBP + CO_2 + H_2O → 2 3PGA (see scheme below)

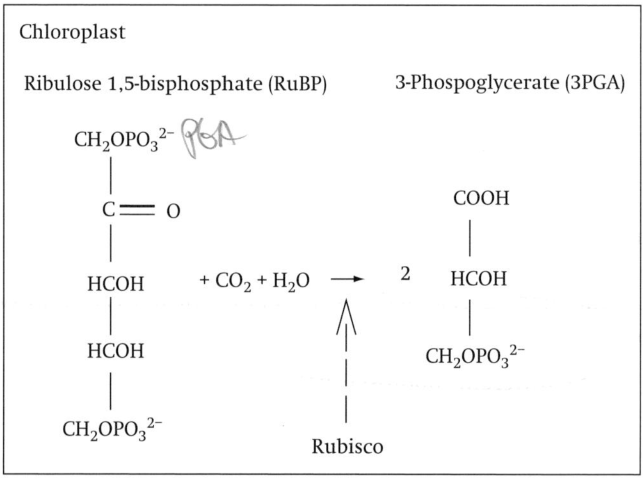

Chloroplast

Ribulose 1,5-bisphosphate (RuBP)   3-Phospoglycerate (3PGA)

$CH_2OPO_3^{2-}$ *[handwritten: PGA]*

$C = O$

    COOH

HCOH   + CO_2 + H_2O →   2   HCOH

HCOH $CH_2OPO_3^{2-}$

$CH_2OPO_3^{2-}$ Rubisco

> CO_2 transport in C4 plants is facilitated

[handwritten: $C_4 \to$ Oxolatecid acid (4C)]

(2) *C4* derives its name from the first organic compound in the photosynthetic process, the four-carbon chain, oxaloacetic acid (OAA). In contrast to C3 plants, this first reaction occurs in the mesophyll cells and involves no gain in energy. Once carbon dioxide is fixed into OAA, a series of transformations occurs,

which varies between plant species, but leads to a transfer of the carbon dioxide and finally its release in the chloroplasts, where the same reaction occurs as in C3 plants. The important ecological difference between C3 and C4 is that this transport mechanism in C4 plants (compare the passive diffusion of carbon dioxide in C3 plants) results in much higher carbon dioxide concentrations around Rubisco. C4 plants are evolutionarily younger species than C3 plants and are typically grasses from tropical and sub-tropical regions (e.g. maize, sorghum). The C4 mechanism has evolved in several different regions and therefore several varieties of this mechanism exist. The first key step in C4 photosynthesis is:

$$PEP + CO_2 \rightarrow OAA + PO_3{}^{2-}$$

which then is followed by the same step as in C3 photosynthesis (see scheme below):

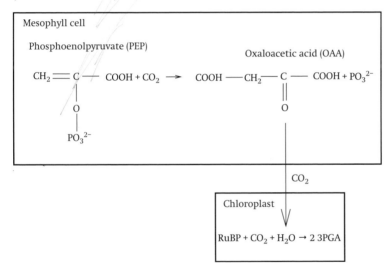

(3) *CAM*, crassulacean acid metabolism, is a specialisation for extremely dry environments where carbon dioxide is fixed by PEP carboxylase into C4 acids during the night. During the day stomata are closed to prevent water loss, but carbon dioxide in the acids is released and enters a normal C3 photosynthetic cycle.

The three different photosynthetic systems give rise to different niches. CAM plants are obviously specialised for dry environments because of their water-saving photosynthetic mechanism. The niche differentiation between C3 and C4 plants is more subtle and is coupled to temperature. The high CO_2 concentration at Rubisco in C4 plants results in a quantum yield that is insensitive to temperature (Figure 6.3). With increasing temperature, O_2 binds more strongly than CO_2 to Rubisco in C3 plants, which results in decreasing quantum yield with temperature (Figure 6.3). However, the

C3 plants are favoured by higher atmospheric CO_2. C4 plants are favoured by higher temperatures

CO_2 concentrating mechanism in C4 plants has an energy cost such that in low light, where quantum yield is most important for photosynthesis, C3 plants may have the fastest photosynthetic rate at low temperatures, but above some crossover temperature, C4 photosynthesis is the fastest (Figure 6.4a). Under light-saturating

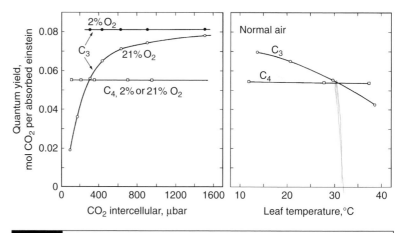

Figure 6.3 The effect of internal carbon dioxide concentration and temperature on quantum yield for C3 and C4 plants. From Björkman (1981) with kind permission from Springer Science + Business Media.

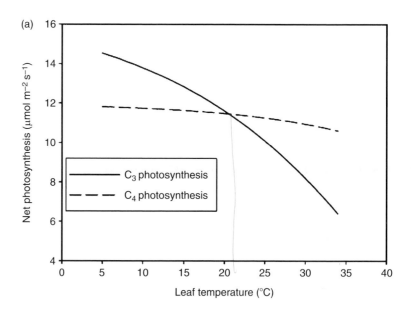

Figure 6.4 Temperature response of net photosynthesis of leaves in C3 and C4 plants at (a) low light levels (250 μmol m^{-2} s^{-1}) and (b) light saturation. From Still et al. (2003) with kind permission from American Geophysical Union.

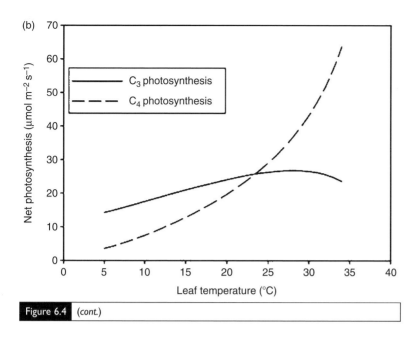

Figure 6.4 (cont.)

conditions, C4 plants respond more strongly to temperature than C3 plants, but again C4 plants have lower rates at low temperatures and higher rates at high temperatures (Figure 6.4b). As a result, temperature creates a niche differentiation between C3 and C4 plants, confining C4 plants to warmer (and moister) environments (Figure 6.5). Increasing atmospheric carbon dioxide concentration should favour C3 plants because they have the potential to respond. On the other hand, the higher temperatures accompanying the increasing carbon dioxide concentration will favour C4 plants, making the final outcome of the ongoing climatic change less certain.

Leaf area index and specific leaf area

The amount of leaves in a canopy can, depending upon the purpose, be described by leaf biomass (or contents of elements like C and N) or by the leaf area. Leaf area is usually expressed as *leaf area index* (LAI), which means the area of leaves above 1 m² of ground. There are two forms of LAI, *projected* and *total*. The projected leaf area is obtained when leaves are laid flat on a surface and their projection on the surface measured. Total leaf area measures the leaf area of all sides of the leaf. Total leaf area is, therefore, often approximately twice the projected leaf area. Conifer needles that resemble cylinders more than sheets have total leaf areas approximately three times (π) the projected leaf area. Because there

LAI
leaf area index:
leaves above 1 m²
of ground

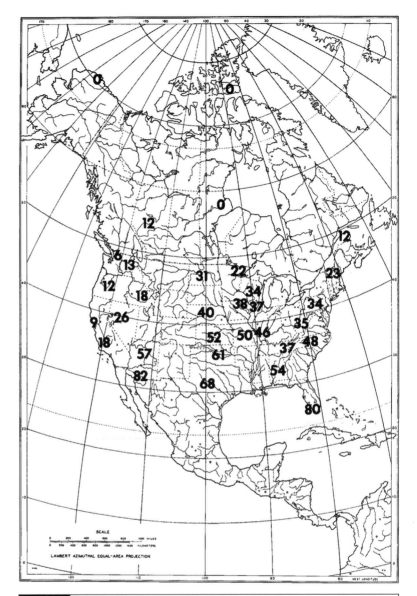

Figure 6.5 Per centage C4 species in the grass flora of North America. From Teeri & Stowe (1976) with kind permission form Springer Science + Business Media.

is no consistent use of the two forms of LAI it is necessary to check which definition is used in each particular case. In what follows we will always use projected leaf area. Typical values of leaf area are 1 to 8 m^2 (leaf) m^{-2} (ground).

The relation between leaf area and leaf biomass is given by the *specific leaf area* (SLA)

$$SLA = \frac{\text{leaf area}}{\text{leaf biomass}} \ (m^2 \ kg^{-1}) \tag{6.6}$$

Box 6.1 | The Farquhar–von Caemmerer model of photosynthesis

Since both carbon dioxide and oxygen can bind to Rubisco, the net rate of carbon dioxide assimilation (A_c) is the balance between the rate of carboxylation (V_c) and oxygenation (V_o). In the latter, one CO_2 is produced per two oxygenation reactions. The rate of respiration during photosynthesis (R_{day}) needs also to be accounted for and may differ from ordinary dark respiration, giving

$$A_c = V_c - 0.5V_o - R_{day} = V_c\left(1 - 0.5\frac{V_o}{V_c}\right) - R_{day} \qquad (6.7)$$

When Rubisco is ribulose 1,5-bisphosphate (RuBP) saturated and the assimilation rate is limited by carbon dioxide, the rate of carboxylation can be described by a Michaelis–Menten function

$$V_c = V_{cmax}\frac{c_i}{c_i + K_m} \qquad (6.8)$$

However, the competitive inhibition of carboxylation from oxygen needs to be included in K_m

$$K_m = K_c(1 + O/K_o) \qquad (6.9)$$

where K_c and K_o are the Michaelis–Menten constants for carboxylation and oxygenation, respectively, and O is the oxygen partial pressure.

The ratio V_o/V_c can be expressed in terms of the CO_2 compensation point in the absence of R_{day} (Γ^*) as

$$V_o/V_c = 2\Gamma^*/c_i \qquad (6.10)$$

giving

$$A_c = V_{cmax}\frac{c_i - \Gamma^*}{c_i + K_c(1 + O/K_o)} - R_{day} \qquad (6.11)$$

When the rate of photosynthesis is limited by the rate at which RuBP is regenerated in the light reaction of photosynthesis (J_{max}), the rate of carboxylation is determined by the relative rate of oxygenation and carboxylation.

$$A_J = J_{max}\frac{V_c}{V_c + V_o}(1 - \Gamma^*/c_i) = J_{max}\frac{c_i - \Gamma^*}{c_i + 2\Gamma^*} \qquad (6.12)$$

The realised rate of photosynthesis is the minimum of A_c and A_J. Under certain circumstances the regeneration of RuBP may also be limited by availability of phosphate.

The variation in SLA can be caused by both differences in leaf thickness (sun leaves are thick, while shade leaves are thin) and differences in leaf density. The variability between species is large, extending at least between 1 and 50 m^2 kg^{-1}. Specific leaf area is not only important for connecting leaf area and leaf biomass, but turns out also to be an important characteristic of plant properties. Fast-growing species tend to have high SLA, i.e. large but thin leaves. Net photosynthesis per unit leaf area is rather insensitive to SLA, but as a consequence net photosynthesis per unit mass decreases with SLA. Longevity of leaves is also correlated with SLA such that longer-lived leaves have lower SLA than short-lived ones. These adaptations are interpreted as fast-growing species investing in a large light-capturing area with little cost of biomass (carbon). As a result such leaves have low levels of protection against hazards and consumers. In contrast, slow-growing plants invest large resources in creating long-lived, but, per unit of biomass, less rapidly working leaves. However, seen over the entire life span of leaves, the differences in cumulative photosynthesis between leaves of different types is not that large. The inverse of SLA (= 1/SLA) or leaf mass per area is also frequently used to characterise leaves.

Light extinction within a canopy

The photosynthesis of single leaves can be described in detail, as has been discussed above. Application of this knowledge to whole canopies requires that we take into account the variability of environmental factors within the canopy (Figure 6.6). The major cause of variation within a canopy is the distribution of leaves within the canopy, and the variable most affected by the distribution of the leaves is, of course, light intensity. The simplest way to describe the variation of light intensity within the canopy is to assume a horizontally homogeneous canopy. If the leaf area density at a depth z

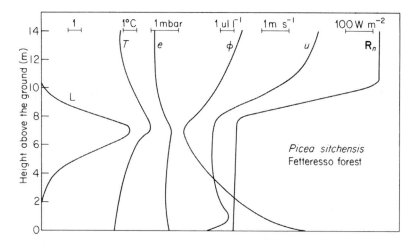

Figure 6.6 Distribution (from left) of leaf area and gradients of temperature, water vapour density, carbon dioxide, wind speed and radiation within a coniferous canopy. From Jarvis et al. (1976) with kind permission from Elsevier.

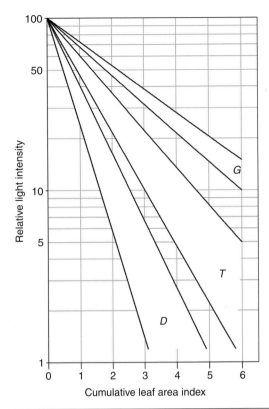

Figure 6.7 Relationship between cumulative leaf area index and light intensity for three typical types of canopies. G = grasses with small k (< 0.5). T = trees with $0.5 < k < 0.65$. D = broadleaved dicotelydons with large k (>0.7). From Larcher (1995) with kind permission from Verlag Eugen Ulmer.

leaf area density at depth z

(counted from the top of the canopy) is $l(z)$, the total leaf area (L) for a canopy of length H is

$$L = \int_0^H l(z)\,dz \tag{6.13}$$

With a constant light extinction per unit leaf area, k, the light intensity at depth z is

$$I(z) = I_0 e^{-k\int_0^z l(z')\,dz'} \tag{6.14}$$

i.e. the light intensity depends only on the quantity of leaves above (Figure 6.7). The major plant property determining the light extinction coefficient is the orientation of the leaves. Horizontal leaves lead to large values of k (0.7 to 0.8) and vertical leaves to small values (0.3 to 0.5). Perfectly randomly oriented leaves give $k = 0.5$. A more detailed description of light extinction requires consideration of solar angles, the partitioning of light into direct and diffuse light and the reflective properties of the leaves.

Light extinction is determined by leaf orientation

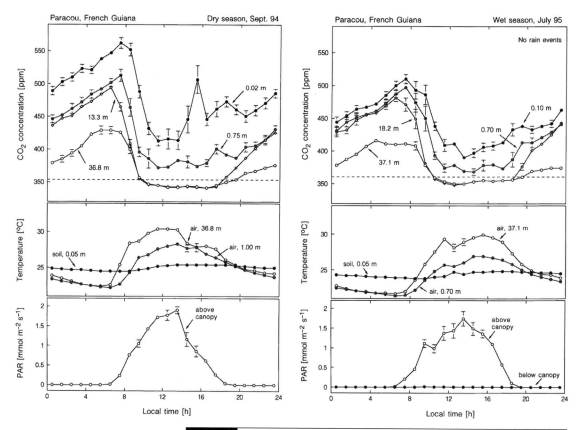

Figure 6.8 Variation in canopy CO_2 concentration, air temperature and PAR in a 25–35 m tall forest stand. Before the Sun rises the rate of soil respiration and autotrophic respiration is faster than the exchange of CO_2 with the surrounding atmosphere. When the Sun comes up and photosynthesis starts the CO_2 concentration within the canopy drops rapidly and the CO_2 concentration just above the canopy drops, even below the average daytime tropospheric CO_2 concentration (dashed line). Close to the soil surface, soil respiration can still maintain a higher CO_2 concentration than in the surrounding atmosphere. From Buchmann et al. (1997) with kind permission from Springer Science + Business Media.

As a consequence of the different light intensities on different leaves, as well as the effect of the leaf distribution on the wind profile, there will also be a gradient in leaf temperature. Transpiration, which increases with amount of leaves, also causes a variation in humidity. The same applies to the carbon dioxide gradient, where more leaves can absorb more carbon dioxide. However, the carbon dioxide profile is also strongly influenced by soil respiration, and respiration by other vegetation components, such that within a stand, large diurnal variations in carbon dioxide concentrations can occur (Figure 6.8).

There is also adaptation of leaves to the conditions to which they are exposed such that leaves exposed to sunlight are thicker than leaves growing in shade. The temperature and light response curves of physiological processes such as photosynthesis also adjust to ambient conditions. In particular, the nitrogen concentration will vary within a canopy in order to optimise the use of this often limiting resource (Figure 6.9). In an ideal situation the leaf nitrogen concentration will follow the light intensity in the canopy (Box 6.2).

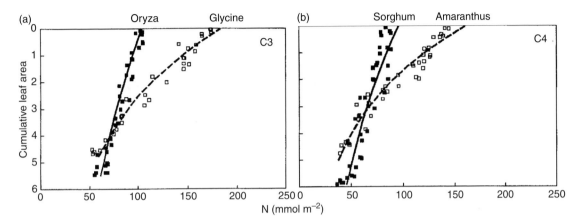

Figure 6.9 Nitrogen concentration in canopies of four plant species as a function of cumulative leaf area. Note that the top of the canopy corresponds to the top of the graph. (a) Two C3 species. (b) Two C4 species. From Anten et al. (1995) with kind permission form Springer Science + Business Media.

Box 6.2 | Optimum nitrogen distribution in a canopy (advanced)

How should a given amount of nitrogen, N_c, be distributed within a canopy? Nitrogen is a mobile element, so evolution should have favoured those plant phenotypes that can distribute the available nitrogen in a way that maximises net photosynthesis. Starting from Equation (6.4) we can give an answer. Let the nitrogen amount per unit leaf area at depth z in the canopy be $c_N(z)$. The maximum net photosynthesis occurs when no change in the nitrogen distribution within the canopy increases net photosynthesis. Expressed in mathematical terms

$$\frac{dA_n}{dc_N} = \text{constant} \tag{6.15}$$

which means that a certain amount of nitrogen makes an equal contribution anywhere in the canopy.

The maximal photosynthetic rate and the dark respiration both depend on nitrogen concentration whereas the quantum yield and the shape parameter can be regarded as independent of nitrogen concentration.

$$P_m = \alpha_P(c_N - c_{NPmin}) \tag{6.16}$$

$$R_d = r(c_N - c_{Nrmin}) \tag{6.17}$$

Differentiating (6.1) with (6.5) gives

$$\frac{dA_n}{dc_N} = \frac{1}{2\theta}\left[\alpha_P - \frac{\alpha_P(\alpha I + P_m) + 2\theta\alpha I\alpha_p}{\sqrt{(\alpha I + P_m)^2 + 4\theta\alpha IP_m}}\right] - r$$

(6.18)

$$= \frac{\alpha_P}{2\theta} - r - \alpha_P\frac{\alpha + P_m/_I + 2\theta\alpha}{\sqrt{\left(\alpha + P_m/_I\right)^2 + 4\theta\alpha P_m I}}$$

This expression is independent of z only if $P_m \sim I$.

When light follows Lambert–Beer's law

$$I(z) = I_0 e^{-kl(z)}$$

(6.19)

we have

$$I_0 e^{-kl(z)} = \omega(c_N(z) - c_{NPmin})$$

(6.20)

where ω is a proportionality constant. This expression can be integrated over the whole leaf area (L)

$$\int_0^L I_0 e^{-kl(z)} dl(z) = \int_0^L \omega(c_N(z) - c_{NPmin}) dl(z)$$

(6.21)

$$= \frac{1}{k}\left(1 - e^{-kL}\right) = \omega(N_c - c_{NPmin}L)$$

ω can be eliminated from this expression to finally give

$$c_N(z) = \frac{N_c - c_{NPmin}L}{1 - e^{-kL}}e^{-kz} + c_{NPmin}$$

(6.22)

Therefore the nitrogen concentration follows the light distribution in the canopy; more light should have more nitrogen and in the special case where light declines exponentially with depth, so will the nitrogen concentration.

This optimisation can be taken further. At the bottom of the canopy the contribution from a nitrogen atom to photosynthesis can be marginal to the extent that it can be advantageous for a plant to shed leaves at the bottom of the canopy and move the nitrogen released in this way to more illuminated positions in the canopy. This can work even if some nitrogen is lost with the senescent leaves (Franklin & Ågren 2002).

Photosynthesis at canopy level

When only the variation in light intensity is taken into account and all leaf properties can be assumed to be equal in the canopy, it is possible to calculate the canopy photosynthesis from Equation (6.5), with $\theta = 0$, and Equation (6.14)

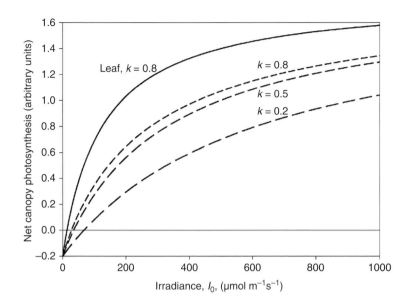

Figure 6.10 Net canopy photosynthesis as a function of incoming light at the top of the canopy for LAI = 2 and three levels of light extinction coefficients ($k = 0.2, 0.5, 0.8$). $P_m = 1$, $a = 0.01$, $R_d = 0.1$. The light response curve of the single leaf producing the canopy response at $k = 0.8$ is also included for comparison (solid line).

$$A_c = \int_0^H \left[A_g(z) - R_d(z)\right]l(z)\mathrm{d}z = \int_0^H \frac{P_m \alpha k I_0 e^{-k\int_0^z l(z')\mathrm{d}z'}}{\alpha k I_0 e^{-k\int_0^z l(z')\mathrm{d}z'} + P_m} l(z)\mathrm{d}z - R_d L \qquad (6.23)$$

$$= \frac{P_m}{k} \ln \frac{\alpha k I_0 + P_m}{\alpha k I_0 e^{-kL} + P_m} - R_d L$$

An example of canopy photosynthesis is shown in Figure 6.10. A major difference between the single leaf and the canopy is that the photosynthetic response of the canopy saturates much more slowly.

Light-use efficiency

Since most plants are based on the same biochemical principles it is not surprising that plants convert the light that they can intercept with approximately the same efficiency. This has led to a very simple relationship between plant production and light: plant production is proportional to the amount of intercepted light during the growing season. The proportionality factor is called light-use efficiency, LUE, often designated ε. What determines plant production is hence the light available at a given site and the amount of leaf biomass that is displayed during the growing season. The amount of leaf biomass is, however, also under control of nutrient availability, water stress, climatic variables etc., and in this way plant growth becomes also connected to other environmental factors. Since it is possible to estimate leaf areas by remote sensing, light-use efficiency provides a means of estimating plant production over large areas.

The light-use efficiency can be used to analyse how a plant community develops and responds to variations in the environment

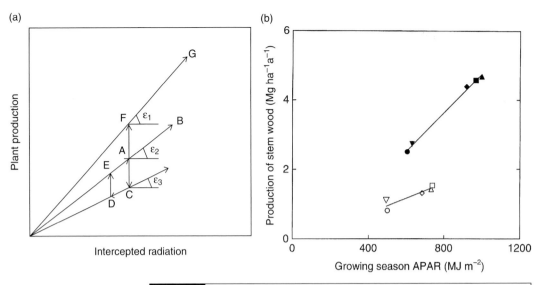

Figure 6.11 (a) The relation between plant production and intercepted light when leaf biomass is changing or when stresses are added or released. See text for detailed explanation. From Linder (1987) with kind permission from Springer Science + Business Media. (b) An example of the relation between plant production (stem wood production) and intercepted light in a Norway spruce stand. Solid symbols represent irrigated and fertilised stands where both nutrient and water limitations have been lifted compared to the untreated stands (open symbols). Different shapes of symbols correspond to different years. From Bergh et al. (1999) with kind permission from Elsevier.

(Figure 6.11). Consider a plant community that is still increasing its leaf biomass, point A in the figure. Normally this plant community will keep on increasing its leaf biomass until it reaches the maximum consistent with the other site conditions, point B, and plant production will increase along the line defined by the normal light-use efficiency ε_2. If the community at point A is released from all other stresses (fertilisation, irrigation), the light-use efficiency can rapidly increase up to an optimum ε_1 at point F and the biomass production will be higher. If left under these unstressed conditions, the leaf biomass will increase such that in the end (point G) the intercepted radiation will be larger than under normal conditions. The increased plant production in this case is thus a result of both a larger leaf biomass and an increase in the light-use efficiency.

Short-term stresses, like a temporary water shortage, will decrease the light-use efficiency, from point A to point C. If this stress is released, the plants will return to point A. Under a stress of long duration, the plant community will also respond by decreasing its leaf biomass. Plant production will then decrease along the line defined by the light-use efficiency line ε_3 (C→D) until the stress is released and the plant community can return to the normal operation defined by ε_2 (D→E). The recovery will in this situation also require the restoration of the lost leaf biomass, i.e. E→A.

Table 6.1 Water-use efficiencies in terms of NPP (g (dw) kg^{-1} (H$_2$O)) of various plant groups. From Larcher (1995) with kind permission from Verlag Eugen Ulmer

	NPP
C4 plants	3–5
Herbaceous C3 plants	
Cereals	1.5–2
Legumes	1.3–1.4
Potatoes and root crops	1.5–2.5
Sunflowers, young plants	3.6
Sunflowers, flowering plants	1.5
Woody plants	
Tropical broadleaved trees (cultivated)	1–2
Temperate zone broadleaved trees	3–5
Sclerophyllous shrubs	3–6
Coniferous trees	3–5
Oil palms	3.5
CAM plants	6–15

Water-use efficiency

Because stomata have to be open to let carbon dioxide in, water vapour will also leak out. This inexorable link between photosynthesis and transpiration can be expressed in terms of *water-use efficiency*, WUE, which expresses the cost for a plant in terms of water loss relative to the gain in carbon. There are several ways of defining WUE. At the physiological, short-term level, WUE is defined as the slope of the relation between net assimilation (A) and stomatal conductance (g_s) – dA/dg_s. At the leaf level, WUE is defined as the ratio between net assimilation and transpiration (E_l) – A/E_l. At the crop scale, long-term level, WUE is defined as the ratio of net primary production (NPP) to transpiration (E_a) – NPP/E_a. There are also other definitions, in particular, in agronomic contexts, where yields rather than NPP are in focus. Some values for WUE are given in Table 6.1.

Water is also the reaction medium in the cells and a growing plant must therefore also take up water to fill the new cells and replace water that has been lost. The amount of water required depends on the growth conditions of the plants such that more rapidly growing plants have higher water contents than slowly growing ones (Figure 6.12).

The water-use efficiency can be compared with the amount of water used to fill the cells. Although the water content of plants varies with their growth rate and type of tissue, green parts can contain around 80% water. In other words, each gram of new cells (dw) produced requires an additional 0.004 kg of water (equivalent to a WUE of 250), which is negligible compared to the amount of water used in transpiration.

WUE, how efficiently a plant can use water

Plants need water to keep cool

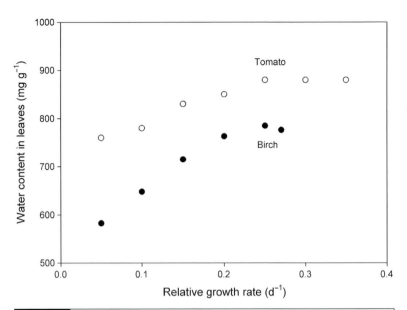

Figure 6.12 The water content in the leaves of tomato and birch plants, respectively, at different relative growth rates. Data from Ingestad *et al.* (1994b).

Because an increasing atmospheric carbon dioxide concentration will cause a larger difference in carbon dioxide concentration across the stomatal aperture, a plant can take up carbon dioxide at the same rate, but with a smaller stomatal aperture and lower stomatal conductance (see Figure 6.1), which decreases transpiration losses and hence increases water-use efficiency.

Plant respiration

About 50% of gross photosynthesis is used for autotrophic respiration. It is therefore of interest to understand the sources of respiration. Several components of respiration can be identified, but three sources are normally considered to be the most important: *growth respiration*, *maintenance respiration* and *root respiration* associated with ion uptake. Plant respiration is strongly dependent on temperature and this dependence is often described as an exponential function with a doubling in the rate for an increase in temperature of 10 °C ($Q_{10} = 2$). This is an oversimplification, as the rate of increase in the respiration rate with temperature becomes slower as temperature increases (Atkin & Tjoelker 2003); at high enough temperatures respiration rates will even go down.

Growth respiration

To grow, a plant must respire

Whenever an organism grows it needs to convert one type of substrate into another. This is inevitably associated with energy losses, the second law of thermodynamics. If we know from which substrates to start and know which substrates form the end products, it is possible to calculate from thermodynamic information the respiratory losses. A major step forward in this area was taken by Penning de Vries (1974), who calculated respiratory costs for several major plant compounds (Table 6.2).

One of the contributing factors to changes in plant composition is the growth rate of the plant. These changes occur not only within a plant as it varies its growth rate, but also between groups of plants adapted to different growth rates. Poorter *et al.* (1991) give examples of typically slow-growing and typically fast-growing species (Table 6.3). In this example the slow-growing plant has to use 93 mg C of photosynthates (respire) to produce a biomass containing 398 mg C, equivalent to a growth cost of 24%. The costs are higher for the fast-growing

[handwritten margin note: Ex: 93 mg of C photosynthates to produce 398 mg C of biomass = growth of 24%]

Table 6.2 Energetic costs of producing different major plant compounds. The costs are expressed as g C respired when producing compounds containing 1 g C. Initial substrates are glucose, ammonia and hydrogen sulfide. The negative carbon cost for producing organic acids should be understood as that this process is energetically favourable and that excess energy can be used for other processes. Depending on the specific composition of the different classes of compounds, the values can vary. Adapted from Thornley & Johnson 1990, Table 12.8

[handwritten note: → C respired]
[handwritten note: ↳ C containing products]

Classes of compounds	Carbon concentration g g^{-1}	Respiratory cost g g^{-1}
Carbohydrates	0.442	0.059
Nitrogenous compounds	0.462	0.835
Lignin	0.667	0.184
Organic acids	0.368	−0.311
Lipids	0.774	0.465

Table 6.3 Respiratory cost associated with production of roots of typically slow-growing and typically fast-growing plant species. Data from Poorter *et al.* (1991)

Classes of compounds	Slow-growing			Fast-growing		
	Composition mg g^{-1}	C cont. mg g^{-1}	Respiration mg g^{-1}	Composition mg g^{-1}	C cont. mg g^{-1}	Respiration mg g^{-1}
Carbohydrates	605	267	16	439	194	12
Nitrogenous compounds	177	82	68	284	131	110
Lignin	44	29	5	27	18	3
Organic acids	18	7	−2	41	15	−5
Lipids	16	12	6	24	19	9
Soluble phenolics[a]	3	2	0.3	3	2	0.2
Minerals	140	0	0	185	0	0
Total		400	93		379	128

[a]Calculated as lignin

plant. Here 128 mg C is required to produce a biomass with 377 mg C, a growth cost of 34%. Typical values for growth respiration should therefore be around 25–30%.

Maintenance respiration

To keep alive, a plant must respire

Since a plant is operating in a state far from chemical equilibrium it must continuously invest energy in the maintenance of that state. The major contributors to that cost are resynthesis of proteins that have degraded and maintenance of the ion balances against concentration gradients. Proteins are the main consumers of nitrogen in the plant. The resynthesis of proteins is therefore essentially proportional to the amount of nitrogen in the plant. Moreover the stability of the proteins decreases with temperature, which leads to a temperature dependence. In consideration of the high cost of maintenance respiration, why has evolution not led to more stable proteins? However, the turnover of proteins may not only be a bad thing for the plant. Through the turnover of proteins, amino acids are released and become available for incorporation into other proteins that might be more needed for the moment. The plant has, therefore, to find the optimal solution between saving energy by having stable proteins and being flexible by having less stable proteins. There are no simple ways, similar to the method for growth respiration, to calculate maintenance respiration, but estimates are that it costs 20–25% of gross photosynthesis.

Root respiration and ion uptake

To take up ions, a plant must respire

Cannell & Thornley (2000) provide estimates of carbon costs for ion uptake:

Ammonium	0.17 g C/g N
Nitrate	0.34 g C/g N
Other ions	0.06 g C/g mineral

To this should be added the cost of reducing nitrate, once taken up, 1.72 g C/g N.

A plant with a nitrogen concentration of 30 mg/g dw, 50 mg/g dw of other ions and 500 mg C/g dw has then invested, depending upon whether it has taken up only NH_4^+ or only NO_3^-, between 0.060 to 0.130 g C for each g C it has grown, or 6–13% of net photosynthesis. The major difference in cost between ammonium and nitrate uptake is in nitrate reduction. This estimate of the cost may be exaggerated because some plants can use energy for nitrate reduction that otherwise would have been wasted in the leaves.

Plant nutrient relationships

Plants need nutrients

Plant growth in natural ecosystems is always limited by nutrient availability. As a good approximation we can assume that it is only

Table 6.4 Relative element ratios in plants. N is set to 100. Values are derived from experiments with birch (*Betula pendula*) but are of high generality. From Ingestad & Lund (1986)

Element	N	K	P	Ca	Mg	S	Fe	Mn	B	Zn	Cu	Mo
Mass basis	100	65	13	7	8.5	9	0.2	0.04	0.05	0.05	0.02	0.007
Molar basis	100	23	5.9	2.5	5.0	3.9	0.05	0.01	0.08	0.01	0.004	0.001

one nutrient that limits growth at any time; this is referred to as *Liebig's law of the minimum* (see Box 6.3 for a more complex picture). Sometimes other factors like temperature and light are also included, but we consider this wrong because these factors limit plant growth independently of nutrient availability. The reason that only one nutrient at a time limits growth is that plants have strict requirements for element ratios. Almost all plant species have approximately the relative requirements of elements (*optimum nutrient ratios*) shown in Table 6.4.

Some other elements, like Na, Cl, Si and Al, might be needed in trace quantities and by certain species.

Hence, if all the elements but one are present in the ratios just given, increasing the concentration of this particular element beyond this ratio has no effect on growth, but when the ratio is lower, this element limits growth. The values for the micronutrients have to be treated with caution, as it is experimentally difficult to establish exact limits for these elements. The amounts required to satisfy plant growth are so small that minuscule impurities in the experimental equipment can cause erroneous results.

Nutrient productivity

The strict dependence on one mineral nutrient as limiting can be used in simple growth equations for plants. Let W be the plant biomass and n the amount of the limiting nutrient in the plant. The growth rate of the plant can then, in its simplest form, be written

$$\frac{dW}{dt} = P_n(n - c_{n,min}W) \tag{6.24}$$

where P_n is the *nutrient productivity* and $c_{n,min}$ a minimum nutrient concentration required for growth of the plant. The nutrient productivity expresses the rate at which a unit of an element can produce new biomass. The idea was initially developed with nitrogen as the key element and its importance as a major element in enzymes in mind. Because enzymes are not consumed during growth, growth does not change the amount of enzymes/nitrogen available for growth, but only its concentration through dilution. A minimum concentration of an element in non-growth-promoting structures might also be necessary to consider. The equation can be rewritten in terms of the *relative growth rate* (R_W) and plant nutrient concentration, c_n

Nutrient availability determines plant growth

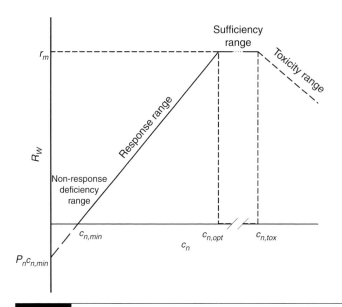

Figure 6.13 Relation between relative growth rate and nutrient concentration of the limiting nutrient. The slope of the line for the response range is the nutrient productivity. Changes in environmental variables, other than nutrients, change this slope. It is not known how the concentrations $c_{n,min}$ and $c_{n,opt}$ are affected, but it is expected that they are insensitive to other environmental variables. From Ågren & Bosatta (1998).

$$R_W = \frac{1}{W}\frac{dW}{dt} = P_n\left(c_n - c_{n,min}\right) \tag{6.25}$$

Above a certain concentration, plants no longer benefit from additional quantities of an element and the growth response levels off; over a range of concentrations nothing happens. At still higher element concentrations, toxicity begins to appear. This is normally associated with plant species being moved to environments outside their normal ecological range or in situations where, for some reason, the concentration of an element in the root medium increases to levels much higher than those normally encountered. The response is summarised in Figure 6.13.

When plants grow bigger, internal shading starts to effect the efficiency with which nutrients can drive growth. It has been found that a convenient way of expressing this negative feedback is to let the nutrient productivity decline with the size of the plant or the stand of which it is a part. This has been applied to the production of new foliage for which the nutrient productivity can be written

$$P_n = a - bW_L \tag{6.26}$$

where a and b are two species- and site-specific parameters and W_L is the leaf biomass.

For a canopy with a constant mortality rate, μ_L, this leads to the following dynamic equation

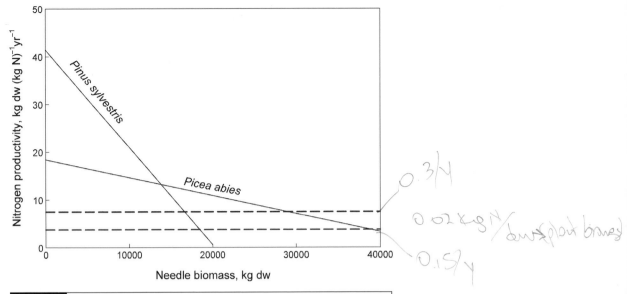

Figure 6.14 Nitrogen productivity for Scots pine (*Pinus sylvestris*) and Norway spruce (*Picea abies*) as functions of needle biomasses (solid lines). The broken lines correspond to the lines for $n^*_L/W^*_L = 0.02$ kg N (kg dw)$^{-1}$ and $\mu_L = 0.3$ yr^{-1} (upper line), and $\mu_L = 0.15$ yr^{-1} (lower line), which could be typical values for these two species. From Ågren & Bosatta (1998).

$$\frac{dW_L}{dt} = (a - bW_L)n_L - \mu_L W_L \qquad (6.27)$$

The steady-state leaf biomass is then given by the equation (we use a star to denote steady-state values)

$$(a - bW^*_L) = \frac{\mu_L}{n^*_L/W^*_L} \qquad (6.28)$$

The steady-state needle biomass is thus also determined by the inverse of the nutrient concentration in the leaf biomass. The nutrient concentration in the leaf biomass is in its turn a function of the nutrient availability at the site, hence connecting plants and soil. These relationships are illustrated in Figure 6.14.

Nutrient-use efficiency

An alternative way of looking at limitation by nutrients is to see how much carbon (or biomass) can be fixed per unit of nutrient taken up, *nutrient-use efficiency* (NUE). Measurements of nutrient uptake are generally difficult so NUE is often estimated from the ratio of carbon to nutrient in litterfall under the assumption that the plant biomass is approximately in a steady state.

NUE, how efficiently a plant can use nutrients

Nutrient-use efficiency and nutrient productivities are related through the *mean residence time* of the nutrient in the plant, (τ_r)

$$NUE = P_n \tau_r \qquad (6.29)$$

Table 6.5 Nitrogen and phosphorus productivities, mean residence times of nitrogen and phosphorus, and nitrogen- and phosphorus-use efficiencies in populations of *Erica tetralix, Calluna vulgaris* and *Molinia caerulea*. From Aerts (1990) with kind permission from Springer Science + Business Media

	Wet heathland		Dry heathland	
	Erica	*Molinia*	*Calluna*	*Molinia*
P_N (g g^{-1} yr^{-1})	77	110	61	141
τ_N (yr)	1.16	0.80	1.46	0.64
NUE_N (g g^{-1})	90	89	89	91
P_P (g g^{-1} yr^{-1})	2900	4440	2170	4780
τ_P (yr)	0.96	0.87	1.38	0.66
NUE_P (g g^{-1})	2790	3860	2990	3160

(handwritten margin notes: "net photosynthesis" → P_N; "mean residence time" → τ_N; "nutrient use efficiency" → NUE_N)

Nutrient-use efficiencies are less variable between species than nutrient productivities and residence times (Table 6.5), where the latter reflect different growth strategies – grow fast and be short-lived or grow slowly and be long-lived.

An important component of the residence time of an element is resorption before tissue is shed as litter. Resorption can be expressed in two ways: (i) *resorption efficiency*, by which is meant the element level in senesced tissues relative to green tissues (the fraction of the element resorbed) and (ii) *resorption proficiency*, by which is meant the absolute level to which the element is reduced before senescence (the absolute level of resorption). Resorption can also be more or less complete, leading to interannual variation in resorption as a result of, for example, a sudden extreme weather event that interrupts the process of senescence. Typical values of element concentrations after complete resorption are for nitrogen 7 mg g^{-1}dw and for phosphorus 0.5 mg g^{-1}dw for deciduous trees, and 0.4 mg g^{-1}dw for evergreen trees (Killingbeck 1996). Resorption efficiency and resorption proficiency are not necessarily correlated. Plants growing on infertile sites have, by necessity, low element concentrations, even in green tissues, and although they may have high resorption proficiencies, can never attain high resorption efficiencies. Vice versa, plants growing on fertile site have high levels of elements in green tissues and can withdraw large amounts, and hence have high efficiencies, without necessarily reaching high proficiency.

(handwritten margin note: "Resorption,")

Plant allocation

Since plants require several types of resource for their growth and these resources are acquired by different tissues, it has been suggested that plants should adjust the growth of different resource-acquiring organs such that all resources are equally limiting (the multiple limitation hypothesis, Bloom *et al.* 1985). This hypothesis is

(handwritten margin note: "Organ development → according to resource limitation/needs")

Box 6.3 | Plant growth and nutrient availability (advanced)

Equation (6.24) gives a simple way of connecting plant growth to nutrient availability. However, a more complete description takes into account that nutrients interact in determining growth. We will here consider the interaction between nitrogen and phosphorus and what consequences this has. Nitrogen is the dominating element in proteins responsible for photosynthesis and subsequent metabolism. It is therefore reasonable to start as before with the relation between plant growth rate and plant nitrogen content (N)

$$\frac{dW}{dt} = \Phi_{CN}(N - c_{N,min}W) \tag{6.30}$$

However, N does not in this case represent just any nitrogen but nitrogen present in proteins. Proteins are produced in ribosomes, which are characterised by their high content of phosphorus, and the rate at which proteins are formed will therefore depend on the amount of phosphorus in the plant, according to a similar relation

$$\frac{dN}{dt} = \Phi_{NP}(P - c_{P,min}W) \tag{6.31}$$

If we combine these two equations we find that the N:P ratio r_{NP} in the plant varies with the relative growth rate of the plant

$$r_{NP} = \frac{R_W \Phi_{NP} + c_{N,min}\Phi_{CN}\Phi_{NP}}{R_W^2 + c_{P,min}\Phi_{CN}\Phi_{NP}} \tag{6.32}$$

Figure 6.15 shows two examples of how this relationship can look (solid line) and also how it will change if the environmental conditions change, for example by a temperature change (both Φ_{NP} and Φ_{CN} change, broken line) or a change in light intensity only (only Φ_{CN} changes, dotted line).

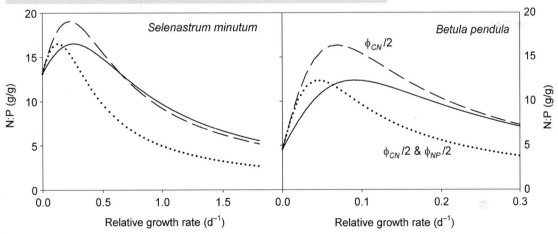

Figure 6.15 Predicted relations between plant N:P ratio and relative growth rate for a freshwater alga (*Seelenastrum minutum*) and a tree seedling (Silver birch, *Betula pendula*). From Ågren (2004).

[handwritten margin note: ↑ photosynthesis ↳ ↑ P demand > N demand]

The important point is that over large ranges of relative growth rate, increasing the relative growth rate increases the demand for phosphorus more rapidly than for nitrogen; the nitrogen:phosphorus ratio is declining. This is called the *'growth rate hypothesis'* (Sterner & Elser 2002).

Box 6.4	Nitrogen productivity or photosynthesis and respiration

The Farquhar–von Caemmerer model of photosynthesis can be combined with costs of respiration for different levels of nitrogen in a plant to give a relation between relative growth rates and plant nitrogen concentration. This gives the same relationship as Equation (6.24), although for young plants the maturation of leaves, the time during which they reach their full photosynthetic capacity, is important to take into account. The two approaches to predict plant growth are therefore compatible, although one approach uses a detailed physiological description and therefore requires large amounts of information for estimation of parameters, and the other approach uses a phenomenological description with little demand on information.

[handwritten margin note: ↑ Relative growth]

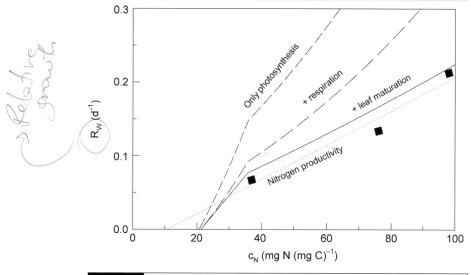

Figure 6.16 The relationship between the relative growth rate of a plant and its nitrogen concentration calculated from photosynthesis only, photosynthesis + respiration, photosynthesis + respiration + leaf maturation, and nitrogen productivity. From Ågren (1996) with kind permission from Oikos.

easily understood. Plants growing in low light can capture more light if they can expand their leaf area by growing more and/or thinner leaves, and in dry environments more roots are needed to obtain water than in wet environments. More roots can also increase the uptake of nutrients. Carbon dioxide in itself is likely to have little effect on allocation because of the rapid rate of diffusion of carbon

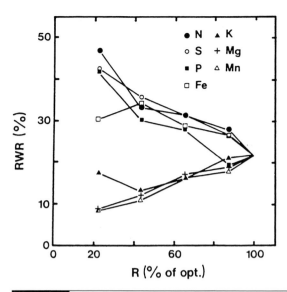

Figure 6.17 The root fraction (RWR) of plants (birch seedlings) as a function of their maximal relative growth rate (R) when the relative growth rate is controlled by one nutrient (N, S, P, Fe, K, Mg or Mn). The relative growth rate is in these experiments a linear (increasing) function of the plant nutrient concentration. The scale on the x-axis could therefore equally well have been plant nutrient concentration. From Ericsson (1994) with kind permission from the *New Zealand Journal of Forestry Science*.

dioxide in the air relative to other limiting rates in a plant. However, indirect effects through water-use efficiency can influence allocation patterns.

Nutrient availability is one of the strongest controls on allocation in plants, in particular allocation between aboveground and belowground growth. Since nutrients normally are acquired below ground, investment in roots or root-associated symbionts (mycorrhiza, nitrogen fixers) can increase the uptake of nutrients. However, plants need carbon to grow their roots, as well as the aboveground tissues that capture carbon. Plants should then partition their resources between aboveground and belowground structures in response to nutrient availability. Many models have been used to show that partitioning between above- and belowground organs that maximises relative growth leads to the desired pattern of allocation (e.g. Ågren & Franklin 2003).

The expected pattern of increasing allocation to roots when nutrients are scarce is observed when nitrogen, phosphorus or sulfur (also iron) is the limiting element (Figure 6.17). However, plants respond opposite to what is expected when potassium, magnesium or manganese limits growth. The explanation for this counter-intuitive behaviour is probably that potassium, magnesium and manganese are elements that are closely coupled to photosynthetic production. Plants may therefore perceive deficiencies in these elements as a

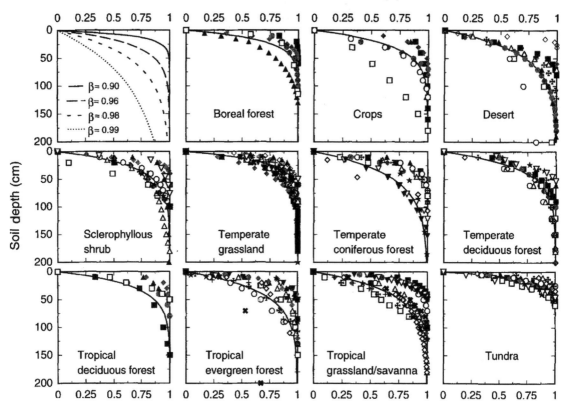

Figure 6.18 Cumulative root distribution as a function of soil depth for 11 terrestrial biomes and for the general model (6.33). Values for the parameter β and total root biomasses as well as root:shoot ratios are given in Table 6.6. The different symbols represent different ecosystems. From Jackson *et al.* (1996) with kind permission from Springer Science + Business Media.

shortage of carbon and hence more resources are be allocated to leaves for more efficient carbon capture. The failure by plants to identify the ultimate limiting resource, a mineral nutrient, is probably a result of plants rarely being exposed to serious limitations by these elements, in contrast to shortages of nitrogen and phosphorus. Hence, the evolutionary pressure to respond properly has been lacking.

The physical distribution of roots with depth is also important for uptake of minerals and water, and the distribution varies between biomes (Figure 6.18, Table 6.6). The cumulative fraction of roots (Y) with depths (d, m) can empirically be described by the function (Jackson *et al.* 1996)

$$Y = 1 - \beta^d \tag{6.33}$$

where $\beta < 1$ is a parameter characteristic of a biome. As Figure 6.18 and Table 6.6 show, in most biomes the major part of the roots is located in the upper 30 cm of the soil. The most notable exceptions

Table 6.6 | Values for the parameter β, the percentage of roots in the upper 30 cm, root biomasses and root:shoot ratios for the biomes in Figure 6.18. From Jackson *et al.* (1996) with kind permission from Springer Science + Business Media

Biome	β	% Root biomass in upper 30 cm	Root biomass kg m^{-2}	Root: shoot ratio
Boreal forest	0.943	83	2.9	0.32
Crops	0.961	70	0.15	0.10
Desert, warm	0.975	53	1.2	4.5
Desert, cold	0.975	53	0.4	0.7
Sclerophyllous shrubs	0.964	67	4.8	1.2
Temperate coniferous forest	0.976	52	4.4	0.18
Temperate deciduous forest	0.966	65	4.2	0.23
Temperate grassland	0.943	83	1.4	3.7
Tropical deciduous forest	0.961	70	4.1	0.34
Tropical evergreen forest	0.962	69	4.9	0.19
Tropical grassland savanna	0.972	57	1.4	0.7
Tundra	0.914	93	1.2	6.6

are deserts, some temperate coniferous forests and tropical grassland savannas. The reason can be found in the demand for access to larger water reserves.

Plant nutrient uptake

Plant mineral nutrient uptake depends on two main factors: (i) the availability of the nutrient in the soil and (ii) the rate at which the nutrient gets into contact with the root. The availability of nutrients in the soil is normally low at any one moment and a continuous supply requires continuous replenishment of the nutrient. The replenishment can come from various sources. Mineralisation of organic matter and subsequent release of mineral nutrients is a major source. In an ecosystem at steady state, mineralisation must equal uptake; other sources will match losses from the system. Since most ecosystems generally recycle (Chapter 9) much more of mineral nutrients than is recycled externally it is clear that mineralisation must dominate availability. However, for nutrients bound on exchange surfaces, the equilibrium between nutrients in soil solution and those bound on exchange surfaces

Table 6.7 Potential contribution of mass flow to nutrient uptake relative requirement for a Norway spruce stand in southern Sweden. Soil solution concentrations are from the upper mineral horizon (Andersson et al. 1998). The uptake is based on a water-use efficiency of 4.8 g kg^{-1} calculated as an average for a range of European Norway spruce and Scots pine stands (van Oijen et al. 2008). The required amounts of nutrients are calculated per kg of produced new biomass and based on the relative requirement of elements in Table 6.4 and an average nitrogen concentration of 4.29 g kg^{-1} in newly produced biomass

Element	Soil solution concentration mg L^{-1}	Potential uptake through mass flow g kg^{-1}	Requirement g kg^{-1}	Potential uptake/ requirement
K	1.77	0.37	2.79	0.13
Mg	0.87	0.18	0.36	0.50
Ca	2.43	0.51	0.30	1.69
Mn	0.44	0.09	0.02	53.4
N	0.09	0.02	4.29	0.00
S	5.04	1.05	0.39	2.72

can be an important buffering mechanism. For the long-term availability external inputs through deposition/fertilisation and weathering are crucial, but in the short term it is only fertilisation that matters.

The transport from the soil to the root has three potential mechanisms: (i) transport with the transpiration stream (mass flow), (ii) diffusion and (iii) roots growing to the nutrients; which of the three mechanisms dominates depends on the specific conditions. Combining our knowledge about water-use efficiency, requirement for different mineral nutrients and some soil chemistry we can estimate for which nutrients mass flow alone can supply the neeccessary amounts (Table 6.7). Water-use efficiency gives the amount of water required by a plant to produce 1 kg of biomass, and multiplying by the soil solution concentration gives the amount of the nutrient that can be transported as mass flow. For the conditions in the forest stand in Table 6.7 mass flow suffices to supply calcium and sulfur and yields a large excess for manganese. About half of the required magnesium can be supplied by mass flow, but only a minor portion of potassium, and in particular nitrogen. In other plant communities with different mineralogy the conditions might also differ.

It is not as easy to separate how much diffusion relative to root growth can contribute because the two processes are intertwined. Root growth can take roots into soil volumes that are rich in nutrients, but for the nutrients to actually reach uptake sites on the root surface diffusion is required. An example of a semi-quantitative analysis of the relative importance of root growth vs. diffusion is as follows (Ingestad and Ågren 1988). Consider a growing root of length L at time t. Let the uptake rate per unit length at a distance z from the root tip be $\Phi(z)$. At time t', the root has reached z. The total uptake rate of that root can then be written as

$$U(t) = \int_0^{L(t)} \Phi(z)dz = \int_0^{L(t)} \Phi(L(t) - L(t'))dL(t')$$

$$= \int_0^t \Phi_a(t - t')\frac{dL}{dt'}dt' = \frac{dL}{dt}\int_0^t \Phi_a(t - t')dt' \qquad (6.34)$$

where subscript a indicates that the uptake rate refers to the age of the root segment and the last equality applies for constant length growth of the root.

The uptake rate of a root segment declines for two reasons. First of all, uptake depletes the amount of nutrients around the root. This can be approximated as an exponential decay with a time constant equal to the slowest decaying Fourier component of diffusion in a cylinder, $T_d = ab/(\pi D)$, where a and b are the inner and outer radii of the cylinder and D the diffusion constant. With realistic values for a, b and D, $T_d = 0.05$–5 days; i.e. diffusion to a root will deplete $2/3$ (e^{-1}) of the nutrients in the vicinity of the root in this time period. Second, the uptake capacity of a root segment declines with age. An approximately exponentially declining uptake capacity with a time constant (T_a) of 10 to 30 days has been observed (Christie & Moorby 1975). The uptake rate (Equation 6.34) then becomes (with k some proportionality factor)

$$U(t) = \frac{dL}{dt}\int_0^t \Phi_a(t - t')dt' = k'\frac{dL}{dt}\int_0^t e^{-(1/T_d + 1/T_a)(t - t')}dt'$$

$$= k\frac{dL}{dt}\left[1 - e^{-(1/T_d + 1/T_a)t}\right] \qquad (6.35)$$

Over short periods of time Equation (6.35) implies that uptake is proportional to root length, and the diffusion rate and ageing are important for the uptake rate. Over longer periods of time the exponential function in Equation (6.35) becomes small, and root exploration of unexploited soil volumes determines the nutrient uptake rate.

A plant can also increase the availability of nutrients. Almost all plants have mycorrhizal symbionts. Since mycorrhizal hyphae are thinner than plant roots, the plant can invest in mycorrhizal hyphae instead of its own roots to increase growth length for the same investment in biomass. Another advantage of mycorrhiza is that they can penetrate volumes where roots are too thick to do so.

Exudation of acids changes the pH in the vicinity of the root and can increase the solubility of minerals. Exudation of phosphatase enzymes in particular is important for releasing phosphate from organic compounds. Associations with nitrogen fixers increase the nitrogen uptake of plants. However, this association comes at a cost such that in the presence of high availability of inorganic nitrogen, nitrogen fixation is suppressed (Figure 6.19). In nutrient-rich environments the cost of nitrogen fixation is so high that non-fixers will outcompete the nitrogen fixers.

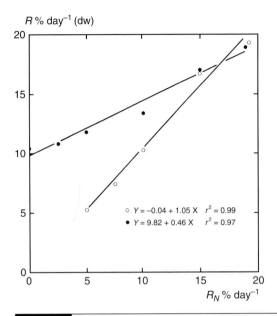

R % day^{-1} (dw)

$Y = -0.04 + 1.05\ X \quad r^2 = 0.99$
$Y = 9.82 + 0.46\ X \quad r^2 = 0.97$

R_N % day^{-1}

Figure 6.19 In a laboratory experiment with the nitrogen-fixing grey alder, inoculated seedlings (●) and uninoculated seedlings (○) were grown with different relative addition rates of nitrogen (ammonium plus nitrate), R_N. At low addition rates, inoculated seedlings compensated for the low supply of nitrogen and increased their nitrogen content by fixation, and could grow faster than the uninoculated ones that were constrained in their growth rate by the rate of nitrogen supply. At high rates of nitrogen supply, nitrogen fixation was switched off and both types of plant grew at rates equal to the rate of supply. The nodule weight decreased in the inoculated seedlings from 24% of root dw, when no nitrogen was supplied, to 1.2% at the highest supply rate. From Ingestad (1980) with kind permission from John Wiley & Sons.

Nutrient uptake is also a matter of charge balance. A plant taking up nutrients in the proportions given in Table 6.4, will, when we for the moment leave nitrogen uptake out, have the following charge balance per uptake of 100 g N (7.14 mol) (phosphorus is taken up as PO_4^{2-} and sulfur as SO_4^{2-}):

$$K + P + Ca + Mg + S : 7.14/100(23 - 2 \times 5.9 + 2 \times 2.5 + 2 \times 5.0 - 2 \times 3.9)$$
$$= +1.3\ mol_c$$

If nitrogen is taken up as ammonium, an additional $100/14 \approx 7\ mol_c$ of excess is taken up. To maintain charge balance in the root, this excess of positive charge has to be balanced by exudation of protons, which leads to acidification around the root. In contrast, if the nitrogen uptake is in the form of nitrate, there will be a similar extra uptake of negative charge, which has to be compensated by exudation of OH^- and hence an alkalisation of the soil. Since plants normally take up an excess of K, Ca and Mg relative to nitrogen, the pH effect of the nitrogen source tends to be greater when ammonium is the nitrogen source. In some ecosystems, typically arctic plants, amino acids can be a major source of nitrogen (Chapter 9).

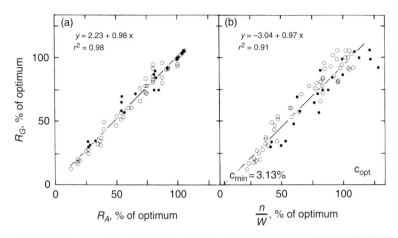

$y = 2.23 + 0.98 x$
$r^2 = 0.98$

$y = -3.04 + 0.97 x$
$r^2 = 0.91$

$c_{min} = 3.13\%$

c_{opt}

R_A, % of optimum

$\frac{n}{W}$, % of optimum

Figure 6.20 (a) Experimental relationship between relative growth rate (relative to maximum), R_G, vs. relative addition rate of nitrogen (relative to maximum) for birch (○) and different conifer seedlings (●) growing under different light intensities and day lengths. (b) Relationship between relative growth rate (relative to maximum) vs. plant nitrogen concentration (relative to optimum) for the same experiment, see Figure 6.13. From Ingestad & Ågren (1992).

Steady-state nutrition

Plant nutrient concentration is clearly a critical expression of the performance of a plant. One may expect that uptake of nutrients and biomass development may not always stay in phase, such that nutrient concentrations are changing, with repercussions on many plant traits. Torsten Ingestad (e.g. Ingestad & Ågren 1988, 1992) introduced the concept of steady-state growth to describe the conditions under which plants are growing at constant nutrient concentrations. For a plant with biomass W and nutrient content n, a constant nutrient concentration implies

$$\frac{d}{dt}\frac{n}{W} = \frac{1}{W}\frac{dn}{dt} - \frac{n}{W^2}\frac{dW}{dt} = \frac{n}{W}\left[\frac{1}{n}\frac{dn}{dt} - \frac{1}{W}\frac{dW}{dt}\right] = 0 \qquad (6.36)$$

or

$$\frac{1}{n}\frac{dn}{dt} = \frac{1}{W}\frac{dW}{dt} \qquad (6.37)$$

The relative change in nutrient content and the relative growth rate of the plant must therefore be equal. The easiest way to achieve this is to supply plants with nutrients at an exponential rate (R_A). As a result the plants will also be growing at an exponential rate (Figure 6.20).

Global plant traits

Plants have solved the problem of optimum use of resources in many different ways, but the solution to the optimisation problem always requires a trade-off between traits. Favourable properties are, for example, long-lived leaves, which conserve the resources invested in

Different leaf properties are strongly correlated

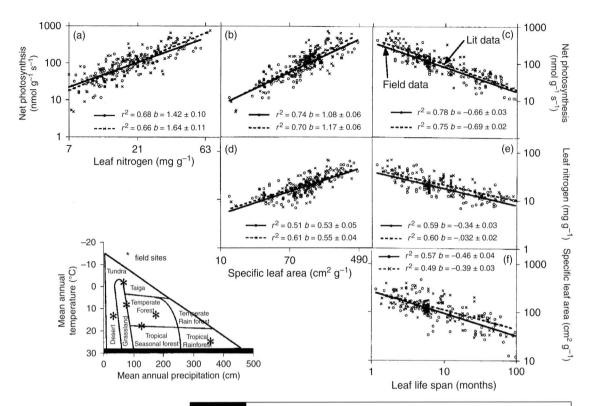

Figure 6.21 Relationship between different leaf traits from Reich et al. (1997) with kind permission from National Academy of Sciences, USA. o (broken lines, lit. data) are data from a global data base and x (solid lines, field data) are data from Reich et al. sampled at six different biomes (∗). The value b in the graphs shows the slopes of the regression lines.

constructing them, and thin, nitrogen-rich leaves, which capture large amounts of light per investment. However, thin leaves tend to be fragile and nitrogen-rich leaves are desirable to herbivores; such leaves tend to have short life spans. On the other hand, when a lot is invested in constructing a leaf, the plant should retain it for a long time to get a large return on the investment. The result is that several leaf traits are strongly correlated (Figure 6.21). Some of the most important relations are between net photosynthesis and leaf nitrogen concentration (on a mass basis), which is a result of more nitrogen, implying more investment in photosynthetic machinery. The increase in net photosynthesis with specific leaf area is also obvious; the same photosynthetic machinery is spread out over a larger area and hence captures more light. The decrease in photosynthetic rate with leaf life span is, on the other hand, not obvious, but is a result of negative coupling between leaf life span and specific leaf area; long-lived leaves are thicker. The long-lived leaves also have a lower nitrogen concentration. This is a result of plants having to invest more in structure to make the leaves long-lived.

The major variability in leaf properties is between species. Climate has little influence, although in warmer and drier climates there is a tendency towards thicker leaves. Since specific leaf area and nitrogen concentration correlates with decomposability (Chapter 7), changes in species composition can also affect the element cycling in an ecosystem.

FURTHER READING

Ågren, G.I. & Bosatta, E. 1998. *Theoretical Ecosystem Ecology – Understanding Element Cycles*. Cambridge: Cambridge University Press.

Lambers, H., Chapin III. F.S. & Pons, T.L. 1998. *Plant Physiological Ecology*. New York: Springer-Verlag.

Larcher, W. 1995. *Physiological Plant Ecology*. Berlin: Springer-Verlag.

Mengel, K. & Kirkby, E.A. 2001. *Principles of Plant Nutrition*. Dordrecht: Kluwer Academic Publishers.

Nye, P.H. & Tinker, P.B. 1977. *Solute Movement in the Soil-Root System*. Oxford: Blackwell Scientific Publications.

Schulze, E.D., Beck, E. & Müller-Hohenstein, K. 2002. *Plant Ecology*. Berlin: Springer.

Thornley, J.H.M. & Johnson, I.R. 1990. *Plant and Crop Modelling: A Mathematical Approach to Plant and Crop Physiological Modelling*. Oxford: Clarendon.

Chapter 7

Soil organic matter dynamics

Dead organic matter from plants, litter, has to be decomposed in order to release its content of elements for use by other plants. This chapter discusses how the release of different elements is related and the factors regulating the release. A simple mathematical model provides a framework that lets us identify how different properties of the decomposer organisms, mainly bacteria and fungi, control the rate and fate of the decomposition process.

Litter and soil organic matter

Litter and *soil organic matter* represent different forms of a continuous transition of organic matter from newly shed, or even still attached, plant tissue or tissues from other living organisms, to an amorphous mixture of organic compounds. Since soils (with litters and soil organic matter) in general contain more of the most important elements than other stores in global element cycles (see Figures 9.21–9.24), the dynamics of soil pools are critical for the functioning of the element cycles. For simplicity, in this chapter we will include litters in soil organic matter, SOM for brevity (see Chapter 4 and the partitioning of soils into horizons).

Intrinsic and external variables control decomposition rates

One of the controls on SOM is its chemical composition, which is a result of the original litter components and conversion caused by soil organisms. Quality is an integrated term which we use to describe how the chemical composition determines the rate at which SOM can be used by the *decomposer organisms*. In addition, the abiotic environment, in terms of temperature, moisture and chemical composition of the soil minerals, exerts an influence which can act directly or indirectly through the activities of soil organisms.

In spite of the enormous richness of litter types, and physical and chemical environments, the dynamics of SOM displays much regularity. This regularity is derived from the triangular interaction: organic matter properties–decomposer organisms–abiotic environment. Fresh litter generally contains many carbon compounds that are easily assimilated by soil organisms, but is low in many other elements. During the progression from litter to SOM the carbon compounds become less and less digestible, but the concentrations of other elements, notably nitrogen and phosphorus, increase. Abiotic factors may modify this path, but their clearest influence is on the rate at which this route is travelled.

A model of litter decomposition

Decomposition of litter and formation of soil organic matter is a well-studied area and we will start with a theoretical perspective to help us identify which are the key features of the decomposition system. There is a basic structure to all descriptions of litter and soil organic matter dynamics. The decomposer community assimilates organic matter and converts it into own biomass and inorganic compounds. The stoichiometry of the assimilated organic matter is rarely in balance with the stoichiometry of the decomposers. As a consequence, what is released in inorganic form (*mineralisation*) will have a different stoichiometry to that assimilated. For elements other than carbon, bacteria and fungi can also take up inorganic forms of the elements from the soil solution (*immobilisation*) to match their stoichiometric requirements. This chapter is about describing and understanding the controls on these mineralisation–immobilisation processes and we will do this with the aid of a simple model.

Use a model to structure the problem

We start by describing the fate of a *litter cohort* (a single type of litter that starts to decompose at the same time). The litter cohort consists of carbon and other elements. The major changes in a litter cohort occur when it is consumed by decomposer organisms.

We describe the substrate by its content of carbon (C) and some other nutrient under consideration (n); in most applications this will be nitrogen. The decomposers have a biomass B, which we measure in units of carbon, and a nutrient:carbon ratio (r_d). When decomposers use (assimilate) substrate they can use only a fraction (e) of the carbon for production of new biomass; the rest must be used for respiration and is therefore converted to CO_2. We call the fraction going into new biomass *decomposer efficiency* or *production-to-assimilation ratio*. When decomposers assimilate substrate, they will not only get carbon, but also the nutrients attached to the carbon. For simplicity, the amount of nutrients is assumed to be the average nutrient concentration in the substrate.

Assume the following:

Decomposition is energy (carbon) limited. This assumption is based on observations that what limits growth of decomposer biomass most is access to energy or equivalently carbon, whereas other essential elements are available in surplus. The basic decomposer organisms, bacteria and fungi, need organic carbon as an energy source, but can use both organic and inorganic forms of other elements. In practice this means that the decomposers live in a soil where nitrate/ammonium and phosphate are readily available. In a soil with SOM consisting of a mixture of material from various sources and ages this is a reasonable assumption, although locally there may be deficiencies of other elements than carbon.

All organisms use carbon as an energy source

As a corollary it follows that when decomposers use a substrate, they obtain nutrients at the average concentration in the substrate.

Let the rate of assimilation of carbon into new decomposer biomass (production) be P and the decomposer mortality M. The dead

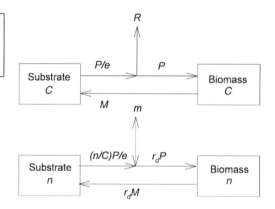

Figure 7.1 Diagram of the processes in the decomposition of a litter cohort. See text for explanation of symbols.

Heterotrophs have limited flexibility in stoichiometry

decomposer biomass, in which we also include excreta, with a nutrient: carbon ratio of r_d is returned to the substrate and becomes food for other decomposers. We can then write three equations describing the turnover of decomposer biomass (B), substrate carbon (C) and nutrient (n) as in Figure 7.1

$$\frac{dB}{dt} = P - M \tag{7.1}$$

$$\frac{dC}{dt} = -\frac{P}{e} + M \tag{7.2}$$

$$\frac{dn}{dt} = -\frac{n}{C}\frac{P}{e} + r_d M \tag{7.3}$$

The term P/e in Equations (7.2) and (7.3) appears because for each unit of carbon that is assimilated by the decomposers only a fraction e ends up as new biomass, whereas the fraction $1 - e$ is lost as respiration. To get P units of new decomposer biomass carbon, P/e units of substrate carbon are therefore required. The net fluxes of carbon (respiration, R) and nutrients (mineralisation, m) are

$$R = \frac{P}{e} - P = \frac{1-e}{e}P \tag{7.4}$$

$$m = \frac{n}{C}\frac{P}{e} - r_d P = \left(\frac{n}{C} - er_d\right)\frac{P}{e} = (r - r_c)\frac{P}{e} \tag{7.5}$$

where we define the substrate nutrient:carbon ratio as

$$r = \frac{n}{C} \tag{7.6}$$

and the critical nutrient:carbon ratio as

$$r_c = er_d \tag{7.7}$$

Since the efficiency e always is <1 and production $P > 0$, respiration R is always positive and the use of the substrate leads to a decreasing carbon amount, *carbon mineralisation*.

The cycle for nutrients is more complex. The loss of nutrients from the substrate (*gross mineralisation*, $(n/C)P/e$) will, in general, not match the decomposers' nutrient uptake ($r_d P$). The difference between these two fluxes (*net mineralisation*) can be both positive (in which case we call it *mineralisation, m > 0*) and negative (in which case we call it *immobilisation, m < 0*). The gross mineralisation can be much larger than the net mineralisation. This exchange of nutrients with the environment is also important when using isotopes to investigate these nutrient fluxes.

The critical nutrient:carbon ratio in the substrate is just the ratio at which the system switches between mineralisation and immobilisation. This switch is an important ecosystem property because immobilising substrates means that the decomposers are appropriating nutrients that plants could otherwise have taken up. It is generally assumed that decomposers are more efficient competitors for nutrients than plant roots, such that decomposers will satisfy their need for nutrients before plants can access any surplus. Mineralisation occurs when the substrate has a sufficiently high nutrient:carbon ratio relative to the decomposers; note that r_c depends only on decomposer properties and that $r_c < r_d$. If we can assume that decomposers do not change over time, the question becomes how r, the substrate nutrient:carbon ratio, can change in magnitude relative to the critical nutrient:carbon ratio r_c. Let us therefore calculate

> To mineralise or not to mineralise, that's the question

$$\frac{dr}{dt} = \frac{d}{dt}\frac{n}{C} = \frac{1}{C}\frac{dn}{dt} - \frac{n}{C^2}\frac{dC}{dt} = \ldots = (r_d - r)\frac{M}{C} \tag{7.8}$$

Equation (7.8) tells us that as long as the substrate nutrient:carbon ratio (r) is less than the decomposer nutrient:carbon ratio (r_d), the substrate nutrient:carbon ratio will increase. When the substrate nutrient:carbon ratio is larger than the decomposer nutrient:carbon ratio, the substrate nutrient:carbon ratio will decrease. In other words, the substrate nutrient:carbon ratio converges towards the decomposer nutrient:carbon ratio. This is not surprising because when carbon and nutrients are cycled back and forth between substrate and decomposers, the composition will become more and more like that of decomposer biomass.

We can now distinguish three different cases depending upon how the nutrient:carbon ratio (r_0) in the initial substrate is in relation to r_d and r_c (Figure 7.2):

(1) $r_0 > r_d$: This leads to a monotonously decreasing r and $r > r_c$ all the time. There is mineralisation from the beginning and with a decreasing substrate nutrient:carbon ratio.
(2) $r_d > r_0 > r_c$: In this case there is also mineralisation all the time, but with increasing substrate nutrient:carbon ratio.
(3) $r_c > r_0$: In this case substrate nutrient:carbon ratio increases all the time, but is initially sufficiently low that there is a phase of immobilisation. However, as the substrate nutrient:carbon ratio must increase, it will eventually reach the critical value and immobilisation is turned into mineralisation.

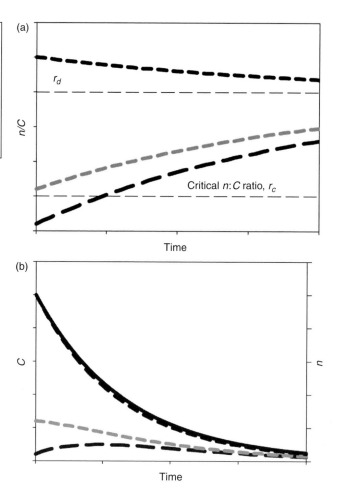

Figure 7.2 Graphs describing the possible developments of $n{:}C$ ratios (a) and absolute amounts (b) of carbon (C, solid line) and a nutrients (n, broken lines) for different initial nutrient:carbon ratios. The ratios and amounts with the same pattern are the development of the same cohort.

The qualitative behaviour of decomposition is therefore rather simple. Carbon will constantly be lost. Nutrients may be immobilised or released from the start of the decomposition; this depends only upon the nutrient requirement of the decomposers relative to the substrate nutrient concentration. The nutrient concentration in the substrate increases or decreases monotonically towards that of the decomposers, depending upon if the initial nutrient concentration in the substrate was lower or higher than that in the decomposers. Since decomposers are nutrient rich there are few substrates, and in particular no natural plant substrates, that have higher nutrient concentrations than the decomposers.

Further development of the model requires that we specify the production and mortality functions. Because most decomposer organisms are short-lived relative to the turnover time of the substrate, the decomposer biomass will rapidly adjust to the level of available substrate, and production and mortality will, therefore, be close to equilibrium, or $P = M$. Another consequence and a logical application of the assumption of carbon limitation is that the production of decomposer biomass should be proportional to the amount of available substrate, or

$$P = uC \tag{7.9}$$

where u is the decomposer growth rate per unit of carbon.

We can then rewrite Equations (7.2) and (7.3) as

$$\frac{dC}{dt} = -\frac{1-e}{e}uC = -kC \tag{7.10}$$

where k is the *specific decomposition rate* and

$$\frac{dn}{dt} = -\frac{u}{e}n + r_d uC \tag{7.11}$$

The solution of (7.10) when k is constant gives the negative exponential decay function, which is often used to describe litter mass loss from an initial amount C_0

The negative exponential is the simplest model

$$C(t) = C_0 e^{-kt} \tag{7.12}$$

Rather than solving Equation (7.11), we integrate (7.8) to get the nutrient:carbon ratio

$$r(t) = r_d - (r_d - r_0)e^{-ut} \tag{7.13}$$

and from which we obtain the nutrient amount in the litter cohort

$$n(t) = r(t)C(t) = r_d C_0 e^{-kt} - (r_d - r_0)C_0 e^{-ut/e} \tag{7.14}$$

We are particularly interested in how long it takes before a litter cohort switches from immobilisation to mineralisation, i.e. when r changes from being less than r_c to being larger than r_c. This length of time, the critical time (t_c), follows from Equation (7.13) when $r(t_c) = r_c$

$$t_c = -\frac{1}{u}\ln\frac{r_d - r_c}{r_d - r_0} \tag{7.15}$$

In an ecosystem with a constant, continuous influx of litter to the soil, we can use Equations (7.12) and (7.14) to calculate how much carbon (C_{ss}) and nutrients (n_{ss}) will be stored in the soil at steady state; it is the sum of what is left of each litter cohort

$$C_{ss} = \int_0^\infty I_0 e^{-kt}dt = \frac{I_0}{k} = \frac{e}{(1-e)u}I_0 \tag{7.16}$$

$$n_{ss} = [r_c + (1-e)r_0]C_{ss} \tag{7.17}$$

All the analysis so far requires that the two parameters u and e are, indeed, constant. Climatic variations is one cause of variability in decomposer growth rate u, but this can be included by letting k be an average over the climatic variability. However, as we will show below, there is a continuous change in the chemical composition of a substrate during decomposition and in general towards lower qualities, which can be interpreted as u decreasing with the amount of substrate. This limits the range over which the simple approach above is applicable. In spite of that, this simple model is useful for qualitatively understanding the decomposition process. More complete descriptions are still based on the simple scheme shown in Figure 7.1, but what have here been taken as constant parameters now become functions. For example, in addition to u we expect the

Table 7.1 | Major organic components in some litters, mg g^{-1}. From Swift *et al.* (1979) with kind permission from Wiley-Blackwell

	Deciduous leaf: young	Deciduous leaf: old	Conifer needle: old	Grass leaf	Grass stem	Deciduous wood
	Quercus sp.	*Quercus* sp.	*Pinus* sp.	*Deschampsia flexuosa*	Zea mais	
Lipids	80	40	240	20	20	20–60
Metabolic carbohydrates	220	150	70	130	150	10–20
Polysaccharides	130	160	190	240	180	190–240
Cellulose	160	180	160	330	30	450–480
Lignin	210	300	230	140	110	170–260
Protein[a]	90	30	20	20	10	–
Ash	60	50	20	–	80	3–11

[a] Protein contains 16% nitrogen

decomposer efficiency to depend on quality and possibly also abiotic environmental factors, but information with regard to such factors is limited. We will now look at what determines the parameters used in the model.

Litter quality

Litter properties vary greatly between plant species

In almost all terrestrial ecosystems plant production ends up as plant litter and only a minor fraction enters the soil decomposer system through other pathways; in marine and limnic ecosystems this can be different, with important stoichiometric repercussions. Plant chemical composition therefore determines the properties of fresh litter. There exists, of course, an enormous number of different chemical compounds in a plant, but with regard to their importance for litter properties they can often be grouped into a few categories (Table 7.1). The chemical composition of plant litter varies foremost between species and tissues within a plant, but also between location of growth and between growing seasons. The chemical composition of plant litter is of major importance for its use as a substrate by decomposers and as such the decomposer growth rate (u) will change with the type of litter (Figure 7.3). These differences in decomposition rates between species at a given locality can be larger than the variability in decomposition rate caused by climatic differences between different localities (Cornwell *et al.* 2008). Under a changing climate, species replacement may, therefore, be more important for changes in decomposition rates than the changes in climate itself.

As decomposers feed on the litter, the chemical composition is modified because the decomposers will not use the composition proportionally. The most easily accessible and digestible compounds, we

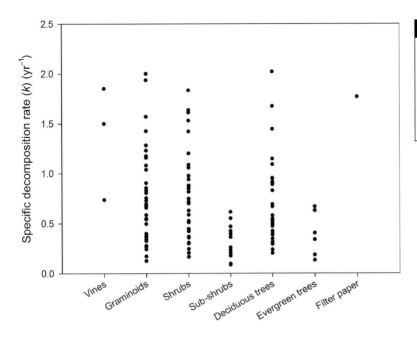

Figure 7.3 Decomposition rates under equal climatic conditions (Sheffield, England) for 126 different species and filter paper. Specific decomposition rates are estimated from 20 winter weeks of decomposition. Data from Cornelissen (1996).

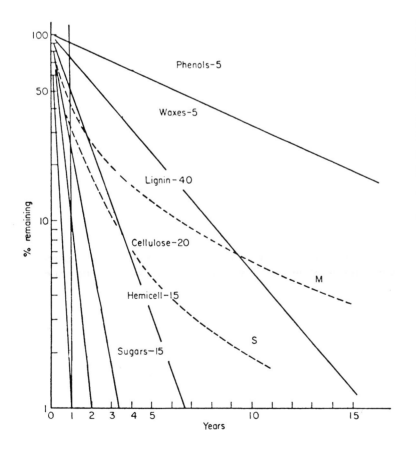

Figure 7.4 Change in remaining amounts of some chemical components in decomposing litters. The number to the right of a component shows its initial concentration (%). The solid lines show the expected curves of disappearance if the component disappears exponentially (Equation 7.12). The broken line marked S is the sum of these expected curves, whereas the broken curve marked M is observed, showing that new components are also formed during decomposition. From Minderman (1968) with kind permission from John Wiley & Sons.

call them high quality, will be used most rapidly, leaving behind the lower quality compounds. Simultaneously, the decomposers produce a variety of new compounds, in general with lower quality than the substrate from which they were produced (Figure 7.4).

Box 7.1 | Experimental techniques to determine SOM quality

There exist a large number of techniques for determining litter and SOM quality. *Wet chemical fractionation* (Figure 7.5) is one of the oldest methods and uses sequential separation with different solvents, producing a series of chemical fractions (see Table 7.1). A typical result, with changes in the chemical composition

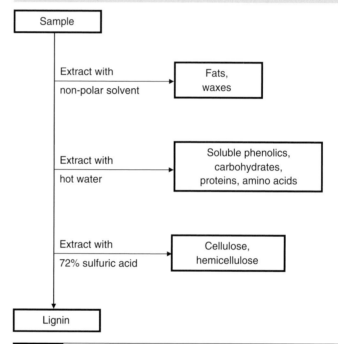

Figure 7.5 Scheme for fractionation of litter using wet chemical fractionation. The exact procedures including choices of solvents varies.

during decomposition is shown in Figure 7.6. Over the very first days the decrease in mass may be due to leaching of water-soluble substances and such a decrease should not be counted as decomposition because these substances are only moved to another part of the ecosystem where their decomposition takes place. The increase in lignin during decomposition is a result of microbially produced recalcitrant compounds. The term lignin is conventionally used in this context for residue that is resistant to digestion in concentrated sulfuric acid, but is actually a mixture of different lignins in a strict chemical sense and recalcitrant microbial products. To avoid confusion, the term Klason lignin is often used for this fraction. Highly decomposed litter where the physical identity of the sub-strate has been lost and the molecular composition is a mixture of original litter

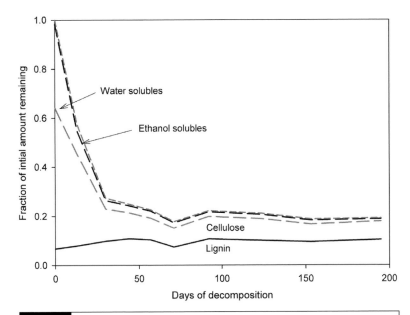

Figure 7.6 Changes in composition of compounds during decomposition, with roots of red clover (*Trifolium pratense*) as an example. Polysaccharides are included in the cellulose category. From Berg *et al.* (1987) with kind permission from Elsevier.

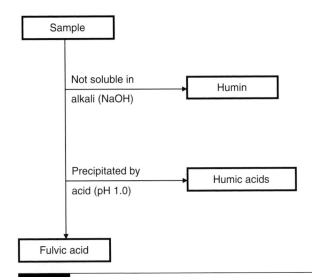

Figure 7.7 Scheme for fractionation of humus.

components, decomposer residues and chemical reaction products form *humus*. The molecular structure of humus is therefore not well determined, but is dominated by high-molecular-weight polymers, with a high content of phenolic rings. It is also high in nitrogen, but it is unclear in which form nitrogen is bound in the humus. To analyse humus or soil organic matter a different fractionation scheme to that for litters is used (Figure 7.7). *Humins* are characterised by long chains of non-polar groups and are the group most strongly bound to mineral particles. *Humic acids* are large (molecular weight up to 300 000),

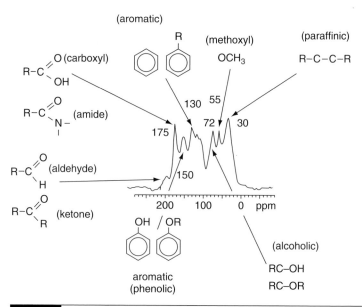

Figure 7.8 A typical NMR spectrum of humic acid showing how different peaks can be identified with characteristic groups. From Bortyatinski *et al.* (1996) with kind permission from the American Chemical Society.

relatively insoluble compounds with extensive networks of aromatic rings. Humic acids are common products in forest soils. *Fulvic acids* (molecular weight 2 000–50 000) are more water soluble than the other two groups because of their extensive side chains and charged groups. Fulvic acids are more common in grasslands. Humic acids are nitrogen-richer than fulvic acids.

Nuclear magnetic resonance (NMR) measures the magnetic field around atomic nuclei created by the electrons in a molecule. Since different chemical groups have different electron structures the magnetic field varies slightly between components and characteristic bonds (Figure 7.8). Only nuclei with an odd nucleon number (i.e. ^{13}C and ^{15}N) can be observed, because in nuclei with an even number, nucleons pair up such that their magnetic moments cancel out. Since the concentration of ^{15}N is much lower than that of ^{13}C in plants, studies of changes in nitrogen compounds are most easily done on plants grown on ^{15}N-enriched fertilisers. The changes in the NMR spectra follow a typical pattern during decomposition (Figure 7.9). Carbohydrates (the peak at 110–60 ppm) decrease while aliphatic structures (the peak at 45–0 ppm), aromatic structures (160–110 ppm) and carboxyl/carbonyl groups (220–160 ppm) increase.

Near-infrared spectroscopy (NIRS) measures vibrational and rotational distortions of chemical bonds and gives information about the frequency of typical chemical groups. Reflected light in the near infrared (800–2500 nm) and visible (400–800 nm) regions of organic matter (OM) gives a unique signature, with important biochemical information about the character and number of functional groups, such as –CH, –OH and –NH chemical bonds. In decomposition studies NIRS has not been used to identify changes in specific chemical fractions, but rather the whole spectrum has been used to characterise the chemical properties of the substrate, Figure 7.10 (Joffre *et al.* 2001).

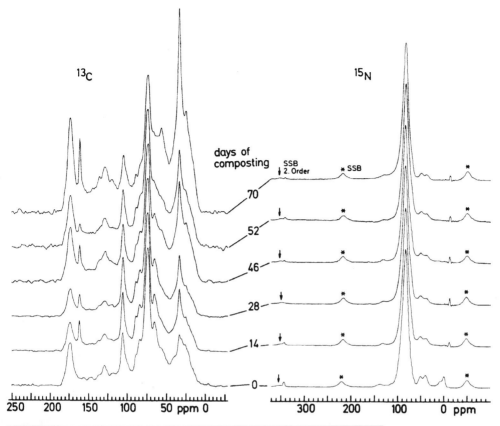

Figure 7.9 Changes in the composition of an NMR spectrum during decomposition of litter (*Lolium rigidum* plants). Almost 80% of the carbon has been lost at the end of the composting period, but almost none of the nitrogen. From Almendros *et al.* (1991) with kind permission from Elsevier.

Density fractionation is based on the observation that older SOM tends to be more associated with minerals and therefore appears in higher density fractions than fresh litter that is purely organic matter.

Abiotic controls

Temperature is one of the most powerful controls over the rate of decomposition, as well as many other soil processes, such as nitrogen mineralisation. It is common to describe the temperature effect on the rate of decomposition (r) with an exponential function of temperature (T)

Temperature controls decomposition rate

$$r(T) = r_0 e^{kT} = r_0 Q_{10}^{\frac{T-T_0}{10}} \qquad (7.18)$$

The exponential function is often replaced by a Q_{10}-function, which shows the relative change in response over a 10 K temperature change.

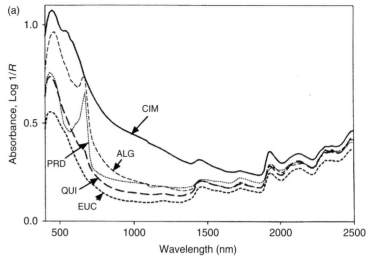

Figure 7.10 Absorption of near infrared light for different types of leaf litter (a: *Quercus ilex*, QUI; *Eucalyptus camaldulensis*, EUC; *Cistus monspeliensis*,CIM; *Alnus glutinosa*, ALG and *Prunus dulcis*, PRD; from Gillon *et al.* (1999) with kind permission from the Ecological Society of America) and for one type of litter (b: *Quercus pubescens* leves; from Joffre *et al.* (1992)) decomposed over 0.5, 2, 4, 4 and 14 months.

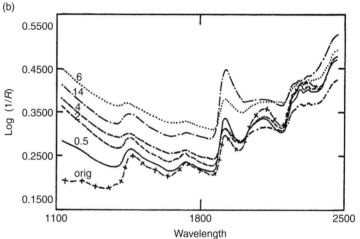

Water controls decomposition rate

It should be noted, however, that although Equation (7.18) can give a reasonable description of the temperature response, a more careful analysis shows that k or Q_{10} increases with decreasing temperature (Figure 7.11).

Water is another important environmental variable controlling the rate of decomposition. In particular, the extremes of very dry and very wet conditions can drastically reduce the rate of decomposition (Figure 7.12). Wet conditions cause anaerobicity and a completely different environment for the decomposition, and methane rather than carbon dioxide may be the end product of decomposition. Similarly, the turnover of nitrogen in the soil is sensitive to the soil water content (Chapter 9). There is also an interaction between temperature and water availability that needs to be taken into account. At temperatures around and just below 0 °C water starts

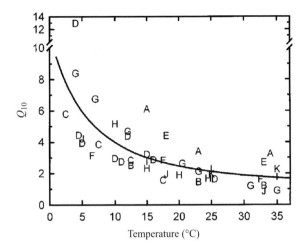

Figure 7.11 Variation in Q_{10} with temperature for decomposition of soil organic matter or litter in different studies. From Kirschbaum (2000) with kind permission from Springer Science + Business Media.

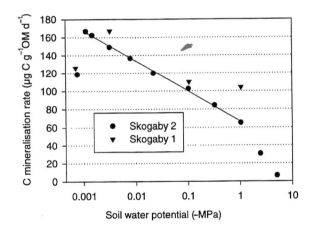

Figure 7.12 Rate of decomposition of two different samples of humus from ecosystem-type 5 as a function of soil water potential. From Seyferth (1998).

to freeze and its availability for soil organisms decreases rapidly; what appears to be a temperature response is actually a response to water (decreasing water potential).

Mineralogy can control decomposition because different minerals can differentially bind to organic matter, making the organic matter more or less difficult to access for the decomposer organisms. The most commonly used variable to describe this interaction is soil texture, because the particle size distribution determines the size of the surfaces onto which particles can be adsorbed.

Texture controls decomposition rate

Extracellular enzymes

The principal decomposers, fungi and bacteria, can only ingest small molecules. They have also difficulty moving to locations where

Enzymes are the ultimate agent for decomposition

Table 7.2 | Important exoenzymes

Enzyme	Function
Hydrolytic enzymes	
Endocellulases	Break up cellulose fibres into smaller pieces
Cellobiohydrolase	Releases cellobiose (a disaccharide) from cellulose
β-Glucosidase	Releases glucose from cellobiose
Xylanase	Degrades hemi-cellulose
Chitinases	Degrades chitin
Proteases	Degrades proteins into polypeptides
Aminopeptidases	Degrades polypeptides into amino acids
Acid (alkaline) phosphatase	Hydrolyses phosphate from phosphosaccarides and phospholipids
Oxidative enzymes	
Phenol oxidases	Breaks down phenolic compounds
Peroxidases	Breaks down lignin and other recalcitrant substrates

their food can be found. Their solution to this problem is to exude a range of enzymes, extracellular enzymes or *exoenzymes*, which are small enough that they can diffuse rapidly in the soil, attack organic matter and break it up into small pieces. These smaller pieces can then diffuse back and be assimilated by the decomposers. There is a variety of exoenzymes, some specialised and others generic (Table 7.2).

The hydrolytic enzymes are specialised to break a single type of chemical bond, whereas the oxidative enzymes can attack a variety of chemical structures, although some of them are more specific (e.g. laccases that break up phenolic rings). A consequence is that the hydrolytic enzymes can operate faster, but are restricted to their special bond. The oxidative enzymes operate more slowly but are versatile. The decomposers can optimise their production of the different enzymes in order to most efficiently use the available substrate. For example, production of peroxidases is often suppressed in the presence of high nitrogen availability because the decomposers' need for nitrogen can then be satisfied more easily than by excavating it from recalcitrant, nitrogen-rich substrates.

In the simple model described earlier in this chapter the exoenzymes are not visible. However, they are hidden in the parameter u, which describes the rate at which carbon is used by the decomposers. More elaborate models include the exoenzymes explicitly (Schimel & Weintraub 2003, Allison *et al.* 2010). Because enzyme production depends on decomposer biomass, the decomposer efficiency, e, becomes even more important when we want to use models to investigate environmental changes. Any factor that decreases the efficiency also decreases the enzyme production and thus u, thereby slowing down the use of carbon and creating a negative feedback from e to u. Temperature increases, which will normally increase u,

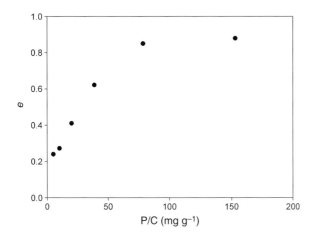

Figure 7.13 Bacterial growth efficiency as a function of nutrient supply (inorganic phosphorus/ DOC) in a lake ecosystem. Data from Jansson *et al.* (2006).

are thought to decrease *e*. As a result, the negative feedback counteracts the primary temperature response in *u*. The net effect of a temperature increase on the decomposition rate is, therefore, difficult to predict because of the complicated way in which *e* and *u* interact.

Other controlling factors

There is an increasing amount of evidence that the decomposer efficiency increases with nutrient availability (Figure 7.13). Such an effect is to be expected because with increasing availability of nutrients, the decomposers need to invest less energy in acquiring them and hence more resources can be used for growth.

We can also expect nutrient availability to affect the growth rate of the decomposers, as well as the type of metabolites that they produce. The latter may have large repercussions on the build-up of the stores of carbon and nutrients in the soil, as the formation of substances resistant to decomposition is a factor of major importance (see below under Models of soil organic matter).

Element concentration in decomposers

As shown above, the relation between nutrient concentrations in the decomposers and their food determines whether the food in itself can supply them with all they need, or if the decomposers need to rely on other, inorganic sources to satisfy their need for nitrogen and phosphorus; other elements are generally in surplus in the food. Element concentrations vary, not only between organism groups, but also with the substrate upon which they are feeding (Table 7.3).

Table 7.3 Element concentrations in some decomposer organisms (mg g^{-1}). Carbon concentration can be set to 0.5 g g^{-1}. From Swift *et al.* (1979) with kind permission from Wiley-Blackwell

	Species	N	P	K	Ca	Mg
Fungal mycelium on leaf	*Mycena galopus*	36.0	2.4	5.7	–	–
Fungal mycelium on wood	*Stereum hirsutum*	13.4	0.9	4.1	7.9	1.0
Bacteria on leaves	Mixed	40.0	9.1	15.0	9.5	1.5
Oligochaeta		105	11	5.0	3.0	2.0
Diplopoda		58	19	5.0	140	2.0
Insecta		85	69	7.0	3.0	2.0
Detritivores		77.4	8.0	1.3	103.0	2.7
Fungivores		77.4	13.9	4.0	39.5	4.6

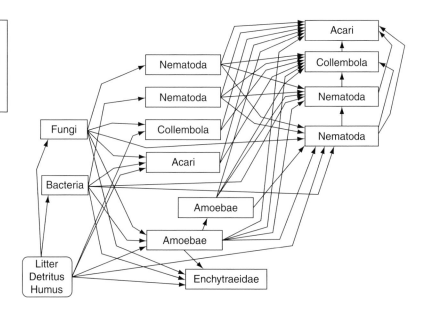

Figure 7.14 An example of a soil food web with some major organism groups and their feeding behaviour. From Schröter *et al.* (2003) with kind permission from John Wiley & Sons.

Soil food webs

The decomposer community is made up of a very large number of species, each with its food preference. An example is shown in Figure 7.14. The most important feeders on the (dead) soil organic matter (litter, detritus, humus) are the fungi and bacteria, although there are also other groups using this as a food source. The major pathway of carbon is therefore from soil organic matter to fungi and bacteria, and then on to their consumers. The nitrogen concentrations in fungi and bacteria are generally much higher than that of their food (Tables 7.1 and 7.2), and as a consequence they may need to immobilise nitrogen to satisfy their metabolic requirements. On the other hand, the consumers of the fungi and bacteria have nitrogen concentrations only 2–3 times higher than their food items and since their efficiencies in converting carbon into biomass are low, similar to those of the fungi and bacteria, they will always acquire a surplus of nitrogen. Hence, the organisms higher up in the food web can dominate the mineralisation of nitrogen.

Models of soil organic matter

There are several ways in which the problem with changing chemical composition during the decomposition process can be handled. Most commonly, litter and soil organic matter are represented by a number of discrete compartments with different rates of turnover, and the single differential equation (7.10) is replaced by a system of ordinary differential equations, which are solved numerically. Two different such models, the Century model and the Rothamsted model, are shown in Figures 7.15 and 7.16, respectively. As these two models

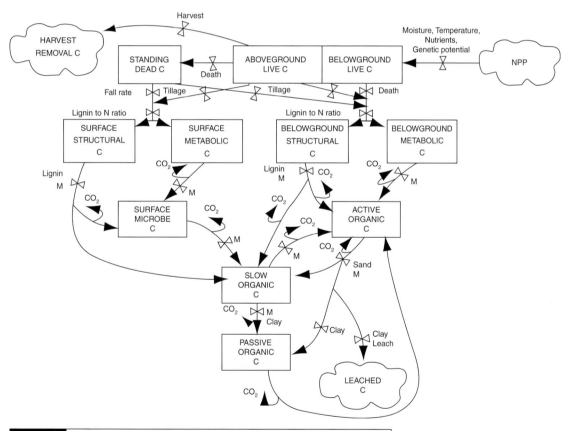

Figure 7.15 Schematic representation of the carbon sub-model of the Century model. The soil organic matter part is the three compartments: Active organic C, Slow organic C and Passive organic C. Decomposer organisms are included in the Active organic pool. The other compartments represent transformations of litter. Note that there are no fluxes back from the soil organic matter compartments to the litter compartments. The factors considered most important are also indicated in the figure (M = moisture, temperature and cultivation). From Metherell et al. (1993) with kind permission from Colorado State University.

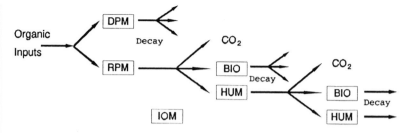

Figure 7.16 Schematic representation of the Rothamsted carbon model. In this model soil organic matter, including litter, is represented by only four compartments, of which one is constant (IOM), and one decomposer compartment. From Coleman & Jenkinson (1999) with kind permission from IARC-Rothamsted.

RPM : Resistant Plant Material

DPM : Decomposable Plant Material

BIO : Microbial Biomass

HUM : Humified OM

IOM : Inert Organic Matter

show, there is no unique way of partitioning the soil organic matter into discrete classes and the correspondence between this kind of model and empirical ways of fractionating the material is often low. In spite of that, this type of model can often reproduce observed dynamics of soil organic matter, both carbon and nitrogen. Another approach is to consider the soil organic matter as consisting of such a large number of different components that the partitioning of carbon into a small number of different pools of different qualities can be replaced by a continuous distribution of qualities (Box 7.2). The advantage with such an approach is that the model is described by a much

---

Box 7.2 | A more elaborate model of soil organic matter turnover

A major problem with the basic model is that it does not account for the changing composition of the substrate during decomposition or, in other words, the quality of the decomposer rest products are assumed to be equal to those of the fresh litter cohort. This can be accounted for in a more elaborate model, which here we will show only for carbon. Such a model requires that we assign to each carbon atom a quality. A litter cohort is then described by a distribution, $\rho_C(q,t)$, which gives the amount of carbon with qualities in the interval $[q, q + dq]$. The turnover of the carbon is described as in the basic model, with one important exception. When carbon is returned to the substrate through decomposer mortality, the quality (q) is no longer the same as the quality (q') of the carbon assimilated by the decomposer. The decomposers convert carbon of one quality into a range of other qualities. This requires the introduction of another distribution (a *dispersion function*) that tells what fraction of carbon of quality q' is produced from one unit of carbon of quality q. Call this function $D(q,q')$. Equation (7.2) is then replaced by $(P = M)$ (Figure 7.17)

$$\frac{\partial \rho_C(q,t)}{\partial t} = -\frac{u(q)}{e(q)}\rho_C(q,t) + \int D(q,q')u(q')\rho_C(q',t)dq' \qquad (7.19)$$

Note that if u and e are independent of q, Equation (7.15) is equal to (7.12) because $\int \rho_C(q,t)dq = C(t)$ and $\int D(q,q')dq = 1$.

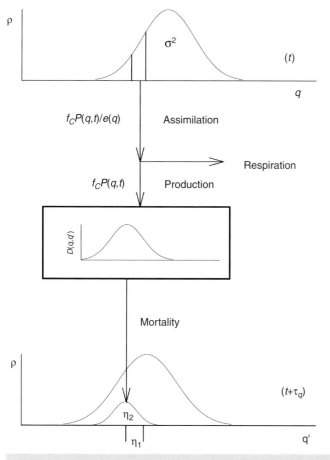

Figure 7.17 Description of litter decomposition when the litter is described by a distribution of carbon qualities. Carbon is assimilated by decomposers from a distribution of carbon in the substrate. Part of the assimilated carbon is respired and a part forms new decomposer biomass. In the process of forming new decomposer biomass, carbon compounds with qualities other than those assimilated are produced and the quality of carbon returned as substrate upon decomposer death is therefore different. From Ågren & Bosatta (1998).

To solve Equation (7.19) requires that we specify the three functions $u(q)$, $e(q)$ and $D(q,q')$. There are several ways of doing this, but one way leads to the following function for the carbon remaining in a litter cohort, compare Equation (7.12)

$$C(t) = \frac{C_0}{\left(1 + p_u p_q t\right)^p} \tag{7.20}$$

The initial specific decomposition rate with this model is then

$$\frac{1}{C}\frac{dC}{dt} = -\frac{p p_u p_q}{1 + p_u p_q t} \rightarrow -p p_u p_q \text{ as } t \rightarrow 0 \tag{7.21}$$

where p is a parameter that can be coupled to decomposer efficiency and how rapidly substrates become more recalcitrant. The parameter p_u can be associated with environmental conditions and p_q with initial litter quality. Over short time spans Equations (7.12) and (7.20) do not differ much, but over long time spans, (7.20) decays much slower and leads to much larger steady-state carbon stores (C_{ss}). For a constant rate of litter input, l_0

$$C_{ss} = \frac{1}{p p_u p_q}\frac{p}{p-1}l_0 \tag{7.22}$$

Since p can be close to 1 (but larger!), the steady-state store calculated with this more elaborate model will be much larger than the corresponding store calculated from the simpler model (7.16)

smaller number of parameters and results can be derived analytically and explicitly. The cost is a larger demand on mathematical knowledge of the user.

FURTHER READING

Ågren, G.I. & Bosatta, E. 1998. *Theoretical Ecosystem Ecology – Understanding Element Cycles*. Cambridge: Cambridge University Press.

Berg, B. & McClaugherty, C. 2003. *Plant Litter – Decomposition, Humus Formation, Carbon Seequestration*. Berlin: Springer.

Berg, B. & Laksowski, R. 2006. Litter decomposition: A guide to carbon and nutrient turnover. *Advances in Ecological Research* **38**:1–428.

Swift, M.J., Heal, O.W. & Anderson, J.M. 1979. *Decomposition in Terrestrial Ecosystems*. Oxord: Blackwell Scientific Publications.

Chapter 8

Organisms and ecosystem processes

We discuss here different concepts of the stability of ecosystems and how they are related to the populations composing the ecosystem. It is possible that in the end stability of ecosystem processes comes at the expense of the stability of the individual species within the ecosystem.

Species and ecosystems

The importance of the identity of the species forming an ecosystem is far from a resolved issue. In certain respects the exact identities of the species matter little because they all perform the same functions: plants photosynthesise, whilst fungi and bacteria decompose organic matter in the soil. In other respects the identity of the species is crucial because only certain species can perform specific and important functions. Examples of such species, *keystone species*, are nitrogen fixers and nitrifiers. The stability, whatever is implied in that term, may also depend on the identity and diversity of species.

Concepts of stability

An ecosystem can be *stable* or *unstable* with respect to disturbances in several senses. We will discuss the most important ones. A convenient analogue for understanding ecological stability is a ball in a landscape with hills and valleys (Figure 8.1). Note that the terminology in this area is sometimes confusing and different schools may use different terms for the same property or the same term for different properties (Peterson *et al.* 1998). First of all, the question is whether an ecosystem returns to the same state as before a disturbance. The ability to recover after a disturbance is often referred to as *resilience* (this term is sometimes used for the rate of return and then called engineering resilience as opposed to ecological resilience as used here). A more technical way of expressing resilience is to look at the range over which the system can be disturbed and still return to its initial state, its *basin of attraction*.

Ecosystems can have one or more equilibrium points; when the axis is soil water the equilibrium points I and II could in our example correspond to pine or spruce forests, with spruce at position I and

Stability has several components

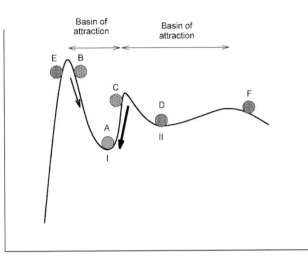

Figure 8.1 Schematic representation of the stability of an ecosystem
represented by a ball in a landscape
with two equilibrium positions
(I and II). At points A and D the ball
is at equilibrium, whereas it is at
different states of non-equilibrium at
the other points. However, the ball at
D can more easily be moved out of its
equilibrium compared to the ball at A;
the steepness of the slope around a
position is a measure of resistance.
The arrows indicate different
elasticities. The balls at E and F have
different persistencies.

pine position II, as spruce has a narrower niche with respect to water
than pine. The extent of disturbance a system can tolerate will in
general be different in different directions, e.g. adding or removing
nutrients. It is also a question of how difficult it is to move the system
from its equilibrium point. Moving the ball in Figure 8.1 from position A towards B should be easier than towards C because the hills
are less steep in the first direction; it may be easier to add nutrients to
an ecosystem than to remove them. This property is called *resistance*.
Similarly, the steeper hill in the direction of C from A should
imply that once the disturbing force is removed, the system returns
more rapidly than had it been disturbed in the direction of B. In the
absence of nitrogen fixers it may take a very long time for an ecosystem to restore nitrogen lost, whereas losing excess nitrogen could be
a rapid affair.

The rate at which the system returns towards its equilibrium
position is called *elasticity*. It is also possible that the environment
has changed in such a way that an ecosystem is about to disappear
and be replaced by another system. However, such changes can be
slower or faster. It is therefore meaningful to look at how long it takes
before the ecosystem has changed (*persistency*). Ecosystems dominated
by long-lived individuals like certain forests may not be able to regenerate because the required climatic conditions for seedling establish-
ments are no longer prevalent, but adult individuals survive; such
ecosystems can be very persistent.

Most analyses of stability can only be qualitative. A major problem
is to define what is meant by an ecosystem retuning to the same state.
If after a disturbance the ecosystem returns to a state with 99% of the
carbon content and with one species less than before the disturbance,
should we then consider the ecosystem as the same? If we accept this
as the same ecosystem, what if the ecosystem has only returned to
95% of its earlier carbon content? Or 90%? Or 50%?

We have here discussed stability as if ecosystems should be con-
fined to one single state. This is, of course, not the case, but most

ecosystems are continuously changing, and stability can mean that the ecosystem properties remain within certain boundaries. In the simplified Figure 8.1 stability is only discussed in one dimension. However, ecosystems exist in a multidimensional world (temperature, water, several nutrients), and stability has to be considered for all these dimensions; stability properties can vary greatly between dimensions, having high stability in some dimensions but low stability in others.

When we observe an ecosystem away from its equilibrium point, it is also important to take into account how it is moving relative to this equilibrium point. Is it moving towards it or away from it? If it is moving away from the equilibrium point, is this because there is some external force pushing it away, such as an ongoing decline in water supply and the ecosystem will start to recover as soon as rain starts to fall? Or is the system moving because its internal inertia has not yet allowed it to reach its new equilibrium point? The latter would be the case when the force comes from the accumulation of some compound like nitrogen deposition over many years or increased atmospheric carbon dioxide concentration. Even removing the force by stopping the nitrogen deposition or halting the increase in atmospheric carbon dioxide concentration will not halt the changes in the ecosystem (Ågren *et al.* 2008). It is then not enough to consider the instantaneous condition of the ecosystem, but projections of its future development are necessary to evaluate its stability. We have what we can call *committed changes* (Jones *et al.* 2009).

Species matter

For a long time a controversial issue in ecology has been the relationship between species diversity or species number, and ecosystem properties. In early times it was assumed that an ecosystem with more species present should be more stable than an ecosystem with fewer species, because different species would perform different functions and substitute for each other. However, in the mid 1970s it was shown that with random assemblages of species, an increasing number of species rapidly increased the risk of some species being lost from the ecosystem, with the implication that increasing the number of species destabilises an ecosystem (May 1973). Since ecosystems are not random assemblages of species, but combinations of species that have been selected in such a way that they can coexist, the question is in fact more complicated.

Besides ecosystem stability there is also the question of ecosystem function. With function we think in this context of processes like net primary production, net nitrogen mineralisation or nitrate leaching. How will they change when the number of species changes? Several experiments have been conducted to answer this question. A particular problem with these types of experiments is that with the few numbers of species it is possible to include, the inclusion or not of

Ecosystem responses to species richness generally saturates at 10–20 species

Table 8.1 Some properties of a Hawaiian forest with and without the nitrogen-fixing tree *Myrica faya*

Property	Without *Myrica faya*	With *Myrica faya*
N input[a]	5.5	23.5
Earthworm biomass $(g\ m^{-2})$[b]	3.3	25.8

[a] From Vitousek *et al.* (1987)
[b] From Aplet (1990)

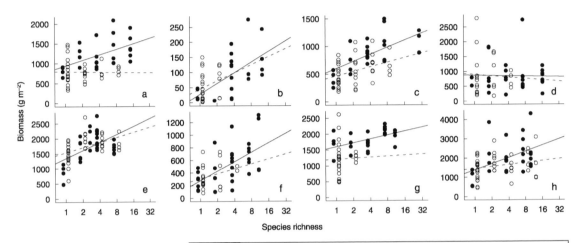

Figure 8.2 Relation between sown species richness and total biomass (above plus below ground) at the end of the third growing season in the international BIODEPTH project for communities with (closed symbols and solid lines) and without (open symbols and broken lines) legumes. In almost all experiments the biomass increased as more species were included. The different sub-figures represent experiments conducted in eight different countries. From Hector *et al.* (2007) with kind permission from John Wiley & Sons.

a particular species can dominate the response. Figure 8.2 shows results from a large species-richness experiment. In this experiment plant biomass increased in most cases in the experimental plots when the number of species increased. The increase occurred independently of the presence or not of nitrogen-fixing legumes, although the increase tended to be larger when legumes were present.

The presence or absence of a species with a particular property (keystone species) can drastically change the functioning of an ecosystem. When a young, nitrogen-limited Hawaiian forest was invaded by the exotic nitrogen-fixer *Myrica faya*, the nitrogen input increased fourfold (Table 8.1). Among the responses observed was a nearly eightfold increase in earthworm biomass. The very specific function of a single species, nitrogen fixation in this case, could therefore cause a large shift in system properties.

Table 8.2 Effects of orbital forcing with and without vegetation feedback on climate during the Holocene epoch at latitudes 60 to 90 °N. The control corresponds to Earth's orbit today and a snow-covered tundra. The orbital forcing corresponds to Earth's orbit 6000 years ago and a snow-covered tundra. In the vegetation feedback the snow-covered tundra in the orbital forcing scenario is replaced by a coniferous forest. Data from Foley *et al.* (1994)

	Control	Orbital forcing	Vegetation feedback
Surface albedo, annual	0.364	0.356	0.265
Absorbed solar radiation, annual (W m^{-2})	111.2	115.3	123.3
Annual surface temperature (°C)	−8.4	−6.6	−5.0

Another example of a species effect on ecosystem properties comes from the vegetation–climate feedback that occurred at the end of the last glaciation (Table 8.2). When the Laurentide ice sheet retreated over North America it left space for the boreal forest to expand northward. Compared to today, the insolation was also different because the Earth's orbit around the Sun was different (orbital forcing, see Chapter 11). Foley *et al.* (1994) calculated the effect on the local climate as a result of the orbital forcing alone or in combination with a change in albedo resulting from replacing snow-covered tundra with a coniferous forest. Their conclusion is that the change in orbit increased the absorbed solar radiation by 4.1 W m^{-2} and the annual average temperature by 1.8 °C. When a coniferous forest replaced the tundra, the absorbed radiation resulting from the lower albedo increased by an additional 8 W m^{-2}. The temperature increased an additional 1.6 °C. A consequence of this strong vegetation feedback on the local climate is that once the ice sheet started to retreat and a forest could establish itself, the additionally warmer climate sped up the retreat of the ice sheet; 'The spruce trees weren't *following* the ice north ... they were *chasing* it!' (J. Harte pers. comm.).

... Or maybe not

Although it is clear that keystone species can alter ecosystem properties and that a large number of species can increase the productivity of an ecosystem by more fully utilising all niche space, this does not necessarily lead to a greater stability. Another way of looking at stability is to investigate how much productivity, for example, varies when the number of species increases. In a long-term experiment in a grassland in Minnesota, the year-to-year variability in total plant biomass was expressed as the coefficient of variation (CV)

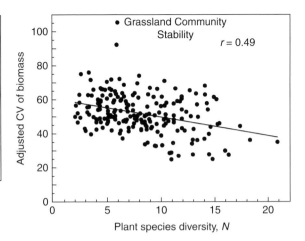

Figure 8.3 The relation between coefficient of variation in total biomass and plant species diversity in grassland plots at Cedar Creek, Minnesota. The decreasing variability with increasing species diversity means that biomass will stabilise with more species. From Tilman (1999) with kind permission from the Ecological Society of America.

(Figure 8.3). With increasing number of species in the plots, the between-year variability decreased, showing that a larger number of species stabilised the production. The interpretation of this result was that the species had complementary properties such that during a drought year certain species were more abundant and could substitute for species suffering from the drought. The idea is that different species respond differently to environmental variability and where one species suffers, another will thrive, such that the overall response remains stable. With an analogy from the stock market, this is called the *portfolio effect*.

The final word on the relation between stability and diversity has not yet been said, and the picture is more nuanced than when much of the discussion started in the 1960s. The current view can perhaps be summarised as: diversity stabilises many processes at the ecosystem level but increases the variability/risk for the individual species (May 1999).

FURTHER READING

Loreau, M., Naeem, S. & Inchausti, P. (eds) 2002. *Biodiversity and Ecosystem Functioning – Synthesis and Perspectives*. Oxford: Oxford University Press.

Chapter 9

Element cycles

A major characteristic of terrestrial ecosystems is element cycles. We first discuss different modes of cycling based on the nature of the participating processes. Cycling is then presented for two different scales – local and global, respectively. The following elements are treated in detail: carbon, nitrogen, phosphorus, potassium, magnesium, calcium and sulfur. Cycling in a temperate Norway spruce forest gives an insight into details and a comparison of cycling characteristics of ecosystems of major biomes in different climates – arctic, boreal, temperate and tropical – provides the broad picture. Major methods for measuring the different elements are also presented.

A major function in terrestrial ecosystems is the cycling of nutrients or mineral elements. A number of processes are responsible for the gradual changes in organic and inorganic materials, which eventually lead to the release of elements in forms that can be taken up by plants; thus maintaining the production of plant matter and sustaining life for other organisms in the ecosystem. Components of these cycles were discussed in Chapters 6 and 7 in relation to plant growth and soil organic matter turnover. Here we will consider the complete cycles of the major elements.

There are two major types of cycle: a gaseous type, where the elements predominantly cycle via the atmosphere, and a sedimentary type, where the cycling is via the soil. Depending on the temporal and spatial scales of the cycles and the participating biotic and abiotic actors we can also identify three different modes of cycling (Figure 9.1). Element cycles can then be described by the modes in which they operate:

Spatial and temporal scales determine which type of cycles to consider

- the *geochemical mode* deals with fluxes across the ecosystem boundary, such as input in terms of precipitation, dry deposition, soil mineral weathering and losses by leaching, erosion and gaseous losses; both hydrological and biological processes contribute on this scale. The contribution to the cycling of an element in this mode is a measure of the openness of this element's cycle.
- the *biogeochemical mode* deals with cycling within the ecosystem or with soil–plant relationships. It includes uptake of elements from the soil by plants and microbes, and the contribution back by litter fall, detritus and leaching from plants.
- the *biochemical mode* deals with transport or translocation of elements in the plants – to developing tissues and from senescing tissues.

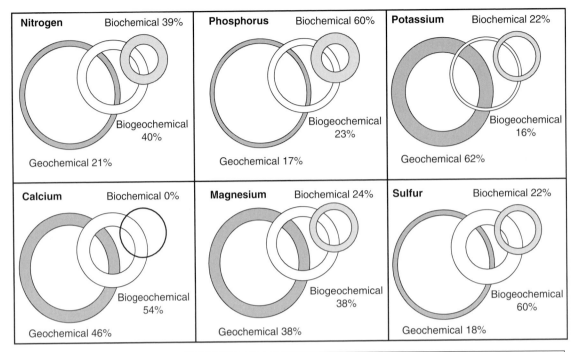

Figure 9.1 An example from a 20-year-old *Pinus taeda* stand of how the different modes of cycling contribute differently depending upon element. The biochemical contribution to the cycling has been estimated as the amount resorbed by trees before senescence of needles. The biogeochemical contribution to the cycling has been estimated as the amount released during litter decomposition. The contribution from geochemical cycling is what remains. The thicknesses of the rings are proportional to the contributions to cycling. The partitioning between modes will be different in other ecosystems. Modified from Switzer & Nelson (1972). Carbon is in this context essentially only cycled geochemically.

The first two modes operate at two scales: small-scale, ecosystem-specific or local, and global scale. The ecosystem scale will describe processes in detail, whereas the global scale will deal with the more general aspects. The third mode operates at the plant level and has already been covered in Chapter 6.

Most elements are highly dynamic at short time scales and small spatial scales, with fluxes that can vary several-fold within a day and also change direction. There is also a large spatial variability, for some processes distances of less than a millimetre can be important. Many of the processes at this scale are well understood at a biochemical level, but integration or averaging to the level of the ecosystem can be difficult because the processes respond non-linearly to environmental conditions and other processes in the ecosystem.

In contrast, the global element cycles have shown an amazing constancy over thousands of years. Well known is the variability in the atmospheric carbon dioxide concentration [CO_2], where the Vostok ice cores show that during the past 400 000 years the

Understanding decreases with increasing scale

atmospheric carbon dioxide concentration has only varied in the interval 180 to 300 ppmv. However, the human use of fossil fuels and large-scale conversion of forests to agricultural land has over as short a period as 200 years brought the concentration up to over 380 ppmv (IPCC 2001, 2007). In view of the stoichiometric constraints on ecological processes discussed in previous chapters we have every reason to believe that global cycles of other elements have also remained within narrow limits, although the empirical evidence for this is more limited.

The summary of global cycles draws from many different sources with different resolutions and ranges. Although the global cycles for the individual elements may be reasonably accurate, combining values from the different cycles can compound errors. Stoichiometric relations may, therefore, not be in agreement with values from local studies or theoretical considerations. We will be using the terms cycles and fluxes (flows) interchangeably. A cycle should always form a loop, closed or open, consisting of links in the form of fluxes. In some cases a chain of fluxes might actually form a cycle and we may use the term cycle, although the cyclic nature of the flux is not emphasised.

Ecosystem scale

We start with an analysis of the carbon and nitrogen cycles – two elements which are in focus in this textbook. The cycles of these elements are both of the gaseous type and have to various degrees biochemical and biogeochemical modes. In fact, the fate of carbon in the ecosystem is rather a flux than a closed cycle. Nitrogen, on the other hand, represents a true cycle. Carbon provides the energy to the system; nitrogen, as a macronutrient, is necessary for many life functions. We will also take up the cycles of phosphorus, potassium, magnesium, calcium and sulfur. These elements are also macronutrients, but of a sedimentary type. They also differ considerably in the modes of cycling.

The carbon cycle

A general representation of carbon fluxes at the ecosystem level is shown in Figure 9.2. It is important to remember that ecosystems are dynamic, that the numbers given are only gross averages over long periods and that specific ecosystems can differ considerably at any given instance (see Figure 3.1). An example of the carbon fluxes through three Norway spruce forests is given in Table 9.1. The exchange of carbon with the surrounding environment is dominated by carbon dioxide fluxes (removal in harvests excluded) characterising the carbon cycle as being of the gaseous type. The biochemical mode contributes little to the carbon cycle in the plant compartment, as carbon once laid down in structural tissues is not recycled within the

The carbon cycle is open

Table 9.1 Carbon fluxes in three 40-year-old Norway spruce (*Picea abies*) stands in Sweden. The flux values are a combination of directly measured values (italic) and values estimated using a simulation model. Eddy-covariance measurements of the NEE at Flakaliden give an annual flux of 0.98–1.08 (Mg ha^{-1} yr^{-1}), which has been used to constrain the simulation model. The simulation model results in a perfectly balanced carbon cycle and the deviations from directly measured values indicate the accuracy with which this type of budget can be established (e.g. NPP – litter $\neq$ change in vegetation). Values within parentheses are percentage of GPP. Data from Berggren Kleja *et al.* (2008)

	Flakaliden (64° N, 19E)	Knottåsen (61° N, 16E)	Asa (57° N, 15E)
Flux (Mg ha^{-1}yr^{-1})			
GPP	7.90	9.16	14.37
trees	7.03	8.60	14.37
field layer	0.87	0.56	0
Autotrophic respiration	4.69	5.59	9.38
trees	4.25	5.28	9.38
field layer	0.44	0.31	0
NPP	3.21 (46)	3.57 (42)	4.99 (35)
Aboveground litterfall	*0.70*	*0.80*	*1.02*
trees	*0.60*	*0.68*	*1.01*
field layer	*0.10*	*0.12*	*0.01*
Belowground litter production	*0.98*	*1.32*	*1.01*
trees	*0.57*	*0.82*	*0.84*
field layer	*0.41*	*0.50*	*0.17*
Heterotrophic respiration	2.14 (27)	2.15 (24)	3.11 (22)
NEE/NEP	1.07 (14)	1.42 (16)	1.87 (13)
Change in vegetation	*2.19*	*1.99*	*4.05*
Change in soil	*−0.08*	*−0.06*	*0.09*
DOC leaching	*0.001*	*0.002*	*0.004*

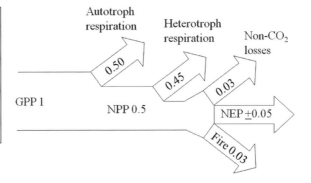

Figure 9.2 Carbon fluxes in an ecosystem with approximate relative long-term partitioning between components. Over very long periods NEP = 0, but can over thousands of years be >0 or <0. The relative contributions from fire and non-CO$_2$ losses vary greatly between ecosystems.

plant. The conversion of carbon to different qualities during decomposition (Chapter 7) is, on the other hand, an important biochemical mode of the carbon cycle. The biogeochemical mode contains, in contrast to other elements, only a unidirectional flux from plants to soil. Uptake of organic acids is a flux of carbon from soil to plants, but negligible compared to carbon uptake through photosynthesis.

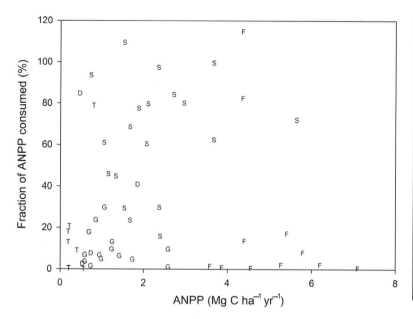

Figure 9.3 Fraction of aboveground net primary production (ANPP) consumed by herbivores for various ecosystems (T = tundra, D = desert, G = grassland, F = forest, S = savanna). The fraction not consumed by herbivores will be consumed in other processes. It should also be noted that belowground production can in several ecosystems be larger than aboveground production and that some of the data in the figure represent outbreak values and are not representative of long-term consumption. Data from McNaughton et al. (1989).

Gross Primary Production (GPP) is the total gross photosynthesis in the ecosystem, i.e. it represents all conversions of carbon dioxide to organic carbon. We have discussed this process in detail in Chapter 6.

Net Primary Production (NPP) is what is left over when the autotrophs have used their share of the GPP for their own respiration. There seems to be a rather stable 50% of the GPP being used in this way, but respiration seems to increase with age in forest stands and there are differences between different types of forests (DeLucia *et al.* 2007). Autotrophic respiration, which loses carbon as carbon dioxide, was also discussed in detail in Chapter 6.

Net Ecosystem Exchange (NEE) is the net carbon dioxide flux in an ecosystem. It is what is left over after heterotrophic respiration has taken its share of the NPP. Heterotrophic respiration is dominated by decomposition by soil organisms; in particular bacteria and fungi. In many ecosystems herbivores consume less than 10% (Figure 9.3). In terrestrial ecosystems the NEE will in the long term be a small positive fraction of the GPP, but can under certain conditions, e.g. following a windfall, have a large negative value when the GPP becomes small. It will, on the other hand, never attain large positive values because there are no situations where heterotrophic respiration would be low without a simultaneous low GPP.

Before the *Net Ecosystem Production* (NEP) can be calculated it is necessary to include carbon transfers over the ecosystem boundary in forms other than respiratorily derived carbon dioxide. The most important of these are carbon losses through fire, uptake and emissions of methane and other volatile organic compounds (VOC), lateral and vertical transfers of dissolved organic carbon (DOC) and particulate carbon by erosion (PIC). Most of these fluxes are never more than a small percentage of the NPP, although fire, when it occurs, can

It is not only CO_2 that contributes to the carbon cycle

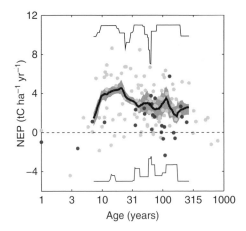

Figure 9.4 Net ecosystem production (NEP) as a function of stand age. Dark grey dots show temperate forests and light grey dots boreal forests. The thick line is the average NEP and the thin lines the 95% confidence intervals. From Luyssaert *et al.* (2008) with kind permission from the Nature Publishing Group.

consume much larger quantities. Fire can also compete with herbivory for consumption of carbon. Herbivores, which reduce fire frequencies and intensities, can in fact maintain the productivity of certain ecosystems at higher levels than otherwise would be the case by preventing nitrogen loss as nitrogen oxides in fires. Dissolved inorganic carbon (DIC) might also have to be considered; as much as 20% of the soil heterotrophic respiration in arctic Alaska may be lost this way (Kling *et al.* 1991). In the long run losses as DOC can be important for ecosystem carbon stores because, although small, this flux will be competing with a slow build-up of the most recalcitrant soil organic substrates. Otherwise the loss of carbon as DOC from terrestrial ecosystems is more important as a source of carbon to downstream aquatic environments.

Are there any ecosystems in which NEP is close to zero such that the ecosystems may be considered at steady state with respect to, at least, carbon? Old-growth forests, where the death of old individuals can be expected to be compensated by the birth of new individuals, have long been assumed to represent such a state. However, there are examples of undisturbed forests as old as several hundred years that continue to accumulate carbon (NEP > 0) (Figure 9.4).

The methane flux is a special case, not because it occurs in larger quantities than the other carbon forms, but as a result of its potentially large GWP (see Box 5.2). Methane is produced during decomposition of organic matter under anoxic conditions. Its production is therefore generally restricted to wetlands and water-logged soils (Figure 9.5). However, methane can, during transport through the soil, encounter aerobic areas in the upper soil horizons and there efficiently be oxidised to carbon dioxide by specialised organisms using methane as an energy source. The net methane release from an area is, therefore, particularly sensitive to the position of the water table, and upland soils with low-lying water tables are in effect consumers of methane. In addition to diffusion through the soil, methane can also be transported in bubbles through the water column (ebullition) and through the stems of certain plant species. The latter process makes the net release sensitive to plant species composition because plant species differ in their capability to conduct gases. Plant species composition is also important because of differences in root exudates that serve as carbon substrates for the methane consumers. An example from an arctic mire of the importance of plant species, as well as of the time horizon for the global radiation balance is shown in Figure 9.6. Where the ecosystem is dominated by *Eriophorum angustifolium*, a large fraction of NPP is released as methane, which has a large effect on the radiation balance over a 20-year time horizon, but because of the short residence time for methane in the atmosphere, the effect is lost with a 500-year time horizon. In contrast, a species like *Carex rotundata*, which causes most of the NPP to return as carbon dioxide and little as methane, will have a smaller, but longer lasting, impact on the radiation balance.

Box 9.1	Measuring terrestrial carbon cycling at the ecosystem level

MEASURING GPP AND AUTOTROPHIC RESPIRATION

Measurements of GPP use cuvettes (Figure 9.5) in which leaves or other photosynthesising tissues are enclosed. An air stream is passed through the cuvette and the incoming and outgoing carbon dioxide concentrations are

Figure 9.5	Net photosynthesis measurement with a cuvette. Photo G.I. Ågren.

measured. The difference represents the uptake/loss of carbon dioxide from the leaf. However, because a leaf in light is both photosynthesising and respiring at the same time these measurements give only the net photosynthesis. Another set of measurements is therefore done with the leaf in darkness, but under other otherwise equal conditions, and from these measurements dark respiration is estimated. Alternatively, the respiration is estimated from measurements made at night. Together these measurements give the gross photosynthesis of the leaf (Equation 6.1). For long-term measurements of photosynthesis and respiration, such cuvettes are coupled to automated measuring systems that day and night follow the carbon dioxide fluxes and a number of environmental variables (e.g. temperature, radiation, humidity). The GPP is then estimated by summing the contribution from all photosynthesising tissues. This involves upscaling of the spot measurements by interpolating and extrapolating to cover the environmental variability within canopies (see Figure 6.6). Cuvettes are also used to measure respiration from other non-photosynthesising tissues.

Figure 9.6 Flux tower for measuring gas exchange over a Norway spruce forest at Knottåsen, central Sweden. Photo: Achim Grelle. See also colour plate section.

MEASURING NPP

The techniques used for measuring the GPP and autotrophic respiration also give the NPP in principle, but direct measurements are preferred because of the uncertainty resulting from upscaling. Depending upon the kind of vegetation, different techniques are required. With annual plants, sampling of the biomass at its peak represents the NPP, although care has to be taken to include losses from earlier senescence, herbivory or other similar causes. Perennials can in principle be handled in the same way, but litter production becomes important to include. Repeated harvesting of perennials can also mean a large disturbance to the ecosystem and non-destructive measurements are desirable. Most such non-destructive measurements rely on allometric relations (see Box 4.3). Establishment of allometric relations are time-consuming and hence costly, which is why standard, species-specific relations are used, although they can for certain vegetation components vary considerably between sites. Because plant roots are hidden in the soil they pose particular problems for measurement and there are currently no really good measurement techniques. Estimates of the NPP with non-destructive techniques (e.g. by measurement of stem diameters) can only be done over longer time intervals because short-term fluctuations in variables not directly coupled to NPP can overshadow the contribution from NPP (e.g. the diurnal swelling and shrinking of tree stems from changes in water content can be as large as the annual increase in stem diameter from growth).

MEASURING NEE

With a micrometeorological technique called eddy-covariance, in which the flux of air and the gradients of gas concentrations above a canopy are measured, it is possible to estimate the NEE (neglecting other routes of carbon dioxide flux). Such measurements are done by erecting towers with sensors at different heights (Figure 9.6). To provide good estimates it is necessary for the environment around the tower to be homogeneous because air movements transport molecules long horizontal distances and mix gases from different locations upwind. Depending upon wind direction and horizontal wind speed the measurement system will therefore estimate the NEE for different areas of the surrounding ecosystems (different footprints). The measurements are done with a high frequency (several times per hour) and provide very detailed temporal information about changes in ecosystem carbon, water vapour and other gaseous fluxes.

Box 9.2 | Ecosystem experiments

Carbon availability in the form of carbon dioxide is one of the most difficult environmental variables to manipulate because whatever carbon dioxide is added in an ecosystem it will rapidly be mixed with the huge atmospheric reservoir. Different types of enclosures are used to avoid this problem and to maintain a constant carbon dioxide concentration around the leaves (Figure 9.7 and 9.8).

The problems with such enclosures are that they can modify the environment in other ways; in particular large coolers may be required to keep the temperature at the ambient level. To avoid such artefacts the canopies can be enclosed in a ring of carbon dioxide sprayers (FACE = free air CO_2

Figure 9.7 Open-top chambers for measuring gas exchange in a marshland at the Chesapeake Bay, MD, USA. Photo: Bert Drake. See also colour plate section.

Figure 9.8 Closed chambers for measuring gas exchange of Norway spruce trees in Flakaliden, northern Sweden. Photo: Bengt-Olof Wigren. See also colour plate section.

Figure 9.9 FACE experiment in a loblolly pine (*Pinus taeda*) stand in Duke Forest, NC, USA. Photo: Chris Hildreth/Duke Photography. See also colour plate section.

enrichment) (Figure 9.9). The uses of such systems are mainly limited because of the extremely high cost of the added carbon dioxide.

The nitrogen cycle

Nitrogen is the key element for all biological activity because it is required in proteins, which serve both as enzymes and structural elements, as well as in nucleic acids (Chapter 3). Nitrogen plays, therefore, an essential role both in the short-term functioning of organisms (enzymes) and in long-term evolution (DNA). It is then not surprising that many organisms respond strongly and rapidly to changes in nitrogen availability, a theme explored for plants in Chapter 6, and have evolved mechanisms for efficiently acquiring nitrogen.

The major nitrogen fluxes in terrestrial ecosystems are shown in Figure 9.7. The main pathway by which nitrogen enters ecosystems in useable forms (often named *reactive nitrogen*) is through nitrogen fixation, although in polluted areas deposition of reactive nitrogen can dominate; other sources such as weathering are negligible. The losses from an ecosystem are mostly as nitrogen oxides or leaching of nitrate or dissolved organic nitrogen (DON). However, the nitrogen leached from one ecosystem will eventually be lost in gaseous form from downstream ecosystems. The nitrogen cycle is therefore mostly of the gaseous type. Nitrogen cycles operate in all three modes (geochemical, biogeochemical, biochemical). A particular feature of the nitrogen cycle is that the importance of these modes can shift in time, even for a given ecosystem.

The nitrogen cycle can be both open and closed

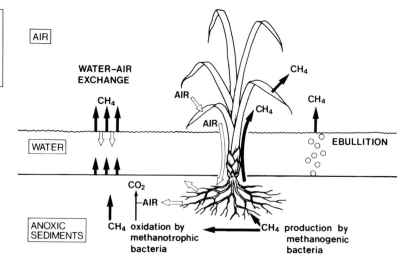

Figure 9.10 Processes of methane production, consumption and transport in wetland soils. From Schütz et al. (1991) with kind permission from Academic Press.

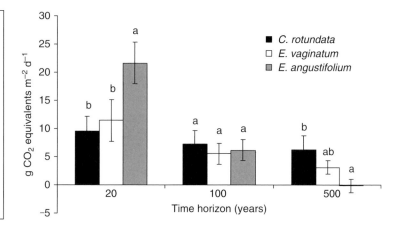

Figure 9.11 The combined radiative forcing from carbon dioxide and methane emissions from arctic ecosystems dominated by three different species (Carex rotundata, Eriophorum vaginatum and Eriophorum angustifolium) and with three different time horizons. The methane emissions represent around 3% of carbon flux in GPP. Bars with different letters are significantly different. From Ström & Christensen (2007) with kind permission from Elsevier.

The atmosphere contains huge quantities of biologically almost inaccessible nitrogen

Only certain types of bacteria are capable of breaking the strong triple bond in N_2 and convert it to ammonium, *biological nitrogen fixation*. The high energy cost for nitrogen fixation, estimated at 9 g C per g N (Gutschick 1981), means that only nitrogen-fixing bacteria well supplied with energy can fix larger quantities of nitrogen. *Rhizobium* (legumes) and *Frankia* (woody plants) use symbiosis with plants to acquire the necessary energy. The rates of nitrogen fixation can for these species be 50 to 200 kg ha^{-1} yr^{-1}. Free-living, photosynthesising bacteria (e.g. the genera *Nostoc*, *Anabaena*, *Rhodospirillum*) can also reach high rates of nitrogen fixation, typically 20 to 100 kg ha^{-1} yr^{-1}. In contrast, free-living non-photosynthesising bacteria (e.g. the genera *Azotobacter*, *Bacillus*, *Clostridium*) are severely limited by energy and do not fix more than 1 to 5 kg ha^{-1} yr^{-1}. Besides energy, nitrogen fixation requires phosphorus, iron and molybdenum, and the key enzyme nitrogenase must be protected from oxygen. For that reason nitrogen fixation often occurs in specialised cells where oxygen is excluded.

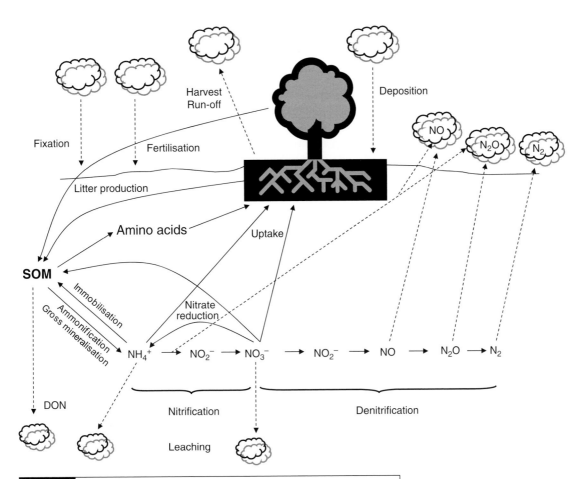

Figure 9.12 The terrestrial nitrogen cycle. Internal fluxes are shown by solid lines and exchanges with the environment by broken lines.

Nitrogen deposition can be as low as 1 kg ha^{-1} yr^{-1} in areas remote from human activities and where the sources are emissions from various neighbouring ecosystems and nitrogen oxides produced by lightning. In areas with intensive farming and dense human populations, such as Central Europe, the deposition can be 80 kg ha^{-1} yr^{-1} or more, e.g. downwind from a pig farm. Deposition can come with ions dissolved in precipitation, *wet deposition*. Gases and particles are also adsorbed on vegetation surfaces as the wind blows past or through sedimentation (*dry deposition*). In the latter case leaf area and the structure of the vegetation is important for the ecosystem's efficiency in scavenging nitrogen. Coniferous forest will in general receive more dry deposition than deciduous forest as a result of being evergreen. Mountaintops and coastal areas can also receive nitrogen from fog. The size of the particle carrying the nitrogen is also important because large particles are more easily deposited. The major forms of nitrogen in deposition are ammonium and nitrate, but the proportions of the two forms vary considerably, depending upon sources; from predominantly ammonium in regions with high agricultural activities to mostly nitrate in regions downwind from industrial regions with high levels of fossil-fuel burning.

The form of nitrogen deposition affects ecosystem processes. Nitrate deposition leads to more nitrogen leaching than ammonium deposition, and nitrogen deposited in the form of ammonium will, if it is taken up directly or first nitrified (see below) by an organism, lower the pH of the soil. Nitrate that leaches out of the ecosystem can remove essential base cations (K^+, Ca^{2+}, Mg^{2+}). There is also an energetic cost associated with reduction of nitrate before it can be used in organisms (Chapter 6). An increased nitrogen deposition in a nitrogen-limited area will stimulate primary production, but all species will not respond equally. A consequence is therefore a change in species composition. For example, nutrient-poor heathlands may be converted to grasslands.

The ammonium released in mineralisation of SOM can be converted by *nitrification* to nitrate. Nitrate can be further converted in a series of reactions, *denitrification*, to several nitrogen gases (N_2, NO, N_2O). The proportions of the various end products vary with environmental conditions, and the entire process has been compared to a leaky pipe because losses can occur at several steps along the reaction chain (Firestone & Davidson 1989).

The ecological significance of nitrification is that it converts the rather immobile ammonium ion to the much more mobile nitrate ion and hence opens the nitrogen cycle. Nitrification can also be an important source of acidification because for each oxidised ammonium molecule two protons are released. Autotrophic nitrification, in which the organism derives energy from the reactions, is a two-step process, where ammonium is first oxidised to nitrite by ammonium-oxidising bacteria (*Nitrosomonas* and 'Nitroso-'genera)

$$NH_4^+ + 1.5O_2 \rightarrow NO_2^- + 2H^+ + H_2O$$

In a second step, nitrite oxidisers (*Nitrobacter* and 'Nitro-'genera) complete the process to nitrate

$$NO_2^- + 0.5O_2 \rightarrow NO_3^-$$

The dominant rate-regulating factor is, as the two reaction formulas indicate, the availability of substrate (ammonium and oxygen). Considering that nitrification increases acidity it is surprising that the autotrophic nitrifiers are sensitive to low pH (pH < 4.5), particularly in agricultural soils. The occurrence of nitrification in acid (forest) soils can therefore either be a result of acid-tolerant autotrophic nitrifiers or the action of heterotrophic nitrifiers, which use organic carbon as the energy source. However, the importance of heterotrophic nitrification is still unclear

The fraction of ammonium that is nitrified varies from almost nothing in acid forest soils, where plant production is nitrogen limited and plant uptake therefore minimises build-up of ammonium pools. Increasing nitrogen deposition or fertilisation can lead to such high concentrations of ammonium in the soil that nitrification starts, in spite of otherwise unfavourable conditions. In phosphorus-limited ecosystems, e.g. many tropical forests, and agricultural soils the conditions are such that almost all mineralised nitrogen is nitrified.

Another important side-effect of nitrification is that nitric oxide (NO) and nitrous oxide (N_2O) can be produced as by-products; the latter is a potent greenhouse gas ($GWP_{100} = 296$, Chapter 5). Under aerobic conditions less than 1% of the ammonium oxidised ends up as nitrous oxide, but as oxygen availability decreases relatively more nitrous oxide is produced, although the overall rate may be going down.

Denitrification is the four-step reaction shown in Figure 9.12. A large variety of bacteria are involved in these processes. Most of them are facultative anaerobes and use oxygen rather than the nitrogen oxides as electron acceptors. For this reason denitrification occurs only under anaerobic conditions and energy (carbon) sources are also necessary. The proportion of the three nitrogen gases emitted during denitrification and nitrification varies depending upon soil water content (Figure 9.8). As soil water content goes up, the proportion of gases with less oxygen increases, but at the same time the production of the substrate, nitrate, goes down such that the maximum emissions of nitrous oxide from denitrification occur at soil water contents of 60–80% of water-filled pore space. The enzymes responsible for the four steps are differentially sensitive to pH such that low pH favours nitrous oxide (N_2O) production at the expense of dinitrogen N_2).

The total emissions of nitrogen gases are extremely variable in time and space, and can change by a factor of 100 from one day to the next. This variability is caused by small-scale changes in soil water, which affect the diffusion rate of oxygen. Nitrous oxide is also very soluble in water and changes in soil water can therefore drive both direct changes in the amounts stored in the soil and affect the retention time and hence the possibility that nitrous oxide is reduced to nitrogen gas. A consequence of this variability is that estimates of nitrogen losses in gas form from soil are uncertain, but are in the range 0.1–$2\,kg\,ha^{-1}\,yr^{-1}$. Losses associated with fertilisation are estimated to be up to 2% of the added nitrogen, but the actual losses are strongly dependent on the timing with weather. The IPCC (2006) recommends that 1% of nitrogen added as fertiliser should be assumed to be lost as nitrous oxide in national greenhouse budgets as a default value.

Under anaerobic, dissimilatory *nitrate reduction*, nitrate can also be reduced to ammonium by certain bacteria.

The carbon and nitrogen cycles in the soil are strongly coupled and the release of nitrous oxide has been shown to be coupled to mineralisation of carbon (Table 9.2) (Xu *et al.* 2008). There are large differences in how these two fluxes are coupled, but the dry conditions in some of the ecosystems favour emissions of NO rather than

Table 9.2 Relation ($y = ax + b$) between N_2O emissions (y, µg N m^{-2} h^{-1}) and CO_2 emissions (x, mg C m^{-2} h^{-1}) in eight different ecosystem types. Data from Xu *et al.* (2008)

Ecosystem type	a	b	r^2	Max. rate[a]
Bogs and fens	0.218	−3.77	0.80	30
Boreal and temperate forests	0.198	0.60	0.66	140
Temperate grassland	0.017	0.86	0.52	11
Dry cropland	0.163	−5.36	0.79	85
Rice paddy	0.663	8.63	0.79	180
Tropical savanna and grassland	0.071	1.14	0.84	12
Sub-tropical and tropical dry forest	0.182	19.55	0.70	70
Sub-tropical and tropical moist forest	0.069	6.56	0.68	120

[a] Maximal observed rate of N_2O emissions in this study

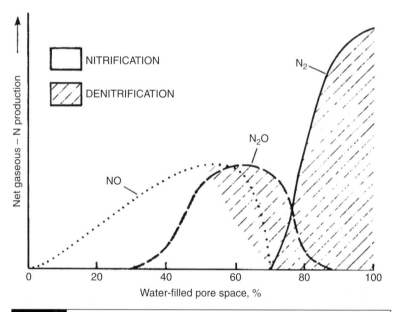

Figure 9.13 Relative contributions to nitrogen gases from nitrification and denitrification as a function of soil water content. From Davidson (1991) with kind permission from the American Society for Microbiology.

N_2O (Figure 9.13). The complete submersion of the soil in rice paddies ought to lead to low N_2O emissions, but these are in fact the highest. However, rice has evolved special transport systems for supplying the roots with oxygen under flooded conditions and the oxygen concentration in the vicinity of rice roots can therefore be

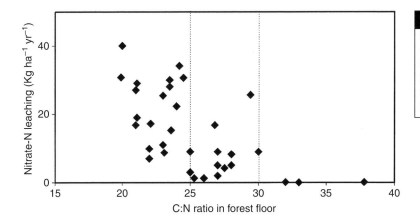

Figure 9.14 Nitrate leaching vs. forest floor carbon to nitrogen ratio (C:N) at 35 forest sites in Northwest and Central Europe. From Gundersen *et al.* (2006) with kind permission from NRC Research Press.

high (see Figure 9.5), leading to conditions that are favourable for N_2O production. Although N_2O has a large GWP, it is still the emissions of carbon dioxide that dominate the greenhouse effect in all ecosystem types; it would take a slope (*a*) of more than 3 to bring the effect of N_2O on a par with carbon dioxide. The intercept (*b*) in the relation between N_2O and carbon dioxide emissions indicates a potential release of N_2O even without carbon mineralisation, and a negative intercept shows that some ecosystems might even be sinks for N_2O.

When the rate of nitrogen mineralisation exceeds the vegetation's capacity for uptake, or under high deposition levels, there will be a build-up of inorganic nitrogen in the soil. If this nitrogen is in the form of nitrate there is a risk that part of this nitrogen is lost through *leaching* to the groundwater. Because of this coupling between nitrogen leaching and mineralisation the status of the soil matters. Soils low in nitrogen relative to carbon will be more efficient in retaining nitrogen (Figure 9.14) although this natural property can be overridden by high deposition of nitrogen. In unpolluted areas, where the natural inputs of nitrogen are low, organic nitrogen can account for 90% of the leached nitrogen (Perakis & Hedin 2002) and be a mechanism that maintains an ecosystem in a continuous state of nitrogen limitation. Organic nitrogen can be more difficult for plants to take up than nitrate and ammonium. Nitrogen losses in organic form are therefore more difficult for the plants to respond to and effective feedback mechanisms (e.g. increased root growth) to retain the nitrogen will not develop.

Uptake of nitrogen by plants occurs in three forms: organic nitrogen (amino acids), ammonium and nitrate. The availability of nitrogen in these three forms varies with the productivity of a site (Figure 9.15). In low-productivity sites there is virtually no free inorganic nitrogen and uptake by plants is mostly in organic form. The more productive a site is, the more inorganic nitrogen appears, first as ammonium, but more and more as nitrate, although there can still be high levels of organic nitrogen present in the soil. The shift

Nitrogen loss is not only the loss of a resource, but can also be detrimental to the recipient

Table 9.3 | Total plant N uptake (100%) distributed on NH_4^+, NO_3^- and an amino acid (glycine) along a fertility gradient in a boreal forest. From Nordin *et al.* (2001) with kind permission from Springer Science + Business Media

Forest type	Plant species	NH_4^+	NO_3^-	Glycine
Dwarf shrub	*Pinus sylvestris*	68	3	29
	Vaccinium vitis-idaea	73	10	17
	V. myrtillus	38	17	45
	Average	60	10	30
Low herb	*Picea abies*	67	25	8
	Rubus ideaus	64	27	9
	Oxalis acetosella	74	18	7
	Maianthemum bifolium	79	14	7
	Average	71	21	8
Tall herb	*Aconitum septentrionale*	51	40	9
	Rubus ideaus	42	47	11
	Oxalis acetosella	52	37	11
	Average	48	41	10

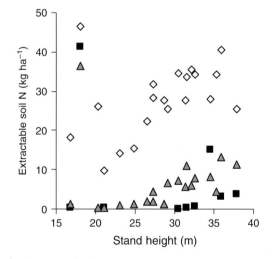

Figure 9.15 Distribution of nitrogen forms along a fertility gradient (asymptotic stand height) after incubation of a boreal forest soil. DON = Dissolved organic nitrogen. From Kranabetter *et al.* (2007) with kind permission from Elsevier.

towards nitrate is, of course, a consequence of fertile sites having high rates of nitrogen mineralisation and thus producing large amounts of ammonium as substrate for nitrification. The role and importance of uptake of organic nitrogen by plants is still unclear, but most plants seem capable of taking up a range of amino acids. However, the form of nitrogen in which it is taken up seems to follow the fertility gradient such that at low-fertility sites amino acids and ammonium are the dominant forms, while at the most fertile sites nitrate dominates (Table 9.3). It is difficult to estimate nitrogen uptake rates because the instantaneous concentrations of different forms of nitrogen in the soil say little about their rate of uptake. At any moment the amounts present in the soil are small compared to the amounts taken up and the flux through these pools is large.

Mycorrhizae help the plants in taking up nutrients by extending the root systems (large surface area per volume) and penetrating volumes inaccessible to the thicker host roots. They can also increase the nutrient uptake by exuding extracellular enzymes that release nutrients from the soil organic matter.

Although primary production in many terrestrial ecosystems is limited by nitrogen and there are mechanisms, as described above, that maintain them in a state of nitrogen limitation, high levels of nitrogen deposition should eventually lead to conditions where other factors limit primary production. When such a state is reached, *nitrogen saturation*, the ecosystem can no longer retain incoming nitrogen, and losses (leaching, denitrification) will be of equal magnitude. Such a situation may be harmful to the ecosystem because of the ensuing changes in soil chemistry. Leaching of nitrate must also be accompanied by the loss of positive ions to maintain electroneutrality. The first ions to be lost are Ca^{2+}, Mg^{2+} and K^+, which can make any of these elements limiting to primary production. When this happens the plant uptake of nitrogen will be still less and nitrate leaching will increase, inducing a positive feedback and aggravating the situation. The base cations that are lost will be substituted by H^+ and various Al ions, causing a decrease in soil pH. Al ions may also be toxic and block uptake of other cations.

The phosphorus cycle

Phosphorus is an essential element for plants and animals (Chapter 3). Examples of phosphorus-containing compounds that are essential in life processes are adenosine triphosphate (ATP), deoxyribonucleic acid (DNA) and ribonucleic acid (RNA). Alongside nitrogen, phosphorus determines the productivity of most terrestrial ecosystems. Shortage of phosphorus leads to reduced growth and development. Phosphorus is found in limited amounts in Nature as calcium phosphate in the minerals apatite and phosphorite. The total quantity of phosphorus in soils is usually low and most of it is in forms unavailable to plants. The organisms in terrestrial ecosystems have therefore developed efficient ways of using phosphorus, as well as of recycling it. Associations with mycorrhiza can be one of the major mechanisms by which plants increase their uptake of phosphorus.

Phosphorus compounds occur both in inorganic and organic form. The proportion between them varies depending on soil conditions, such as clay and organic matter content. The organically bound phosphorus is found in soil organisms, humus and soil organic matter. Through microbial decomposition inorganic phosphorus is released to the soil solution as ionic phosphorus, phosphate, which can be taken up by the plants. The phosphate ion is an anion to

Lack of gaseous or water-soluble forms makes the phosphorus cycle closed

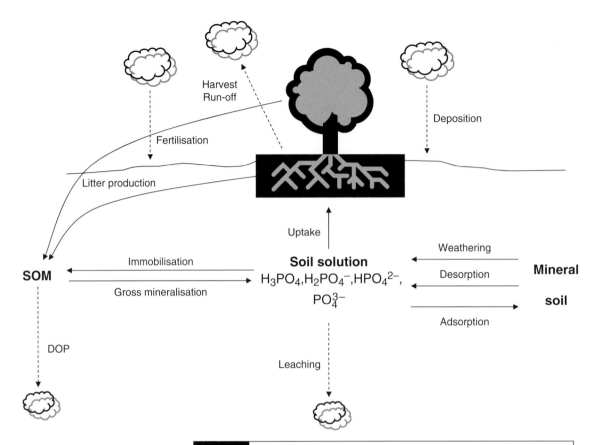

Figure 9.16 The terrestrial phosphorus cycle. Internal fluxes are shown by solid lines and exchanges with the environment by broken lines.

phosphoric acid, H_3PO_4 – a weak acid – which is dissociated, depending on the pH of the soil solution:

$$H_3PO_4 \rightleftharpoons H^+ + H_2PO_4^-$$

$$H_2PO_4^- \rightleftharpoons H^+ + HPO_4^{2-}$$

$$HPO_4^{2-} \rightleftharpoons H^+ + PO_4^{3-}$$

At higher pH PO_4^{3-} becomes more frequent and a decrease in HPO_4^{2-} and $H_2PO_4^-$ occurs. The solubility in the soil solution of the different ionic forms of phosphorus is limited, as they bind strongly to calcium, iron and aluminium complexes (Chapter 4).

The cycling of phosphorus is shown in Figure 9.16. The phosphorus cycle has a dominant biochemical mode (Figure 9.1). The inputs to the phosphorus cycle come from atmospheric deposition, fertilisation and weathering of primary soil minerals. The phosphorus ion is taken up by plants from the soil solution and then returned in litter from aboveground parts and roots to the soil to be become included in the soil organic matter. Through the mineralisation process the phosphorus is released and is made available in the soil solution for uptake, but it can also again be immobilised in the soil organic

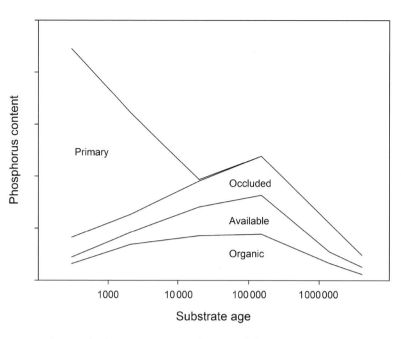

Figure 9.17 Changes in phosphorus fraction in a temporal sequence from Hawaii. The observations for the different substrate ages are on substrates from volcanic lava flows of different ages. Modfied from Vitousek (2004).

matter in much the same way as nitrogen (Chapter 7). The phosphate ion can also be adsorbed onto soil mineral particles and form complexes with calcium, iron and aluminium. This process is reversible – desorption. The form and solubility is, as mentioned, pH dependent. Soils with high pH have higher availability of phosphorus as compared to soils of low pH. The loss of phosphorus from ecosystems is dominated by phosphorus bound to particulate matter that leaches to groundwater, or run-off to surface water (DOP); only minor fractions are lost in ionic form because of the low solubility of the phosphate ions. Gaseous losses of phosphorus essentially do not occur. Harvésts can also remove considerable amounts of phosphorus.

Because the only major source of phosphorus in an ecosystem is the primary minerals the losses will eventually lead to phosphorus deficiency. However, the availability of phosphorus to plants and other organisms changes considerably during soil development (Figure 9.17) (Walker & Syers 1976). The primary minerals weather and the released phosphorus is either taken up by plants or binds to minerals in less accessible forms (occluded). Plant litter returns phosphorus in organic forms, which mineralises and adds to the available phosphorus. The rate at which these processes proceed depends strongly on climate (precipitation, temperature), pH and the type of primary rock. Once the phosphorus content in the soil has been depleted, some major reshaping of the landscape is necessary to expose fresh minerals. Such events can be glaciation or, as in the case of Hawaii, volcanic eruptions.

The potassium cycle

Potassium comes next after nitrogen and phosphorus in importance for the productivity of terrestrial ecosystems. Potassium is essential for life processes as activator of a large number of enzymes and an osmotic constituent of the cytoplasm of plant cells (Chapter 3). The potassium status is also important to plants for drought tolerance and winter hardiness, as well as resistance to fungal diseases.

The origin of potassium is usually weathering of silica minerals such as biotite and muscovite – primary minerals – but only a minor fraction of the potassium in the soil is available to plants, as the potassium ion can be fixed and firmly bound to clay minerals – secondary minerals. Other sources of potassium are atmospheric dry and wet deposition. Because of the lack of minerals in certain natural forest ecosystems, such as forests on ditched peatlands, productivity can be severely limited by potassium, as well as phosphorus, deficiencies. Cultivated crops need the addition of potassium because of the large removal in harvests. Other losses from the ecosystem occur through leaching, run-off and erosion, but the gas phase is not involved.

Potassium is a small ion, which does not bind strongly to organic matter. It is, therefore, easily leached from plants, as well as the soil. Leaching of potassium from the canopy can even be larger than losses with litterfall. Release of potassium from soil organic matter to the soil solution occurs with mineralisation, but also through direct leaching. As a result the potassium cycle is dominated by the geo-chemical mode (Figures 9.1 and 9.18).

The calcium cycle

Calcium is an interesting element. It is both an essential plant nutrient and an important element for creating the soil environment for plants and animals (Chapters 3 and 4). Calcium is a component of the cell wall of plants. It also regulates cell elongation and division, as well as membrane permeability, and activates a number of enzymes. Calcium can be precipitated in plant tissues such that its concentration can increase with the age of the tissue. For animals it is an essential element as it is a part of the bones in the skeleton and protective structures.

Calcium regulates the acid–base status of the soil, which affects the availability of plant nutrients, as well as the structural properties of the soil. This also regulates the ability of the soil to store nutrient elements as well as water. The acid–base status or the calcium status of the soil determines the species composition of ecosystems, as well as the productivity level. Plants favoured by a good soil calcium status are called *calcicoles*, and those not favoured, *calcifuges*.

The calcium cycle has a dominating geochemical and biogeochemical mode (Figures 9.1 and 9.18). Calcium occurs in three different soil pools: mineral soil, complexes with organic matter and bound to colloids of clay-humus in exchangeable form. Through the weathering of primary minerals such as calcite and plagioclase, calcium becomes available to plants in ionic form. Intermediate forms of secondary minerals, clay, will also form complexes with humus. Calcium is also released during min-eralisation of soil organic matter, and also brought to the ecosystem in dry and wet deposition. An important measure in managed soils is to

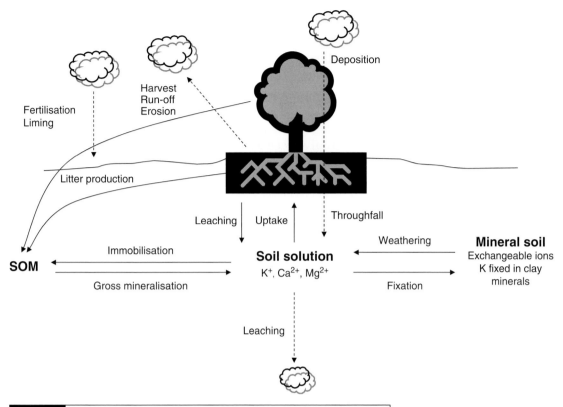

Figure 9.18 The terrestrial potassium, calcium and magnesium cycles. Internal fluxes are shown by solid lines and exchanges with the environment by broken lines. Immobilisation has no significance for these elements.

maintain a good calcium status, which occurs through liming. Losses from the ecosystem occur in ionic form through leaching and run-off, as well as calcium in particulate matter. Like potassium there are no gaseous phases with calcium.

The magnesium cycle

Magnesium is an essential element, it is the core of chlorophyll and thus of fundamental importance to photosynthesis (Chapter 3). It also has a key role in formation of oils and proteins, as well as activation of enzymes responsible for energy metabolism, especially processes in the cell leading to phosphorylation. Deficiency symptoms are characterised by yellowing leaves and needles.

The magnesium cycle is similar to that of calcium. It has dominating geochemical and biogeochemical modes, but also an obvious biochemical one (Figures 9.1 and 9.18) because it is, in contrast to calcium, mobile within the plant and can be retranslocated before senescence. There are, in the same way as for calcium, three major pools of magnesium: primary minerals, secondary minerals and soil organic matter. The origin of magnesium is weathering of primary

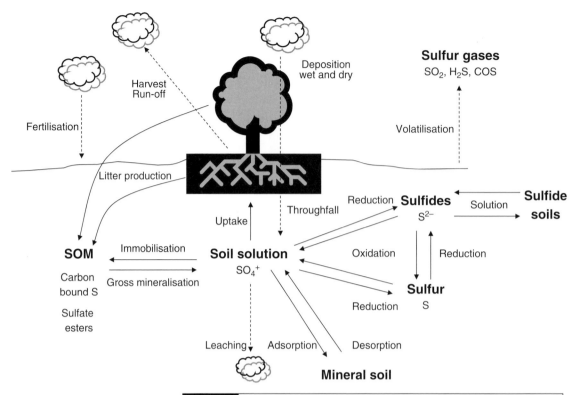

Figure 9.19 The terrestrial sulfur cycle. Internal fluxes are shown by solid lines and exchanges with the environment by broken lines.

minerals such as dolomite, biotite, hornblende and serpentine, and later release from clay-humus complexes and clay minerals. Magnesium is also brought to ecosystems by dry and wet deposition where coastal areas have a higher fall-out than inland areas when the source is marine spray. Fertilisation is another input to soils. Losses occur through leaching and run-off, and erosion of magnesium in ionic and particulate forms. Losses occur also with harvests.

The sulfur cycle

Sulfur is an important constituent of amino acids such as methionine, cysteine and cystine, and as such part of many proteins regulating processes like photosynthesis and nitrogen fixation (Chapter 3). Sulfur is also found in a number of vitamins. The managing of the sulfur cycle is particularly important in agriculture to avoid malnutrition of humans.

The sulfur cycle has a dominating biochemical and biogeochemical mode (Figures 9.1 and 9.19). There are three major sources of sulfur: soil minerals, soil organic matter and sulfur gases in the atmosphere.

Sulfur in soils is not as frequent in inorganic as in organic forms. The most common inorganic ones are sulfates and sulfides. Sulfate

Figure 4.8.1 The Stordalen mire with declining palsa. Photo: Dan Hammarlund.

Figure 4.8.2 The Jädraås boreal coniferous forest. The forest is dominated by 150-year-old Scots pine (*Pinus sylvestris*) trees, but younger Norway spruce (*Picea abies*) trees are slowly invading. Photo: Linnea Berglund.

Figure 4.8.3   The Pawnee temperate short grass prairie with pronghorns (*Antilocapra americana*). Photo: Paul Stapp.

Figure 4.8.4   The Solling temperate deciduous forest (European beech, *Fagus sylvatica*) – a classical ecosystem investigation started in the 1960s and still ongoing. Photo: Folke Andersson.

Figure 4.8.5 The Skogaby temperate evergreen forest (Norway spruce, *Picea abies*). The large leaf area of trees leaves little light for any ground vegetation. Photo: Ulf Johansson.

Figure 4.8.6 The H.J. Andrews temperate rain forest (Douglas fir, *Pseudotsuga menziesii*) an early ecosystem investigation now continued within the framework of the US Long-Term Ecosystem Research, LTER. Photo: Folke Andersson.

Figure 4.8.7 The Pointe Noire tropical savanna with experimental equipment from the CARBOAFRICA project. Photo: Laurent Saint-André and Agnes de Grandcourt.

Figure 4.8.8   The Chamela tropical dry forest. Photo: Gerardo Carreón.

Figure 4.8.9 The San Carlos tropical rain forest – multilayered, trees with buttress stems, lianas and epiphytes. Photo: Folke Andersson.

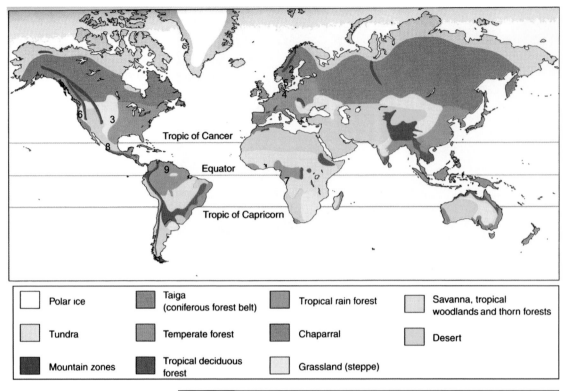

	Polar ice		Taiga (coniferous forest belt)		Tropical rain forest		Savanna, tropical woodlands and thorn forests
	Tundra		Temperate forest		Chaparral		Desert
	Mountain zones		Tropical deciduous forest		Grassland (steppe)		

Figure 4.11 Map of biomes of the world. Numbers show the locations of the biomes in Figure 4.10. From Solomon & Berg (1995) with kind permission from Cengage Learning.

Figure 9.6 Flux tower for measuring gas exchange over a Norway spruce forest at Knottåsen, central Sweden. Photo: Achim Grelle.

Figure 9.7 Open-top chambers for measuring gas exchange in a marshland at the Chesapeake Bay, MD, USA. Photo: Bert Drake.

Figure 9.8 Closed chambers for measuring gas exchange of Norway spruce trees in Flakaliden, northern Sweden. Photo: Bengt-Olof Wigren.

Figure 9.9 FACE experiment in a loblolly pine (*Pinus taeda*) stand in Duke Forest, NC, USA. Photo: Chris Hildreth/Duke Photography.

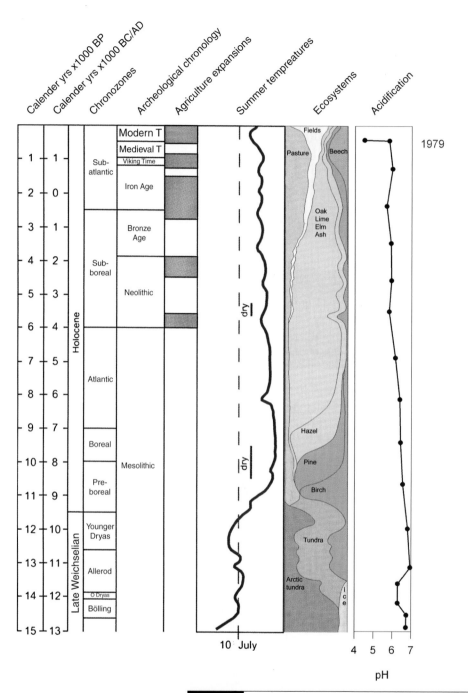

Figure 12.2 Late- and Postglacial development of southern Swedish terrestrial ecosystems in relation to climate (given as mean July temperature, the temperature range in the figure is approximately 10–15°C). Acidification is expressed as lake acidification deduced from analysis of sub-fossil diatoms in sediments, Lake Gårdsjön, west Sweden. Modified from Anonymous (1982), Liljegren (1999) and Berglund et al. (2008).

KRAGEHOLMSSJÖN

Analyst: Marie–José Gaillard

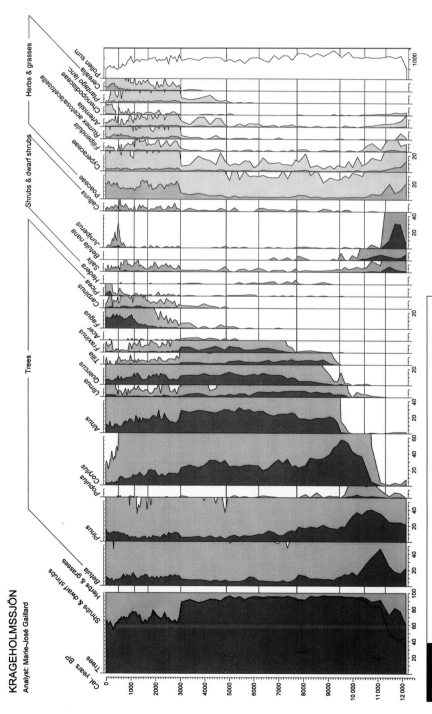

Figure 12.3 Pollen diagram from Krageholmssjön, Scania, southern Sweden showing the development of vegetation from 13 000 years before present (BP) to the present day for species representing forests (trees and shrubs), open land (dwarf shrubs, herbs and grasses) and areas of cultivation (ceralia). For species with two colours – the left part indicates % and right part ‰, i.e. magnified 10 times. From Berglund et al. (2008) with kind permission from Springer Science + Business Media.

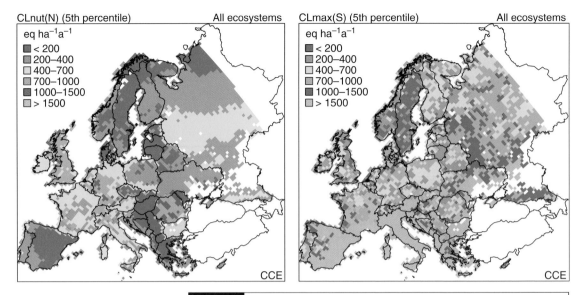

Figure 14.9 European maps of critical loads for eutrophication by nitrogen (left) and acidification by sulfur (right), which protect 95% of natural areas (all ecosystems) in 50 × 50 km EMEP grid. In red-shaded areas deposition needs to be lower than 200 eq ha^{-1} yr^{-1}. From Hettelingh *et al.* (2008).

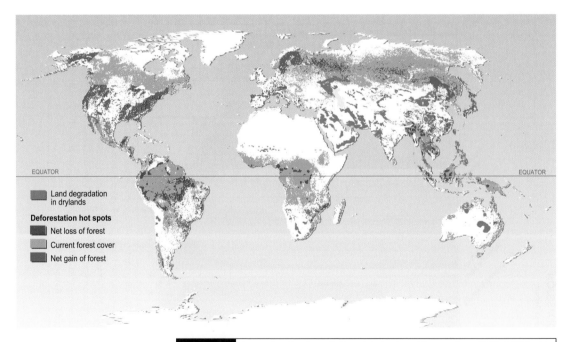

Figure Epi. 4 Areas showing degradation of drylands and forests. From MEA (2005) with kind permission from the World Resources Institute.

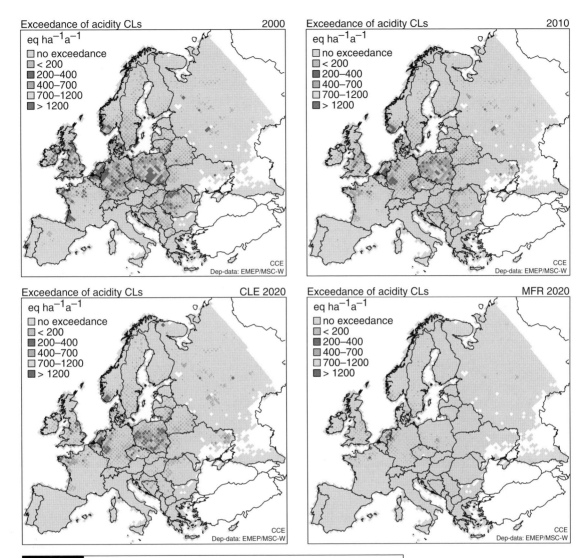

Figure 14.10 Exceedance of critical load for acidification by deposition in 2000, 2010 and 2020. The first three maps are valid for Current Legislation (CLE) to reduce emissions. The lower right map is based upon Maximum Feasible Reductions (MFR). From Hettelingh *et al.* (2008).

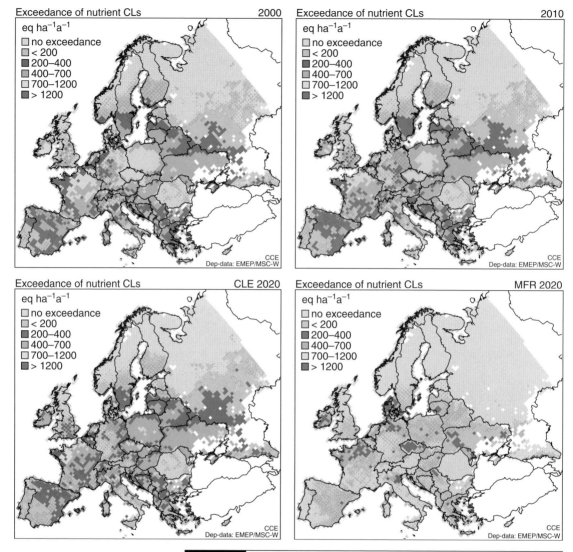

Figure 14.11 Exceedance of critical load for eutrophication by deposition of nitrogen in 2000, 2010 and 2020. The first three maps are valid for Current Legislation (CLE) to reduce emissions. The lower right map is based upon Maximum Feasible Reductions (MFR). From Hettelingh *et al.* (2008).

minerals are easily soluble and sulfate ions are readily taken up by plants. They are mostly found in soils in more arid areas. Sulfides, on the other hand, are found in more humid areas. In order to be taken up by plants the sulfide ion must be oxidised into sulfate. The oxygen or redox condition of the soil is a major regulating factor for the dynamics of soil sulfur.

As much as 90% or more of the soil sulfur is present in organic forms. Compared to nitrogen the forms in which they occur are not so well defined. The oxidation state varies depending on the organic chemical composition. Soil microorganisms decompose the organic sulfur compounds into soluble forms, but only a small share is available for uptake by plants as sulfates.

A number of activities, natural and man-made, generate sulfur compounds in the atmosphere. It may happen through volcanic eruptions, volatilisation from soils, sea spray, and combustion of sulfur-containing biomass, coal and oil, as well as metal smelters. In the atmosphere various sulfur compounds are oxidized into sulfate. In recent times industrialisation and energy production have been the major sources of sulfates leading to formation of sulfuric acid – the acid rain story (Prologue, see also Figure 9.26).

The atmospheric sulfur will be deposited in ecosystems as dry or wet deposition. Wet deposition is dominated by sulfuric acid and is absorbed in the soil. A small share can be taken up directly by the canopy of plants. The same holds for dry-deposited sulfur. The degree of direct uptake by plants depends on the general sulfur status of the plants. If there is a deficiency, more sulfur will be taken up by the plant cover.

Element cycling in a temperate Norway spruce forest

As an example of element cycles we will take the temperate, planted evergreen forest in Figure 4.10, part 5 (Figure 9.20). The forest is located in south-west Sweden with almost exclusively Norway spruce (*Picea abies*) trees. It is a young forest of 21 years in 1987, with a tree density of 2347 trees ha^{-1}, a mean height of 9.8 m, a basal area of 24.7 m^{-2} ha^{-1} and a standing volume of 147 m^3 ha^{-1}. The fertility or production level is high; the expected tree height when the stand reaches 100 years is 32 m. The dense canopy allows only a sparse bottom layer, with mosses (*Hylocomium splendens*, *Pleurozium schreberi* and *Dicranum scoparium*) and a few herbs such as *Maianthemum bifolium* and *Oxalis acetosella*, to develop. The soil type is a poorly developed spodosol (Bergholm *et al.* 1995).

Compared to the average plant biomass and production (carbon cycle) of temperate evergreen forests this Norway spruce forest is representative (Table 4.5), with a plant biomass above and below ground of 43 and 12 Mg C ha^{-1} (or t ha^{-1}), respectively (Figure 9.20a). The ground vegetation contributes less than 1 Mg C ha^{-1} to the carbon stock and around 30 kg N ha^{-1}. The plant production above

Figure 9.20 Element cycling in a young temperate Norway spruce forest (*Picea abies*) in southern Sweden. Fluxes to and from vegetation components are only shown as exchanges with the environment. No internal translocations are shown. Values within parentheses represent annual changes in stocks.
A horizontal arrow from the right to 'soil available' shows weathering, while the vertical arrow shows deposition. A vertical arrow to 'canopy' indicates direct uptake of deposition. Solid arrows without values indicate large fluxes for which no empirical data are available. Dashed arrows indicate small, but important, fluxes for which no empirical data are available. Data are not available for partitioning mineralisation fluxes from 'forest floor' and 'mineral soil' but their sum must balance in- and outfluxes from 'soil available'. Some values are estimated from mass balances. In some cases different sources have been used that are not consistent with mass balances. Most data refer to conditions in 1987, but some fluxes are averages over several years. Stores in Mg ha^{-1} or kg ha^{-1}. Fluxes in Mg ha^{-1} yr^{-1} or kg ha^{-1} yr^{-1}. Data sources: Bergholm et al. (1995), Nilsson & Wiklund (1995), Persson & Nilsson (2001).

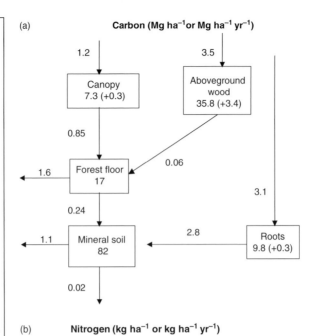

(a) Carbon (Mg ha^{-1} or Mg ha^{-1} yr^{-1})

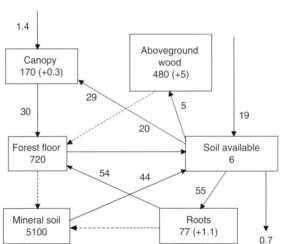

(b) Nitrogen (kg ha^{-1} or kg ha^{-1} yr^{-1})

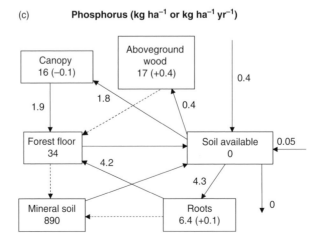

(c) Phosphorus (kg ha^{-1} or kg ha^{-1} yr^{-1})

(d) **Potassium (kg ha⁻¹or kg ha⁻¹ yr⁻¹)**

Figure 9.20 (cont.)

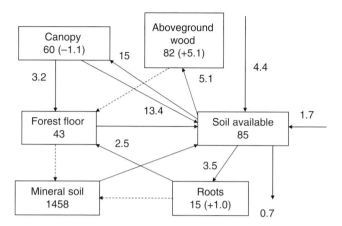

(e) **Magnesium (kg ha⁻¹or kg ha⁻¹ yr⁻¹)**

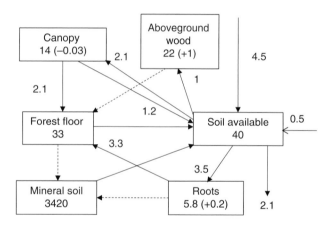

(f) **Calcium (kg ha⁻¹ or kg ha⁻¹ yr⁻¹)**

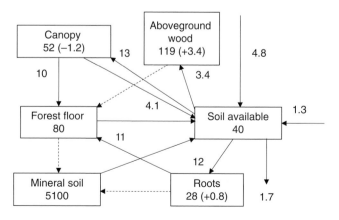

Figure 9.20 (cont.)

(g)   **Sulfur (kg ha^{-1}or kg ha^{-1} yr^{-1})**

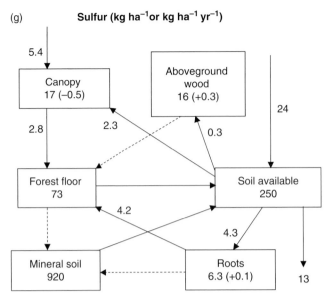

and below ground is 4.7 and 2.7 Mg C ha^{-1} yr^{-1}, respectively. The forest floor, litter and humus layer contains 17 Mg C ha^{-1}, and the mineral soil (0–50 cm) stores 82 Mg C ha^{-1}. At this age of the stand the trees and soil are comparable stores for carbon, but trees will soon become dominant because both above- and belowground plant biomass are rapidly increasing; the ecosystem is in an aggrading state (Bormann & Likens 1979).

As for *total nitrogen* (Figure 9.20b) in the forest, the aboveground parts have 650 kg ha^{-1} with a major portion in the woody parts; this represents a considerable amount of nitrogen that is basically withdrawn from circulation. The root biomass contains 77 kg ha^{-1}. The largest store of nitrogen is found in the forest floor and the mineral soil (0–50 cm) with 720 and 5100 kg ha^{-1}, respectively. This forest is located in an area with high input of nitrogen through dry and wet deposition, 10–15 kg ha^{-1} yr^{-1}. The input from nitrogen fixation is negligible. Not all nitrogen deposition reaches the ground, but 1.4 kg ha^{-1} yr^{-1} is directly absorbed in the tree canopy. In areas with very high nitrogen deposition this uptake mechanism can give rise to extreme nitrogen concentrations in the canopy. Only a minor share of the soil nitrogen is available for uptake; all is bound as organic nitrogen. In this type of forest there is limited loss of nitrogen through leaching.

The *phosphorus* cycle (Figure 9.20c) shows great similarities to the nitrogen cycle. However, the store in aboveground wood (17 kg ha^{-1}) equals that in the canopy (16 kg ha^{-1}). The mineral soil is by far the largest store (890 kg ha^{-1} or 92%). There is also a small input through weathering, although currently it is only 1/10 of the input from deposition.

Table 9.4 Comparison of canopy nutrient status for the Skogaby stand with reference values for limitation (cf. Table 6.4)

	N	P	K	Ca	Mg	S
Canopy (kg ha^{-1})	170	16	60	52	14	17
Relative N = 100	100	9.4	35	31	8	10
Reference		10	35	2.5	4	5

The cycles of potassium, magnesium and calcium are similar, as was pointed out earlier. The potassium (Figure 9.20d) as well as the magnesium cycle (Figure 9.20e) have an evident biogenic nature, as the living part, the canopy, stores 40% of the aboveground content of these elements. The soil-available pool is generated from mineralisation of organic matter in the forest floor and in the mineral soil, as well as from weathering. There is a considerable input by deposition of these elements. However, for potassium there is internal cycling in the ecosystem through leaching from the canopy, which exceeds the input by deposition. This illustrates that the potassium ion is easily mobile, which may lead to losses. The plants can however 'conserve' the potassium by rapid uptake. There are limited losses by leaching from the soil. The calcium cycle (Figure 9.20f) exhibits a more biogeochemical nature, as a smaller share (30%) of the aboveground store is found in the canopy. The aboveground woody parts have a high share of calcium, often bound to bark. There is a limited input of calcium by deposition, often dust, as well as leaching from the soil.

The main features of sulfur cycling are shown in Figure 9.20g. The aboveground parts contain 33 kg ha^{-1}, with equal parts in the canopy and in the woody parts, 17 and 16 kg ha^{-1}, respectively. The root biomass contains 6 kg ha^{-1}. The input of sulfur through dry and wet deposition was 24 kg ha^{-1} yr^{-1} in 1988–1993, but has decreased to less than half that level at the beginning of the twenty-first century. The losses of sulfur by leaching are almost of the same order as the input.

Let us consider the canopy nutrient status (Table 9.4). The concentrations of calcium, magnesium and sulfur relative to nitrogen are all well above the reference values for limitation. On the other hand, potassium and phosphorus are both just at the level at which they take over from nitrogen in being limiting. Forests in the temperate and boreal zones are generally expected to be limited by nitrogen availability, in particular with young soils as in this case. The reason for this shift in limiting element from nitrogen to potassium/phosphorus is the high nitrogen deposition that this forest has experienced over the last decades. Note that the relative proportions of nitrogen, potassium and phosphorus in the deposition show an excess of nitrogen relative to the reference proportions.

Another aspect that we want to emphasise is the difference between where in the ecosystem you find the different elements. In this ecosystem 35% of the carbon is bound in the vegetation (trees), but because this is a young, rapidly growing stand it will not be long before more carbon is bound in the vegetation. Relatively large fractions of nitrogen and potassium, 11 and 9%, respectively, are also found in the vegetation. In contrast, almost all the stocks of the other elements are found in the soil: phosphorus 96%, calcium 96%, magnesium 99% and sulfur 97%.

Comparison of element cycling in different terrestrial ecosystems

We will now consider how ecosystems can differ with respect to element cycling. We will use our nine ecosystems from Figure 4.10 to discuss reasons for differences and ecological implications. Element cycles can be characterised in many different ways and we will use nine different properties related to resource utilisation (Figure 9.21). The individual values need to be treated with caution because some estimates are uncertain and this is particularly true for estimates of belowground vegetation properties. Similarly, the global averages are uncertain because of the difficulties in obtaining accurate estimates.

Biomass
Biomasses (Figure 9.21a) in forest ecosystems are clearly larger aboveground, up to two orders of magnitude, than in other ecosystems. However, the major difference occurs as a result of the large woody parts of trees. When we look at only the canopy (leaves), the differences are much smaller, ranging from 1.8 Mg C ha^{-1} in temperate deciduous forest (Solling) to 7.3 Mg C ha^{-1} in temperate evergreen forest (-Skogaby). The larger aboveground biomasses in forests are also reflected below ground, but it is not as pronounced. Most of the forests have 20% or less of their biomass located below ground compared to non-forest ecosystems that have most of their biomass belowground; in temperate grassland (Pawnee) almost three times as much. The larger biomasses in forests are coupled to two factors associated with water balance. First of all, from an evolutionary perspective and partly speculative, a large biomass creates a large fuel load, which will lead to more intensive fires when they occur. Forests must, therefore, be restricted to wetter areas with less risk of fires. Second, with larger biomasses the canopies must be high up in the air and there exposed to higher wind speeds and concomitant larger evapotranspiration (Chapter 5). The differences in allocation between above- and belowground components is also due to life history. In forests the aboveground parts are perennial, whereas in the other ecosystems the aboveground parts are renewed every year. The larger allocation to belowground biomass in non-forest ecosystems is also an adaptation to water stress.

Production
The variation in production (Figure 9.21b) between our nine ecosystems is most clearly coupled to the climatic gradient, with low

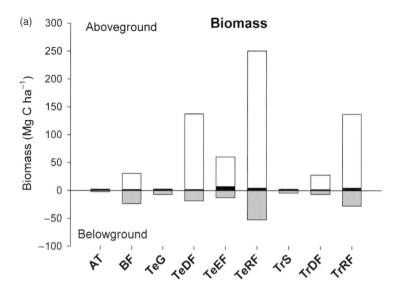

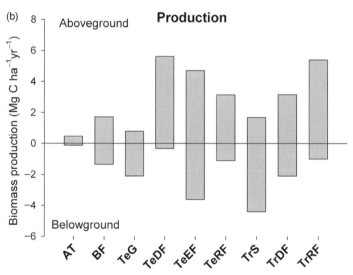

Figure 9.21 Different indices of resource utilisation for the nine ecosystem types, also representing features of their respective biomes. Broken lines represent global averages according to the values in Figures 9.22 and 9.24. The asterisks in the Biomass turnover panel indicate that turnover values are calculated only for aboveground biomass. The white portion of the bar for biomass is woody biomass and the black portion leaf biomass. See text for further explanation. AT: Arctic Tundra (Stordalen). BF: Boreal Forest (Jädraås). TeG: Temperate Grassland (Pawnee). TeDF: Temperate Deciduous Forest (Solling). TeEF: Temperate Evergreen Forest (Skogaby). TeRF: Temperate Rain Forest (H.J. Andrews). TrS: Tropical Savanna (Pointe Noire). TrDF: Tropical Dry Forest (Chamela). TrRF: Tropical Rain Forest (San Carlos).

productivity in cold environments and high productivity in warm environments. The two grasslands stick out by their large allocation of growth below ground. We can also consider production in relation to the photosynthetic capacity in terms of canopy biomass. The arctic tundra remains at the bottom as a result of climatic constraints. The boreal forest, the temperate grassland, the temperate evergreen forests and, somewhat surprisingly, the two rain forests form an intermediate group with 4–6 times as high production per unit canopy. Finally, the temperate deciduous forest, the tropical savanna and the tropical dry forest form a group with about 10 times as high production per unit canopy as the arctic tundra. Except for the arctic tundra, where climate is the dominating factor for productivity, the differences between the other ecosystems reflect different

Figure 9.21 (cont.)

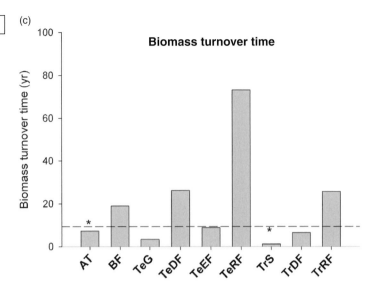

(c)

Biomass turnover time

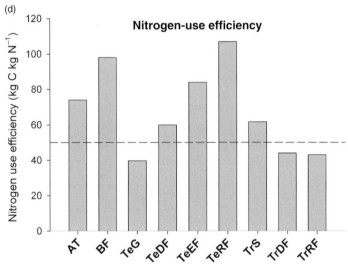

(d)

Nitrogen-use efficiency

growth strategies. High production may not always be the best strategy. To some extent our ecosystems here may not be representative because both the tropical forest ecosystems are at the low end of productivity in their categories (see Table 4.5).

Plant biomass turnover

We define here plant biomass turnover time (Figure 9.21c) as the ratio between standing (annual maximum) biomass and annual production. There is a huge difference in the turnover times of the biomass, from approximately 1 year in the tropical savanna to 73 years in the temperate rain forest. The global average of 9 years is more typical for the rest of the ecosystems, but again the forest ecosystems distinguish themselves from the others with considerably longer turnover times.

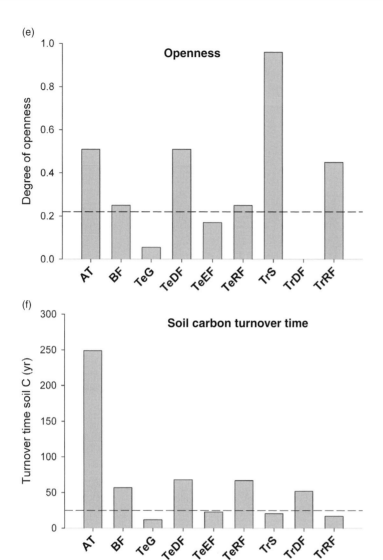

Figure 9.21 (cont.)

The short turnover time of 7 years for the temperate evergreen forest is an underestimate and will increase as this forest ages. On the other hand, there is no climatic gradient involved in the turnover rates except the one that separates forest ecosystems from other types of ecosystems.

Nitrogen-use efficiency: NUE
Here we define nitrogen-use efficiency (Figure 9.21d) as the ratio between annual production and annual nitrogen uptake. Compared to other properties this is the one that varies least between ecosystems. We consider this a result of convergent evolutionary processes that have resulted in similar efficiencies in the utilisation of a very strongly limiting resource. The somewhat lower NUE in tropical forests can be a sign of phosphorus being more important than

Figure 9.21 (cont.)

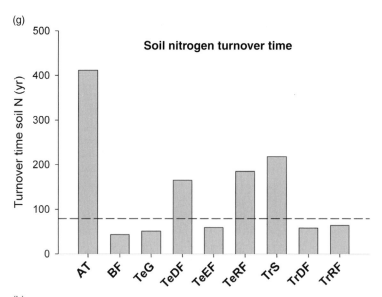

(g)

Soil nitrogen turnover time

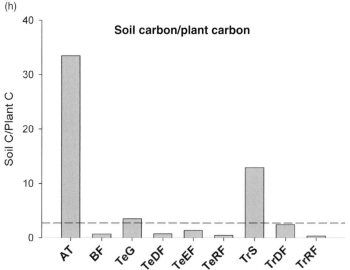

(h)

Soil carbon/plant carbon

nitrogen in these environments. The high NUEs in temperate forests is a result of the large allocation of growth to wood, which is a cheap product in this context and can therefore be produced in large quantities with little use of resources.

Degree of openness
We define degree of openness (Figure 9.21e) as the ratio between the annual nitrogen influx (deposition plus fixation) and the annual flux of nitrogen in the litters; other elements could have been chosen, but most data are available for nitrogen, and nitrogen is at the same time the element most likely to be limiting. There are huge differences in openness, which arise from different specific conditions; from the

(i)

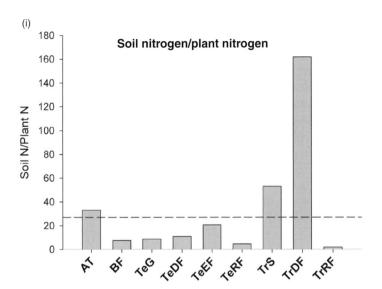

Figure 9.21 (cont.)

temperate grassland that seems to lose no nitrogen, to the tropical grassland that loses as much nitrogen as comes in. The other ecosystems position themselves in between these extremes. The large openness in the temperate deciduous forest is explained by the location of this forest in an area with high nitrogen deposition. The temperate evergreen forest is located in a region with rather high nitrogen deposition, but because this forest is rapidly expanding its biomass it has also a large capacity to absorb this deposition. The relatively open character of the tropical rain forest can be attributed to phosphorus limitation, which constrains the capacity to take up nitrogen, while the harsh climatic conditions set the limit in the arctic tundra.

Turnover time of soil carbon

The turnover times of soil carbon (Figure 9.21f) fall into three groups. Slow turnover occurs in the arctic tundra and results from a combination of a cold climate and a high water table, creating anaerobic conditions for decomposition. Faster turnover in grassland ecosystems than in forest ecosystems is a result of the lower quality, more recalcitrant, litter produced in forests. Climate is also important, as can be seen in the faster turnover in the tropics relative to the temperate zone. However, the type of ecosystem seems to be more important than differences in climate. Changing climatic conditions can therefore be expected to have larger impacts on ecosystem processes when they also cause a change in ecosystem type.

Turnover time of soil nitrogen

The turnover of soil nitrogen (Figure 9.21g) follows closely that of soil carbon. The major difference is the turnover time, which is approximately twice as long. This is a consequence of the mineralisation–immobilisation cycle that exists for nitrogen, but not for carbon, as we discussed in Chapter 7.

Soil carbon/plant carbon ratio

For distribution of carbon (Figure 9.21h) the arctic tundra, grasslands and forests also form three separate groups. In grasslands, and even more so in the arctic tundra, the soil completely dominates the carbon storage of the ecosystem. In forest ecosystems the plants tend to dominate, but it now becomes a question of stand age (Figure 3.1). In the young temperate evergreen forest (Skogaby) there is almost twice as much carbon in the soil as in the vegetation. There is also more carbon in the soil in the dry tropical forest, in this case probably a result of long dry periods slowing down decomposition. In the other forests, with mature trees and sufficient humidity to be non-limiting for decomposition, the vegetation contains about twice the carbon in the soil.

Soil nitrogen/plant nitrogen ratio

The distribution of nitrogen between soil and vegetation (Figure 9.21i) follows much the same pattern as the distribution of carbon although the temperate grassland (Pawnee) is similar to the forests.

Global scale

The carbon cycle

The global carbon cycle (Figure 9.22) operates at several time scales. At the short end, the daily exchange of carbon dioxide in photosynthesis–respiration dominates (Chapter 6). On an annual basis, plant production and litter decomposition dominate, be it terrestrial or marine, although human activities perturb the carbon cycle at this scale (see Figure Pro.2). At a time scale of several hundred years the exchange between sea surface waters and deep waters becomes important. The deep water of the seas is also a major pool of carbon, containing 50 times as much as the atmosphere. On a geological time scale sedimentation removes carbon from, and carbonate weathering adds carbon to, the terrestrial cycle. One should in this context note that although the mean residence time for a carbon atom in the atmosphere is 3 to 4 years, the time taken to remove an extra carbon atom from the atmosphere is much longer, probably of the order of thousands of years, but our lack of understanding of all feedbacks in the global carbon cycle prevents precise estimates; this is one of the factors behind uncertainties in GWP values.

There is a regular variation in the atmospheric carbon dioxide concentration of about 10 ppmv at northern latitudes and a few ppmv from the equator southwards (Figure 9.23). These oscillations follow the seasons, such that during the summer, with maximum photosynthetic uptake of carbon to terrestrial ecosystems, photosynthesis dominates over respiration. In the winter cold air and lack of light slows down photosynthesis, but decomposition of soil organic matter can still proceed, as soil temperatures are less affected. The variability

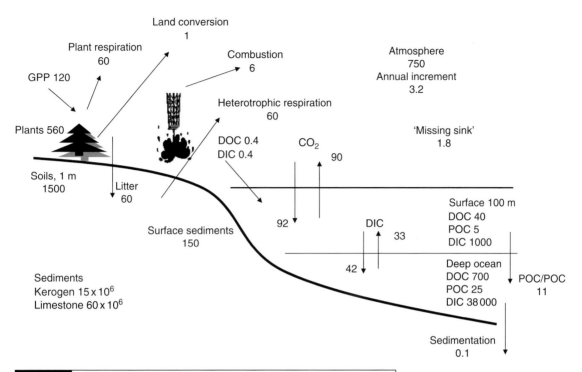

Figure 9.22 The global carbon cycle. Stores in Pg and fluxes in Pg yr⁻¹. The estimate of the soil carbon stock is likely a gross underestimation, as Tarnocai *et al.* (2009) have shown that the northern circumpolar permafrost region contains around 1400 Pg more carbon than the previous estimates used for this figure. Sources: Reeburgh (1997) and Schlesinger (1997).

is less pronounced over the southern hemisphere than over the northern hemisphere, because the south is dominated by sea with less climatic variability than the terrestrially dominated north. The global weather patterns are also such that mixing of gases between the hemispheres is reduced, whereas mixing in the longitudinal direction is rapid.

Human activities have in recent years emitted annually about 6 Pg carbon as carbon dioxide to the atmosphere. Approximately half of that carbon dioxide has remained in the atmosphere and about a quarter is estimated to have been absorbed by the oceans. It is not well known where the remaining quarter of the emissions (the residual) is absorbed; it is therefore often labelled the *'missing sink'*. Regrowth, increased atmospheric carbon dioxide and nitrogen (through deposition) fertilisation of forest in the northern hemisphere are probably the major causes of this sink, although there are also reports of increased growth rates in tropical forests (Lewis *et al.* 2009). It is possible that both terrestrial ecosystems and oceans will become weaker sinks in the future, and hence a larger

We still do not know where all emitted CO_2 ends up

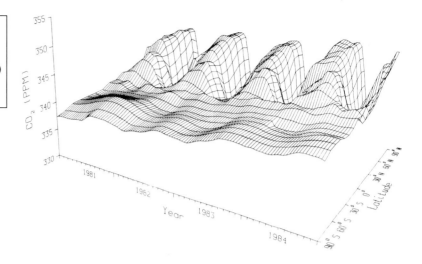

Figure 9.23 Variation in atmospheric carbon dioxide concentration with time and latitude. From Conway et al. (1988) with kind permission from John Wiley & Sons.

fraction of emitted carbon dioxide will remain in the atmosphere (Fung et al. 2005).

Although the global carbon cycle is dominated by exchanges of carbon dioxide and organically bound carbon in biomass and soil organic matter, there are other carbon compounds of importance. Methane, with a residence time of 9 years and a concentration of 1.8 ppmv (1745 ppb in 1998, Table 5.5), is not quantitatively important as a carbon pool, but is important through its potent effect as a greenhouse gas. Carbon monoxide has a still lower atmospheric concentration and shorter residence time (45 to 250 ppb and 2 months, respectively) than methane. It shows limited absorption of infrared radiation, but is indirectly important for the energy balance of the Earth because it slows the destruction of methane. It is also involved in tropospheric ozone production. Volatile organic compounds (VOC) of both natural (terpenes) and anthropogenic sources constitute other minor pools, but with strong effects on atmospheric chemistry.

The nitrogen cycle

Human activities and natural processes add approximately equal quantities of reactive nitrogen to the global cycle

The global nitrogen cycle (Figure 9.24) is characterised by tight internal cycling within terrestrial and aquatic ecosystems. In terrestrial ecosystems organically bound nitrogen dominates completely because any inorganic nitrogen is rapidly taken up by nitrogen-starved organisms. In contrast, inorganic nitrogen dominates over organic nitrogen in the oceans, but almost all of this nitrogen is found below the biologically most active surface waters. The exchange through nitrogen fixation and denitrification with the dominating atmospheric pool is a key feature that can replenish and deplete the reactive nitrogen forms. With the advent of fossil-fuel burning and industrial production of ammonia for fertiliser use there have been drastic increases

Table 9.5 Emissions of nitrogen-containing gases to the atmosphere, Tg yr^{-1}. NO$_x$ are in this table all nitrogen oxides except N$_2$O. Data from Galloway *et al.* (2004)

	NO$_x$ Mid			N$_2$O Mid			NH$_3$ Mid		
	1860	1990	2050	1860	1990	2050	1860	1990	2050
Anthropogenic	2.6	36.2	41.8	1.4	4.7	7.6	7.3	47.2	108.1
Food	2.0	9.0	14.8				6.6	44.3	106
Energy	0.6	27.2	27.0				0.7	2.9	2.1
Natural	10.5	9.7	9.7	10.6	10.6	10.6	13.3	11.0	10.0
Total	13.1	45.9	51.5	12.0	15.3	18.2	20.6	58.2	118.1
Per cent anthropogenic	20	79	81	12	30	42	35	81	92

The global nitrogen cycle Tg or Tg yr^{-1}

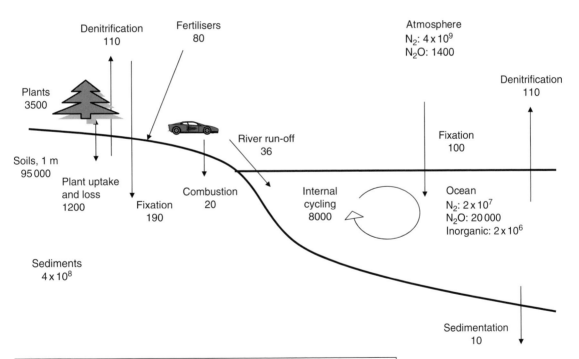

Figure 9.24 The global nitrogen cycle. Stores in Tg and fluxes in Tg yr^{-1}. Sources: Reeburgh (1997) and Schlesinger (1997).

in the emissions of nitrogen gases to the atmosphere (Table 9.5). The lifetimes of NO$_x$ (summary term for nitrogen oxides) and NH$_3$ in the atmosphere are only a few days. Most of these emissions will therefore be deposited close to their sources and the global spatial pattern of nitrogen deposition is therefore very unevenly distributed.

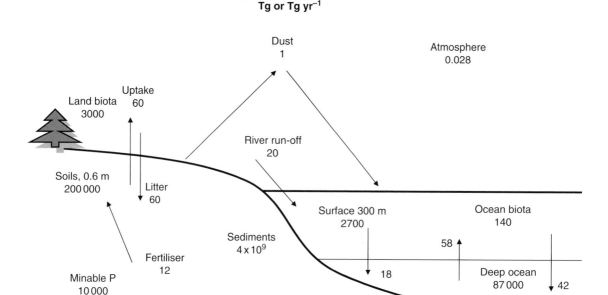

The global phosphorus cycle
Tg or Tg yr^{-1}

Figure 9.25 The global phosphorus cycle. Stores in Tg and fluxes in Tg yr^{-1}. Sources: Reeburgh (1997) and Schlesinger (1997).

On geological time scales sedimentation can remove some nitrogen, but the huge atmospheric store acts as a buffer. Because the soil (organic) pool of nitrogen is large relative to the carbon pool, the turnover of soil nitrogen is slower, in contrast to the turnover in the plants, which is faster for nitrogen. The latter is explained by the large, long-lived and nitrogen-poor woody plant components. The existence of gaseous nitrogen compounds and water-soluble nitrate opens up exchange of nitrogen between ecosystems.

The phosphorus cycle

The global phosphorus cycle (Figure 9.25) is characterised by the lack of important gaseous and water-soluble components. For this reason internal cycling within ecosystems is tight, although over long periods erosion will remove phosphorus from land ecosystems and sedimentation from aquatic ones. Phosphorus lost through sedimentation is only returned to biologically active pools through geological uplift, and hence moves in a very slow cycle. Because of technical difficulties in separating soil phosphorus fractions, the soil pool also contains inorganic forms of phosphorus, explaining the large pool size relative to nitrogen. On the other hand, the almost

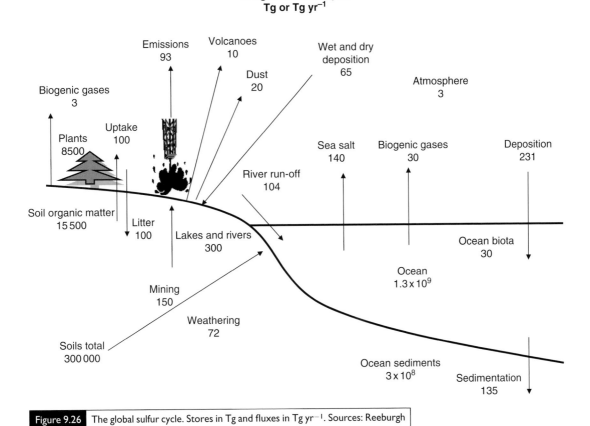

The global sulfur cycle
Tg or Tg yr^{-1}

Figure 9.26 The global sulfur cycle. Stores in Tg and fluxes in Tg yr^{-1}. Sources: Reeburgh (1997) and Schlesinger (1997).

equal sizes of terrestrial plant nitrogen and phosphorus pools reflect the difficulties in obtaining accurate global estimates of these elements. From ecological stoichiometry one expects the plant phosphorus pool to be approximately 1/10 of the nitrogen pool (see Table 6.4).

The sulfur cycle

The global sulfur cycle (Figure 9.26) has many similarities with the nitrogen cycle, in terms of both pool sizes and turnover rates. The major difference is that there is virtually no atmospheric sulfur pool (the residence time of sulfur dioxide in the atmosphere is of the order of days), but geological cycling, with emissions through volcanism, is more important. The sulfate dissolved in the oceans is also an important biologically active reservoir.

Human influence on element mass balances

Over the past 250 years human activities have drastically altered global element cycles, with approximately 405 ± 30 Pg carbon emitted as carbon dioxide into the atmosphere as a result of fossil-fuel

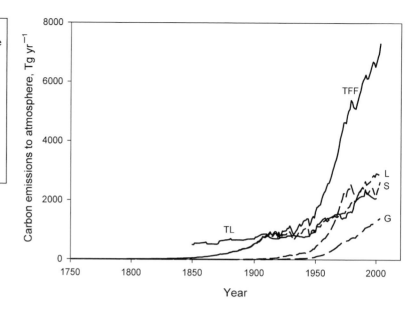

Figure 9.27 Carbon emissions from use of fossil fuels and land-use conversions. TFF = total emissions from fossil fuels and cement production. L = emissions from liquids. S = emissions from solids. G = emissions from gas. TL = total emissions from land-use changes. Complied from Houghton & Hackler (2002) and Marland et al. (2006).

burning and cement production (75%), and land use and land-use change (25%), predominantly deforestation (IPCC 2001) (Figure 9.27). Conversion of forest to agricultural land in North America as a result of European immigration was, up until 1900, the dominant cause of carbon emissions. This conversion eventually ceased, and from around 1920 North America has been a sink for carbon. Instead, land-use changes in China and Latin America took over the role of dominating carbon emissions, but from around 1980 China's role has been replaced by Tropical Africa and Tropical Asia (Houghton & Hackler 2002). Industrial use of coal became the main carbon emitter around 1900 and despite a steady increase, the explosive increase in liquid fossil fuels after 1950 has made it the largest emitter today. There has also been a rapid and important increase in carbon emission from gas fuels since 1950 (Marland et al. 2006).

As a result of anthropogenic emissions, the global average atmospheric CO_2 concentration, $[CO_2]$, has risen from 280 ± 5 ppmv in preindustrial times to 383 ppmv in 2004 (WMO 2008) (i.e. by about 35%). This increase in $[CO_2]$ accounts for about 40% of these anthropogenic emissions, the remainder being absorbed by the oceans and terrestrial ecosystems. On average during the 1990s, annual global emissions of carbon dioxide amounted to 6.4 ± 0.3 Pg (C) from fossil fuels, plus 1.7 ± 0.8 Pg (C) from land use and land-use change, mainly deforestation in the tropics. There are four main global sinks for these emissions: the atmosphere (3.2 ± 0.1 Pg (C)), the oceans (1.7 ± 0.5 Pg (C)), tropical vegetation (1.9 ± 1.3 Pg (C)), and temperate and boreal vegetation, mainly forests (1.3 ± 0.9 Pg (C)) (Read et al. 2001). In particular, plant photosynthesis is responding to this increase in $[CO_2]$.

Deposition of nitrogen (wet and dry, oxidised and reduced) to forests is between 1 and 80 kg ha^{-1} yr^{-1}, smaller amounts occurring

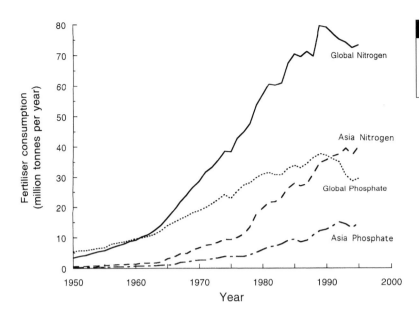

Figure 9.28 Global and Asian use of nitrogen and phosphorus fertilisers. From Mackenzie *et al.* (1998) with kind permission from Cambridge University Press.

in the more remote forests, particularly in rural areas at high latitudes, and large amounts in industrialised central Europe (Jarvis & Fowler 2001). The additions of reactive nitrogen to the global nitrogen cycle from fertiliser use (Figure 9.28) and from combustion processes are currently on a par with additions from the natural processes. The NO_x produced in combustion processes can come from nitrogen in the fuel when the combustion temperature is low (< 1000 K) and the fuel is nitrogen rich (coal, biomass), but at higher temperatures and in low-nitrogen fuels (liquid fuels) reactions between N_2 and O_2 also occur (Bowman 1991). The global increase in [CO_2], temperature and nitrogen that has occurred so far has also most probably contributed to a current carbon sink in forests of the north temperate and boreal regions; nitrogen especially has been identified as a driving factor in European forests (Binkley & Högberg 1997, Kahle *et al.* 2008).

The anthropogenic additions to the global phosphorus cycle through fertiliser use are also on a par with many natural cycles. The current values of phosphorus fertiliser use in Figure 9.27 are higher than those in Figure 9.25 for the global cycle, because the latter are based on earlier data. The large difference, about a factor of 2, is indeed a sign of how rapidly human use of natural resources are increasing.

The global trend in sulfur emissions followed the pattern of steadily increasing emissions of nitrogen and phosphorus until 1970, when the acidifying effects of sulfur deposition became such an important issue in Europe and North America, the major emitters at that time, that drastic reduction measures were initiated, with subsequent declines in emissions (Figure 9.29; see also Prologue). The collapse around 1990 of many Eastern European economies, which were based on high-sulfur-containing coal, was also a major reason for the

(a)

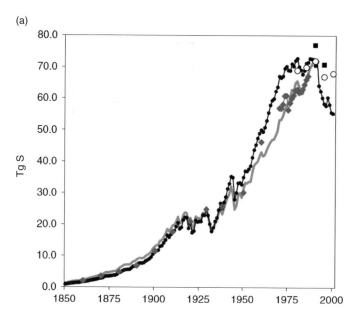

(b)

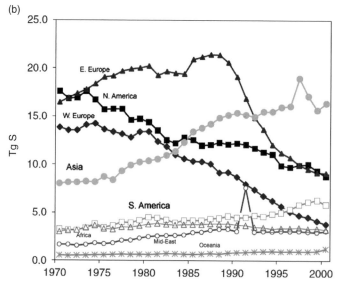

Figure 9.29 The global trend in annual sulfur emissions (a) as estimated in different studies, and emissions partitioned over regions (b). Note the steady declines in Western Europe and North America and the abrupt decline in Eastern Europe around 1990, as well as the increasing trend in Asia. Redrawn from Stern (2006) with kind permission from Elsevier.

decline in emissions. The sulfur emissions are still declining despite rapidly increasing emissions, particularly in China. The human effect on the global sulfur cycle also differs in another respect from those of nitrogen and phosphorus; the anthropogenic enhancement of the sulfur cycle is considerably larger than the natural introduction of new sulfur.

Box 9.3 | Ecosystem chemistry: material, sampling, treatment of samples and determinations

The purpose of this box on ecosystem chemistry is to give major features of sampling procedures and techniques used in examining chemical properties of ecosystems. There are many methods available and the aim of the investigation will determine the method. The text is based on long experience from the Department of Biology, Section of Plant Ecology and Systematics, University of Lund. For more detailed information on sampling and analyses we refer to available books on methodology (see Further reading).

We take ecosystem chemistry in a wide sense, covering aspects essential for describing and analysing ecosystem structure, function and dynamics. In focus for our scientific philosophy are the four cornerstones (Chapter 3), where we emphasise the role of the chemical elements as nutrients, the usefulness of their mass balances and stoichiometric relationships. The major elements (Box 3.1) and the form in which they appear is a starting point. We consider the different elements as such, as well as their stable and unstable (radioactive) isotopes (Box 9.4). Chemical analyses are needed for the quantification of the biogeochemical cycles of the elements, as well as providing the information needed when looking at relationships between mineral nutrition and production of biomass. Isotopes can be used for tracing pathways and estimating residence times of elements in organisms, as well as the whole ecosystem. It is also possible to establish the age of different materials, which can give insights into evolutionary, historical and actual developments. A number of applications are given in the different chapters.

MATERIAL

The materials that we have to deal with cover a range of aggregation forms. We consider gases, water, organic compounds in plants, water and soils, as well as inorganic constituents/elements. Analysing an ecosystem (Box 4.3) will, as shown, as a minimum require information on nutrient elements in plants, water and soils.

SAMPLING

Fundamental for sampling is the statistical design. Sample areas and samples should be replicated. A classical example is fertilisation experiments with randomised blocks, often three or four with control and treatment plots.

Air and water samples are usually taken by volume. Plant material is collected on an area basis. Soil material is usually collected on a volumetric basis, but can be converted to an area basis with appropriate supplementary information, e.g. bulk soil density.

Terrestrial ecosystem properties often show a great variation in time (Figure 3.1) and space. It is important to include this variation in the system description. The variation observed in tree biomass and production in a deciduous forest in southern Sweden can serve as an example (Andersson 1970b). Based on the methods described in Box 4.3, the sampling error was $\pm$ 6.3% for tree biomass and $\pm$ 8.6% for tree production, respectively. Soil properties may have a greater variation (Andersson 1970a). The errors in the chemical analyses are generally small compared to the sampling error.

TREATMENT OF SAMPLES

It is recommended that analyses are made on *fresh samples*. This is particularly important if the aim is to investigate properties that can be affected by microbial activities such as nitrate and ammonium levels.

Water samples may be of different origins: precipitation, soil water, lake water and groundwater. Depending on the purpose of the analyses, different treatments may be required. Sensitive to transport and storage are pH, bicarbonate, phosphate, nitrate and ammonium. The two first variables need to be analysed immediately. When immediate analysis is not possible, the samples can be stored cold in darkness or deep frozen.

Total content of elements in *plant and organic soil material* is determined after digestion with usually a 20% excess of pure nitric acid at 200 °C. The analysed material needs to be dried at 40 or 85 °C. The residue after digestion is dissolved in measuring flasks. The major elements are usually determined by the ICP technique.

Soils are analysed chemically in order to determine plant-available elements, as well as the total amount of elements. The available elements are analysed after extraction with solutions of different strengths. A water-soluble fraction may be extracted, which only gives a minor share of the available elements (< 0.01%). Stronger agents, ranging from neutral salts to acid or basic solutions, are mostly used to determine what are considered as plant-available elements. The total amount of elements is determined after dissolution with strong acids. Some extraction methods with stronger solutions may simulate a weathering rate.

The analyses should be done on fine soil (<2 mm particle size). The sample, usually a volume-determined sample, needs to be weighed fresh and sieved. Material not passing the sieve is weighed. A sample of the sieved soil is dried in order to determine its water content, followed by extraction for analyses of available elements. Usually loss on ignition – organic matter – is also determined.

DETERMINATIONS

Some commonly analysed elements/substances are summarised in Table 9.6, as well as some techniques and equipment applied for analyses of gases, water, plants and soils.

Table 9.6 | Major techniques for chemical analyses of gases, water, plants and soils

Medium/Element	Major analysis techniques and instruments
Gases	
CO_2	UV absorbance/Gas
CH_4	chromatography/Infrared
NOx	spectroscopy
NH_3	
O_3	
SO_2	

Table 9.6 (cont.)

Medium/Element	Major analysis techniques and instruments
Water	
pH	Electrometric
Conductivity, electrolytic	
HCO_3^-	Titration
Total carbon, TOC	Infrared spectroscopy
Cl^-, SO_4^{2-}, F^-, NO_3^-	Ion chromatography
NH_4^+	FIA
Na, K, Ca, Mg, Al, Fe	ICP or ICP-MS
Mn, S, P, Cu, Zn, Cd	
Conductivity	Calculated
Plants, peat and humus layer – organic matter	
Organic matter	Loss on ignition 550 °C
C, N, H, O	Infrared spectroscopy
N-total	Kjeldahl-N
Mineral soils	
Water content	Gravimetric 105 °C
Loss on ignition	Ignition 550 °C
C-total	Infrared spectroscopy
N-total	Kjeldahl-N
pH_{H_2O} and pH_{BaCl_2}	Electrometric
Na, K, Ca, Mg, Al, Fe, Mn,	ICP or ICP-MS
B, S, P, Cu, Zn and others	
e.g. Co, Cr, Ni, Pb, Rb, Sr,	
Ti, V	
Extractables	With e.g. $BaCl_2$, EDTA
Total	Digestion with e.g. nitric acid

FIA – flow injection analysis
ICP – inductively coupled plasma spectrophotometer
MS – mass spectroscopy

Box 9.4 | Isotopes in ecological research

Because isotopes have different masses they move with different velocities and react with different rates. As a result there will in many processes be a fraction-ation of isotopes that we can measure. Technological advances have made mass spectrometers both more powerful and cheaper, such that nowadays analyses of several isotopes are standard methodology in ecological research.

There are different ways of using isotopes. There are on the one hand *stable* and *unstable* isotopes. For unstable isotopes to be useful they must have half-lives comparable to the rates of the processes being studied. There are only a few of ecological interest (^{3}H: half-life 12.3 yr, ^{14}C: half-life 5700 yr, ^{32}P: half-life 14 d); others decay too rapidly or too slowly to match ecological processes, with typical rates expressed in days or years. Stable isotopes can either be used at their *natural abundances* or be *added experimentally*.

For almost all elements of interest the lighter isotope dominates. To get convenient numbers to talk about, isotope ratios are usually expressed relative to a reference, the δ-value

$$\delta^H X = \left[\frac{R_{sample}}{R_{standard}} - 1 \right] * 1000 \qquad (9.1)$$

where R_{sample} and $R_{standard}$ are the ratios of the heavy to the light isotope in a sample and some standard reference, respectively. By multiplying by a factor the 'units' of δ-value become permil (‰; cf. per cent, %).

The most commonly used isotopes (besides the dominating one) are:

Hydrogen: ^{2}H or D, average natural abundance 0.016%. Mostly used for tracing water movements.

Carbon: ^{13}C, average natural abundance 1.11%. Strong fractionation between ^{12}C and ^{13}C occurs during photosynthesis, giving C3 and C4 plants (Chapter 6) unique isotopic signatures. Effects of water stress on photosynthesis can also be detected. Fractionation also occurs during respiration/decomposition. The equilibrium between CO_2 in the atmosphere and the surface waters of oceans involves chemical fractionation.

Carbon: ^{14}C, average natural abundance in the atmosphere before 1950, 0.0 000 000 001%. The radioactive decay of ^{14}C makes it possible to determine the time at which a carbon compound was produced from atmospheric CO_2. The aboveground nuclear bomb tests conducted between 1955 and 1963 have added a strong signal of ^{14}C to the atmosphere that can be used to track organic matter produced after 1955. The extremely low concentration of this isotope makes analyses very expensive and limits its use.

Nitrogen: ^{15}N, average natural abundance 0.36%. During decomposition of organic matter ^{14}N is released faster than ^{15}N. Both nitrification and denitrification have large isotopic effects. ^{15}N is frequently added experimentally to follow components of the nitrogen cycle (Chapter 9).

Oxygen: ^{18}O, average natural abundance 0.20%. Mostly used for tracing water movements. This isotope was used to show that O_2 released in photosynthesis comes from the water rather than from CO_2.

Phosphorus: ^{32}P, no natural abundance. Half-life 14.28 d.

Sulfur: ^{34}S, average natural abundance 4.21%.

FURTHER READING

Balsberg-Påhlsson, A.M. (ed.) 1990. *Handledning i kemiska metoder vid växtekologiska arbeten.* 6th edn. (Manual for chemical analyses in plant ecological work) Meddelanden från Växtekologiska avdelningen, Lunds Universitet No 52. ISSN 0348–2456.

Brady, C.B. & Weil, R.R. 2007. *The Nature and Properties of Soils.* 14th edn. Upper Saddle River, NJ: Pearson, Prentice Hall.

Galloway, J.N., Dentener, F.J., Capone, D.G. *et al.* 2004. Nitrogen cycles: Past, present, and future. *Biogeochemistry* **70**:153–226.

ICP Forestry UN-ECE 2003–2007. Manuals for sampling and analyses of soils (2006), soil solution (2003), leaves and needles (2007), tree growth and yield (2004), litterfall (2004). www.ICP.Forest-manual.com.

Klute, A. (ed.) 2006. *Methods of Soil Analysis. Part 1. Physical and Mineralogical Methods*. American Society of Agronomy and Soil Science Society of America Book Series No. 5. Madison, WI: American Society of Agronomy and Soil Science Society of America.

Schimel, D.S. 1995. Terrestrial ecosystems and the carbon cycle. *Global Change Biology* **1**:77–91.

Schlesinger, W.H. 1997. *Biogeochemistry: Analysis of Global Change*. San Diego, CA: Academic Press.

Schulze, E.D., Beck, E. & Müller-Hohenstein, K. 2002. *Plant Ecology*. Berlin: Springer.

Sparks, D.L. (ed.) 2005. *Methods of Soil Analysis. Part 3. Chemical Methods*. American Society of Agronomy and Soil Science Society of America Book Series No. 5. Madison, WI: American Society of Agronomy and Soil Science Society of America.

Chapter 10

Principles

In the previous chapters we have dealt with processes in terrestrial ecosystems in detail. In this chapter we take a broader view and summarise what has been discussed previously in *principles*. We divide the principles into five categories according to the processes they encompass. For each principle we start with stating the principle, continue with a discussion of the reason and validity behind the principle, and end with examples demonstrating the use of the principle.

In Chapter 3 we introduced some cornerstones in ecosystem science. Chapters 4–9 have dealt in detail with structures and functions of terrestrial ecosystems. Here we take a broader view and derive from these chapters 17 principles, which can serve as a point of departure when analysing questions about ecosystem behaviour (Figure 10.1). The principles are divided into five classes, depending upon which component of the ecosystem they are dealing with:

(1) Boundary conditions (B1–B5). These principles pertain to the interaction between the ecosystem and its environment.
(2) Energy and water processes (A1). This principle relates to abiotic (energy and water) constraints on ecosystem processes.
(3) Plant processes (P1–P5). These principles deal with constraints on plant growth.
(4) Soil processes (S1–S3). These principles deal with the turnover of soil organic matter.
(5) Element cycling processes (E1–E3). These principles couple plants and soils through the element cycles.

Principles pertaining to boundary conditions (B)

Principle B1. On boundaries and storage

The conditions on the boundary to an ecosystem constrain the storage of elements in the ecosystem.

This is also an application of the principle of mass balance

The total storage of an element in an ecosystem depends on the balance between fluxes over the ecosystem boundary. As long as these fluxes do not change, the total storage will remain the same, although the internal distribution can change. For many elements an ecosystem can be described as a series of n pools (X_i) interconnected by fluxes (F_{ij}). Some

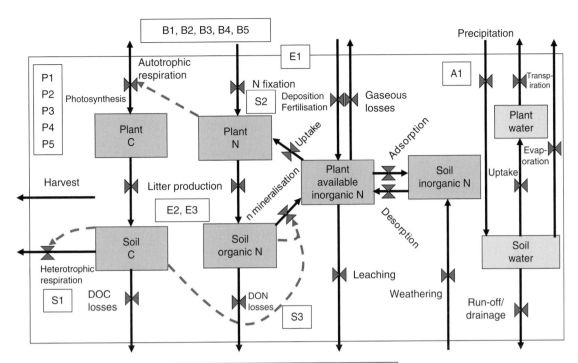

Figure 10.1 A number of principles can be coupled to the terrestrial cycles of carbon, nutrients, and water. We have grouped these into five different categories: boundary conditions (B), energy and water – abiotic (A), plant production (P), soil processes (S) and element cycles (E).

of these pools are also connected to the surrounding environment. In the simplest of cases there is an inflow (I) to only one of the pools, say 1, and an outflow from one of the pools, say n. Let the inflow be constant and independent of the state of the ecosystem, as would be the case with nitrogen in wet deposition, and let the outflow be proportional to the size of pool n (kX_n), which might be the case if this flow represents nitrate leaching. A model of such an ecosystem could be

$$\frac{dX_1}{dt} = \sum_{i=1}^{n} F_{1i} - \sum_{i=1}^{n} F_{i1} + I$$

$$\frac{dX_j}{dt} = \sum_{i=1}^{n} F_{ji} - \sum_{i=1}^{n} F_{ij}, \quad 1 < j < n \qquad (10.1)$$

$$\frac{dX_n}{dt} = \sum_{i=1}^{n} F_{ni} - \sum_{i=1}^{n} F_{in} - kX_n$$

We then have, for the total amount of the element in the ecosystem $X_T = \sum X_i$

$$\frac{dX_T}{dt} = I - kX_n \qquad (10.2)$$

because the sum of all the internal flows F_{ij} equals zero; a flow into one pool must come from some other pool. At steady state ($dX_T/dt = 0$)

$X_n = I/k$ and the conditions of the ecosystem become determined by the conditions at the boundary, the inflow and the outflow.

An outstanding example of this principle is Earth, where a nearly constant incoming solar energy flux has been matched by a nearly constant atmospheric carbon dioxide concentration.

Principle B2. On perturbing boundaries

Perturbations that change boundary conditions will have different effects to perturbations that affect internal conditions.

This principle is a logical consequence of principle B1. Changing boundary conditions will change the storage capacity of elements, but internal changes are more likely to redistribute the elements within the ecosystem.

Different elements will be affected differently by perturbations

Consider as an example the difference between a storm felling of a forest and a forest fire. In the first case nutrients are mostly redistributed within the system, if not harvested, but with a fire, large quantities of nutrient can be volatilised and thus lost. The long-term recovery can therefore be less complete after the fire unless there are other processes compensating for the losses of limiting elements.

Principle B3. On nitrogen vs. phosphorus limitation

The relative rates of inputs and losses of nitrogen and phosphorus will over long time scales change and as a consequence, which of these elements that is limiting for plant production will change with the age of the site.

The nutrient availability varies at long time scales and is associated with processes of soil formation, release of nutrients from soil minerals and nitrogen fixation. Ecosystems in climate zones that allow the systems to evolve for millions of years will typically be nitrogen limited in the early phases because no nitrogen is available in the bare soil. Nitrogen fixation will add nitrogen to the system, but losses in the form of denitrification and leaching will maintain nitrogen-limited plant production. Over still longer times phosphorus is lost from the system through erosion or transferred to inaccessible (occluded) forms (Figure 9.12).

An example can be found in a 3 000 000-year chronosequence from Hawaii showing how nitrogen and phosphorus concentrations in the foliage of the dominant tree species vary (Figure 10.2). During approximately the first 10 000 years these ecosystems are nitrogen limited. Then a period up to around 75 000 years follows with strong phosphorus limitation. Beyond 75 000 to 100 000 years concentrations of both elements drop as a result of erosion losses of phosphorus. The lack of phosphorus also restricts the uptake of nitrogen and it is difficult to identify either of the elements as clearly limiting.

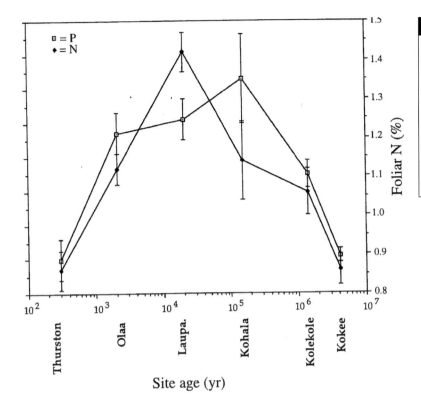

Figure 10.2 Changes in nitrogen and phosphorus concentration in foliage of *Metrosideros polymorpha* across a Hawaiian chronosequence created by volcanic eruptions. The scales for nitrogen and phosphorus concentrations have been chosen such that the lowest line represents the limiting element (see Table 6.4). From Crews *et al.* (1995) with kind permission from the Ecological Society of America.

We also suggest the following two principles for boundary conditions:

Principle B4. On production and openness

Ecosystem production is in the long run determined by the element with the most closed cycle.

The more open an element cycle is, the more easily this element will be replenished and lost from the ecosystem. In the long run we expect therefore that the element that is most strongly retained and recycled will constrain the cycling of the other elements.

Principle B5. On time scales and openness

The time scale at which an element cycle adjusts to changes in the environment is inversely proportional to its degree of openness.

The time it will take for different element cycles to adjust themselves to each other must depend upon how well they can exchange matter with the environment. More open element cycles can rapidly exchange matter and reach their equilibria with other element cycles, whereas more closed cycles need longer times to reach equilibrium.

Principles pertaining to energy and water (A)

Principle A1. On climate and ecosystem distribution

The large-scale distribution of ecosystems and biomes is determined by a combination of the abiotic factors, temperature and precipitation.

Climate, in terms of temperature and precipitation, determines on a global scale the short-term boundaries for ecosystem production. Temperature reflects the available energy in sunlight, but is also in itself a strong rate regulator, and higher temperatures will, in most cases, increase reaction rates. Water is also a critical factor because, in contrast to nutrients, it cannot be recycled and used over and over again within the ecosystem. Once water is evaporated from an eco-system there is no immediate replenishment, in contrast to carbon dioxide, which is always available at a fairly constant level. These features make water unique as a limiting resource.

On maps of primary production or biome distributions (Figure 4.9), the climatic effects can be seen as latitudinal bands reflecting the temperature component of climate and precipitation visible as the distance from oceans (Figure 4.9). As a result production correlates with temperature and precipitation (Figure 10.3) but with a lot of variability. The sources of this variability are due to problems in cor-rectly estimating productivity, but also an expression of other factors of importance, mainly nutrition. At a given location, it is therefore not sufficient to know temperature and precipitation to accurately esti-mate primary production.

Principles pertaining to plant processes (P)

Principle P1. On element availability

The utilisation of an element in an ecosystem depends on whether its availability is determined by its concentration or by the rate at which it is made available by some other mechanism.

The availability of an element to an organism, of which there exists such a large stock in the environment that the organism cannot exhaust it, is controlled by the concentration of the element. We call such elements *non-depletable* or *concentration limited*. If, on the other hand, the organism or the assembly of organisms in the ecosystem regularly exhausts an element, the availability of that element is inde-pendent of its concentration and is instead controlled by how fast the supplying mechanisms operate. Such elements are called *depletable* or *replenishment-rate limited*. Depletable/non-depletable is, of course, not a true dichotomy, but the two end-points of a continuum.

This is also an application of the principle of optimisation

Carbon in the form of carbon dioxide is again a typical example of an element, the availability of which is unlimited for terrestrial plants. Without drastically changing how the world looks, it is difficult to

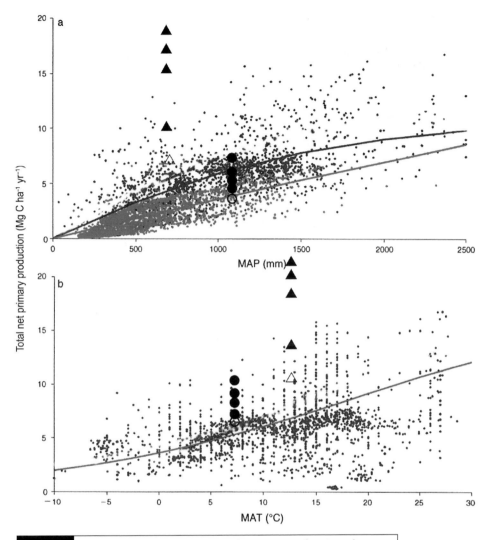

Figure 10.3 Net primary productivity in terrestrial ecosystems as functions of mean annual precipitation (MAP) and mean annual temperature (MAT). Upper regression line in (a) and regression line in (b) represent tree-dominated ecosystems and lower regression line in (a) represents non-tree ecosystems. Modified from Del Grosso *et al.* (2008) with kind permission from Ecological Society of America. Fertilising ecosystem and/or irrigating can greatly increase the productivity. (●,○) and (▲,Δ) are results from fertilisation/irrigation experiments in a *Picea abies* stand in Sweden (Persson & Nilsson 2001) and a *Pinus radiata* stand in Australia (Raison & Myers 1992), respectively. The unfilled symbols represent untreated conditions.

imagine how plants could more than marginally alter the atmospheric carbon dioxide concentration; at least in the short term. Most resources acquired in the soil by plants (water and mineral nutrients), on the other hand, are often exhausted by the existing vegetation. Water stress is a common phenomenon and most mineral nutrients in the soil are found in only low concentrations. The important implication of this principle for an organism striving to optimise its resource allocation is that with resources that are limiting through their concentration, an increased allocation to structures that increase the acquisition of this element always pays off. A plant can increase its leaf surface and thereby increase its carbon dioxide uptake. With elements that are controlled by their supply rate, the maximum uptake is out of the control of the organism. No matter how much root biomass a plant produces, when all nitrate and ammonium is removed from the soil solution, the plant has to wait for the decomposers to release more. However, it may still pay off for an individual plant to increase its root biomass beyond what should be required for complete uptake of nutrients available in the soil if this prevents a competing plant individual from acquiring these nutrients.

Principle P2. On light limitation

Plant growth is limited by intercepted radiation.

Light is a necessary resource for plant growth. Light is therefore one of the resources that can become limiting for growth. Plant growth in relation to light was analysed in detail in Chapter 6.

Principle P3. On nutrient limitation

Plant growth is limited by some nutrient.

Nutrients are necessary resources for plant growth. Nutrients are therefore one of the resources that can become limiting for growth. Plant growth in relation to nutrients was analysed in detail in Chapter 6.

Principle P4. On water limitation

Plant growth is limited by water availability.

Water is a necessary resource for plant growth. It is therefore one of the resources that can become limiting for growth. Plant growth in relation to water was analysed in detail in Chapter 6.

Principle P5. On resource use efficiency and acquisition

Plant production in an ecosystem depends on the product of the efficiency of the use of a limiting resource and the rate of acquisition of the resource.

This is an extension of the principle of limiting nutrients

We showed in Chapter 6 that plant production can be related to light-use efficiency (ε, Principle P2), nutrient-use efficiency (NUE, Principle P3) or water-use efficiency (WUE, Principle P4). If LU, NU and WU are the rates of uptake/absorption of light, nutrient and water, respectively, we can calculate three expressions for NPP depending upon which of the three production factors we consider. The actual NPP is then given by

$$NPP = \min\{LU * \varepsilon, NU * NUE, WU * WUE\} \tag{10.3}$$

It is the most limiting factor that determines NPP; the other terms express only the production potential of the other resources. One use of Equation (10.3) can be to estimate the potential for growth increase. For example, in a nutrient-limited system there is no point in fertilising more than to reach the NPP where the next limiting resource takes over. Expression (10.3) can also be used to analyse the reasons behind production changes. A change in the availability of a limiting resource causes a change in production. This is what happens when nitrogen deposition increases nitrogen availability or when a drought decreases water availability. In these cases, the basic plant physiology remains unchanged. Alternatively, the plant physiology changes, in which case it is the resource-use efficiency that changes. An example is that an increasing atmospheric carbon dioxide concentration permits a plant to take up carbon dioxide at the same rate, but with a smaller stomatal aperture, which decreases transpiration losses and hence increases water-use efficiency.

When resource-use efficiencies are calculated from NPP and the rate of resource acquisition, the efficiencies of the non-limiting resources are by necessity lower than those obtained when the resource is limiting. This may be seen as luxury consumption by the plant, but in the case of mineral resources it can also be a way of obtaining reserves for the future. In an ideal, optimal world a plant would allocate its resource acquisition such that all resources were equally limiting. In practice, there are costs associated with changing allocation and certain resources are acquired simultaneously, i.e. allocation to roots can increase uptake of both water and several mineral nutrients.

Principles pertaining to soil processes (S)

Principle S1. On decomposition – energy limitation

Decomposition is energy limited.

As explained in Chapter 7, energy is generally the most critical resource for decomposers because it can only be obtained from the soil organic matter. Other essential resources such as nitrogen and phosphorus are also obtained from the soil organic matter, but other sources in inorganic forms are also available. The primary energy sources are all the various carbon compounds, and when carbon is used as energy its end product is generally carbon dioxide, which cannot be recycled in the soil. The use of other element resources and their conversion mostly produces a state where the elements can be recirculated within the soil, e.g. the conversion of organically bound nitrogen to ammonium.

The addition of an easily useable carbon (energy) source to the soil will therefore stimulate decomposer growth. Higher decomposer activity can also lead to increased attack on older, more recalcitrant, carbon. As a result there will be an overall increased decomposition of soil organic matter; this is an example of positive *priming*.

Principle S2. On nitrogen fixation

Nitrogen fixation cannot remove the limitation by nitrogen, but only reduce it.

Nitrogen fixation is an energetically costly process. Ecosystem development based on nitrogen fixation will therefore come to an end when it is less costly for the organisms to obtain more nitrogen by investing in more efficient uptake of soil inorganic nitrogen than in nitrogen fixation (Rastetter *et al.* 2001). In the long run nitrogen fixers will be outcompeted in most ecosystems, or they will switch off nitrogen fixation (see Figure 6.19).

Principle S3. On nitrogen leaching

The ratio of dissolved organic nitrogen to dissolved inorganic nitrogen in leachates from an ecosystem is important for the carbon storage in the ecosystem.

Plants growing in nitrogen-limited ecosystems can diminish their nitrogen limitation by allocating more resources to nitrogen uptake if the losses are in inorganic form. In contrast, if the losses are in the form of organic nitrogen they are, in general, in a form that is less readily taken up by plants. Hence, the allocation mechanisms within the ecosystem do not function to reduce losses of organic nitrogen (Rastetter *et al.* 2005). One result is that in unpolluted areas nitrogen losses are mostly in organic form (Perakis & Hedin 2002), whereas in polluted areas inorganic forms dominate because the ecosystem does not have the capacity to retain all incoming nitrogen. A lower storage capacity for carbon also follows with nitrogen losses.

Principles pertaining to element cycles (E)

Principle E1. On openness of element cycles

Different element cycles have different degrees of openness.

In a given ecosystem, some elements are circulated very tightly within the system, undergoing very little exchange with the environment, whereas other elements move freely in and out of the system. A major determinant of the openness of an element cycle is the existence or absence of gaseous forms of the element and how water soluble different forms of the element are.

Carbon, of which there is a huge gaseous reservoir in the form of carbon dioxide in the atmosphere, is a typical element, with respect to which all ecosystems are entirely open. Sodium and chlorine, which are highly water soluble, also move easily in and out of ecosystems. Phosphorous, on the other hand, which has neither gaseous nor highly water-soluble forms, remains tightly bound in an ecosystem. Nitrogen is an element that normally, and in most ecosystems, is retained rather

Table 10.1 Degrees of openness for two forest ecosystems (Skogaby and Hubbard Brook, a mature deciduous forest in the eastern USA). Degree of openness is calculated as the ratio of annual element losses to plant uptake (kg ha^{-1} yr^{-1}). Data for Skogaby from Figure 9.21 and Hubbard Brook from Likens & Bormann (1995)

	Skogaby			Hubbard Brook		
Element	Uptake	Loss	Degree of openness	Uptake	Loss	Degree of openness
N	89	0.7	0.007	79.6	4.0	0.05
P	6.6	0.0	0	8.9	0.01	0.001
S	6.9	13	1.46	24.5	17.6	0.72
K	23.6	0.7	0.03	64.3	2.4	0.04
Ca	28.4	1.7	0.06	62.2	13.9	0.22
Mg	6.6	2.1	0.32	9.3	3.3	0.35
Na	34.8	7.4	0.21			
Cl	0	4.6	∞			

tightly, but has both gaseous (N_2O, NO, NO_2) and water-soluble phases (NO_3^-) and can therefore shift between closed-system and open-system behaviour, depending upon the circumstances. This also provides a feedback that prevents an excessive accumulation of the element in an ecosystem. In the case of nitrogen, when high levels of the less mobile form (ammonium) build up, mechanisms are switched on (nitrification) which convert the immobile form into a mobile one. Other elements show varying degrees of openness, which can depend on both the status of the ecosystem (steady state or aggrading) and high input levels that exceed the capacity for internal cycling, as well as underlying bedrock with differing weathering rates. Two examples from two different forest ecosystems are given in Table 10.1.

The elements interact with regard to their openness. In an ecosystem where plant production is, for example, nitrogen limited, an increase in nitrogen deposition that stimulates growth will also lead to an increased requirement for other elements. As a consequence, an increased plant uptake of the other elements may reduce their losses, e.g. phosphorus (Perring *et al.* 2008).

Principle E2. On element distributions

Different elements have different distributions within an ecosystem.

Elements in an ecosystem occur as organic and inorganic forms, as well as being bound in components with very different turnover times. In terrestrial ecosystems, it is only the organic form of carbon that is of interest. Carbon as CO_2 is only a transitory phase in rapid exchange with the environment. In some ecosystems there can be considerable amounts of carbon as carbonate, but this carbon is biologically inactive, although important as a buffer of soil pH. The other elements

Table 10.2 Distribution of elements between trees and soil and element:C ratios in trees and soil in the Skogaby forest ecosystem. Data from Figure 9.21. C in Mg ha^{-1}, other elements in kg ha^{-1}

Element	C	N	P	S	K	Ca	Mg
Tree:soil ratio	0.53	0.13	0.043	0.032	0.099	0.038	0.012
Tree element:C ratio		13.7	0.7	0.7	3.0	3.8	0.8
Soil element:C ratio		58.8	9.3	12.6	16.0	52.7	35.3

are distributed between organic and inorganic forms, but the fraction belonging to each of these groups varies between elements. For some of the quantitatively most important elements (N, P and S) the organic forms are most abundant. There is also a distribution over different inorganic forms with varying biological availability. Again, elements differ in this respect with important ecological consequences.

The elements are also partitioned between plants and soil. Normally the ratio of organically bound elements to C is higher in the soil than in the plant, but for some elements the difference is not as large. It can also be important to consider the partitioning between active tissues like leaves and fine roots relative to structural tissues like wood. In all cases, the element:C ratio is rather constrained and clearly different between different components. Table 10.2 illustrates the differences in partitioning.

Principle E3. On ecosystem carbon storage

Changes in ecosystem carbon accumulation are determined by:

(1) *The ecosystem's ability to reallocate N between vegetation and soil*
(2) *The flexibility of the N:C ratio in vegetation and in soil*
(3) *The changes in total ecosystem N.*

This is an example where steady state is a useful reference situation

A perturbation of an ecosystem will change the storage and distribution of N within the ecosystem. As a consequence, C storage will also change. These changes can be attributed to three mechanisms. The first is a change in the relative distribution of N between the plant component and the soil component. Since in the soil each kg of N is bound to 15–40 kg C, but in the vegetation to 50–200 kg C (Table 10.2), moving 1 kg of N from soil to plant increases the total amount of carbon bound by 10–185 kg C. Such a redistribution can occur if mineralisation increases, and if this extra mineralisation is taken up by the plants and not lost from the ecosystem. Second, plants have a certain flexibility in their N:C ratios; N fertilisation generally increases and CO_2 fertilisation generally decreases this ratio. Larger changes in N:C can occur if vegetation types change, in particular in a succession between woody and non-woody species. The N:C ratio in the soil can also change. This can happen as a result of changes in the N:C of the litter and thus be driven by changes in the vegetation. It can also change because of changes in N cycling in the soil. The decomposers may change their competitiveness relative to other processes (plant uptake, losses), retaining a smaller or larger share of mineralised N and external inputs of N can be bound to the soil organic matter. Finally, if the total amount of N changes, the amount of carbon also has to change. This principle can also be applied to other changes in partitioning in an ecosystem, e.g. woody biomass vs. active biomass.

How much the three mechanisms contribute can be calculated as follows (from Rastetter *et al.* 1992).

Let C_s, C_v and $C_e = (C_s + C_v)$ be the carbon in the soil, in the vegetation and in the total ecosystem, respectively. N_s, N_v and N_e are the corresponding pools of nitrogen and $\psi_i = C_i/N_i$ ($i = s, v, e$) the corresponding C:N ratios. The addition of a 0 to a subscript indicates an initial value. The change in C storage resulting from a change in N:C ratio, given unchanged amounts of N in vegetation and soil is

$$\Delta C_{e,N:C} = N_{v0}\Delta\psi_v + N_{s0}\Delta\psi_s \qquad (10.4)$$

where the N:C in the subscript indicates that this is a change associated with a change in N:C ratio. Similarly, by assuming that ψ_v and ψ_s do not change and that the ratio N_v/N_s remains constant, we can calculate the carbon storage change from a change in total N storage as

$$\Delta C_{e,N} = \psi_{e0}\Delta N_e \qquad (10.5)$$

Changes in C storage resulting from reallocation within the ecosystem are less straightforward because we need to separate changes resulting from changes in ecosystem N from changes resulting from changes in allocation. We find (see Box 10.1 for derivation)

$$\Delta C_{e,a} = \frac{\Delta N_v N_{s0} - \Delta N_s N_{v0}}{N_{e0}}(\psi_{v0} - \psi_{s0}) \qquad (10.6)$$

We also need to add a fourth term to account for interactions among the three factors. For example, a net gain in N will result in a larger increase in C storage if the C:N ratio of the components of the ecosystem also increases. This term is

$$\Delta C_{e,i} = \Delta N_v \Delta\psi_v + \Delta N_s \Delta\psi_s \qquad (10.7)$$

The total ecosystem carbon change in storage is then

$$\Delta C_e = \Delta C_{e,N:C} + \Delta C_{e,N} + \Delta C_{e,a} + \Delta C_{e,i} \qquad (10.8)$$

Table 10.3 illustrates how a change from a shrubland to a forest redistributes ecosystem nitrogen and alters the ecosystem carbon store. In the shrubland less than 1% of the ecosystem nitrogen is found in the vegetation. In the forest it is still not more than 2%. However, the change in ecosystem type has not changed the ecosystem store of nitrogen; the difference in Table 10.3 is not statistically significant. In spite of small changes in nitrogen distribution the ecosystem carbon store has more than doubled. This increase has two components. First of all, the nitrogen that has been moved from the soil to the vegetation is much more efficient in binding carbon; the trees bind 30 times more carbon per unit of nitrogen than the shrubland soil. Second, the

Table 10.3 Carbon and nitrogen stores in a shrubland and after 35 years of forest (*Pinus halpensis*) in Israel. All values in kg ha^{-1}. Data from Grünzweig *et al.* (2007)

	Forest			Shrubland		
	C	N	C:N	C	N	C:N
Vegetation	17 680	79	225	680	11	65
Soil	40 720	3430	12	23 160	3130	7.4
Ecosystem	58 400	3510	17	23840	3140	7.6

Box 10.1 | Derivation of Equation (10.6)

The changes in C storage resulting from reallocation within the ecosystem are derived in the following way.

Assume that changes in N storage in vegetation and soil are in proportion to the sizes of these variables, i.e.

$$\Delta N_{v,s} = \frac{N_{v0}}{N_{e0}} \Delta N_e \tag{10.9}$$

and

$$\Delta N_{s,s} = \frac{N_{s0}}{N_{e0}} \Delta N_e \tag{10.10}$$

The changes as a result of reallocation are then

$$\Delta N_{v,a} = \Delta N_v - \Delta N_{v,s} = \Delta N_v - \frac{N_{v0}}{N_{e0}} \Delta N_e = \frac{\Delta N_v N_{s0} - \Delta N_s N_{v0}}{N_{e0}} \tag{10.11}$$

and

$$\Delta N_{s,a} = \Delta N_s - \Delta N_{s,s} = \Delta N_s - \frac{N_{s0}}{N_{e0}} \Delta N_e = \frac{\Delta N_s N_{v0} - \Delta N_v N_{s0}}{N_{e0}} = -\Delta N_{v,a} \tag{10.12}$$

The change in carbon storage is obtained by multiplying the changes in N storage with the corresponding C:N ratios, finally giving

$$\Delta C_{e,a} = \frac{\Delta N_v N_{s0} - \Delta N_s N_{v0}}{N_{e0}} (\psi_{v0} - \psi_{s0}) \tag{10.13}$$

changes in litter properties have increased the amount of carbon per unit of nitrogen by over 60%. Given that trees in forests may contain around 10% of the ecosystem nitrogen (see Figure 9.22) one should expect that with time this ecosystem will continue to redistribute nitrogen and still increase its carbon store.

FURTHER READING

Dodds, W.K. 2009. *Laws, Theories, and Patterns in Ecology*. Berkley, CA: University of California Press.

Section III

Ecosystem dynamics at different time scales

Two major features of the terrestrial ecosystems have been dealt with so far, structure and function. A third major feature is dynamics, development and changes over time, and also the reaction of the ecosystems to perturbations – natural or man-made. It is a question of the stability of ecosystems and their ability to accommodate changes. Changes occur on different temporal and spatial scales. There are changes at the global scale, which have occurred since the Earth's early history, as well as those occurring in recent times. The very early history of the Earth has a flavour of 'science fiction' and today we have the issue of 'climate change', which is experienced as dramatic and to some extent uncertain.

We will deal with historical changes as well as more recent changes of terrestrial ecosystems, with a focus on northern areas. To a great extent the dynamics of terrestrial ecosystems are a question of the dynamics of vegetation, but we will show that there is also a question of changes in other parts of the ecosystem and their function.

Ecosystem changes occur at many different temporal scales. Some of these scales are entirely set by external forces, but others are due to the response times of the ecosystem components. Dynamics in ecosystems can also be driven by large catastrophic events like fires and wind.

The clear-felling of a forest takes less than a year and the responses in terms of a new forest succession may take more than a century. Climate fluctuations occur on both short and medium- to long-term time scales. The development of a new soil type combined with changes in vegetation and animal communities will require a time span of 1000 to 10 000 years. In this time perspective we should also expect changes in the genetic speciation of biota. Over a longer time perspective we have more drastic changes resulting from, for example, plate tectonics.

We can identify five different time scales with related dominating driving mechanisms, rates of change and changing factors, which will be dealt with in Chapters 11–13:

Time scale	Dominating driving mechanism	Rate of change	Changing factors
Tectonic	Plate tectonics, volcanic activity	>Millions of years	Climate, migration patterns
Orbital	Changes in Earth's orbit around Sun	100 000s to 1000s of years	Climate, glacial–interglacial cycles, ecosystem development
Millennial	Solar variability, changes in ocean circulation patterns, biotic and natural site factors, man-made disturbances	1000s to <100s of years	Climate, ecosystem development, land use, other human activities
Centennial-Decadal	Sun-spot activity, changes in ocean circulatory patterns, biotic and natural site factors, man-made disturbances	100s to <10s of years	Climate, land use, ecosystem development, other human activities
Annual	Solar radiation	Between- and within-year variation	Temperature, precipitation

Chapter 11

Tectonic to orbital changes

The long-term development of Earth is a combination of physical and biological processes. The early production of atmospheric gases, tectonic drift and slow changes in the position of the Earth relative to the Sun are major physical forces. Production of oxygen and consumption of carbon dioxide are major biological forces.

Changes during the development of the biosphere

The Earth is approximately 5 milliard (5×10^9) years old and the development on Earth can be described by a 'biogeological clock' (Figure 11.1). The first atmosphere around the Earth is assumed to have been formed when the planet started to cool off. Earlier it was too hot for gases to be retained around the Earth. The first atmosphere was formed from volcanic outgassing from the Earth's interior and consisted probably of helium, hydrogen, ammonia and methane. Later, water vapour, carbon dioxide, nitrogen and sulfur gases became the dominant gases. The water vapour together with particles (condensation nuclei) led to cloud formation and rain, forming rivers, lakes and filling the oceans. The water bodies became sinks for carbon dioxide, as they are today, and through biological, chemical and physical processes sedimentary rocks were formed. As nitrogen is not very chemically active it accumulated in the atmosphere. The new atmosphere with clouds and water vapour regulated the energy balance of the Earth and thus became an important climatic regulator.

Life, which appeared around 3.8 milliard years ago or perhaps even earlier (Des Marais 2000), has played an important role in the development of the atmosphere. Here life means that the first living organisms capable of performing processes leading to energy fixation in organic matter appeared, in other words photosynthesis. The earliest photosynthesis occurred without the production of oxygen.

About 2.8 milliard years ago phototrophic bacteria producing oxygen as a by-product of photosynthesis appeared. With the occurrence of true phototrophic bacteria, oxygen began to be produced in large quantities. The prerequisites for higher life were now present. However, iron oxide formation and reaction with gases in the atmosphere consumed most of the oxygen produced such that atmospheric oxygen concentration was absent until about 2 milliard years ago,

The early environment was a result of chemical reactions

Figure 11.1 The biogeological clock indicated in milliard (10^9) years. From Des Marais (2000), reprinted with kind permission from the American Association for the Advancement of Science.

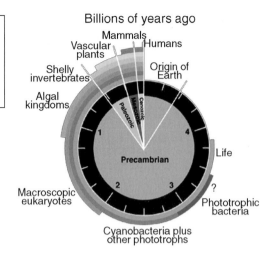

Figure 11.2 Changes over tectonic time scale in atmospheric CO_2. The different lines represent different ways of estimating historical atmospheric CO_2 concentrations. The shaded area to the right is expanded in Figure 11.4. From IPCC (2007) with kind permission from Cambridge University Press.

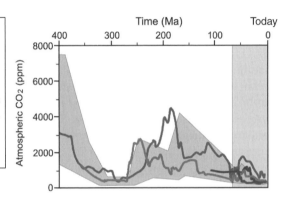

when a slow increase started. Around 500 million years ago, when terrestrial plants began to appear, there was a jump in the atmospheric oxygen concentration to present levels. This increase coincided with a dramatic decline in atmospheric carbon dioxide (see Figure 11.2).

An alternative way of presenting the geological and biological development is seen in the more conventional geological time scale with eras, periods, epochs and their time domain (Figure 11.3). In the diagram some important events in the development of plants are given as well the development of major plant groups.

At 2 milliard years ago macroscopic eukaryotes appeared (organisms with their genetic material within a cell nuclei separated from the cytoplasm by membranes). Evolution continued with the occurrence of algae. In the beginning of the Palaeozoicum (225–570 million years ago) invertebrates with a protective structure existed. The vascular plants also appeared. In the Mesozoicum (65–225 million years ago) mammals appeared and in the Cenozoicum (from 65 million years ago and on), as a latecomer, Man entered the scene.

During the development of the Earth several environmental changes have occurred. These changes have been caused by shifts in

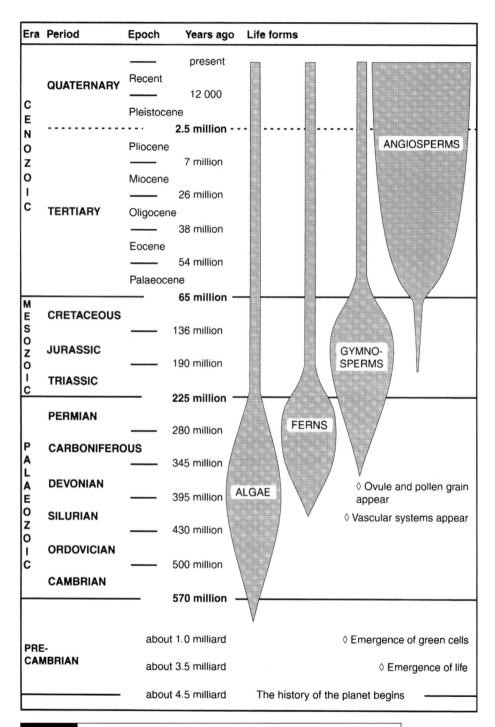

Era	Period	Epoch	Years ago	Life forms

CENOZOIC
QUATERNARY — Recent — present, 12 000
Pleistocene — 2.5 million
TERTIARY — Pliocene — 7 million
Miocene — 26 million
Oligocene — 38 million
Eocene — 54 million
Palaeocene — 65 million

MESOZOIC
CRETACEOUS — 136 million
JURASSIC — 190 million
TRIASSIC — 225 million

PALAEOZOIC
PERMIAN — 280 million
CARBONIFEROUS — 345 million
DEVONIAN — 395 million
SILURIAN — 430 million
ORDOVICIAN — 500 million
CAMBRIAN — 570 million

ANGIOSPERMS

GYMNO-SPERMS

FERNS

ALGAE

◊ Ovule and pollen grain appear
◊ Vascular systems appear

PRE-CAMBRIAN
about 1.0 milliard — ◊ Emergence of green cells
about 3.5 milliard — ◊ Emergence of life
about 4.5 milliard — The history of the planet begins

Figure 11.3 The geological time scale and development of major plant groups.
From Andersson & Lhoir (2005) with kind permission from Elsevier.

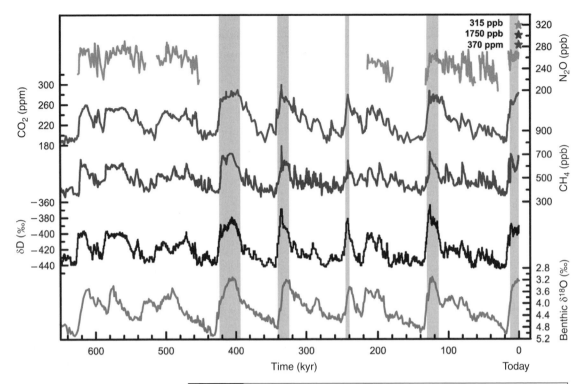

Figure 11.4 Changes over orbital time scale in δD (second from bottom, a proxy for local temperature), atmospheric CH_4 (third from bottom), atmospheric CO_2 (fourth from bottom) and atmospheric N_2O (top) derived from air trapped in ice cores from Antarctica. Changes in benthic $\delta^{18}O$ (bottom) are a proxy for global ice volume fluctuations with downward trends reflecting increasing ice volumes on land. Stars indicate atmospheric values in 2000. The shading indicates interglacial warm periods. Horizontal scale in kyr. Note that the entire x-axis in this figure is less than one unit on the x-axis in Figure 11.2. From IPCC (2007) with kind permission from Cambridge University Press.

the positions of the continents over time – continental drift. The planetary position of the Earth in relation to the Sun is constantly changing, with accompanying changes in light and temperature. The changes occur on three different time scales (*Milankovitch cycles*): the ellipticity of the Earth's orbit (eccentricity) changes with a period of 100 000 years; the angle of the Earth's axis relative to the plane of orbit (tilt) changes with a period of 41 000 years; the orientation of the Earth's axis of rotation (precession) changes with a period of 23 000 years. The consequences of these cycles are that the strength of the seasonality varies and that the insolation of the northern and southern hemispheres vary relative to each other. Since the two hemispheres differ in their proportions of land and sea, this modifies the global climate. In addition, solar radiation has increased by around 30% since the birth of the Sun.

The long-term development of atmospheric CO_2 from the Devonian to the Tertiary is shown in Figure 11.2. The more recent changes, in the last 600 000 years, in atmospheric CO_2 and Earth surface temperature associated with orbital changes are shown in Figure 11.4.

(a)

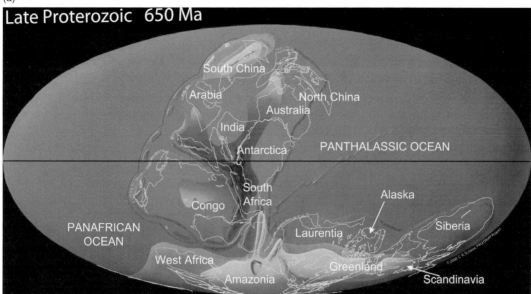

(b)

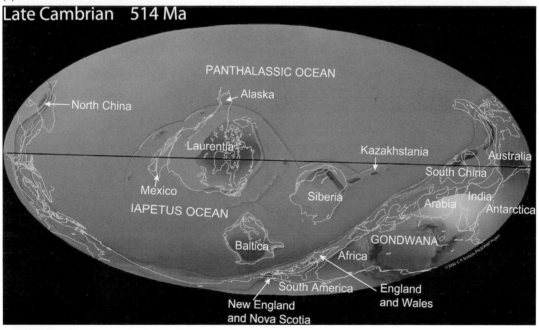

Figure 11.5 The drift of the continents – from the Precambrian (Late Protoerozoic), Palaeozoic, Mesozoic and Cenozoic eras to the present time (a) as well as a projection 50 million years into the future. Dark shaded areas indicate land during the eras and thin lines present land areas. Note that during the last glacial maximum there were land connections between several of today's islands in Southeast Asia. From Scotese (2001) (full colour maps, www.scotese.com).

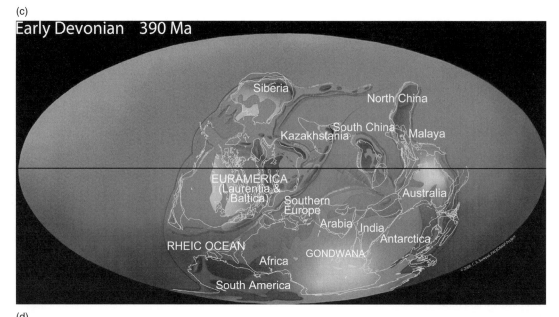

(c)
Early Devonian 390 Ma

(d)
Late Permian 255 Ma

Figure 11.5	(cont.)

Movements of the continents, the continental drift, shaped the Earth as we know it

In early geologic times continental land masses collided and formed supercontinents. During the Precambrian era, about 1.1 billion years ago, a supercontinent, Rodina, was assembled. Its actual size is difficult to state as clear evidence is lacking. The major land masses were concentrated around the poles, and ice ages were common (Figure 11.5a). During the Cambrian period North America, Laurentia, moved northwards towards the equator. The continent was

(e)

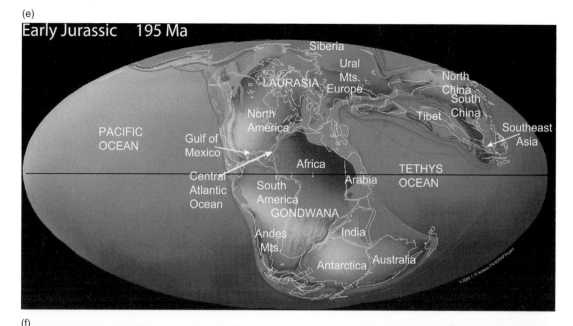

(f)

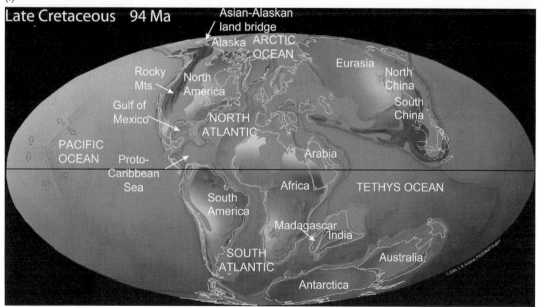

Figure 11.5 *(cont.)*

flooded by a tropical, shallow sea. At the South Pole a large continent, Gondwana, existed – a remnant of the earlier Rodina continent (Figure 11.5b).

During the Devonian period, 390 million years ago, the land masses of Gondwana and Euamerica approached each other, but remained separated by water (Figure 11.5c). The two continents collided and formed another new supercontinent Pangea, 255 million

(g)

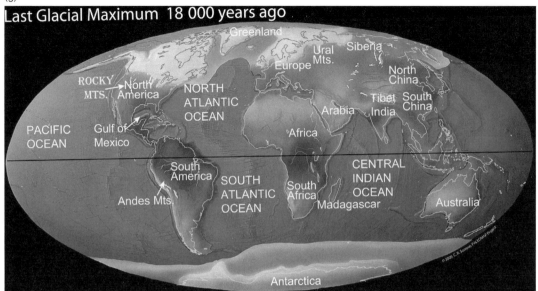

(h)

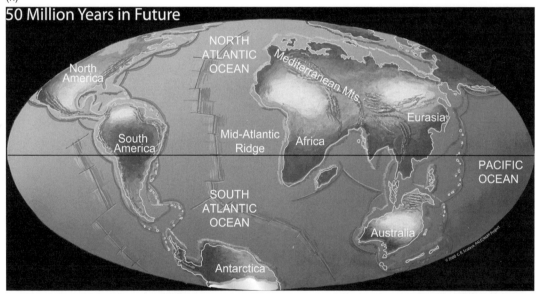

Figure 11.5 (*cont.*)

years ago, in the Permian period (Figure 11.5d). As a result of the collision, mountain ranges were formed. The mountains created rain shadows and parts of the continents had desert conditions.

Pangea broke apart 195 million years ago during the Jura period (Figure 11.5e) and its northern part, Laurasia, moved northwards. Continent-like islands were formed, separated by seas. The populations of species with an earlier wide distribution became isolated and reduced. Towards the end of the Mezosoic era, new species evolved. During the Cretaceous period 95 million years ago the continents took their present shapes and positions, although Antarctica, Australia and India were still close to Africa (Figure 11.5f). The present layout is shown for the situation 18 000 years ago, during the Pleistocene, when the northern hemisphere and the Antarctic were covered by inland ice sheets (Figure 11.5g).

Continental drift will also continue in the future. From the present directions of movement of the continental plates we can make an educated guess of what may happen (Figure 11.5h). The Atlantic and the Indian oceans will continue to widen. North America will move anti-clockwise and Eurasia clockwise. Africa will collide with Europe and the Mediterranean Sea will be replaced by a new mountain range. Australia is coming closer to India. It is likely that the movement with time will go in the direction of the formation of a new 'Pangea supercontinent'!

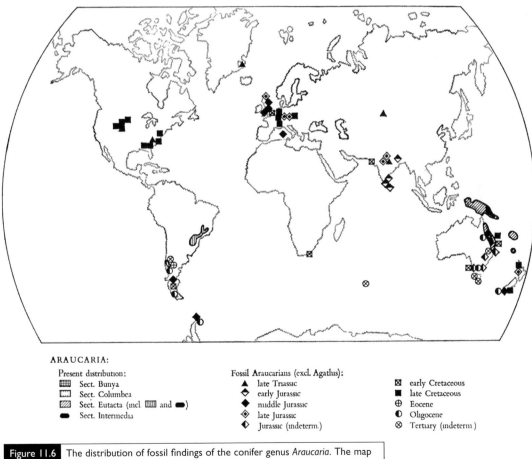

ARAUCARIA:

Present distribution:
▦ Sect. Bunya
▭ Sect. Columbea
▨ Sect. Eutacta (incl. ▦ and ⬤)
⬤ Sect. Intermedia

Fossil Araucarians (excl. Agathis):
▲ late Triassic
◆ early Jurassic
◆ middle Jurassic
◈ late Jurassic
◈ Jurassic (indeterm.)

⊠ early Cretaceous
■ late Cretaceous
⊕ Eocene
◑ Oligocene
⊗ Tertiary (indeterm.)

Figure 11.6 The distribution of fossil findings of the conifer genus *Araucaria*. The map illustrates the historical links between South America, Antarctic, South Africa and Australia. It also shows that there have been earlier links to other areas. From: Florin (1964).

Similarities of plant fossils between continents verify earlier links

It is intriguing to see how the contours of the continents fit together, e.g. South America and Africa, and how they link to the Antarctic. It is further fascinating that these links can be verified by the distribution of fossil plants, such as the conifer genus *Araucaria* occurring in South America, South Africa, Australia and even on the Antarctic continent (Figure 11.6).

FURTHER READING

Fredén, C. (ed.) 1994. *Geology. National Atlas of Sweden*. Stockholm: SNA Publishing.

Chapter 12

Millennial to centennial or postglacial changes

As a result of the retreat of the last glaciation, the last 20 000 years have involved dramatic changes in landscapes. Using Sweden as an example, we describe the development of these changes, at first driven only by the climate, but later more and more under the influence of humans, in particular through agriculture and forestry.

Postglacial development

We will now turn to the changes in more recent times. As an example we take the development of terrestrial ecosystems in south Sweden. But first some notes on driving forces – changes in climate with glaciations. During the geologic development of the Earth there have been a number of glaciations, with interglacial periods in between (Figure 11.4). The last glaciation extended from approximately 100 000 years ago to 10 000 years ago, with a maximum 20 000 years ago. During this period, massive ice fields covered large parts of the continents. At its maximum extent, the Weichselian Ice Sheet covered eastern Denmark, Finland, Norway, Sweden and the Baltic states, as well as northern Germany, northern Poland and western Russia. The Laurentide Ice Sheet covered Canada and the northern United States, and the Patagonian Ice Sheet southern Chile and Argentina. The ice started to leave south Sweden 17 000 years ago and the whole country was free from inland ice approximately 7000 years ago.

Information on the development of terrestrial ecosystems since the last glaciation is obtained from analyses of lake sediments and peat with their contents of pollen, fruits and other plant remains. The conditions and development of ecosystems after the last glaciation in south Sweden, as well as elsewhere, attract great interest. We have chosen to follow two main sources: Birks (1986) and Berglund *et al.* (2007). The first gives a review of late-quaternary biotic changes in terrestrial and lake environments, in particular north-west Europe. The second summarises changes in vegetation over 17 000 years in the southernmost province of Sweden, Scania (Skåne).

Ecological development during glacial and interglacial periods can in principle be described in five major phases (Figure 12.1), mainly governed by the climate, as follows:

Ecosystems change with changing climate

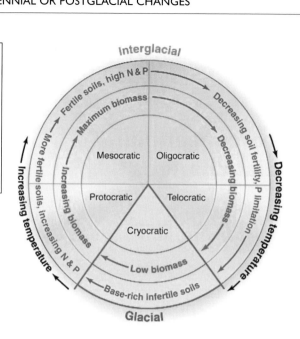

Figure 12.1 Principle phases of ecosystem development – vegetation and soil types – during a glacial and interglacial cycle adapted to south Sweden from Late glacial and Postglacial times to present day. From Birks & Birks (2004) with kind permission from the American Association for the Advancement of Science.

1. *Cryocratic phase* during Older Dryas and Bölling times up to 14 000 BP

The climate is cold, glacial and considered to be dry and continental. The vegetation is open with sparse assemblages of arctic-alpine, steppe and ruderal herbs growing on arctic, base-rich mineral soils, often disturbed by frost and other soil movements.

2. *Protocratic or pioneer phase* during Alleröd and Preboreal times 14 000–10 000 BP

The interglacial phase starts with increasing temperature. Base-demanding and shade-intolerant herbs, shrubs and trees immigrate and expand rapidly to form species-rich grasslands, scrubs and open woodlands on unleached, fertile soils low in humus. Species and populations are of different origins and expand rapidly, even speciation occurs. Competition is generally low; although light and nutrients are abundant, the space is still not fully occupied.

3. *Mesocratic phase* during Boreal, Atlantic and Sub-boreal times 10 000–2500 BP

The climate can be the same as in the previous phase or warmer. This phase is characterised by temperate deciduous forests growing on fertile brown forest soils (alfisols). With the development of dense vegetation cover, shading and competition for light increases. Shade-intolerant species are rare or absent due to competition and loss of habitat. The development of the ecosystems can be seen as a response to climatic changes, as well as delayed immigration. The first human impacts on ecosystems can be seen.

4. *Oligocratic phase* during Sub-atlantic times 2500–1500 BP

This phase starts with decreasing temperature and also increased humidity. The previous dense and biomass-rich forests open up and the vegetation becomes dominated by coniferous forests, dwarf-shrub heaths and bogs. The major soil type changes into nutrient-poor podsols (spodosols).

5. *Teleocratic phase* from 1500 BP to the present day

This phase has a still colder climate and the vegetation becomes more open. The soils are changing independently of climate due to bio-logical acidification and leaching. Human impacts on ecosystems become still more evident. With time a new glacial phase will develop as the climate becomes colder – a new cryocratic phase will follow.

We will now describe the development of ecosystems in more detail for south Sweden (Figure 12.2) in terms of the general development of ecosystems, climate and the impact of humans, with associated acidification. Chronozones and archeological chronology are also indicated.

Before 15 000 BP the area was an arctic desert or tundra with scattered vegetation of lichens, mosses and dwarf-shrubs, such as *Salix polaris*, as well as a few herb species, such as *Minurtia*, *Papaver* and *Saxifraga*. Around 15 000 BP, the start of the Bölling time, the summers became warmer. The arctic tundra developed into a sub-arctic steppe-tundra with a rich flora, a mixture of sub-arctic-mountain plants and continental steppe species of a south-eastern origin. There were also dwarf-shrubs and shrubs such as *Salix* spp., *Juniperus communis*, *Betula nana* and *Hippophaë rhamnoides* – the latter today a plant growing on newly exposed seashores. During a short period with a colder climate around 14 000 BP this vegetation was forced back.

Then follows a warmer period, the Alleröd, 14 000–12 800 BP, when a shrub-forest tundra developed and the first trees invaded: birch (*Betula*), related to our present mountain birch, rowan (*Sorbus aucuparia*), aspen (*Populus tremula*) and even pine (*Pinus sylvstris*) in the southernmost parts. Towards the end of the period *Empetrum*-heaths were common, indicating more stable soils with a continuous humus layer. Around 12 800 BP it again became colder, the Younger Dryas. The shrub-forest tundra regressed into a sub-arctic tundra with a mosaic of steppe tundra and dwaf-shrub tundra. Towards the second half of the period the landscape was dominated by steppe and dwarf-shrub tundra with *Empetrum nigrum*, *Lycopodium* spp., *Betula nana, Salix*-shrubs and scattered birch trees. A fern, *Gymnocarpium dryopteris*, was common on heathlands in northern Scania. The transition of tundra to forests (11 700–11 500 BP) was characterised by a widespread occurrence of *Junipers*, before the birch forest took over.

Plant remains in lakes and mires bear witness of human activities

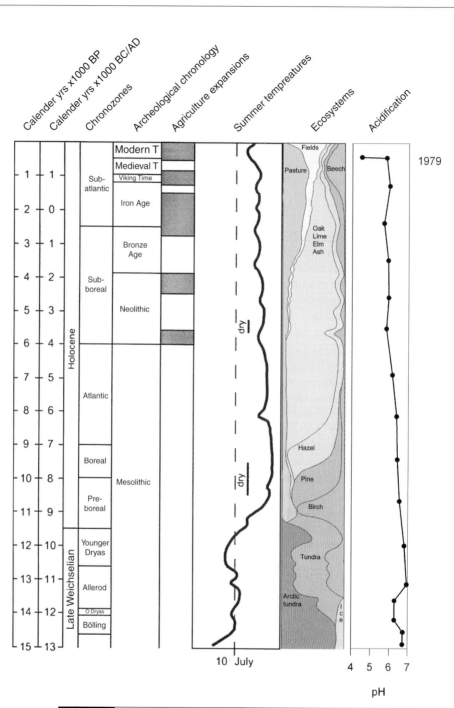

Figure 12.2 Late- and Postglacial development of southern Swedish terrestrial ecosystems in relation to climate (given as mean July temperature, the temperature range in the figure is approximately 10–15°C). Acidification is expressed as lake acidification deduced from analysis of sub-fossil diatoms in sediments, Lake Gårdsjön, west Sweden. Modified from Anonymous (1982), Liljegren (1999) and Berglund et al. (2008). See also colour plate section.

Many of the species in the steppe tundra are today found as relicts in lime-stone areas (Alvar) on the islands of Öland and Gotland, and some other limestone areas. There was a rich variation of site conditions with regard to moisture, nutrients, light and soil movement. Because of frost processes and solifluction the soils were unstable, favouring *r*-selected species. Examples of species found in arctic and sub-arctic areas today are: *Dryas octopetala*, *Saxifraga* species, such as *oppositifolia*, *Silene acaulis*, *Astragalus alpinus* and *Oxyria digyna*. Species related to continental steppe plants with a south-eastern distribution are: *Helianthemum oelandicum* and *H. nummularium*, *Gypsophila fastigiata*, *Oxytropis campestris*, *Artemisia* and *Chenopodium* species. The latter species are today considered weeds along with *Centaurea cyanus* and *Plantago major*. Many of these plants are also nitrogen-fixers, which promoted their existence and the development of the soil.

Around 11 500 BP forests started to dominate, as a result of a rapid increase in summer temperatures of 5–6 °C within a century. Birch, aspen and pine were the main components. 500 years later hazel (*Corylus avellana*) and elm (*Ulmus glabra*) came on the scene (Figure 12.2 and 12.3). Moist forests with birch and willow (*Salix* spp.) were, around 9000 BP, replaced by alder (*Alnus glutinosa*). The landscape had a great variation in site conditions, which, together with a warm climate, favoured the entrance of southern species such as ivy (*Hedera helix*), great fen sedge (*Cladium mariscus*) and royal fern (*Osmuna regalis*) to the area. The soils were rich in bases, even in areas with non-calcareous bedrock.

The warmth-demanding, rich deciduous forests dominated during the period 9000–6000 BP. Elm met competition from oak (*Quercus robur*) and small-leaved lime (*Tilia cordata*), and, from 7 500 BP, also ash (*Fraxinus excelsior*). Even more warmth-demanding species occurred, such as *Tilia platyphyllos* and *Taxus baccata*, as well as *Ilex aquifolium* – today a very rare species in south Sweden. Different soil conditions favoured different trees and other species. Ash and elm dominated on heavy clay soils and oak and limes on lighter, sandier soils.

Around 6000 BP the climate started to be unstable, with fluctuating summer temperatures and precipitation. Now the first action of humans was seen – the 'landnam' – with clearings, small-scale cultivation and grazing land combined with settlements. There was a decrease in elm, ash and limes. Oak and hazel were favoured by a more open landscape. Around 5000 BP hornbeam (*Carpinus betulus*) and beech (*Fagus sylvatica*) were newcomers, with a later expansion. A more open landscape appeared. Several species favoured by cultivation were found: *Rumex acetosa* and *acetosella*, *Plantago lanceolata*, *Artemisia absinthium* and *Ceralia*.

Around 3000 years BP a dramatic change towards a still more open landscape occurred. Forests retreated and elm, lime, ash and hazel decreased, while birch expanded. The two beech species increased around 2000–1500 BP. The open landscape increased further during the Viking age (800–1100 AC). The number of tree species gradually decreased. The beech and oak forests seen today in south Sweden have their origin from this time. During the last 300–400 years Norway spruce (*Picea abies*)

KRAGEHOLMSSJÖN

Analyst: Marie-José Gaillard

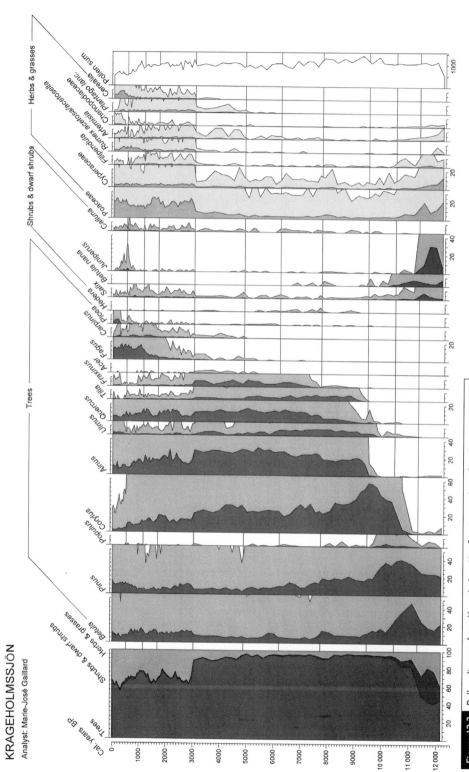

Figure 12.3 Pollen diagram from Krageholmssjön, Scania, southern Sweden showing the development of vegetation from 13 000 years before present (BP) to the present day for species representing forests (trees and shrubs), open land (dwarf shrubs, herbs and grasses) and areas of cultivation (cerealia). For species with two colours – the left part indicates % and right part ‰, i.e. magnified 10 times. From Berglund et al. (2008) with kind permission from Springer Science + Business Media. See also colour plate section.

colonised south Sweden, a process that has, since the second half of the nineteenth century, been favoured by plantations of the species.

Humans, climate and ecosystems

There has been a strong relationship between climate and humans. This can be seen in the way that humans have adapted to more severe climate conditions, as well as being favoured by more benign climatic conditions in the search for resources for survival. As can be seen in the diagrams (Figures 12.2–12.5) the impacts of human activities and climatic changes on landscape development have been concentrated to seven periods (Berglund 2003):

Stage 1 In early Neolithic times (5900 BP) agriculture was introduced and caused a decline in the occurrence of elm in the pollen diagrams. This is also called the 'landnam' period.

Stage 2 Around 5500 BP a short wet and cool period occurred, followed by a 300-year dry period and then a regeneration phase, with concentration of agriculture regionally and locally.

Stage 3 At the end of the Middle Neolithicum, 4500 BP, agriculture expanded around settlements, as well as in more marginal areas. The climate was cool and wet.

Stage 4 At the beginning of the Bronze Age (3800 BP) agriculture with the use of pasture increased, with deforestation and expansion of heathland. Climate changed from continental to oceanic.

Stage 5 During the late Bronze Age, 3000–2800 BP, a period with complex climatic changes followed. Agriculture expanded again, with widespread deforestation as a result.

Stage 6 A period around 1500 BP with rapid decrease in temperature followed. Agriculture retreated and forest increased again during the Late Iron Age. This was the time of migration and also the fall of the Roman Empire.

Stage 7 During the Viking age of the Late Iron Age, 1100 BP, the climate improved again, leading to increased agricultural activities.

We can also add an eighth stage:

Stage 8 Around 600 BP the climate became cool and moist – the Little Ice Age – with detrimental consequences for agriculture. This is well documented, both in geological archives and historical documents.

A result of the changes in vegetation and soils – the ecosystem – as responses to the changing climate and human actions changes in the water quality in watersheds or catchments can be detected. The historical acidification of the water in a small west Swedish clear-water, oligotrophic, lake is shown in Figure 12.2. This lake is surrounded by acid bedrock covered by thin acid soil layers with a small buffer capacity. The water pH has been deduced from sub-fossil diatoms in the lake sediments, which also have been dated. Diatoms are organisms with a low evolution rate and their life requirements are considered not to have changed over time. The pH curve demonstrates the natural acidification of the environment caused by increased biomass growth and decay of organic matter, with leaching of organic acids as well as bases into the lake. The pH declines to approximately 5.5 up to the 1960s when a drastic drop down to 4.5 takes place as a result of the deposition of air-borne pollutants such as sulfur and nitrogen. Renberg *et al.* (2009) described these changes as natural acidification and air pollution-induced acidification, respectively. Through improved diatom analyses Renberg *et al.* also identified a stage with an increase in pH (culturally induced pH increase) for a number of other west Swedish clear-water lakes occurring 2000–1000 BP. This is explained by human activities with clearing, burning with shifting cultivation, grazing leading to increased leaching of bases and decreased transport of organic acids to the lakes.

How did the species and the ecosystems respond to the rapid changes in the environment just described? Theoretically, on a local and region level we can consider three possibilities:

- Decreases and increases in rates of population turnover leading to changes in species richness, abundance and, in extreme cases, extinctions
- Speciation – genetic adaptation to changes in the environment
- Changes in distribution of species.

The rate of change in species composition was analysed by Bradshaw & Lindbladh (2005) through the regional spread of beech and Norway spruce in southern Scandinavia. They used both the information in conventional pollen diagrams, with sampling in lake sediments or peat bogs representing more regional conditions (Figure 12.4), and records of pollen analysis from samples taken in small hollows as a complement, giving more local conditions. The conventional pollen analysis with samples from lake sediments, represents pollen which has long distance transport. To represent local conditions a correction of the regional pollen sedimentation needs to be done (see Gaillard *et al.* 2008) as different species have different degrees of production of pollens, as well as different degrees of dispersal.

The rate of change from the year 4000 to the present time is demonstrated in Figure 12.4. Based on the occurrence of *Ceralia* pollen in the analysed samples, analyses of the samples from the small hollows showed that the spread of beech was favoured by human activities, but the spread of spruce was more a response to a suitable climate.

Centennial to recent changes

Human impact has accelerated over the last 200 years

Changes during the last three to four centuries can be followed in archive materials and available maps. This is well demonstrated for forest development in the province of Halland, south-west Sweden from an investigation by Malmström (1939) and current land-use information (Figure 12.5). With an increasing population

No. years before present

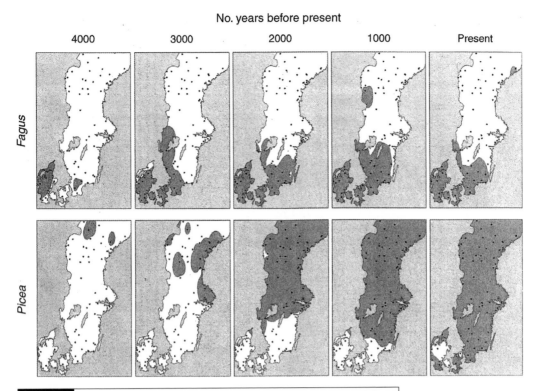

Figure 12.4 South Scandinavian distribution (dark grey shading) of *Picea abies* and *Fagus sylvatica* reconstructed from regional pollen data for the last 4000 years. The points show the location of sites used to construct the distribution. From Bradshaw & Lindbladh (2005) with kind permission from the Ecological Society of America.

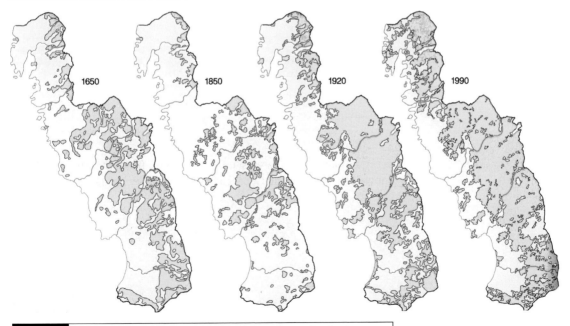

Figure 12.5 Forests (shaded) in the province of Halland, south-west Sweden from 1650–1990. From National Atlas of Sweden/The Forests (www.sna.se), after Carl Malmström (National Atlas of Sweden 1990).

and improved agricultural technology between 1650 and 1850 the demand for and possibility to use the forests and the heathlands for producing fodder and grazing increased. The heaths were regularly burnt to maintain good grazing quality, but with decreased soil fertility as a consequence. The maps show that the landscape had reached a maximum degree of openness in 1850 when the forest area had decreased to a minimum. The need to supply the growing sawmill industry with timber led in 1905 to a law enforcing reforestation in Sweden. The resulting plantations of Norway spruce caused drastic changes in the landscape – a darker landscape (Blennow & Hammarlund 1993).

Chapter 13

Centennial to annual changes

Wind, fire and herbivory are three major forces that alter the dynamics of ecosystems by modifying their element cycles and regulating ecosystem development, in particular returning mature ecosystems to earlier development stages.

Wind

Wind as an ecological factor acts in two ways. At moderate to low speed it has an indirect action by affecting the intensity of, for example, physiological processes. For plants, subtle winds, for example, modify the temperature of plants and other organisms. Transpiration can be increased, as well as carbon dioxide transport to plants, which stimulates photosynthesis (Chapter 5). At higher wind speeds the mechanical impact on the ecosystem is of particular interest for the dynamics of the ecosystem.

Wind affects physiological processes and shapes vegetation structure

Disturbances are a major factor influencing the species composition of ecosystems – wind is no exception (Pickett & White 1985). Extremely high wind speeds usually occur on sea coasts and in mountains. Lowlands may also experience extreme situations or catastrophic events such as tornados and hurricanes. Forests close to the coast in wind-exposed situations are always suppressed and further inland the height increases. The trees lean in the prevailing wind direction. The wind also transports salt, which is deposited on the leaves and has a negative effect on the vegetation. In mountains the wind, together with temperature and snow cover, determines the level of the tree limit.

Catastrophic wind events lead to windbreak and windthrow. These are associated with up-rooting and creation of bare soil surfaces suitable for colonisation of plants. Shade-tolerant and early successional species are then favoured (Loucks 1970, Bormann & Likens 1979). It was realised very early that in the North American temperate deciduous forests wind was an important factor for their dynamics (Smith 1946, Stearns 1949), such that forest regeneration mainly occurred in small gaps created when large trees were overthrown by wind. This is also valid in other parts of the world. Simplistically, ecosystems in wind-disturbed areas return to an earlier successional stage. Today we understand that the frequent, non-catastrophic wind events are important for ecosystem development, which so far is not fully understood. There is a variation in resistance to disturbance among species, which will be of importance for the final changes at local and landscape levels (Papaik & Canham 2006). Windthrows create gaps in the forest, which increase light and offer available nutrients to the remaining trees, as well as other plants. With time fallen trees become a suitable seedbed substrate for small-seeded species. This is an example of the importance of old coarse woody debris as a factor in maintaining biodiversity. The long-distance wind transport of seeds is also of importance.

Thus, these non-catastrophic events create gaps or patches in ecosystems. This phenomenon has been of interest for a long time (Shugart 2002). Modelling of patch or gap dynamics is an active branch of present ecosystem dynamics.

Fire

Fire regulates species composition and affects mineral cycling

Fire, like wind, is a natural disturbance factor. Certain ecosystems require fires for their survival, such as the boreal pine forests both in North America and Eurasia. Other examples are the prairies in North America and steppes in Asia, as well as tropical grasslands – savannas. Natural fires are also a prerequisite for the regeneration of some forests or tree species (Weber & van Cleve 2005), for example, jack pine (*Pinus banksiana*) and giant sequoia (*Seequoiadendron giganteum*), which have big and hard serotinous cones (requiring heat to open in order to release their seeds). These species generally also have a thick fire-resistant bark on the stems. Dense *Eucalyptus* forests in Australia and Tasmania will not regenerate without fire.

Most of the fires in Nature are today caused by Man. Fires caused by lightning are less frequent; recent data for the Canadian boreal forests suggest that they constitute 35% (Weber & Stocks 1998). However, these fires were responsible for 85% of the total burnt area and occurred mostly in remote areas where few resources for fire prevention are available. In areas close to urban regions the fires tend to be more limited in severity, as fire prevention is more accessible.

The effects of fires at the ecosystem level will vary. In a forest, the fire can be restricted to the litter layer, which may be more or less burnt off with few consequences for the mineral soil. The fire may be spread as a 'crown fire', which is detrimental to the tree canopy, usually with death as a consequence. In cases of peat soils there may be a slow-burning 'glowing fire' without flames.

After a fire, a regeneration or succession phase follows, which will vary in length depending on the geographic situation. We illustrate this with two examples. First, a tropical one – the rain forest in San Carlos, Venezuela (Figure 4.10 part 9) – where phosphorous has been found to be the limiting element. This rain forest has been used by native Indian populations for shifting cultivation for centuries. After clear-felling and burning of a forest area, crops were cultivated. Charcoal remains are commonly found in the soil. The available nutrient capital was exploited by the crop, the harvest decreased and the area was abandoned after 5 to 10 years. Fast-growing species, less nutrient-demanding than crop plants, then rapidly invaded the abandoned fields. After some years the production level in the new secondary forest could even be higher than in the native forest. The development of the ensuing succession is determined by the extent to which the organic matter in the soil can be protected and renewed in order to store mineral nutrients. Where there is a limited negative impact the development leads to a stage resembling the original forest. A steady-state condition, where nutrients are bound in the biomass and soil, leads again to a decreased production level corresponding to the native forest. This may take 100–200 years.

The boreal case is taken from an investigation of the effects of fires in northernmost Sweden, Muddus National Park (Uggla 1958). It is an area with a low impact by Man. The fire history has been studied by dating fire scares on Scots pine trees by using annual ring analysis. There have been a number of fires in the area caused by natural factors, such as lightning, but also more recent ones caused by Man. The succession occurring after the fire depends on a number of factors, such as the intensity of the fire and the availability of seeds or diaspores for germination and colonisation. Regeneration can also occur vegetatively from surviving shrubs and other plants.

Species present immediately after a fire have in general colonised the burnt area from outside via wind-spread diaspores. Others may have survived in the soil. As for trees, Scots pine is more resistant to fire than other trees. Birch is a fast coloniser and is spread by wind, making it successful in the start. However, the young, low-stature, Scots pine and the birch are grazed by moose (*Alces alces*) as well as reindeer (*Rangifer tarandus*), delaying the recovery of the vegetation. Compared to the tropical case the successional development towards a 'climax' state should be slower, depending on the climatic conditions.

Fire is used as a management tool for regeneration of forests. An example from north Sweden (Uggla 1957) shows that a weak fire will have a positive effect on nutrient availability and seedling establishment. If only a part of the humus layer is burnt off and the ashes remain in the top soil, mineral nutrients are then adsorbed on the remaining humus and available to the seedlings. Nitrogen mineralisation is increased. The activities of soil organisms are stimulated by the die-off of roots leading to increased availability of organic as well as mineral nutrients ('azzard effect' – Romell 1935).

In general, fire has a more violent effect on the dynamics of nutrients than wind. Fire may destroy the aboveground biomass and then reduce the primary productivity to zero (Bormann & Likens 1979). Fire also leads to a loss of nutrients by volatilisation (Table 13.1). Since different elements are differentially lost with fires, the fire will alter the relative availability of elements. A comparison of Table 13.1 and Table 6.4 indicates that fire might enhance nitrogen limitation, but calcium and manganese losses could be more severe in this particular case. If the humus layer is not burnt off completely,

Table 13.1 | Nutrient losses during low-intensity prescribed burns in three Australian sub-alpine eucalypt forests. Values are the highest and lowest observed. The fraction lost is the percentage of the amount in the litter and understory. The proportion lost is calculated from the average of the highest and lowest values. From Raison *et al.* (1985)

Element	N	P	K	Ca	Mg	Mn	B
Loss (kg ha^{-1})	74–109	1.96–3.04	12.1–21.0	18.7–29.7	4.5–9.7	1.6–4.3	0.08–0.12
Fraction lost (%)	54–75	37–50	43–66	31–34	25–49	25–43	35–44
Proportion relative to N	100	2.7	18	26	7.8	3.2	0.11

an increased decomposition and mineralisation rate may result. Mineral nutrients in the ash will also be readily available, but are exposed to leaching. The final result is usually an even-aged stand. In the case of catastrophic wind damage, an even-aged stand is also the result, but with a contribution from younger trees that survived from the previous stand.

Grazing and other animal impacts

Grazing is an effective regulator of ecosystem structure

Both large and small animals, including phytophagous insects, have an effect on the dynamics of ecosystems. Herbivory and predation can change the food supply and population strategy, and induce physical and chemical defences in organisms. Early work in animal ecology focussed on the relations between animals and plants. Little attention was devoted to what happened in other parts of the ecosystem (Naiman 1988). We will use two cases to illustrate how browsing for food by large animals can cause chain effects in terrestrial ecosystems. The first example is from the Serengeti savannas – a tropical case (McNaughton *et al.* 1988 and literature cited therein) – and the second case from a boreal forest in Canada (Pastor *et al.* 1988 and literature cited therein). The animals have a foraging strategy that leads to a physical change of the habitat, as well as changes in the structure and dynamics of the ecosystem, with effects on soils and nutrient availability, which in turn feeds back on the animal population and ecosystem structure (Figure 13.1).

The tropical case

The Serengeti is most likely one of the best-studied areas of the world, with a spectacular set of large animals. They are ecologically separated in their search for food. The giraffes (*Giraffa camelopardalis*) are browsers, elephants (*Loxodontia africana*) and impalas (*Aepyceros melampus*) are mixed feeders (browsers and grazers), and then there are pure grazers such as wildebeests (*Connochaetes taurinus*) and zebras (*Equus quagga*). As a result of this separation in feeding habits, the available plant species, growth stages, height and the food preferences of the animals, the grazing pressure will be distributed. It is well known that elephants push down tall trees, which favours the growth of grasses.

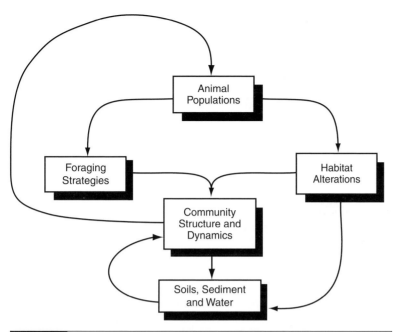

Figure 13.1 Animals influence ecosystem dynamics by their foraging strategies and by physical habitat alterations. These impacts are transferred in the ecosystem, leading to long-term changes in biogeochemical cycles in soils, as well as in sediments and water. From Naiman (1988) with kind permission from the American Institute of Biological Sciences.

Browsers prevent saplings from growing tall and becoming fire resistant. These effects lead to a balance between trees, bushes and open grassland, with fire as an important actor.

The primary production of the savannas shows local differences, depending on the variation in available moisture. The rate of mineralisation of nutrients will therefore vary over time, with consequences for primary production. The dung produced by the grazers may also have an effect, both by redistributing nutrients over the savanna and by changing litter quality; plant material that has been processed by large herbivores will probably have lower carbon quality, but higher nutrient concentration than fresh plant litter (Chapter 7). The vast aerial extent of the savannas also offers a variation in soil type, which also contributes to variation in chemical properties. The recycling of nutrients varies depending on various factors. Fast recycling occurs where grazing is intense for the whole growing season. In areas where neither grazing nor fire occurs, slow recycling dominates. In savannas with periodic heavy grazing or fires, the recycling of nutrients is characterised by pulses.

The variability of the different factors is great and the combination of possibilities for these factors difficult to foresee. A model has been developed to investigate the relationships between different factors. The model consists of three different sub-systems: a plant, a grazer and a decomposition sub-system (Figure 13.2). Grazing stimulates

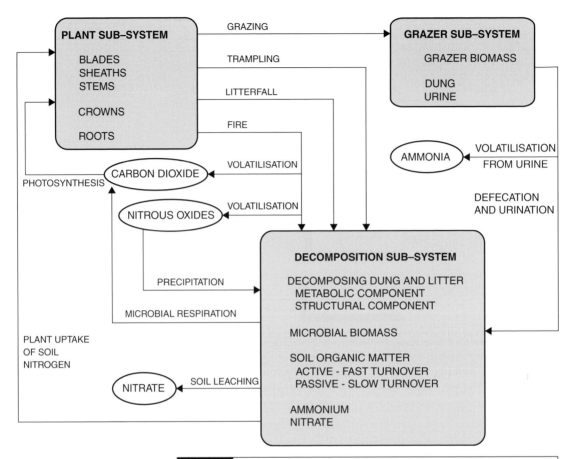

Figure 13.2 Nutrient cycling pathways in Serengeti grasslands supporting abundant large mammals. The live plant sub-system is shown in the upper left, grazing upper right and the soil sub-system lower right. Different pathways of nutrient flows from the plant sub-system to the decomposer subsystem vary in importance within the landscape, depending on the balances between grazing, fire, litter-fall and trampling. Fast cycles are created where the principal pathway is through litter-fall, and pulsed cycles where trampling or fire predominate. Alternative pathways are independent and spatially variable, thus creating landscape mosaics of nutrient cycling types. From McNaughton *et al.* (1988) with kind permission from the American Institute of Biological Sciences.

plant nitrogen uptake and has effects on nitrogen mineralisation and immobilisation, but net nitrogen mineralisation is only slightly affected (Table 13.2). With time, litter and other dead material accumulates leading to a slowdown of the nitrogen turnover processes.

From this model exercise we can draw the conclusion that grazing by large mammals affects not only soil biological processes, but also plant nutrition. This can lead to increased quality of forage or to increased storage of minerals for periods of less availability. Urine and dung can provide ammonium for plant uptake. The uptake of ammonium ions is associated with acidification of the root environment, which may favour the solubility of some ions at low pH (Figure 4.3).

Table 13.2 Characteristics of nutrient cycling in grazed and ungrazed grassland as simulated by the Grassland Research and Serengeti Systems (GRASS model). Simulations were for the intrinsically fast-cycling landscape of the southern Serengeti plains. Varying initial amounts of litter and standing dead plant biomass (0, 30, 60) reflect different periods without grazing or fire. All values are in g m^{-2} for a growing season except for microbial turnover, which is in g day^{-1}. Note that plant nitrogen uptake is only a small part of the nitrogen cycle in the soil. Modified from McNaughton *et al.* (1988)

	Simulated conditions			
	Grazed		Ungrazed	
Initial litter	0	0	30	60
Plant nitrogen uptake	7.95	5.16	4.16	3.39
Microbial turnover	2.08	2.35	1.64	1.65
Nitrogen immobilisation	76.1	60.0	39.8	30.0
Gross nitrogen mineralisation	81.4	65.1	43.7	33.4
Net nitrogen mineralisation	5.34	5.10	3.87	3.4

This abbreviated Serengeti story clearly shows complicated links between grazing animals and other ecosystem processes, which have mutual effects on the components of the savanna ecosystem.

The boreal case

The interaction between moose (*Alces alces*) and vegetation has been studied in a classic area, the Isle Royale National Park, Michigan, USA. The island is situated in Lake Superior and has, depending on soil conditions, both deciduous hardwoods and boreal coniferous forests. The latter, with the highest densities of moose, is dominated by aspen (*Populus tremuloides* and *balsamifera*), birch (*Betula papyrifera*), spruce (*Picea glauca* and *mariana*) and balsam fir (*Abies balsamifera*). Moose arrived on the island more than 120 years ago. At that time there was an ample food supply, but no predators. The moose population increased to more than 3000 animals in the 1930s leading to over-browsing. The population declined. Forest fires occurred in 1936 and 1938 with resprouting of aspen and birch leading to increased food availability. The moose population recovered. In the late 1940s wolves (*Canis lupus*) appeared. The moose population was then kept at a low level with a good food supply as a result. The predators, not the food, became the limiting factor for the moose population.

In order to have a deeper insight into the long-term changes in the vegetation cover in the presence of moose, three exclosures were established on the island with paired plots, grazed and ungrazed. Four of the forest species were browsed regularly: aspen, birch, mountain ash (*Sorbus americana*) and mountain maple (*Acer spicatum*). Where the moose was excluded these tree species were able to grow taller. Changes in the vegetation could also be seen in the quantity of litterfall,

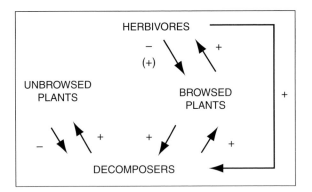

Figure 13.3 Positive and negative feedbacks in the herbivore–plant–decomposer system. Decomposers positively affect all plants by releasing nutrients from plant litter. Some plants are not browsed and can negatively affect decomposers because of high lignin and low nitrogen contents in litter. Other plants positively affect decomposers because of low lignin and high nitrogen contents of tissues and litter. These plants support herbivores, which in turn negatively affect them by browsing. Light browsing may stimulate plant growth. Urine, faeces and carcasses of herbivores are rapidly decomposed, and they may enhance nutrient availability. From Pastor *et al.* (1988) with kind permission from the American Institute of Biological Sciences.

as well as its composition. The changes in litterfall changed soil physical properties and soil biological activity, and then the dynamics of nitrogen and other nutrients. The following relations have been suggested in the herbivore–plant–decomposer system (Figure 13.3).

Eight different properties of the soil were examined in order to trace the effects of browsing (Figure 13.4). At the site where the exclosure had the clearest effect on litter production, the effects on soil biological and chemical properties were also largest. This shows that browsing by moose, soil microbes and plant litter production are related.

Stages in ecosystem development

Functional changes occur in ecosystems during succession

At the time scale of most interest to us, up to a few hundred years, we can identify regularities in the changes in species, populations, communities and ecosystems over time; *succession* and *climax* are key terms. Succession, also understood as *ecosystem development*, means that changes in energy partitioning, species composition and structure, and community/ecosystem processes occur over time. If no strong disturbances from outside occur the changes are usually predictable. When the changes are mainly determined by internal forces there is *autogenic* ('self-regulated') *succession*. In the case when outside forces dominate *allogenic* ('externally generated') *succession* prevails.

A number of stages replace each other during a typical succession. First, there is a pioneer stage dominated by species with short life cycles and high growth rates, e.g. annuals in a grassland or birch in a forest; *r*-selected species. In the end there will be a mature stage,

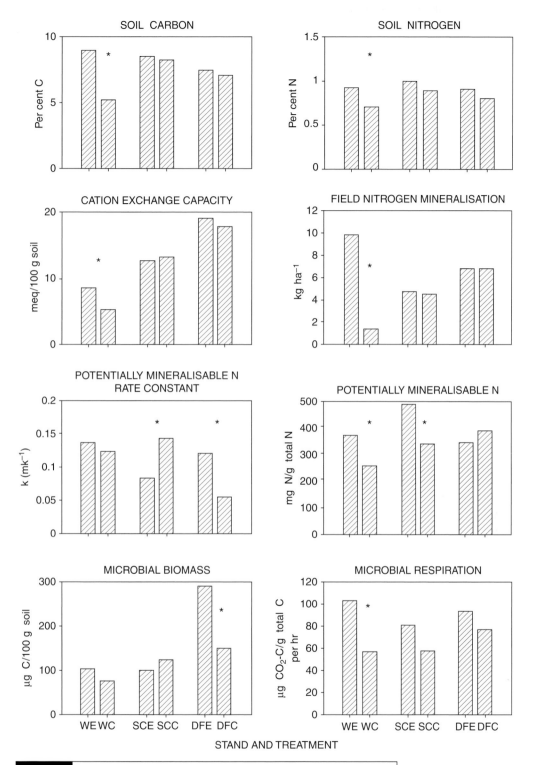

Figure 13.4 Changes in soil biological and chemical properties 40 years after excluding moose by establishing exclosures. W, SC and DF denote the name of exclosures. Treatments: E = exclosure and C = control. Significant differences between treatments are indicated with * above the bars. From Pastor *et al.* (1988) with kind permission from the American Institute of Biological Sciences.

Table 13.3 Expected changes in an ecological succession – autotrophic type. Energy flow is more or less equivalent to carbon flow. Adapted from Odum & Barrett (2005)

Ecosystem characteristics	Trend in ecological development Early stage → Climax Youth → Maturity Growth stage → Pulsing steady state
Energy flow (community metabolism)	
Gross production (P)	Increases during early phases of primary succession; little or no increase during secondary succession
Net community production (yield)	Decreases
Community respiration (R)	Increases
P/R ratio	P > R to P = R
P/B ratio	Decreases
B/P and B/R ratios (biomass supported per unit energy)	Increase
Food chains	From linear food chains to complex food webs
Community structure	
Size of individuals	Tends to increase
Total biomass (B)	Increases
Non-living organic matter	Increases
Biogeochemical cycles	
Mineral cycles	Become more closed
Turnover time and storage of essential elements	Increases
Internal cycling	Increases
Nutrient conservation	Increases
Ecosystem regulation	
Resilience	Decreases
Resistance	Increases

a climax ecosystem, dominated by *K*-selected species. During development from the pioneer stage to the mature stage production (*P*) is higher than respiration (*R*), *autotrophic succession*. This type of succession can occur, for example, when vegetation invades bare soils after an ice sheet of a glacier has melted and is an example of *primary succession*. When succession occurs in an area that has been vegetated previously, *R > P*, there is *heterotrophic succession* or *secondary succession*.

The following table summarises how a number of ecosystem characteristics may change during an autogenic succession. The changes occur in energy flows or community metabolism, community structure and biogeochemical cycles (Chapter 9), as well as natural selection and regulation.

FURTHER READING

Last, W.M. & Smol, J.P. 2001. *Tracking Environmental Change Using Lake Sediments. Vol. 1–5*. Dordrecht: Kluwer Academic Publishers.

Mattsson, W.J. & Addy, N.D. 1975. Phytophagous insects as regulators of forest primary production. *Science* **190**:515–522.

Section IV

Applications

Ecosystem ecology can be an endeavour just to satisfy our intellectual curiosity. However, with mankind appropriating such a large share of all kinds of natural resources and so strongly perturbing many element cycles, it is inescapable that ecosystem ecology has become a tool for analysing and maybe finding remedies to the environmental problems that Man is causing.

We will consider two prominent cases: air pollution and global change. Although sulfur dioxide emission as an air pollutant has decreased in many regions, it is still important in other regions and its historical legacy remains; emissions of other compounds, nitrogen oxides and ozone-forming compounds, are still here. Together with carbon dioxide and Man's conversion of land, this forms global change. Ecosystems respond to these changes and create both negative and positive feedback loops. The analysis of this interaction between Man and his environment is a typical case for ecosystem ecology. Can we be sure that short-term actions intended to mitigate environmental problems actually are beneficial and also function in a longer time perspective?

Chapter 14

Air pollution and forest ecosystems

Air pollution in the form of sulfur dioxide, nitrogen oxides and ozone affects ecosystems, both vegetation and soil. The immediate effects are physiological damage to vegetation and soil organisms, whereas long-term effects occur through changes in soil chemistry, in particular the loss of base cations. To identify the limits to which ecosystems can support the impacts of air pollutants, the concepts of critical levels and critical loads have been developed.

Today's awareness of air pollution and its effects follows observations in early industrialisation when, for example, roasting of iron ore containing sulfur resulted in drastic effects on the surroundings, with the death of vegetation. Our modern society, with combustion of fossil fuels containing sulfur and nitrogen at levels not compatible with a clean environment, has then delivered further unpleasant surprises, e.g. 'dead' lakes and now also a changing climate. This chapter deals with the effects of air pollution on forests – an area which has been the focus of research for a long time at the home institute of the authors.

Air pollution can be a threat to plants and ecosystems

In a basic model we describe a forest with 'forest damage syndrome' (Figure 14.1). The modern version of 'forest damage', observed since the mid 1980s, is expressed as a thinning of the canopy of trees. It is often given the simplistic explanation of being caused by air pollution, but how? Many scientists and laymen presented at that time a depressing future for the affected forests with far-reaching consequences, such as decreased production/forest growth, changes in vegetation and even dying forests. The vitality or health of trees and forests needs to be seen as an interaction between the status of the forest soil, including consideration of earlier history and climate/weather factors such as drought and frost.

The trees are affected directly and indirectly. The direct impact is on the canopy and the stem. Indirect effects come through the soil. The physiological properties of the tree will be altered. The carbon balance, water balance and nutritional balance will be changed. The latter may lead to decreased frost and drought sensitivity, as well as altered resistance to insect and other pest attacks. We will in this chapter investigate the left-hand side of Figure 14.1; the right-hand side, the carbon balance, has been dealt with in previous chapters.

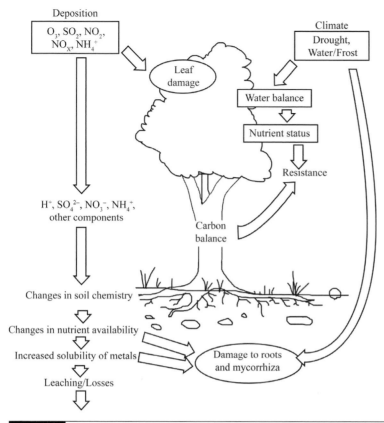

Figure 14.1 Simplistic model of a forest subject to air pollution, but also natural climatic stress, with direct and indirect effects on trees and soils.

The most important of the different air pollutants are the gases SO_2, NO_x and O_3. These cause *direct effects* on plants. There are also pollutants in ionic or particulate form, such as H^+, SO_4^{2-}, NO_3^- and NH_4^+, as well as other elements of importance for the long-term productivity of forests. These latter pollutants in dry and wet deposition lead to *indirect effects* on plants by affecting soil biology and soil chemistry. These effects can be soil acidification, changes in soil biological activity and hence in nutrient availability, and damage to roots and mycorrhiza, as well as increased leaching of elements. Changes in the nutrient status of the vegetation are expected, as well as changes in production or growth of plant biomass – timber or biofuels. Changes in nutritional status of the vegetation also lead to changes in resistance to attacks by pathogens and insects.

We show empirical evidence that over the last 100 years there have been changes in soil chemistry, which can be attributed to air pollution. We will also see if there is evidence for a change in tree nutrition as well as in the rate of tree growth. From here we go on to examine some field experiments, which will help to explain the observations. First, however, we will look at the direct effects of air pollutants.

Direct effects of air pollution on trees

SO_2 enters the leaves mainly through the stomata. It is also deposited on wet leaf surfaces and reacts with cuticular waxes and can then enter the leaf through the damaged cuticula. In and on the leaf SO_2 reacts with water to form sulfuric acid. Visible injuries are seen, such as chlorosis, white spots with eroded pigment. The damage in the leaf is dependent on the ability of the plant cell to buffer the acid. The permeability of cell membranes is also increased and cell solutes are lost. As a result the trees become more sensitive to abiotic stresses, such as snow and frost, as they are less protected. The metabolic changes decrease tree growth as less assimilates are available for growth. Roots are also affected by smaller amounts of assimilates. Changes in the soil chemistry with increasing aluminium levels might also affect the roots negatively by blocking the uptake of cations. In classical cases with high concentrations of SO_2, the trees die, as has been seen around smelters in Falun (Sweden), Sudbury (Canada) and the Black Triangle (Czech Republic and Poland).

NO_x enters the leaves through the stomata and the cuticular resistance is lower than for SO_2 and O_3. NO_x at high concentrations can reduce plant growth, but at moderate levels it usually stimulates growth by adding a limiting element. Prolonged exposure to NO_x can lead to increased sensitivity to drought, frost and pests. Synergetic effects can occur when different gases appear together as SO_2, NO_x and O_3.

In Europe and North America sulfur pollution has decreased drastically, but nitrogen oxides continue to be high (Chapter 9). In countries with growing populations, industries and increasing numbers of cars, the combustion of fossil fuels leads to increased pollution by SO_2 and NO_x. Ozone, O_3, is formed from NO_2 in sunlight, and other pollutants, e.g. hydrocarbons, at high levels can consume the OH radicals that otherwise would have destroyed the ozone (Emberson *et al.* 2003). Hydrocarbons (e.g. terpenes) are also naturally produced by plants, especially forests. Increased attention to ozone and its consequences for health, agricultural crops and forests has made it evident that it has a greater impact then previously realised (The Royal Society 2008). Ozone is also naturally produced in the stratosphere, where it is an important shield against the most energetic UV radiation from the Sun. Some of this ozone is transported down to the troposphere.

The tropospheric ozone production, fluxes and yearly behaviour are summarised in Figures 14.2 and 14.3. O_3 has its maximum occurrence in spring and early summer, seasons when the air contains maximum hydrocarbons and also maximum sunlight. Beside this seasonality there is also a daily cycle with the production and exchange of ozone bound to the presence of sunlight.

Background values of O_3 can be estimated to 10–25 ppb, including a contribution from stratospheric ozone. Maximum hourly mean

Gaseous and particulate pollution affect the leaves

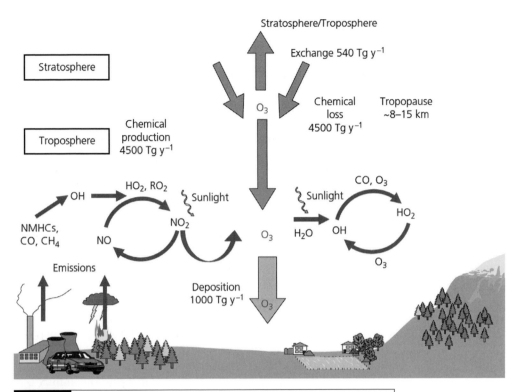

Figure 14.2 Annual fluxes of O_3 in the troposphere. The fluxes include stratosphere to troposphere exchange, photochemical production and loss in the troposphere, and the deposition flux to terrestrial and marine surfaces. From The Royal Society (2008) with kind permission.

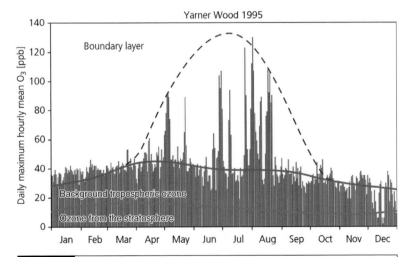

Figure 14.3 A year of surface O_3 concentration measurements in southern England showing maximum hourly values for each day. The peak values occur during spring and summer months. An indication of the sources of observed O_3 is also shown. From The Royal Society (2008) with kind permission.

values and peak values in the English example in Figure 14.3 vary between 80 and 120 ppb. In the *EU Directive on ambient air and clean air for Europe* it is recommended that ozone levels expressed as seasonal (May–July) accumulated exposure above 40 ppb (AOT40) should not exceed 9000 ppb h^{-1} to avoid yield losses of sensitive crops.

The toxicity of O_3 is not as complicated as that of SO_2 and NO_x as ozone is not coupled to an essential nutrient. The major share of the ozone uptake is through the stomata. As it enters the cell it reacts with aqueous constituents of the cell wall and oxidation of sensitive components takes place. An inability to repair the thus altered membrane permeability can lead to symptoms of visible damage, such as chlorosis, necrosis and flecking. Chronic exposure, even without visible damage, can lead to growth reductions and yield losses.

Most experiments investigating the effects of ozone on tree growth have been performed on seedlings and there are few field experiments with mature trees. Generally, broadleaved trees are more sensitive than coniferous, and pioneer species seem to be more sensitive than climax species.

In one Swedish field investigation on mature Norway spruce, a growth reduction related to ozone could be detected (Karlsson *et al.* 2006). The yearly economic loss due to ozone damage for growth of Swedish forests was estimated to be 56 million € per year and for crops (wheat and potato) 32 million € (Karlsson *et al.* 2005). The annual economic loss for the USA has been calculated to be 2–4×10^9 US\$ and for the EU to be 4.4–9.3×10^9 € (The Royal Society 2008). Besides the yield losses there are also quality impacts, such as decreased protein content in rape seed, potato and vegetables, and damage to reproductive structures.

Indirect effects of air pollution on forest ecosystems

Empirical evidence

Forest soil acidification: centennial to recent changes

Indirect effects of pollution are mediated through the soil

The consequences of the increased deposition of acidifying sulfur and nitrogen compounds as postulated by Svante Odén (1968) were observed as a reality in 1970 when acid lakes with reduced or absent fish populations were reported in west Sweden (Hultberg 1985). It took longer before effects of the acid rain could be detected in Swedish forest soils because effects were not as clearly visible. However, they could be detected through a number of reinvestigations of earlier pH studies of soils (Nilsson & Tyler 1995). During a search for documents dealing with forest vegetation changes, protocols for soil pH measurements from 1926 and 1927 in the Tönnersjöheden Experimental Forest, south-western Sweden were unexpectedly found (Hallbäcken & Tamm 1986, Tamm & Hallbäcken 1988). The soil could then be resampled in 1982–1984. Simultaneously a comparison could be

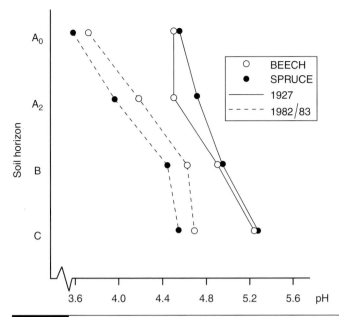

Figure 14.4 Changes in mean soil pH (water suspension) in different soil horizons in beech and Norway spruce forests between 1927 and 1982/83 at Tönnersjöheden Experimental Forest, Halland, Sweden. From Hallbäcken & Tamm (1986) with kind permission from The Royal Swedish Academy of Sciences.

done with conditions in an experimental forest in north Sweden, Kulbäcksliden-Svartberget, where pH measurements of soils had also been made earlier. Both these forests have thorough documentation and earlier sampling points could be located.

At Tönnersjöheden, an area with high deposition of pollutants, a comparison could be done of soil pH changes over 55 years in beech and Norway spruce stands (Figure 14.4). The beech stands have been there for 300 years or more, while the Norway spruce stands represent first or second generation with a rotation period of 60–80 years. In 1927 the pH of the beech and Norway spruce forest soils were equal, but after 55 years the pH in both soils had decreased, by about one unit. The strongest impact of air pollutants was observed in the spruce forest, which can be attributed to it being evergreen and having a higher LAI, thus causing it to capture more air pollutants (dry deposition). The changes were largest in the top soil, but acidification of the whole soil profile had occurred.

The northern site, Kulbäcksliden-Svartberget, represents an area with low deposition of pollutants and is covered by Norway spruce forests (Figure 14.5). Slight acidification of the humus layer could be detected after 60 years. No changes could be detected for the C horizon. The pH is in general higher in the northern site than at Tönnersjöheden.

The comparison of the results from these two reinvestigations represents a kind of experiment, as the two forests have been subject

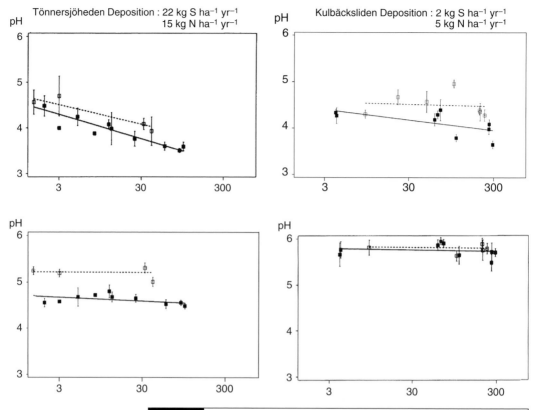

Figure 14.5 Changes in soil pH (water suspension) in the A_0 (top) and C horizons (bottom) of Norway spruce forests of different ages (logarithmic scale) between the 1920s (broken lines) and 1980s (solid lines) at Tönnersjöheden Experimental Forest, south-west Sweden (left) and Kulbäcksliden-Svartberget Experimental Forest, northern Sweden (right) representing two different deposition regimes – high and low. Sulfur given as total (dry + wet) deposition and nitrogen as wet deposition estimated for 1985. From Tamm & Hallbäcken (1988) with kind permission from The Royal Swedish Academy of Sciences.

Acidification changes the activity of soil processes and the availability of nutrients

to different deposition levels – high in the south-west and low in the north.

The soil pH of the two experimental forests could be compared with respect to not only changes over time and soil depth, but also stand age (Figure 14.5). For both the south-western and the northern sites pH is decreasing with age – natural or biological acidification – especially in the top mineral soil. At Tönnersjöheden acidification of the entire soil profile is evident after 55 years compared with Kulbäcksliden-Svartberget, where no changes could be detected in the lower mineral soil. We should also note the differences in pH levels for the C horizon in the two cases. This is a result of the age of the soil and the geographic situation. The soils in south-west Sweden are older than in north Sweden and more organic matter and organic acids have been formed, which has affected the soil formation. However, the higher acid deposition in south-west Sweden has also contributed to the changes in the C horizon. The higher input of mobile anions, SO_4^{2-} and NO_3^-, has led to higher leaching of base cations, such as Ca, Mg and K, and, thus, soil acidification caused by air pollution. This observation has been important in understanding the nature of the effects of acid rain and its consequences. At the international level it has had direct political implications by convincing representatives of countries not concerned about the consequences of air pollution and acid rain and that countermeasures had to be taken.

Associated with the pH decrease is a decrease in exchangeable base cations (Ca^{2+}, Mg^{2+} and K^+), as well as an increase in exchangeable H^+ and Al ions. These acid ions are leached with the surface and ground water to lakes and are responsible for the observed lake acidification. With a decreasing deposition of sulfur, but in many areas still high nitrogen deposition, the consequences for soil and water acidification still remain to be seen and understood. A decrease in pH can also increase the solubility of some heavy metals. The increased availability of these metals may not always be detrimental to the vegetation, but can be damaging to other organisms living on the vegetation.

Biological versus pollution-generated acidification: the hydrogen ion budget approach

There is no single cause for the acidification of soils and water, as a number of processes contribute. One way of examining the two main categories of acidification, biological or internal on one side, and air-pollution-dependent (anthropogenic, external) on the other, is to establish a hydrogen ion budget. In Table 5.2 acidifying (H^+-producing) and alkalinising (H^+-consuming) processes were identified. The balance between these processes will be affected by, for example, deposition, land use as open land versus forests, harvests, ditching, fertilisation etc.

A few comments on the different processes are needed. Values of hydrogen ion deposition range from 10–90 meq $H^+ m^{-2} yr^{-1}$ for open fields (wet deposition) to 5–40 meq $H^+ m^{-2} yr^{-1}$ and 15–350 meq $H^+ m^{-2} yr^{-1}$ under deciduous and spruce forests, respectively. The uptake of mineral nutrients by plants requires an ionic balance. Uptake of a monovalent cation leads to an exchange of one hydrogen ion and uptake of a bivalent cation yields two hydrogen ions. The uptake of anions is followed by an exchange of HCO_3^- or OH^-. Nitrogen is a key element and is taken up to a great extent as NH_4^+ or NO_3^-. In the first case, which is common in acid soils, additional hydrogen ions are added to the soil with increased acidification as a result. In contrast, uptake of NO_3^- results in consumption of hydrogen ions and means neutralisation. The fate of the elements taken and bound in the plant biomass depends on to what degree the plant biomass is broken down later. If it is completely decomposed the mineral nutrients are released. Hydrogen ions are consumed and neutralisation occurs. If there is an accumulation of organic matter as litter and humus the net result is acidification. Removal of cations by harvesting also adds to soil acidification.

By comparing the deposition of hydrogen ions with the equivalent values of accumulated elements in plant biomass and humus we get

Acidification can be generated by human activities or biological processes

Table 14.1 | Comparison of externally and internally generated acidification of soils in Swedish and German forests. Compiled from Andersson *et al.* (1980), Nilsson & Nilsson (1981), Nilsson *et al.* (1982), and Sollins *et al.* (1980)

Ecosystem	External (E) eq H^+ ha^{-1} yr^{-1}	Internal (I) eq H^+ ha^{-1} yr^{-1}	E/I
Scots pine forest 120 yr			
Central Sweden, Jädraås	19	30	0.6
Norway spruce forest			
West Sweden, Lidhult 120 yr	26	140	0.2
Germany, Solling 55 yr	81	48	1.7
Beech			
South Sweden, Kongalund 120 yr	26	39	0.7
Germany, Solling 120 yr	81	68	1.2

an approximate idea of the extent of deposition-dependent and natural biological acidification; in other words, we can compare the effects of external and internal addition of acids (Table 14.1). As we are moving from areas with low deposition (central Sweden) to areas with high deposition (south Sweden and still more so in Germany), the deposition of acids plays an increasing role. The resulting soil acidification, in particular in deeper layers, is dependent on the composition of the soil solution. The more mobile sulfate and nitrate ions it contains, the greater the effect will be on the acidification of the soil because the movement of these anions must be accompanied by cations.

Nutritional changes in trees
The observations of an air-pollution-related increase in soil acidity and a simultaneous decrease in essential base cations (Ca, Mg and K) in soils was a trigger to look for possible changes in tree nutrition. An indication of possible changes should be found in the relative chemical composition of leaves or needles – a diagnostic tool (Chapter 6). This led to extensive examination of the nutritional status of trees in old and ongoing field experiments. By comparing untreated plots from different times it should be possible to find changes. In a study by Aronsson (1985) field experiments with Norway spruce were re-examined and a comparison was made between the nutritional status of needles in the 1950s/1960s and in 1983/1984 (Figure 14.6).

This simple investigation revealed that the nitrogen concentration in spruce needles had increased over a 30–40-year period. During the same period the needle concentrations of phosphorus, potassium and calcium had decreased. The sulfur concentration had also decreased, while magnesium did not show any clear trend. The increase in nitrogen concentration in needles was a response to the continued increase in nitrogen deposition, and the decreases in phosphorus, potassium and calcium were interpreted as a response to changes in

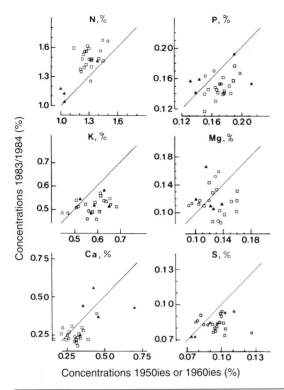

Concentrations 1983/1984 (%)

Concentrations 1950ies or 1960ies (%)

Figure 14.6 Needle concentrations of N, P, K, Mg, Ca and S 1983/1984 vs. concentrations in the 1950s/1960s in Norway spruce stands, mainly from south Sweden. The comparisons are based on samples from untreated plots in field experiments. From Aronsson (1985).

the available pools in the soil. The decrease in sulfur concentration was a result of the reduction in deposition of sulfur.

Similar increases in foliar nitrogen concentrations have also been reported from Germany (Prietzel *et al.* 1997) and later confirmed convincingly by Kahle *et al.* (2008). Increasing levels of nitrogen in needles has also led to an increase in needle weight, which also means greater needle biomass (Figure 14.7). This then results in increased tree growth.

> Is forest growth decreased or increased by pollution?

Growth rate changes in forests

Let us start with a Swedish perceptive by again referring to Svante Odén (1968), who hypothesised that acid deposition could lead to the loss of base cations and a decrease in forest growth (Tamm 1989). This challenging comment led to an investigation of tree growth based on growth rings (Jonsson & Sundberg 1972). Growth rates of Norway spruce and Scots pine were compared for the period 1911–1965 for areas considered as sensitive and less sensitive to acidification. For the period 1950–1965 there seemed to be a negative trend. The authors did not explicitly say that the cause was acid rain, but it was interpreted in this way in the popular press. This study was

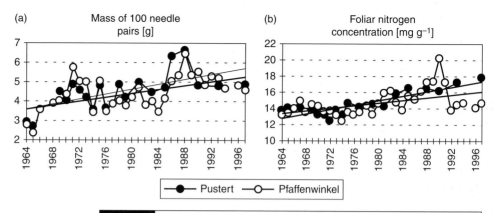

Figure 14.7 Changes in needle weights (a) and nitrogen concentrations (b) of Scots pine in two German field experiments between 1964 and 1994. Samples taken from control plots. From Prietzel *et al.* (1997) with kind permission from John Wiley & Sons.

repeated later and included the period up until 1974 (Jonsson & Svensson 1982). The negative growth trend for sensitive areas was no longer seen, rather the opposite. The first investigation from 1972 suffered from too short an investigation period, 15 years, to permit safe growth trends to be estimated.

Another challenging hypothesis by Odén (1968) was the following: 'Changes in atmospheric conditions such as the increase in carbon dioxide (ca 0.3% per annum) and the increase in deposition of nitrogen compounds (ca 5% per annum) would be expected to increase biological production of natural soils with about 1% per annum. Even if the figure is not very accurate, an accumulated positive effect during the last twenty years ought to come out of the Swedish Forest Survey, especially as improved management would also affect forest yield in a positive direction.'

In Figure 14.8 the mean forest growth in different parts of Sweden can be followed from 1926 to 2004. Improved management is clearly visible in the increased growth rates for the different regions, and as a result the forests today contain more biomass than earlier. The differences between north and south need to be stressed. The question is if increases in growth rates in south Sweden (Götaland and Svealand) in the most recent decades can be attributed to the factors mentioned by Odén.

During the 1990s reports on increased growth rates began to be published. A comprehensive survey showing mostly positive, but also neutral and negative growth trends was published in 1996 (Spiecker *et al.* 1996). The causes are complex and many. It can be a question of increased soil fertility, as earlier land use led to nutrient export by litter raking and grazing. The increased fertility can be a result of the increased deposition of nitrogen, better management of the forest leading to increased release of nutrients. In some cases fertilisers may have been added. The climate is changing – increases in spring and autumn temperatures leading to longer growth periods and shorter

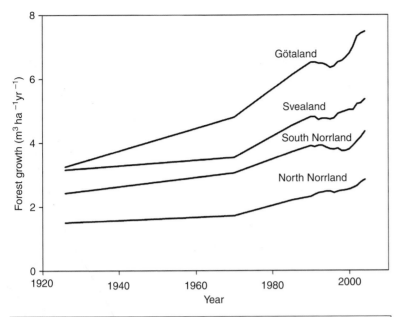

Figure 14.8 Mean forest production/growth in m^3 ha^{-1} yr^{-1} in different regions of Sweden (from south, top, to north, bottom) from 1926 to 2004. From Yearbooks of Swedish Forest Statistics.

periods of water shortage. These changes are species and site specific. The increase in CO_2 in combination with increased nitrogen availability is another stimulating growth factor.

A European study has recently been published with the purpose of elucidating the importance of the various growth factors (Kahle *et al.* 2008). This study dealt with the major tree species Norway spruce, Scots pine and European beech. Results from comparative as well as experimental approaches were used and a set of models were compared. The final outcome was that the most important factor for increased growth so far was nitrogen deposition. With time and changing availability of nutrients, increased levels of carbon dioxide, changes in temperature and the humidity climate will change the importance of each regulating growth factor.

Vegetation changes

How will the indirect effects of air pollution, such as changes in soil acidity, available base cations and nitrogen deposition affect the ground vegetation? This question has been reviewed by Falkengren-Grerup (1989 & 1995) and Tyler (1987). In general we can say that plants forming vegetation are long-lived and that they reproduce in a vegetative way. Sexual reproduction organs are sensitive. Ecosystems with high pH and base saturation usually have high biodiversity. A pH decrease should then lead to a loss of biodiversity. Unprotected organisms, such as lichens and mosses, are sensitive. Nitrogen stimulates the growth of grasses, which might lead to a decrease in the number of herbs.

It is not only the trees in a forest that respond to air pollution

For conditions in south Sweden it has been found that in beech forests as well as oak forests, demanding species decrease and that nitrogen-favoured plants increase. The National Forest Survey follows the ground vegetation and it has been documented that there is a general increase in grass cover in areas with high deposition in Sweden. For lichens and mosses it has been found that oceanic lichens decrease, as well as epiphytic and epigaeic lichens.

Experimental evidence: understanding

Experiments have increased understanding and been a base for model development and analyses

The 'acid rain'and the 'forest decline' problems still call for a better understanding of cause and effect. Scientifically one can pursue two lines of enquiry: comparative approaches and experimental approaches. The previous text has given several examples of the comparative method. There are limitations in the interpretation of the comparative approach. An example is the growth changes in conifers observed in the two south Sweden investigations (Jonsson & Sundberg 1972, Jonsson & Svensson 1982). The alternative, the experimental approach, also has its limitations. The chosen ecosystems should be representative and homogeneous. There must be clear, testable hypotheses. Treatments must be relevant and of good design with replications necessary in order to obtain statistically testable results. Further, field studies must be of a sufficient duration to distinguish between short-term and long-term treatment effects. Different approaches are therefore recommended in order to test different hypotheses. Models should be used to test results and also to generate new hypotheses (van Oene & Ågren 1995). Another dimension of field experiments is their increasing value when they are maintained for longer periods (Högberg et al. 2006).

When the 'acid rain' problem was indentified in Sweden, a limited number of field experiments were set up (Tamm 1989, Tamm & Popovic 1995, Tamm et al. 1999). These were coupled to field experiments for studies of tree and ecosystem behaviour under controlled nutrient regimes – optimum nutrition experiments. Besides having different regimes for N, P and K, the experiments also included treatments with acidification and its counterpart, liming. Acidification was achieved by adding dilute sulfuric acid or sulfur powder. These treatments gave some initial negative effects, such as 'burning' of mosses and other sensitive vegetation. Sulfur powder is also a fungicide, which meant that soil biological processes were affected, with decreased release of nitrogen as a possible consequence.

In the following we will briefly describe one of the field experiments, which have contributed to our understanding of the acid rain problem. The field experiment 'Farabol' was situated in the province of Blekinge, south-east Sweden. It started in 1976 and ended in 1991. It was a factorial experiment with three replications. The treatments and applications of sulfur, nitrogen and lime are given in Table 14.2.

From the beginning it was an extensive experiment with conventional treatments and follow-up of changes in tree growth, tree nutrition and soil chemistry. Towards the end of the experimental period it

Table 14.2 Experimental treatments in the Farabol experiment. From Andersson *et al.* (1995)

| Treatment | Abbreviation | Added amounts 1976–1987 | | |
		Sulfur	Nitrogen	Lime
Control	0	0	0	0
Acidification[a]	S1	600	0	0
Acidification[a]	S2	1200	0	0
Acidification[a] + nitrogen[b]	NS1	600	600	0
Nitrogen[b]	N	0	600	0
Liming[c]	Ca	0	0	6000

[a]Sulfur powder (100% S). Yearly additions 1976–1987, 50 (S1) and 100 (S2) kg ha^{-1}, respectively.
[b]Urea. Addition of 200 kg N ha^{-1} 1975, 1980 and 1985.
[c]Limestone powder. Yearly addition 1976–1987 500 kg ha^{-1}. Total addition was 6000 kg ha^{-1} or as $CaCO_3$, 5400 kg ha^{-1}. The lime also contained: 18 kg Mg, 12 kg K, 2,4 kg P and 1.2 kg S ha^{-1}.

Table 14.3 The Farabol experiment with acidification, liming and nitrogen fertilisation. Changes in soil chemistry between 1975 and 1991 (absolute values for control), total tree biomass, tree production between 1975 and 1991 and productivities after 15 years of treatment. Values for soil chemistry with [†] differ from the control and values for tree variables with different indices are significantly different at $p < 0.05$. From Andersson *et al.* (1995)

Variable/Treatment	0	S1	S2	NS1	N	Ca
Soil chemistry 1975–1991						
pH						
Humus layer	4.2	0	−0.1	0	+0.2	+1.9[†]
Mineral soil 10–20 cm	4.4	−0.1	−0.1	−0.1	0	+0.3[†]
Base saturation %						
Humus layer	13.5	−2.7	−4.4	−1.5	+1.3	+67.3[†]
Mineral soil 10–20 cm	2.7	−0.1	+0.2	0	−0.1	+1.4[†]
Tree biomass 1990						
Total tree biomass (Mg ha^{-1})	207.6[b]	198.0[b]	174.2[c]	207.9[b]	228.2[a]	201.2[b]
Total needle biomass (Mg ha^{-1})	19.4[b]	15.0[c]	13.3[c]	16.7[c]	22.5[a]	16.1[cd]
Tree growth 1975–1990						
Stem volume (m^{3}ha^{-1} yr^{-1})	10.6[b]	10.3[b]	9.3[b]	12.5[a]	13.4[a]	10.4[b]
Total tree biomass (Mg ha^{-1} yr^{-1})	5.0[b]	4.3[b]	3.3[c]	5.0[b]	6.4[a]	4.5[b]
NPP per unit needle biomass (Mg Mg^{-1} yr^{-1})	0.50[bc]	0.56[a]	0.50[c]	0.58[a]	0.55[ab]	0.56[a]
NPP per unit needle nitrogen (Mg Mg^{-1} yr^{-1})	22.2[b]	27.3[a]	22.6[b]	23.5[b]	22.3[b]	26.5[a]
Soil nitrogen mineralisation capacity (kg N ha^{-1} yr^{-1})	35	—	30	—	38	60

was possible to perform a complete ecosystem analysis (Box 4.3) with investigations of soil, tree growth, tree biomass, roots, soil chemistry, soil water and element cycling (Table 14.3).

This field experiment has contributed to a good understanding of the behaviour of trees, soil and soil water when fertilisers (nutrients), acids and lime are added. The addition of acid leads to a decrease in pH and base saturation in the soil and addition of lime the opposite. The extent of the changes is, of course, dependent on the intensity and duration of the treatment. The same holds for addition of nitrogen fertilisers with or without acid. The yearly total aboveground production for the experimental period was highest for N followed by NS, 0, Ca and S1, and lowest for S2.

A continued deposition of nitrogen can lead to 'nitrogen saturation' of soils with leaching of nitrate to watercourses as a consequence. The results of long-term experiments provide us with a base for analysing and modelling future situations (Högberg *et al.* 2006). With decreased deposition of sulfur we can assume that recovery from acidification can occur, a phenomenon which is now happening in earlier acidified lakes with moderate to low deposition of acidity (SNV 2000). Soil conditions in Swedish forests are followed yearly by the National Forest Survey (Stendahl 2007). For the period 1983 to 2003, indications of chemical changes in the soil towards a recovery have been found, in particular for south-west Sweden, where the deposition of pollutants as sulfur had previously been high. The improvement in the acidification status of the soils in the area is reflected by decreases in hydrogen and aluminium ions. No changes in pH and exchangeable base cations such as calcium and magnesium have, however, been detected.

Critical loads and the future

Can we know how much pollution an ecosystem can support?

Air pollution is today an international and transboundary problem as different pollutants are transported over national boundaries. The international community have therefore acted and created rules to regulate the level of pollution. In 1979 the UN-ECE Convention on Long-Range Transboundary Air Pollution (LRTAP) was established. It has gradually been developed and in 1999 this convention was further extended – the Gothenburg protocol. For this purpose the critical load and critical level concepts have been developed (Nilsson & Grennfelt 1988). The critical load was defined as: 'A quantitative estimate of an exposure to one or more pollutants below which significant harmful effects on specified sensitive elements of the environment do not occur according to present knowledge.'

One has first to identify a system (ecosystem or species) which is sensitive to pollution, for example, a forest and its growth rate. Then one must link the status of the system to some chemical criterion. The next step is to develop a model (e.g. a simple mass balance model) in order to be able to calculate a deposition level corresponding to the critical chemical criterion. This is the *critical load*. The difference between current deposition level, when it is higher than the critical load, and the critical load is called *exceedance*. An additional concept is target load, which is the level of deposition set by policymakers to protect a given area of sensitive ecosystem components. The *target load* may be higher or lower than the critical load, based on consideration of economic costs of emissions reductions and time frame, among other things.

The first applications of the critical load concept dealt with single pollutants only, e.g. acidity. Today it is realised that not only sulfur, but also nitrogen leaching contributes to acidification. The critical load is therefore treated as a combination of sulfur and nitrogen deposition (www.mnp.nl/cce).

The critical load concept is a steady-state concept, therefore no information is available on how long it will take until effects are seen. Calculations of critical loads contain many simplifications. It should therefore be seen as a risk concept. The higher the exceedance is, the higher the risk of negative effects. Even if there is zero exceedance there may be negative impacts. Development of the methods is ongoing, with attempts to include dynamic models.

The Gothenburg protocol today includes acidification (surface water and soils) and non-methane volatile organic compounds (NMVOC). The concept of *critical level* is used for gases such as ozone.

Critical loads from a European perspective

The critical loads under which 95% (5th percentile) of natural ecosystems, forests, semi-natural vegetation and surface waters are protected against acidification (maximum sulfur deposition) and eutrophication (nitrogen) in Europe are shown in Figure 14.9. Because of the character of the underlying bedrock, the areas most sensitive to acidification are in the north; acid deposition has to be lower than 200 eq ha^{-1} yr^{-1}

Nitrogen pollution continues to be a problem

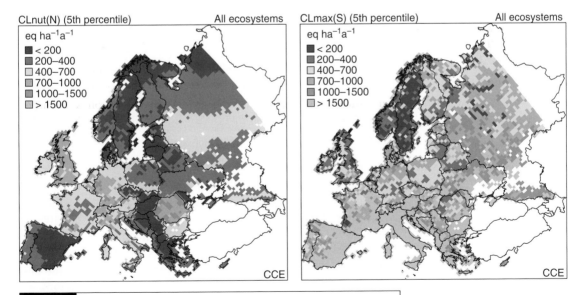

CLnut(N) (5th percentile)   All ecosystems

eq ha^{-1}a^{-1}
- ■ < 200
- ■ 200–400
- □ 400–700
- □ 700–1000
- ■ 1000–1500
- □ > 1500

CCE

CLmax(S) (5th percentile)   All ecosystems

eq ha^{-1}a^{-1}
- ■ < 200
- ■ 200–400
- □ 400–700
- ■ 700–1000
- ■ 1000–1500
- □ > 1500

CCE

Figure 14.9 European maps of critical loads for eutrophication by nitrogen (left) and acidification by sulfur (right), which protect 95% of natural areas (all ecosystems) in 50 × 50 km EMEP grid. In red-shaded areas deposition needs to be lower than 200 eq ha^{-1} yr^{-1}. From Hettelingh *et al.* (2008). See also colour plate section.

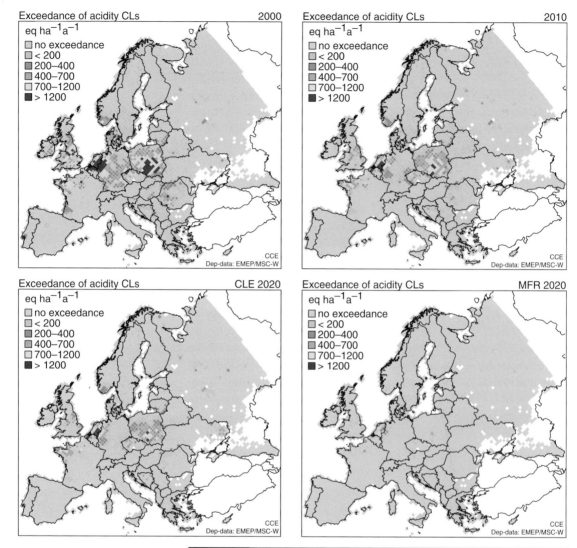

Figure 14.10 Exceedance of critical load for acidification by deposition in 2000, 2010 and 2020. The first three maps are valid for Current Legislation (CLE) to reduce emissions. The lower right map is based upon Maximum Feasible Reductions (MFR). From Hettelingh *et al.* (2008). See also colour plate section.

to protect 95% of the area. The areas most sensitive to eutrophication are found in the north, west and south of Europe.

Today acidity exceedances higher than 1200 eq ha^{-1} yr^{-1} are mostly found in Belgium, Germany, the Netherlands and Poland (Figure 14.10). In 2020 the areas of exceedance will be considerably reduced if current reduction policies for acidifying emissions are followed. In the optimistic MFR scenario, deposition in almost all Europe is below the critical load.

The highest exceedance of critical loads for nitrogen is at present found in West Europe, coastal areas from north-west France to Denmark

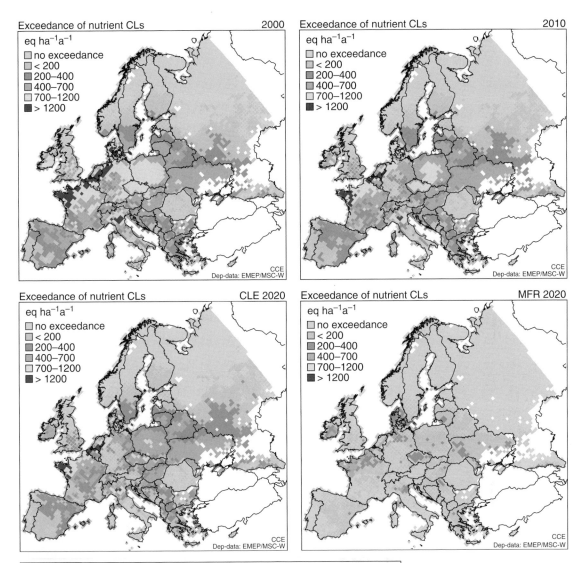

Figure 14.11 Exceedance of critical load for eutrophication by deposition of nitrogen in year 2000, 2010 and 2020. The first three maps are valid for Current Legislation (CLE) to reduce emissions. The lower right map is based upon Maximum Feasible Reductions (MFR). From Hettelingh *et al.* (2008). See also colour plate section.

as well as south-west of the United Kingdom (Figure 14.11). For South Europe high exceedance is found in north Italy. The changes up to 2020 are small. Even with the MFR reductions the areas with the highest depositions currently are still at risk of eutrophication.

FURTHER READING

Netherlands Environmental Assessment Agency. Critical loads. www.mnp.nl/cce

SNV. 2000. *Recovery from Acidification in the Natural Environment. Present Knowledge and Future Scenarios*. Report 5034, Swedish Environmental Protection Agency (Naturvårdsverket). ISBN 91-620-5028-1.

Chapter 15

Global change

Land-use changes, increasing atmospheric concentration of carbon dioxide, with concomitant changes in physical climate, and increasing nitrogen deposition, all contribute to new conditions for ecosystems. The difficulties in predicting the net effects are a result of several factors. Some of the changes can affect the ecosystems in opposite directions. Other factors have different effects depending on the time scale at which they are evaluated. A change in one factor will in most cases cause a chain reaction that eventually leads back to the primary change as a positive or negative feedback.

The use of biofuels as a substitute for fossil fuels is often suggested as a remedy, but the environmental consequences depend to a large extent on which biofuel is considered and under which conditions it is produced.

Global change has several components

All the important element cycles are currently being modified by human activities (Chapter 9). Can we predict the changes this might cause in terrestrial ecosystems? We will here discuss how climatic drivers change ecosystem functioning. What is important to realise is that one driver can have different effects, even with regard to the sign of the effect, depending upon time perspective. The drivers we consider most important are the increasing atmospheric carbon dioxide concentration, $[CO_2]$, in itself, its consequences for the physical climate, with increasing temperature and modified precipitation patterns, and increased nitrogen deposition. The effects will be highly variable between ecosystems because different ecosystems are differentially sensitive to the various components of climate change. Sala *et al.* (2000) estimated how climate change, including effects of land-use change, would affect biodiversity in various ecosystem types (Figure 15.1). The direct effect of human activities through the direct changes in land use dominate, but the indirect effects differ greatly, with some ecosystem types most sensitive to physical climate and others to nitrogen deposition or the introduction of new species. With the exception of grasslands and savannas, increasing $[CO_2]$ was not expected to be important for changes in biodiversity. We will here look more into effects of climate change on the carbon and nitrogen cycles in terrestrial ecosystems.

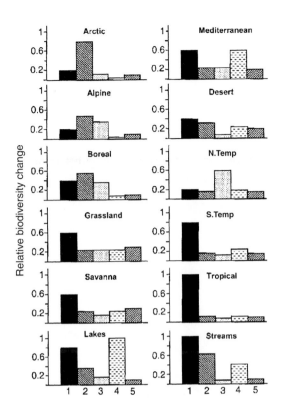

Relative biodiversity change

Figure 15.1 Effect of climate change drivers on biodiversity change between 2000 and 2100 for different ecosystem types. Bars: 1, land use; 2, temperature and precipitation; 3, nitrogen deposition; 4, introduction of new species (biotic exchange); 5, [CO₂]. From Sala *et al.* (2000) with kind permission from the American Association for the Advancement of Science.

Effects on ecosystem carbon balance

Because increasing [CO_2] is a major component in climate change, the response in the carbon balance of ecosystems is important. If ecosystems respond by increasing their carbon dioxide uptake, they will provide negative feedback and slow down the increase in [CO_2], and vice versa if they diminish their carbon dioxide uptake. We will use Figure 9.1 as a framework for discussing the effects of the components of climate change. We start by considering the direct effects and then come back to interactions and feedbacks. Figure 15.2 summarises which carbon fluxes we consider to be affected by these drivers.

Ecosystem responses to global change are modulated by both positive and negative feedbacks

Atmospheric carbon dioxide

The only process on which carbon dioxide will have any direct significant effect is photosynthesis (Figure 15.2a). The short-term increase in net photosynthesis in C3 plants is generally around 30–50% and 10–25% in C4 plants (Soussana & Lüscher 2007). However, when looked at from a longer time perspective the increase in NEE is often less than the response in GPP because much of the increase goes to short-lived tissues and compounds like fine roots and exudates, and is therefore dissipated in heterotrophic respiration. However, a consequence is that, taken on its own, the increased [CO_2] should increase the competitive ability of C3 plants relative to C4 plants.

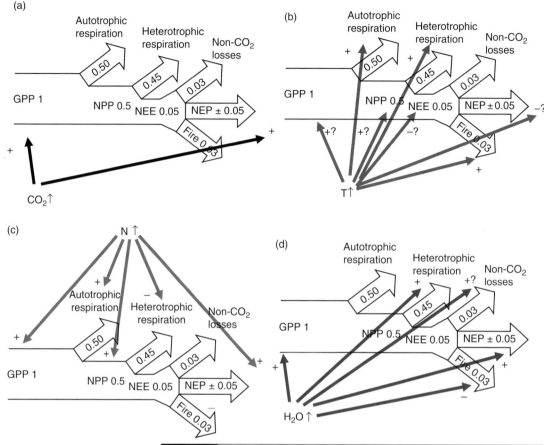

Figure 15.2 The direct effects of carbon dioxide, temperature, nitrogen deposition and precipitation on carbon fluxes in terrestrial ecosystems, see Figure 9.1. A + shows that this flux increases with an increase in the driving variable. A ? shows that there are opposing forces and that it is unclear whether the net result will be an increase or a decrease in the flux.

Temperature

In contrast to carbon dioxide, temperature directly affects many processes in an ecosystem (Figure 15.2b). As discussed in Chapter 6 photosynthesis is strongly temperature dependent, but the relation is not simple because of the interaction between temperature and other factors, such as light intensity. Moderate temperature increases are likely to increase net photosynthetic rates, but the increases might be less than expected from short-term experiments because plants can acclimate, such that the response curve of photosynthesis to temperature has its maximum at the prevailing temperature. The large difference in temperature response of photosynthesis between C3 and C4 plants should also be noted (Figure 6.4).

We showed also in Chapter 6 that autotrophic respiration increases with temperature and this will counterbalance the increase in gross photosynthesis. In fact, it seems that there are feedbacks operating inside plants such that photosynthesis and autotrophic respiration increase more or less in tandem to maintain autotrophic respiration around 50% of the GPP (Dewar *et al.* 1999). To the extent that there is an increase in photosynthesis in response to temperature, the NPP will also increase.

Because decomposer activity is stimulated by increasing temperatures the heterotrophic respiration will go up with increasing temperature, and strongly so (see Chapter 7). What is less clear is if heterotrophic respiration will increase more or less than the NPP in the short term. Considering that we are uncertain that the GPP will actually increase it seems probable that heterotrophic respiration will increase more than the GPP and that the NEE will become negative with a temperature increase; ecosystems will lose carbon and we have a positive feedback on climate. In the long run this loss of soil carbon decreases the available substrate for the decomposers and their activity has to go down to match the influx of fresh litter; the equilibrium level of soil carbon will now be lower.

There will also be non-biological effects of a higher temperature. Most notably we should expect a higher incidence of fires as a result of more efficient drying out of dead organic matter.

Nitrogen

Because nitrogen is, in general, limiting plant production we can foresee a higher GPP as a result of higher nitrogen deposition (Figure 15.2c). An accompanying effect is of course an increase in both growth and maintenance respiration, but always less than the increase in GPP such that NPP will go up.

Although the mechanisms are not well understood it seems clear that decomposers react to increasing nitrogen deposition with a decrease in heterotrophic respiration. This may be a result of decreased overall activity or of greater efficiency, see parameter *e* in Chapter 7, substrate use, or some combination of the two. The net effect is that the NEE increases and, because other processes are not affected, the NEP goes up.

Precipitation

The effects of changing precipitation patterns are more difficult to generalise (Figure 15.2d). First of all, a warmer climate will increase evaporation and hence precipitation (what goes up has to come down). However, the predictions of where this increased precipitation will occur are uncertain and there will even be many areas of the world with less precipitation; the differences between wet and dry areas are probably going to be reinforced (IPCC 2007). Second, the effects of a change in precipitation will depend on the current relation between precipitation and evaporative demand. For simplicity we will consider a situation where there is some shortage of water and there is an

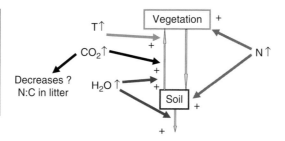

Figure 15.3 The direct effects of carbon dioxide, temperature and nitrogen deposition on nitrogen fluxes in terrestrial ecosystems. A + shows that this flux increases with an increase in the driving variable.

increase in precipitation. Under such conditions the GPP will increase, but autotrophic respiration will not be affected as such. Heterotrophic respiration will also increase as long as the increased precipitation does not lead to water logging (see Figure 7.12). We expect the effect on the GPP to be larger than that on heterotrophic respiration and the NEP will increase. There can be effects on non-CO_2 losses as well, because wetter soils can increase the release of carbon as methane, and although this may be a small change in the ecosystem carbon budget it can be important in a greenhouse gas perspective (see Box 5.2). More precipitation should also increase run-off and drainage and hence transport of DOC out of the ecosystem. Again this may be a small change in the ecosystem carbon budget, but will be more important for recipients. Wetter environments will also be less susceptible to fire.

Effects on ecosystem nitrogen balance

There are relatively few direct effects on the ecosystem nitrogen cycle from climate change (Figure 15.3); climate-change effects will be more manifest in indirect and long-term effects. The main effect of a temperature increase is through the increased turnover of soil organic matter, which will increase nitrogen mineralisation and hence nitrogen uptake by the vegetation. As a consequence of the increased allocation of carbon to fine roots when the carbon dioxide concentration goes up, the plants will become more efficient competitors for nitrogen and their nitrogen uptake will increase. Although it is commonly observed that plants growing in elevated carbon dioxide environments have lower nitrogen concentrations in their foliage this does not seem to carry through to their litters, presumably because retranslocation of nutrients at senescence is independent of the ambient carbon dioxide concentration. However, in plants where the retranslocation is not complete, the N:C ratio of fresh litter could decrease. Nitrogen deposition in itself will, of course, add to the nitrogen stocks of both the vegetation and the soil. Since we counted on increasing mineralisation of carbon as a result of more soil water there will also be increasing nitrogen mineralisation, with a concomitant increase in nitrogen uptake by plants. Also in parallel with increased carbon losses as DOC there will be additional losses of nitrogen, in the form of both organic and inorganic nitrogen, where the increase in nitrogen mineralisation further increases inorganic nitrogen losses.

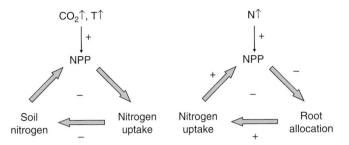

Figure 15.4 The feedback from an increase in $[CO_2]$ or temperature from a short-term perspective (< 1 yr). The signs at the arrows indicate how an increase in the factor at the base of the arrow affects the factor at the arrowhead. For example, if nitrogen uptake increases then soil nitrogen is decreased. By doing a complete turn and counting the number of minus signs we can determine if the loop leads to a reinforcement (positive feedback, even number of minus signs) or if the loop will reduce (negative feedback, odd number of minus signs) the initiating change. In this case we get a negative feedback and soil processes in the form of nitrogen supply restrain the increase in NPP that $[CO_2]$ or temperature alone would have caused. See text for further explanation.

Interactions

It is not sufficient to describe the effects of climate change by looking at how the drivers act one by one because the different drivers will interact. One obvious example is that increasing temperatures will increase evaporative demands, such that whenever we consider effects of changes in temperature it is necessary to take changes in water availability into account. The increase in water-use efficiency resulting from increased $[CO_2]$ will decrease transpiration and increase soil moisture. Moreover, there will be chains of reactions and feedbacks that can amplify or dampen the direct impacts. Moreover, these chains and feedbacks will be different depending on the time scale of observations and can even reverse the sign of the effect when going from instantaneous to long-term observations. We will here consider some of the more important feedbacks at different time scales.

The short–term effect (< 1 yr) of increasing $[CO_2]$ or temperature is an increase in NPP (Figure 15.4). To match this extra NPP, more nitrogen has to be taken up from the soil; the stoichiometric relations in the plant must be maintained. This leads to a decrease in the pool of nitrogen available for uptake because there are no processes in the soil that can match this additional demand for nitrogen on this short time scale (Principle P1). When the pool of available nitrogen in the soil decreases, the uptake has to go down and this restricts the increase in NPP.

At a time scale of a few years additional processes come into play (Figure 15.5). An increase in $[CO_2]$ will still stimulate NPP, but the limitation from nitrogen uptake that could not keep pace (Figure 15.4) causes a decrease in nitrogen concentration in the plant. As a result the plant will respond by increasing its allocation to root growth (see Chapter 6), which increases nitrogen uptake and which

Positive feedbacks will eventually be constrained by other limiting factors

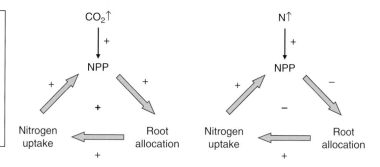

Figure 15.5 The feedback from an increase in [CO$_2$] or nitrogen deposition from a time perspective of a few years. In this case we get a positive feedback from the increased [CO$_2$], but a negative one from the increased nitrogen deposition. See text for further explanation.

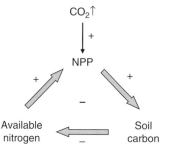

Figure 15.6 The feedback from an increase in [CO$_2$] from a time perspective of decades. In this case we get a negative feedback from the increased [CO$_2$]. See text for further explanation.

further stimulates NPP; we have a positive feedback. This circle of ever increasing NPP can, of course, not expand forever, but eventually other factors will exercise their constraints; in that case the pool of available soil nitrogen will be exhausted and no matter how many roots are produced they cannot provide the necessary extra nitrogen. The situation is different when the initial stimulation of NPP comes from nitrogen deposition because in this case the increasing plant nitrogen concentration will lead to a decreased allocation to roots and consequently the nitrogen uptake is limited; a negative feedback.

On a time scale of decades and longer several slow soil processes become important (Figure 15.6). An increasing NPP resulting from an increase in [CO$_2$] produces more litter and this leads to a build-up of soil carbon. However, the increase in soil carbon also ties up nitrogen and less nitrogen will be available for the vegetation, which then restricts the response in NPP. Overall this results in a negative feedback and serves to constrain the response to the driver, in this case [CO$_2$]. Principle C3 can be used to estimate the possible changes in carbon and nitrogen pools in the vegetation and soil in the ecosystem.

Threshold effects

The examples of chains of responses to climate change and feedback mechanisms in ecosystems illustrated above all assume that changes in ecosystems occur smoothly and that existing organisms can adjust to the new conditions. This may not always be the case. There are situations where the consequences of climate change are qualitative changes in ecosystem functioning.

The increasing [CO_2] will favour species with low water-use efficiency because those with already high water-use efficiency have less potential for improving their efficiency. This will be particularly important in areas where C3 and C4 species are competing. However, it is not the photosynthetic pathway per se that is important; a change from C4 to C3 species can also imply a change from grassy species to woody ones and that change has a considerable effect on biogeochemical cycles. Woody species tend to be more recalcitrant to decomposition and have lower nutrient concentrations in their live tissues. This will redistribute carbon and nitrogen between vegetation and soil, but will also increase the storage of carbon in plant biomass.

Temperature and precipitation determine at a large scale the kind of vegetation that is possible (Figure 4.8). In particular, rather small changes in precipitation can shift an ecosystem from a grassland type to a forest and in cold regions the border between tundra and boreal forest depends critically on temperature. Climate change can in both these cases cause drastic shifts in species composition. The consequences in this case will also depend upon whether changes in species composition involve woody species or not. In contrast to the effects of increasing [CO_2], which generally would lead to more forests, changes in temperature and precipitation can lead to either more or less forests. Increasing temperatures without a concomitant increase in precipitation can lead to a too dry climate for forests and there will also be regions with less precipitation.

Increased nitrogen deposition will favour plant species with a potential for fast growth, but this in itself is not likely to cause any threshold effects. However, as the nitrogen pool in the soil builds up there will be an increase in nitrate leaching (Figure 9.14). Although this leaching is probably in itself not harmful to the ecosystem from which the leaching occurs, the nitrate has to be accompanied by cations. This in turn can eventually lead to conditions where vegetation growth is limited by some cation. When this happens, the uptake capacity for nitrogen in the vegetation becomes limited and nitrate leaching increases, which further aggravates the cation deficiency. We end up in a situation with a positive feedback, the hallmark of threshold effects.

Bioenergy: cure or curse?

The emissions of carbon dioxide from fossil-fuel burning will alter conditions for all ecosystems on Earth. An alternative energy source, avoiding the addition of fossil carbon to the global carbon cycle, is more intensive use of bioenergy. The use of bioenergy is, however, controversial, as it cannot be used without environmental consequences. Even the idea that bioenergy basically implies that the same carbon atoms are used over and over again with minimal increase of carbon in the atmosphere may be questioned. A major problem in the discussions of bioenergy is that bioenergy can be derived from so many sources and their environmental effects differ enormously. First of all, one needs to consider the direct effects when land is converted to bioenergy production. Fargione *et al.* (2008) analysed, for a number of different bioenergy production systems, the time it would require to compensate for the carbon losses from vegetation and soil (Figure 15.7). In the best of their cases (ethanol on marginal cropland) there would be an immediate gain, whereas in their worst case (biodiesel from rain forest peatlands) more than 400 years would be required just to break even.

It is easy to understand that, if we clear a massive forest and replace it with, for example, sugarcane, that a lot of carbon will be lost. Similarly, it is easy to understand that if we plant a short-rotation crop (a crop like *Salix* harvested typically every third to fifth year) on a marginal cropland we are going to first build up a biomass before anything can be harvested; we are removing carbon from the atmosphere. It is much less easy to see the changes that occur below ground and which are often even larger. It is also less obvious what happens when we intensify the use of biomass, for example, by increasing the harvest of residues that previously had been left in place to decompose and contribute to the soil organic matter. The removal of harvest residues is in principle equivalent to a decrease in litter production. We can, therefore, use the model developed in Chapter 7 to estimate the effects on soil carbon. If we are removing ΔI Mg C ha^{-1} yr^{-1}, we can calculate that this corresponds to a long-term loss of soil carbon of $\Delta I/k$ (Equation 7.16). However, this loss of soil carbon must be compared to the amount of fossil fuel that has been substituted. To fully understand this situation we must consider a dynamic situation. We can assume that per unit carbon (and carbon dioxide), biofuels and fossil fuels are equal; this is a very good approximation, except for natural gas (methane) and explains why the mileage is lower when driving a car on ethanol (the extra oxygen molecule) compared to petroleum.

Figure 15.8 explains the process. The left panel shows a typical decomposition curve for one unit of forest harvest residues (branches, tops, coarse roots) when they are left decomposing in the soil. If such harvest residues instead are removed and burnt, the carbon in them will return more or less instantaneously to the atmosphere, rather than taking more than 20 years. Because we need energy every year we will go from place to place and collect harvest residues and burn them. The carbon release from them will then follow the broken line in the middle panel. These are also the emissions that would come from the corresponding use of fossil fuels. However, the broken line does not represent the net emissions of carbon because we have to take into account the decomposition that would have occurred if the residues had been left in the forest. When we come to year two, we can deduct the amount of carbon that the residues from the first year

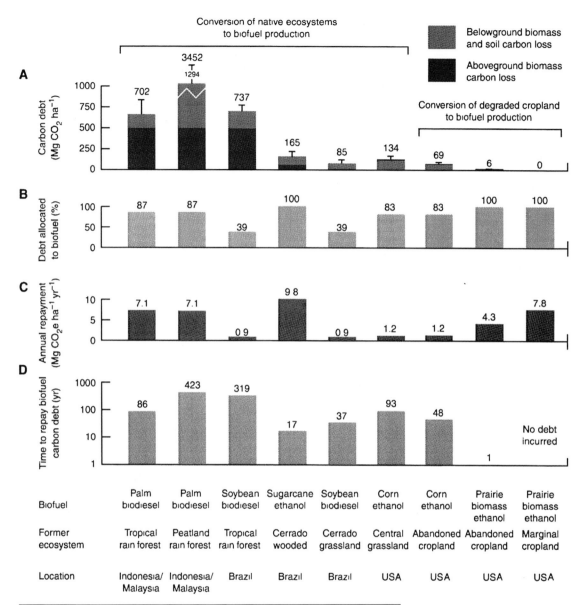

Figure 15.7 Carbon debt, biofuel carbon debt allocation, annual carbon repayment rate and years to repay biofuel carbon debt for nine scenarios of biofuel production, estimated means and standard deviations. (A) Carbon debt, including CO_2 emissions from soils and aboveground and belowground biomass resulting from land-use change. (B) Proportion of total carbon debt allocated to biofuel production. (C) Annual life cycle GHG reduction from biofuels, including displaced fossil fuels and soil carbon storage. (D) Number of years after conversion to biofuel production required for cumulative biofuel GHG reductions, relative to the fossil fuels they displace, to repay the biofuels carbon debt. From Fargione et al. (2008) with kind permission from the American Association for the Advancement of Science.

have lost through decomposition; about 11% of what was harvested, as the left panel of Figure 15.8 shows. The third year we can deduct decomposition losses from harvest residues for the first (11%) and

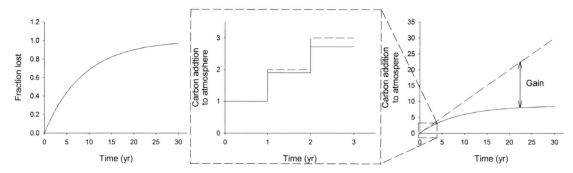

Figure 15.8 Effects of substituting fossil fuels with harvest residues. Left panel: Fraction of residue lost through decomposition with time. Middle panel: Gross and net carbon emissions from use of harvest residues with time. Right panel: Reduction in carbon emissions when substituting fossil fuels with harvest residues. See text for fuller explanation.

second (21%) year cohorts and so on. For each year we can add losses from more and more cohorts giving the solid line in the middle panel. If we extend this for a long time and smooth out the solid line in the middle panel we get the solid line in the right panel. If we had used fossil fuels instead, the carbon emissions would have increased linearly over time (broken line). The difference between the two lines is the reduction in emissions. Initially the gains are very small, but they grow larger and larger every year. If we had used natural gas, the emission line would have had a smaller slope and it would have taken some time to get a net gain from the biofuel.

There are, of course, additional aspects to consider when analysing the consequences of replacing fossil fuels with bioenergy, and a complete life cycle analysis is required. The example above considers only the direct effect in the ecosystem where the harvest takes place. Transport and processing are additional factors that need to be included (also for the fossil fuels). When specifically growing biofuels, fertilisers might be used and their energy costs and possible emissions (N_2O) must be included in the balance. Effects on the landscape (aesthetic values, biodiversity) are other complications.

FURTHER READING

Hyvönen, R., Ågren, G.I., Linder, S. et al. 2007. The likely impact of elevated [CO2], nitrogen deposition, increased temperature, and management on carbon sequestration in temperate and boreal forest ecosystems. A literature review. *New Phytologist* **173**:463–480.

IPCC 2007. *Climate Change 2007. The Scientific Basis.* Cambridge: Cambridge University Press.

Epilogue

Society and terrestrial ecosystem ecology

In this epilogue we will deal with using our knowledge of terrestrial ecosystem ecology. There is always an interest in basic science arising from the curiosity to learn and understand more. However, at the same time there is a demand to apply the knowledge or principles of our discipline for the good of society – a utilitarian demand. Terrestrial ecosystem ecology serves then as a base for understanding, utilising and managing natural resources.

Humanity depends on natural resources. The sustainable use of services which ecosystems provide us with has today come into focus. These ecosystem services are essential components for our wellbeing and while this has increased, it is at the cost of fast degradation of our ecosystems and the loss of ecosystem services. There are international and national rules, laws or constraints setting the framework within which we use our natural resources, but there is an increased need to modify present policies, institutions and practices. Therefore, we need close links between society and science.

Humanity or society depends on Nature and its resources, not the reverse. These resources give a number of benefits: social, economic and environmental. The ecosystem then provides us with a number of functions (ENFORS 2005) or benefits, today often called *ecosystem services*. The global and local economies, as well as our social needs create a demand for resources. The use of a resource is in many cases built upon historical aspects and legacies. A number of factors determine the way we use the resource (Figure Epi. 1). These factors are by their nature social, economic and biological-ecological. They can be seen as forces or constraints.

In which framework are we using the natural resources?

When utilising a resource we are bound by national laws, e.g. Forestry Law, as well as international agreements such as conventions and protocols. For air pollution there is the Convention on Long-Range Transboundary Air Pollution (the LRTPAP Convention) and a Protocol to Abate Acidification, Eutrophication and Ground-level Ozone (the Gothenburg Protocol). For ecosystems there are the Convention on Biological Diversity (CBD), the Convention on Climate Change, the Convention on Wetlands (RAMSAR), the Convention on Migratory Species, the European Landscape Convention and the Convention to Combat Desertification. There are also agreements that are not legally binding. For forests one can mention 'Sustainable Forest Management' with its roots in the UN Rio conference on the 'Environment and Development' as well as the 'Forest Principles' from 1992. There is also an International

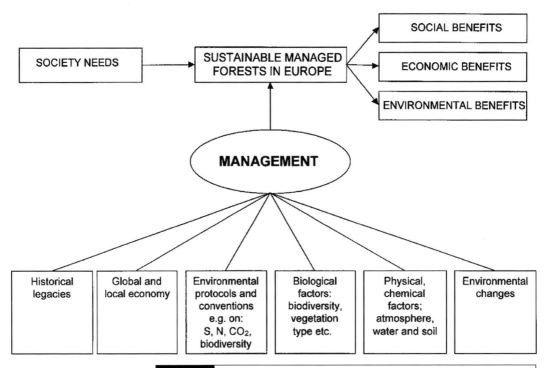

Figure Epi.1 Knowledge and facts determining use and management of a natural resource, forests as an example. From Andersson *et al.* (2000) with kind permission from Elsevier.

Forest Forum under the UN (UNIFF). Several suggestions of instruments or tools are available, such as 'National Forest Plans' and 'Criteria and Indicators for Sustainable Forest Management (C&I)'.

The previous chapters have dealt with the historical aspects, environmental changes and the scientific basis for understanding terrestrial ecosystems and their function in terms of biological structures and processes, as well as chemical and physical factors and processes. Here the focus is on the use and the management of natural resources in a sustainable way, which usually is defined as: Today's use is not allowed to hamper or jeopardise use of the resource for future generations.

What are ecosystem services?

The concept of ecosystem services has gradually developed. It was first used in a report *Man's Impact on the Global Environment* (SCEP 1970). Environmental textbooks by Ehrlich & Ehrlich (1970, 1981) called attention to 'the most subtle and dangerous threat to man's existence – the potential destruction, by man's activities, of those ecological systems upon which the very existence of the human species depends'. Earlier Sears (1956) had described the processes involved in changing ecosystems as a consequence of human actions. He had stressed the importance and ability of the ecosystem to recycle nutrients from waste and other organic materials as a base for human life and welfare.

Global concern for the future of humanity resulted in an activity initiated by the UN: 'The Millennium Ecosystem Assessment' (MEA) carried out 2001–2005 (Millennium Ecosystem Assessment 2005). The intention was to provide a basis for measures related to four of the conventions mentioned (CDB, Desertification, RAMSAR and Migratory Species). The assessment focussed on the consequences of changing ecosystems with regard to human wellbeing and dealt with a range of ecosystems, from relatively undisturbed natural forests to landscapes used by humanity, and intensively managed and modified by humanity, such as agricultural land and urban areas

Ecosystem services are what humanity benefits by or takes from Nature or the ecosystems (Figure Epi. 2). There are four basic services: provisioning, regulating, cultural and supporting services. The provisioning services give us food, fresh water, wood and fibre, fuel, minerals etc. The ecosystem is also a regulator of climate, flooding and disease, and purifies water. The four main services require functioning ecosystems, which primarily means nutrient cycling, soil formation and primary production. A special concern is the biodiversity of life on Earth.

Ecosystem services are the basis for the wellbeing of humanity

The ecosystem services are essential components for human wellbeing. The ecosystems should provide individuals with basic material for a good life, which means adequate livelihoods, sufficient nutritious food, shelter and access to goods. These assets are a must for good health (strength, feeling well, access to clean air and water). Individuals should also feel secure (personal safety, secure resource access and secure from disasters), have good social relations and have freedom of choice for personal development.

Ecosystem changes in the last 50 years

Earlier we described changes in ecosystems over time, ecosystem dynamics (Chapter 13). The Millennium Ecosystem Assessment looks more closely at what has happened on a global scale over the last 50 years. Four major findings are:

(1) In the last 50 years humanity has changed ecosystems more rapidly and extensively than in any period in history in order to meet the demands of a growing population and its demand of food, fresh water, timber, fibres and fuel. The result of this is a loss of biological diversity.

(2) These changes have resulted in a gain in human wellbeing and economic development. The gains have been achieved with growing costs in terms of the degradation of 60% of the ecosystem services, increased risk of non-linear changes and increased poverty

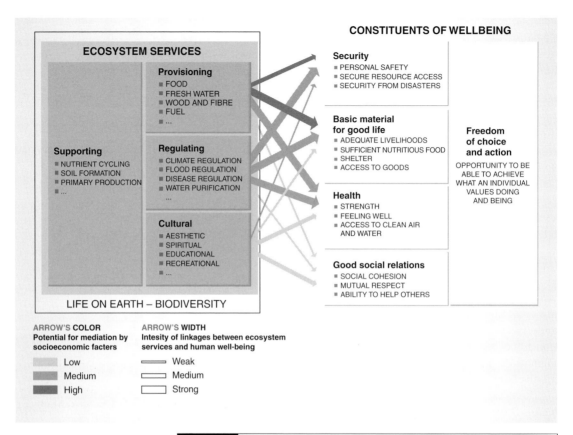

Figure Epi. 2 Linkages between ecosystem services and human wellbeing. Intensity of linkages between ecosystem services and wellbeing are indicated, as well as potential for mediation by socio-economic factors. The strength in the linkages as well as potential to mediate conditions varies between regions. The influence on human wellbeing is also affected by environmental, economic, social, technological and cultural factors. A change in human wellbeing may also affect ecosystems. See further Figure Epi. 3. From MEA (2005) with kind permission from the World Resources Institute.

for particular groups of people. In other words, natural resources have not been used in a sustainable way.

(3) The degradation of ecosystem services described is a threat to developing goals for the next 50 years.

(4) In order to challenge the situation and reverse the degradation, significant changes in polices, institutions and practices need to be achieved, which at present is not at hand.

During the period 1950–1980 more land was converted to agriculture than during the period 1700–1850. Today more than 25% of the Earth's terrestrial surface is utilised for agricultural purposes and at least 30% of this area is used for various forms of cultivation. At the same time degradation of dry land occurs as well as deforestation (Figure Epi. 4).

An attempt has been made to estimate the conversion or loss of original biomes before 1950 and between 1950 and 1990. Mediterranean

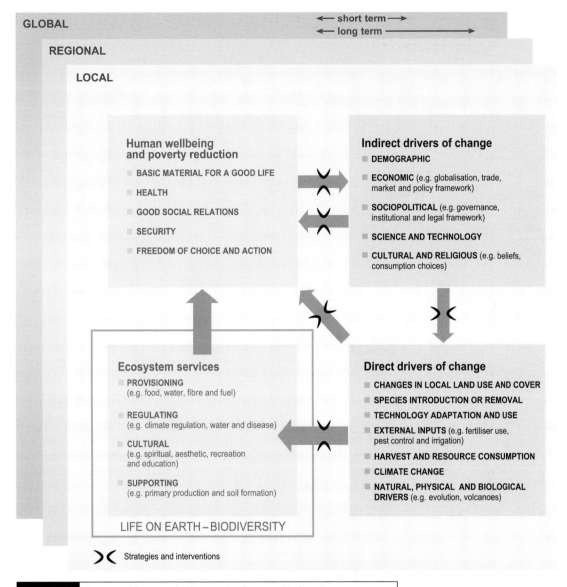

Figure Epi. 3 Conceptual framework of interaction between biodiversity, ecosystem services, human wellbeing and drivers of change. From MEA (2005) with kind permission from the World Resources Institute.

forests, including woodlands and scrubs, as well as temperate forests, with woodlands and steppes, decreased by almost 70%, a change which occurred mostly before 1950 (Figure Epi. 5). During 1950–1990 losses occurred in tropical and sub-tropical forests, as well as drier biomes. The Millennium Ecosystem Assessment has also made a projection of changes by 2050, which indicates that, in particular, forests are at risk in tropical and temperate areas. Further, during the last five decades at least 20% of the world's coral reefs have been lost and at least 35% of mangrove forests.

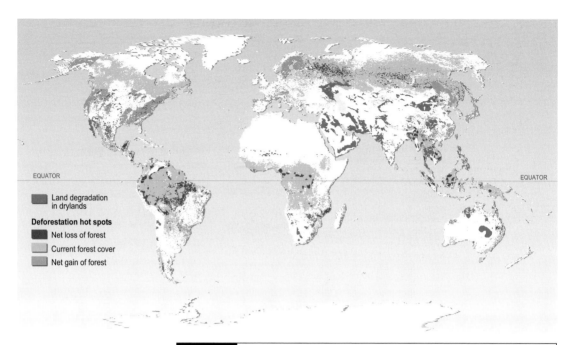

EQUATOR

Land degradation
in drylands

Deforestation hot spots

Net loss of forest

Current forest cover

Net gain of forest

EQUATOR

| Figure Epi. 4 | Areas showing degradation of drylands and forests. From MEA (2005) with kind permission from the World Resources Institute. See also colour plate section. |

The conversion of the biomes leads to changes in biological biodiversity. It has been observed that in general over a range of taxonomic groups the population size and/or area is decreasing and the majority of species are declining. Simultaneously, the distribution of species is becoming more homogeneous. One reason for this is that species are intentionally or inadvertently introduced in connection with increased travel and shipping.

The Assessment concludes that the number of species is declining. Over the past few hundreds of years humans have increased the extinction rate of species by a factor of 1000 over background rates typical over the planet's history (Figure Epi. 6). Currently, 10–30% of mammals, birds and amphibians are threatened with extinction (medium to high certainty = 65–98% probability). Another consequence of the decline of species is a loss of genetic diversity.

Linking society and the scientific community

This book started by describing how the combustion of sulfur-containing oil was found to cause environmental problems. When this was realised a number of hypotheses for possible negative effects were stated. These became then subject to research. Gradually understanding increased and mathematical models could be developed in order to predict which

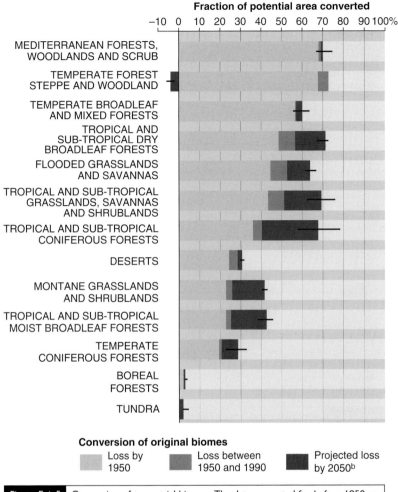

Fraction of potential area converted

Conversion of original biomes

Loss by 1950 Loss between 1950 and 1990 Projected loss by 2050[b]

Figure Epi. 5 | Conversion of terrestrial biomes. The data presented for before 1950 as well as for 1950–1990 are of medium certainty (65–85% probability) and the projection by 2050 of low certainty (52–65% probability). The projections have mean error bars indicated (black lines). From MEA (2005) with kind permission from the World Resources Institute.

changes would occur under different assumptions or future scenarios. This insight was then communicated to society (state governments or local boards) who discussed which future changes were or were not acceptable. In other words, a policy was determined. After some time an assessment needs to be done to see if the suggested policy has worked or not. Two other activities are needed to follow the state of an ecosystem or a natural resource, surveys and monitoring. A survey is needed in order to have information on where different natural resources are found and in which quantities and qualities. Their changes over time will then be followed by monitoring (Figure Epi. 7).

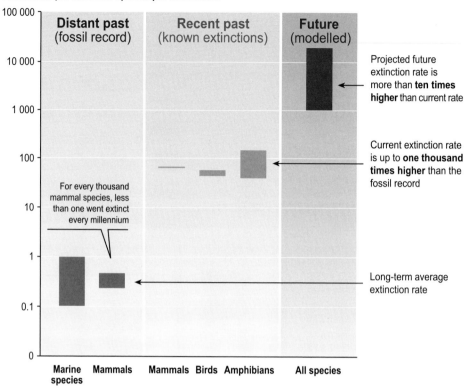

Figure Epi. 6 Species extinction rates. From MEA (2005) with kind permission from the World Resources Institute.

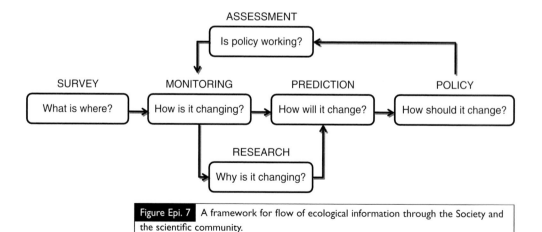

Figure Epi. 7 A framework for flow of ecological information through the Society and the scientific community.

FURTHER READING

Millennium Ecosystem Assessment (MEA) 2005. *Ecosystems and Human Well-Being: Synthesis*. Washington, DC, Island Press.

The Royal Society 2009. *Ecosystem Seervices and Biodiversity in Europe*. European Academies Science Advisory Council Policy Report 09. ISBN 978-0-85403-738-4. www.easac.eu.

Appendix 1

Abbreviations

a	Nutrient productivity
A	Assimilation
AC	After Christ
AD	Anno Domini
ADP	Adenosine diphosphate
AET	Actual evapotranspiration
A_g	Gross photosynthesis
A_n	Net photosynthesis
ANPP	Aboveground net primary production
ATP	Adenosine triphosphate
B	Decomposer biomass
BP	Before Present
BS	Base saturation
$^\circ$C	Degrees Celsius
C	Amount of carbon
c	Speed of light in vacuum
C/n	Carbon/nutrient ratio
C/N	Carbon/nitrogen ratio
C3	Related to the photosynthetic pathway whose initial carboxylation products are three-carbon sugars
C4	Related to the photosynthetic pathway whose initial carboxylation products are four-carbon sugars
c_a	CO_2 concentration outside (ambient) the leaf
c_i	CO_2 concentration inside the leaf
CAM	Crassulacean acid metabolism
CEC	Total cation exchangeable capacity
c_n	Plant nutrient concentration
C_S	Carbon in soil
C_{ss}	Steady-state carbon in soil
C_v	Carbon in plant biomass
C_{vss}	Steady state of carbon in plant biomass
DIC	Dissolved inorganic carbon
DNA	Deoxyribonucleic acid
DOC	Dissolved organic carbon
DON	Dissolved organic nitrogen
DOP	Dissolved organic phosphorus
E	Evaporation rate
$E(\lambda)$	Emitted energy at wavelength λ
EA	Exchangeable acidity
EAC	Exchangeable acid cations

EBC	Exchangeable base cations
e	Base of the natural logarithm
e	Decomposer efficiency
e_o	Reference point of water vapour density
e_{sat}	Saturated water vapour density
g_c	Canopy conductance
GPP	Gross primary production
g_s	Stomatal conductance
GWP	Global warming potential
h	Planck's constant
H	Latent heat loss
HFC	Hydrofluorocarbon
$H/\lambda E$	Bowen ratio
I	Light intensity
I_0	Input rate of litter
IPCC	Intergovernmental Panel on Climate Change
IR	Infrared
k	Boltzmannn's constant
k	Light extinction coefficient
k	Specific decomposition rate
K	Kelvin
L	Total leaf area
L	Growing root length
LAI	Leaf area index
LRTAP	Long-range transport of air pollution
LTER	Long-term ecosystem research
LUE	Light-use efficiency
M	Decomposer mortality rate
MAP	Mean annual precipitation mm
MAT	Mean annual temperature °C
m	Nutrient mineralisation rate
m_s	Mass of soil
m_w	Mass of water
mol_c	Mole charge
mol_e	Mole electrons
n	Amount of (limiting) nutrient
n_{ss}	Steady-state amount of nutrient in soil
NEE	Net ecosystem exchange
NEP	Net ecosystem production
NIRS	Near-infrared spectroscopy
NMR	Nuclear magnetic resonance
NPP	Net primary production
N_s	Nitrogen in soil
N_T	Total amount of nitrogen
NUE	Nutrient-use efficiency
N_v	Nitrogen in plant biomass
P	Decomposer production rate
Pa	Pascal

PAR	Photosynthetically active radiation
PC	Particulate carbon
PET	Potential evapotranspiration
pH	Negative log of H^+ activity
P_m	Maximal photosynthetic rate
P_n	Nutrient productivity
ppb	Parts per billion
ppmv	Parts per million by volume
Q_{10}	Proportional increase in the rate of a process with a 10 °C increase in temperature
R	Respiration rate
R_d	Dark respiration rate
R_{sample}	Isotopic ratio in sample
$R_{standard}$	Isotopic ratio in reference
Rubisco	Ribulose biphosphate carboxylase–oxygenase
R_W	Relative growth rate
SLA	Specific leaf area
r	N:C ratio
r_c	Critical N:C ratio
r_0	Initial N:C ratio of litter
SOM	Soil organic matter
SPAC	Soil–plant–atmosphere continuum
T	Temperature
T	Rate of transpiration
t	Time
U	Nutrient uptake rate
u	Decomposer growth rate
W	Watt ($=$ Js)
W	Plant biomass
W_L	Canopy biomass
VOC	Volatile organic compounds
WUE	Water-use efficiency
yr	Year
α	Quantum yield
Δ	Difference in isotope concentration relative to a standard
ε	Light-use efficiency
λE	Sensible heat loss
μ_L	Leaf mortality rate
μE	Microeinstein
σ	Stefan–Boltzmann's constant
Ψ	Water potential
Ψ_g	Gravitational potential
Ψ_m	Matric potential
Ψ_p	Pressure potential
Ψ_s	Osmotic potential

Appendix 2

Glossary

Term	Explanation (the explanations refer to the use of the terms in the context of ecosystem ecology)
abiotic	Not living
abrasion	Mechanical scraping of a rock surface or soil particle by friction between rocks and soil particles during their transport by wind, glaciers and water
acid–base status	The acid–base status of a soil is described by pH (activity of hydrogen ions) and degree of base saturation (% metallic cations of total exchangeable cations)
acid reaction	Weathering increases when the activity of hydrogen ions from strong and weak acids increases
actual evapotranspiration (AET)	Evapotranspiration at a site, cf. potential evapotranspiration
aerobic	Environment with oxygen present
albedo	Fraction of the incident shortwave radiation reflected from a surface
alfisol	Soil order with grey to brown horizons, medium to high base content, B horizon with clay accumulation, forest and savanna with pronounced seasonal moisture deficit
allometric relation	Regression relation between biomass properties
ammonification	Conversion of organic nitrogen to ammonium during decomposition of soil organic matter; often synonymous with nitrogen mineralisation
anaerobic	Environment free of oxygen
anoxic	Lack or absence of oxygen
aridisol	Soil order with dry soils in dry climate, wet less than three months, low in organic matter
autecology	The ecology of an individual organism or species
autotroph	Organisms producing organic matter from inorganic sources (CO_2, water etc.) and environmental energy, mostly through photosynthesis. Synonymously primary producers

biodiversity	Biodiversity is a measure of the relative diversity among organisms present in different ecosystems
biogeochemistry	The interaction of physical, chemical and biological processes in ecosystems
biomass	The mass of living organisms
biome	A major ecological community extending over a large area and generally characterised by a dominant vegetation
biotic	Relating to living organisms
black body	A hypothetical body capable of absorbing all the electromagnetic radiation falling on it
boreal	From the north, boreal ecosystems are found in the Sub-arctic
boundary layer	A thin layer around a surface, leaf or root, where conditions differ from the bulk environment
Bowen ratio	Ratio of sensible to latent heat flux
calcification-salinisation	Processes of accumulation of calcium carbonate and salts in soils
canopy	The layer of leaves and branches of the vegetation cover
carboxylation	Attachment of CO_2 to another molecule
chlorosis	Loss of chlorophyll in a plant, resulting in normally green leaves becoming discoloured
chronosequence	A sequence of related ecosystems (vegetation and soils) that differ from each other only as a result of time
clay	Soil particles with diameters less than 0.002 mm
climax	End point of succession where element cycles are at steady state
cohort	A group of items of similar properties and age
community	A set of interdependent organisms inhabiting an area
compensation point	The temperature, CO_2 concentration or light intensity at which the net photosynthesis of a leaf is 0
complexation	Inorganic and organic compounds together bind to Al in minerals, thereby decreasing their stability
conductance	The flux per unit driving force; the inverse of resistance
conifer	Cone-bearing plants, e.g. pines, spruces, cedars

crown drip	Water captured in the canopy and then falling to the ground
deciduous	Not permanent, applied to trees that fell their leaves in the autumn
decomposer	Organisms that break down dead organic matter
denitrification	Conversion of nitrate to nitrogen gases (N_2, NO, N_2O)
diffusion	Movement of atoms in a gaseous mixture or of ions in a solution, primarily as a result of their own random motion
dissolution	Process when molecules of a gas, solid or liquid dissolve in a liquid and become completely and uniformly dispersed in the liquid's volume
dry weight/mass	The mass of an object when all water has been removed.
dynamic	Not in equilibrium
ecology	See page 19
ecophysiology	Physiology at the scale of ecosystems
ecosystem	A system consisting of a community of organisms and their environment
entisol	Soil order with little if any profile development
eutrophic	Rich in nutrients
evaporation	Conversion of liquid water to water vapour
evapotranspiration	Water loss from an ecosystem by transpiration and evaporation
evergreen	Plants that retain leaves throughout the year
fetch	The length/area over which wind has blown before reaching a target
field capacity	The amount of water held by a soil after gravitational water has drained
foliage	The leaves in a canopy
food web	The network of transfers of energy and nutrients between organisms in a community
forest floor	The forest soil O horizons, including litter and unincorporated humus, on the mineral soil surface
fresh weight	The mass of an object in its natural state, without drying
friction velocity	An empirical velocity used to describe wind profiles
gelisol	Soil order in areas with permafrost
growth respiration	Respiration coupled to an increase in biomass

guard cells	Cells surrounding the stomata and regulating the stomatal conductance
herbaceous	Pertaining to herbs
heterotrophs	Organisms that live on organic matter produced by other organisms (decomposers, consumers etc.)
histosol	Soil order; organic soils without permafrost
holism	The idea that the whole is more than the sum of its parts
homeostasis	The keeping of an even level
humidity	Relation between precipitation and evapotranspiration
humus	Amorphous soil organic matter. Also used to designate the part of the organic matter on top of the mineral soil
hydration	Chemical union between an ion or compound and one or more water molecules, the reaction being stimulated by the attraction of the ion or compound for either the hydrogen or the unshared electrons of the oxygen in the water
hydrolysis	A reaction with water that splits the water molecule into H^+ and OH^- ions
immobilisation	Conversion of inorganic nutrients to organic forms
inceptisol	Soil order; soils with few diagnostic features
interception	The process of stopping, e.g. light through a canopy
keystone species	Species that have a larger impact on ecosystem processes than would be expected from their biomass
latent heat	The amount of energy in the form of heat absorbed or released during a phase transition (e.g. evaporation of water)
laterisation	Weathering of primary soil minerals in a way where silica is first leached and aluminium and iron are accumulated
leaf area	The total area of the leaves of a tree or stand. Leaf area can be both projected and total
leaf area index (LAI)	The leaf area per unit ground area
lessivage-melanisation	Processes of transport of clay to B horizon and humus coloration of A horizon in soils, respectively
light compensation point	Light intensity at which net photosynthesis is 0

light extinction coefficient   Fraction of light absorbed per unit of leaf area along a light ray

light saturation   Light intensities at which photosynthesis is insensitive to light intensity

light-use efficiency   Ratio of primary production to absorbed radiation

limnology   The study of lakes and fresh waters

litter   Dead plant material that is sufficiently intact to be recognisable

loam   See Figure 4.10

maintenance respiration   Respiration used to maintain living biomass

mass balance   Conservation of mass

mass flow   Movement of nutrients with the flow of water to plant roots

material volume   The volume percentage of the total soil bulk occupied by solid particles

matric potential   The component of the water potential caused by adsorption of water to surfaces

methanotrophs   Methane-oxidising bacteria

mineral soil horizon   Leaching or eluvial horizon and accumulation or illuvial horizon

mineralisation   Conversion of carbon and nutrients from organic to inorganic forms

mollisol   Soil order; dark, soft soils of grasslands, black and rich in humus, base saturation often >50%

mycorrhiza   The fungal part of symbiosis between and fungi and roots of plants. The fungal hyphae surround the root (ectomycorrhiza) or penetrate the root (endomycorrhiza)

niche   The relational position of an organism in an ecosystem

nitrification   Conversion of ammonium to nitrate

nutrient   Element needed for life

nutrient productivity   Plant production per unit of nutrient

nutrient-use efficiency   Primary production per unit nutrient taken up

oligotrophic   Poor in nutrients

osmotic potential   Component of the water potential caused by substances dissolved in water

oxidation-reduction   Loss of electrons in a substance leading to a gain in positive charge and a gain of electrons giving a loss of positive charge, respectively

oxisol	Soil order in tropical climates, with accumulation of low-active clay, highly leached with free oxides and quartz
oxygenation	The process of adding oxygen
parent soil material	The unconsolidated and more or less chemically weathered mineral or organic matter from which the soil is developed by soil-forming processes
photosynthesis	The biochemical process that converts CO_2 and water to sugars
phytosociology	The branch of science which deals with plant communities, their composition and development and the relationships between the species within them
podsolisation	Weathering of primary soil minerals in a way where aluminium, iron and humus are leached to the B horizon; humus and silica remain in upper part of the soil
pore volume, porosity	The volume percentage of the total soil bulk not occupied by solid particles
portfolio effect	Increasing biodiversity increases ecosystem stability by minimising effects by individual species
precipitation	Water input to an ecosystem as rain and snow
priming	Change of the rate of a process by addition of another component. Priming can be both positive and negative
primary producer	Organism that converts CO_2, water and solar energy into biomass (plants); synonymously autotroph
pyramid of numbers	Many small organisms are required to support a few large organisms
quantum yield	Amount of CO_2 fixed per absorbed light quanta; the initial slope of the light-response curve of photosynthesis
radiative forcing	The change in the radiation balance of Earth caused by a radiative active gas
resorption efficiency	The fraction of nutrients withdrawn from senescing plant tissue
resorption proficiency	The lowest nutrient concentration that can be reached in senescing plant tissue
respiration	Biochemical reaction in which the chemical bonds of energy-rich molecules such as glucose are converted into energy usable for life processes and CO_2 and water
root interception	Acquisition of nutrients by a root as a result of the root growing into the vicinity of the nutrient source

roughness length	A parameter describing the effect of the roughness of a surface on the wind profile
Rubisco	Ribulose bisphosphate carboxylase–oxygenase; photosynthetic enzyme that catalyses the initial carboxylation in photosynthesis
sensible heat	Heat energy that can be sensed and involves no phase transition
silt	Soil particles with diameters between 0.002 and 0.05 mm
site factor	Property that affects the growth rate of the dominating vegetation
soil	A dynamic natural body composed of mineral and organic solids, gases, liquids and living organisms, which can serve as a medium for plant growth
soil order	Soil type occurring over larger geographic regions
soil organic matter	Dead organic matter in the soil, recognisable parts may be excluded from the term
soil organic matter horizon	Horizon with accumulated litter and some living material, as well as partly decomposed material
soil solution	The aqueous liquid phase of the soil and the solutes, consisting of ions dissociated from the surface of the soil particles and of other soluble materials
soil structure	The arrangement of soil particles creating the pore system
soil texture	The relative proportions of different sizes of mineral particles in the soil
soil type	A soil formed from a specific set of soil-forming factors such as vegetation and climate
solifluction	Downslope flow of water-saturated soils over a frozen layer
specific leaf area	The ratio between the area of a leaf and its mass
spodosol	Soil order of humid and cool or temperate climates; acid and coarse textured soils, accumulation of humus, aluminium, iron in B horizon
stemflow	The flux of water along plant stems from the canopy to the ground
stoichiometry	Relation between elements
stomata (pl.)/stoma (sing.)	The pores on leaf surfaces through which exchange of CO_2 and water between the leaf and the atmosphere takes place

streamflow	The flow of water in streams, rivers and other channels
succession	The directional change in species composition over time
synecology	The ecology of plant and animal communities
texture	Particle distribution in soils
throughfall	Water that drops from the canopy to the ground
transpiration	Water flux through stomata to the atmosphere
trophic level	Position of an organism in a food chain
trophic structure	Organisation of organisms in a food web
turgor	Pressure of cell contents against cell walls
ultisol	Soil order, usually moist, but during warm periods dry, highly leached, low in bases, clay accumulation in B horizon
vegetation structure	Structure of ecosystems/vegetation is characterised by their layering – tree, shrub, field layer of herbs and grasses, bottom or ground layer of mosses and lichens
vertisol	Soil order in areas with distinct dry and wet periods, clayey, swelling and shrinking in dry periods leading to deep cracks
water-use efficiency	Ratio of primary production to water loss; ratio of photosynthesis to transpiration
weathering	Physical and chemical processes converting parent rock into soil
wilting point	The soil water potential at which plants no longer can extract soil water
zero plane displacement	The height at which the logarithmic wind profile is extrapolated to 0

Appendix 3

Some useful values and symbols used to represent them

Radius of Earth	6371 km
Heat of vaporisation of water (at 20 °C), λ	2.44 MJ kg^{-1}
Heat of combustion of glucose	2803 kJ mol^{-1} or 15.6 kJ g^{-1} or 38.9 kJ (g C)$^{-1}$
Heat capacity of water (at 20 °C and 0.103 MPa)	4.175 MJ m^{-3} °C^{-1}
Diffusion coefficient of CO_2 in air (at 20 °C and 0.103 MPa)	1.51×10^{-5} m^2 s^{-1}
Diffusion coefficient of H_2O in air (at 20 °C and 0.103 MPa)	2.42×10^{-5} m^2 s^{-1}
Gas constant, R	8.314 J mol^{-1} K^{-1}
Density of dry air (at 20 °C and 0.103 MPa), ρ_a	1.205 kg m^{-3}
Density of water (at 20 °C)	998.2 kg m^{-3}
Specific heat of air at constant pressure, c_p	1.01 kJ kg^{-1} K^{-1}
Carbon concentration in dry matter (average)	0.5 g g^{-1}
Density of soil particles in soil (typical)	2650 kg m^{-3}

Conversion factors

$\mu g = 10^{-6}$ g
$mg = 10^{-3}$ g
$kg = 10^{3}$ g
$Mg = tonne = 10^{6}$ g
$Gg = 10^{9}$ g
$Tg = 10^{12}$ g
$Pg = 10^{15}$ g
1 kg m^{-2} = 10 tonnes ha^{-1} = 10 Mg ha^{-1}
1 g C = 44/12 g CO_2 = 3.67 g CO_2

Prefixes

$n = 10^{-9}$ (nano)
$\mu = 10^{-6}$ (micro)
$m = 10^{-3}$ (milli)
$k = 10^{3}$ (kilo)
$M = 10^{6}$ (mega)
$G = 10^{9}$ (giga)
$T = 10^{12}$ (tera)
$P = 10^{15}$ (peta)

Appendix 4

Information and data on selected ecosystems

This appendix provides additional information on the examples of terrestrial ecosystems we have chosen to illustrate structural and functional properties. The examples used represent investigations from different periods and of different schools. The completeness of the data also varies for that reason and may not always be completely comparable. This is particularly evident when it comes to belowground plant properties. Estimates of nitrogen deposition can also be more or less complete by not including all components (NO_3^-, NH_4^+, organic N) in dry and wet deposition.

The references in the Further reading section give in general more detailed information than in Table A4.1 below and in other parts of the text.

(1) Arctic tundra: Stordalen, Sweden

The example from the Arctic comes from northernmost Sweden, Stordalen, close to the Abisko Scientific Research Station. This is an area where field investigations and measurements have been carried out since 1903. It is a classic and well-known area. Long-term weather observations are available for Abisko; small-scale microclimate differences may exist relative to Stordalen. Since 1935 the Royal Swedish Academy of Sciences is responsible for the station. Today a modern and well-equipped station serves as base for many biological and environmental investigations. During the 1950s special interest was devoted to the differentiation of mire ecosystems in past and present times. This activity became the base for the Swedish efforts within the international IBP-tundra programme (Sonesson 1980), focussing on the biological functioning of tundra ecosystems. Today the Abisko station hosts the Climate Impact Research Centre and the Lake Torne Träsk Man and Biosphere Centre, among other activities. Thanks to 30-year-old data it has been shown that graminoide-dominated areas increase, while dryer areas with lichens, mosses and dwarf shrubs decrease. The most likely reason is that the extent of permafrost is decreasing.

FURTHER READING

Malmer, N., Johansson, T., Olsrud, M. & Christensen, T.R. 2005. Vegetation, climate changes and net carbon sequestration in a North-Scandinavian subarctic mire over 30 years. *Global Change Biology* **11**:1895–1909.

Olsrud, M. & Christensen, T.R. 2004. Carbon cycling in subarctic tundra; seasonal variation in ecosystem partitioning based on in situ 14C pulse labelling. *Soil Biology & Biogeochemistry* **36**:245–253.

Rosswall, T. & Granhall, U. 1980. Nitrogen cycling in a subarctic ombrotrophic mire. *Ecological Bulletins* **30**:209–234.

Sonesson, M. (ed.) 1980. *Ecology of a Subarctic Mire*. Ecological Bulletins 32. Stockholm: Swedish Natural Science Research Council.

Wielgolaski, F.E. (ed.) 1975. *Fennoscandian Tundra Ecosystems. Part 1. Plants and Microorganisms. Ecological Studies 16.* Berlin, Heidelberg, New York: Springer Verlag.

(2) Boreal coniferous pine forest: Jädraås, Sweden

The boreal example represents a Scots pine (*Pinus sylvestris*) forest, age 120 years. This area is now an experimental forest belonging to the Forest Faculty of the Swedish University of Agricultural Sciences. It was established in 1972 as a post-IBP activity and was a result of concern about the environmental impact of, among other things, air pollution. The long-term productivity and threats to biodiversity were driving forces for establishing research activities, which should give increased knowledge on how 'Nature functions'.

The research forest today has an age series of pine forests where long-term observations of climate, vegetations and soils occur. There have also been experimental efforts with irrigation and fertilisation.

FURTHER READING

Bringmark, L. 1977. A bioelement budget of an old Scots pine forest in central Sweden. *Silva Fennica* **11**:201–237.

NPP Boreal Forest: Jädraås, Sweden 1973–1980. Data set. Available online (www.daacornl.gov) from Oak Ridge National Laboratory Distributed Active Archive Center, Oak Ridge, TN, USA.

Persson, T. (ed.) 1980. *Structure and Function of Northern Coniferous Forests*. Ecological Bulletins 32. Stockholm: Swedish Natural Science Research Council.

(3) Temperate short grass prairie (steppe): Pawnee site, Colorado, USA

In the USA ecosystem research within the IBP concentrated on large-scale efforts in the form of biome programmes. The Pawnee site is one example of a grasslands site within the Grassland biome programme, where long-term investigations have been operated. Today these sites are used by several environmental programmes. The site is a part of the Central Plains Experimental Range, Colorado State University, Fort Collins. The Pawnee site is also an example of the LTER programme – Long Term Ecosystem Research Network.

FURTHER READING

Clark, F.E. 1977. Internal cycling of nitrogen in a shortgrass prairie. *Ecology* **58**:1322–1333.

Clark, F.E., Cole, C.V. & Bowman, R.A. 1979. Nutrient cycling. In Breymeyer, A.I. & Van Dyne, G.M. (eds). *Grasslands, Systems Analysis and Man. International Biological Programme 19*, Cambridge: Cambridge University Press.

Sims, P.L. & Coupland, R.T. 1976. Producers. In Coupland, R.T. (ed.) *Grassland Ecosystems of the World*. International Biological Programme 18. Cambridge: Cambridge University Press.

(4)   Temperate beech forest: Solling (*Heinz Ellenberg*), Germany

The Solling site was established in the early 1960s as a part of the IBP Deciduous Biome Project. It was initiated by one of the prominent advocates for forest ecosystem research, Professor H. Ellenberg, Göttingen. A detailed structured investigation of the major components was the result. The project focussed initially on: primary production of forests in relation to climate, soil and historical factors, secondary production with soil microbes and fauna, as well as element cycling.

   Gradually experiments were established. A roof was built to allow the manipulation of incoming water, acidity and nitrogen. This extension was motivated from the concern for long-term sustainability of forests as a consequence of air pollution.

FURTHER READING

Ellenberg, H., Mayer, R. & Schauermann, J. (eds) 1986. *Ökosystemforschung – Ergebnisse des Solling-Projekts*. Stuttgart: Ulmer.

(5)   Temperate planted spruce forest: Skogaby, Sweden

The Skogaby site was established in 1988 at a time when the effects of air pollution on forest ecosystems were under debate. Changes in soil acidity had been demonstrated in south-west Sweden. There was a need to explain causes of forest damage. It was assumed that the vitality of trees was a result of the interaction between climate and tree nutrition. A field experiment was designed where these factors were manipulated. Roofs were built under the tree canopy and water and nutrient factors were varied through irrigation, drought and fertilisation. Previous experience from large-scale fertilisation and irrigation experiments in the field, e.g. the Jädraås site, was an important background and help.

The site has also been used for additional investigations, among others, carbon dynamics to meet the increased interest in the effects of climate change and the forest ecosystem as a sink or source for carbon. The effects of ozone on trees have also been investigated.

FURTHER READING

Persson, T. & Nilsson, L.O. (eds) 2001. *The Skogaby Experiment – Effects of Long-Term Nitrogen and Sulfur Addition to a Forest Ecosystem (in Swedish)*. SNV Report 5173. Stockholm: SNV.

Schulze, E.D. (ed.) 2000. *Carbon and Nitrogen Cycling in European Forest Ecosystems*. Ecological Studies 142. 500 pp.

(6) Temperate coniferous rain forest: H.J. Andrews, Oregon, USA

The example of the temperate rain forest is taken from Watershed 10 in the H.J. Andrews Experimental Forest in Oregon, USA. The 6400 ha site, established in the 1950s, is located in the western central Cascade Mountains and belongs to the US Forest Service. The forest is dominated by *Pseudotsuga menziesii* and corresponds to a warm mesic site. The investigations were part of the US Coniferous Forest Biome Project belonging to the US IBP programme, Analysis of Ecosystems. Since 1980 it has been part of the National Science Foundation Long Term Ecological Research (NSF-LTER) programme. The H.J. Andrews Experimental Forest has become a leader in the analysis of forest and stream ecosystem dynamics.

FURTHER READING

Greenland, D. 1993. *The climate of the H.J. Andrews Experimental Forest, Oregon, and its Regional Synthesis*. USDA Forest Service, Pacific Northwest Research Station; Cooperative Agreement No. PNW 92–0221. 39 pp.

Grier, C.C. & Logan, R.S. 1977. Old growth *Pseudotsuga menziesii* communities of a western Oregon watershed: Biomass distribution and production budgets. *Ecological Monographs* **47**:371–400.

Sollins, P., Grier, C.C., McCorison, F.M. & Cromack Jr, K. 1980. The internal element cycles of an old-growth Douglas-fir ecosystem in western Oregon. *Ecological Monographs* **50**:261–285.

(7) Tropical savanna: Point Noire (Kondi), Congo

Since 1978 43 000 ha of native savanna has been planted with the exotic *Eucalyptus* on the coastal plains of Congo-Brazzaville. This has caused considerable changes in the element cycles and concern for the

sustainability of the short-rotation forestry. CIRAD (Centre de coopér-
ation internationale en recherche agronomique pour le développement)
has conducted studies in the area since 1997. The studies are also part of
the network of the Center for International Forestry Research (CIFOR).

FURTHER READING

de Grandcourt, A. & Saint-Andre, L. 2008. Evaluating NPP in a savannah of the
    Coastal plains of Congo, Part I: Biomass increment. CarboAfrica, short
    communication, 5th NewsLetter, http://www.carboafrica.net/downs/
    newsletters/05-Carboafrica_Newsletter_05-2008.pdf.
Laclau, J.P., Ranger, J., Deleporte, P. *et al.* 2005. Nutrient cycling in a clonal
    stand of Eucalyptus and an adjacent savanna ecosystem in Congo: 3. Input–
    output budgets and consequences for the sustainability of the plantations.
    Forest Ecology and Management **210**:375–391.
Laclau, J.P., Ranger, J., Nzila, J.D.D., Bouillet, J.P. & Deleporte, P. 2003. Nutrient
    cycling in a clonal stand of Eucalyptus and an adjacent savanna ecosystem
    in Congo: 2. Chemical composition of soil solutions. *Forest Ecology and
    Management* **180**:527–544.
Laclau, J.P., Sama-Poumba, W., Nzila, J.D.D., Bouillet, J.P. & Ranger, J. 2002.
    Biomass and nutrient dynamics in a littoral savanna subjected to annual
    fires in Congo. *Acta Oecologica* **23**:41–50.

(8)   Tropical dry forest: Chamela, Mexico

The Chamela forest is a part of the Biosphere Reserve Chamela-
Cuixmala, Jalisco, and situated near the Pacific coast of Mexico,
2 km inland and about 40 km south of the town of Tomatlan. It
belongs to the Biological Station of the National Autonomous University of Mexico (UNAM). The vegetation is highly diverse, including
about 700 plant species (of which over 180 are trees), and there is a
well-developed understory of shrubs. One of the most remarkable
features is the seasonality of leaf fall, with most species remaining
leafless for several months during the dry season. Tropical deciduous
forests are widespread in Mexico, covering large tracts along the
Pacific slopes from the state of Sonora in the north to Chiapas in the
south; it is also found in the northern part of the Yucatan peninsula.
The Chamela station covers 3300 hectares and is thought to have been
undisturbed for several hundred years; there are no records or evidence of either natural or anthropogenic fire.

FURTHER READING

Maas, M. & Martinez-Yrizar, A. 2001. NPP Tropical Forest Chamela, Mexico
    1982–1995. Data set available online (http://www.daac.ornl.gov) from Oak
    Ridge National Laboratory Distributed Active Center, Oak Ridge, TN, USA.
Martinez-Yrizar, A., Maass, J.M., Pirez-Jiminez, L.A. & Sarukhin, J. 1996. Net
    primary productivity of a tropical deciduous forest ecosystem in western
    Mexico. *Journal of Tropical Ecology* **12**:169–175.

(9) Tropical rain forest: San Carlos, Venezuela

The example of a tropical rain forest comes from San Carlos, in the Amazon province, Venezuela. It represents a low-production rain forest. Ecosystem investigations in San Carlos were started during the 1970s. The starting point was to have a better understanding of sustainability in a tropical rain forest after exploitation by clear-felling. A joint German, US and Venezuelan research effort was established within the Man and Biosphere Project.

FURTHER READING

Jordan, C.F. 1989. *An Amazon Rain Forest: The Structure and Function of Nutrient Stressed Ecosystem and the Impact of Slash–and Burn Agriculture.* Paris: UNESCO and The Parthenons Publishing Group.

Jordan, C.F., Caskey, W., Escalante, G. *et al.* 1982. The nitrogen cycle in a 'Terra Firme' rainforest on oxisol in the Amazon territory of Venezuela. *Plant and Soil* **67**:325–332.

Jordan, C.F., Cuevas, E. & Medina, E. 1999. NPP Tropical Forest; San Carlos de Rio Negro, Venezuela, 1975–1984. Data set available online (http://www.daac.ornl.gov) from Oak Ridge National Laboratory Distributed Active Center, Oak Ridge. USA.

Table A4.1 General characteristics, stocks and fluxes of carbon and nitrogen

Site Biome	1. Stordalen Tundra	2. Jädraås Boreal forest	3. Pawnee Temperate grassland	4. Solling Temperate deciduous forest	5. Skogaby Temperate evergreen forest	6. H.J. Andrews Temperate rain forest	7. Pointe Noire Savanna	8. Chamela Tropical dry forest	9. San Carlos Tropical rain forest
Location	68°22'N 19°03'E	60°82'N 16°50'E	40°49'N 104°46'W	51°43'N 9°36'E	56°33'N 13°13'E	44°13'N 122°13'W	4°07'S 12°00'E	19°30'N 105°011'W	1°93'N 67°05'W
Elevation (m asl)	351	185 650	475	115	115	430–670	100	70	122
Mean temp. (°C)	−0.8	+3.8	+9.6	+6.4	+7.6	+8.5	+25.7	+24.9	+27.0
Precip. (mm)	304	607	332	1088	1237	2224	1206	780	3565
Carbon stocks ($Mg\,ha^{-1}$) and fluxes ($Mg\,ha^{-1}\,yr^{-1}$)									
Aboveground biomass	2.00	35.0	2.67	137	60	250	2.6	27.6	137
Belowground biomass	2.33	23.4	7.17	18.6	13	52.4	4.4	6.7	27.8
Aboveground production	0.47	1.72	0.8	5.62	4.7	3.14	1.69	3.15	5.4
Belowground production	0.12	1.35	2.1	0.33	3.6	1.11	4.4	2.10	1.0
Litter production above ground	0.47	0.68	0.8	1.70	1.1	1.97	0	1.6	3.0
Litter production below ground	0.12	nd	2.1	nd	3.2	nd	4.4	nd	nd

Soil organic matter	145	39.3	34.9	115	99	134	90	83	50.4
DOC leaching	0.005	nd	nd	nd	0.03	0.06	nd	nd	nd
Nitrogen stocks (kg ha^{-1}) and fluxes (kg ha^{-1} yr^{-1})									
Aboveground biomass	63.3	113	84.9	588	293	539	20	42.5	1080
Belowground biomass	40.0	19.3	343	148	99	199	93	nd	979
Aboveground uptake	8.0	6.5	73.0	93.3	29	27.1	27.4	119	127
Belowground uptake	In agu	24.8	In agu	5.9	70	12.3	nd	In agu	22
Litter production above ground	8.3	23.7	nd	49	22	18.9	0	nd	61.3
Litter production below ground	In agu	nd	nd	nd	71	nd	nd	nd	nd
Soil organic matter	3420	1020	3730	8110	5820	3500	5980	6890	3910
Nitrogen fixation	2.0	0.1	nd	nd	nd	2.8	21.6	nd	16.2
Nitrogen deposition	2.2	5.8	4.0	25	17	2.0	4.8	nd	11.5

In agu: Included in aboveground uptake

nd: Not determined

References

Aber, J.D. & Melillo, J.M. 2001. *Terrestrial Ecosystems*. 2nd edn. San Diego, CA: Academic Press.

Aerts, R. 1990. Nutrient use efficiency in evergreen and deciduous species from heathlands. *Oecologia* **84**:391–397.

Ågren, G.I. 1996. Nitrogen productivity or photosynthesis minus respiration to calculate plant growth. *Oikos* **76**:529–535.

Ågren, G.I. 2004. The C:N:P stoichiometry of autotrophs: theory and observations. *Ecology Letters* **7**:185–191.

Ågren, G.I. & Bosatta, E. 1990. Theory and model or art and technology in ecology. *Ecological Modelling* **50**:213–220.

Ågren, G.I. & Bosatta, E. 1996. *Theoretical Ecosystem Ecology – Understanding Element Cycles*. 1st edn. Cambridge: Cambridge University Press.

Ågren, G.I. & Bosatta, E. 1998. *Theoretical Ecosystem Ecology – Understanding Element Cycles*. 2nd edn. Cambridge: Cambridge University Press.

Ågren, G.I., Chertov, O., Kahle, H.P. *et al.* 2008. Analysis of the long-term consequences for sustainability of observed growth changes of the European forests. In Kahle, H.P., Karjalainen, T., Schuck, A. *et al.* (eds) *Causes and Consequences of Forest Growth Trends in Europe – Results of the RECOGNITION Project. European Forest Institute Research Report 21*. Leiden: Brill, 235–238.

Ågren, G.I. & Franklin, O. 2003. Root:shoot ratios, optimisation, and nitrogen productivity. *Annals of Botany* **92**:795–800.

Allison, S.D., Wallenstein, M.D. & Bradford, M.A. 2010. Soil-carbon response to warming dependent on microbial physiology. *Nature Geoscience* **3**:336–340.

Almendros, G., Fründ, R., Gonzalez-Vila *et al.* 1991. Analysis of 13C and 15N CPMAS NMR-spectra of soil organic matter and composts. *FEBS Letters* **282**:119–121.

Amundson, R. & Jenny, H. 1997. On a state factor model of ecosystems. *BioScience* **47**:536–543.

Andersson, F. 1970a. Ecological Studies in a Scanian Woodland and Meadow Area, Southern Sweden. I. Vegetational and Environmental Structure. *Opera Botanica* 27. Lund: CWK Gleerup.

Andersson, F. 1970b. Ecological studies in a Scanian woodland and meadow area, Southern Sweden. II. Plant biomass, primary production and turnover of organic matter. *Botaniska Notiser* **123**:8–51.

Andersson, F.O., Ågren, G.I. & Führer, E. 2000. Sustainable tree biomass production. *Forest Ecology and Management* **132**:51–62.

Andersson, F., Bergholm, J., Hallbäcken *et al.* 1995. *Farabolförsöket – Försurning, Kalkning, och Kvävegödsling av en Sydöstsvensk Granskog (The Farabol Field Experiment – Acidification, Liming and Nitrogen Fertilisation of a Norway Spruce Forest in South-East Sweden*, English legends to figures and tables). Department of Ecology and Environmental Research, Swedish University of Agricultural Sciences, Uppsala. Report 70. ISBN 91-576-5139-9.

Andersson, F.O., Brække, F.H. & Hallbäcken, L. (eds) 1998. *Nutrition and Growth of Norway Spruce Forests in a Nordic Climatic and Deposition Gradient*. TemaNord 1998: 566. Copenhagen: Nordic Council of Ministers.

Andersson, F., Fagerström, T. & Nilsson, I. 1980. Forest ecosystem responses to acid deposition – hydrogen ion budget and nitrogen growth model approaches. In Hutchinson, T. & Havas, M. (eds) *Effects of Acid Precipitation on Terrestrial Ecosystems*. New York: Plenum, 319–334.

Andersson, F.O., Feger, K.H., Hüttl, R.F. *et al.* 2000. Forest ecosystem research – priorities for Europe. *Forest Ecology and Management* 132:111–119.

Andersson, F. & Lhoir, P. 2005. Introduction. In Andersson, F. (ed.) *Ecosystems of the World 6. Coniferous Forests*. Amsterdam: Elsevier, 1–22.

Andersson, F. & Lundkvist, H. 1989. Long-term Swedish field experiments in forest management practices and site productivity. In Dyck, W.J. & Mees, C.A. (eds) *Research Strategies for Long-Term Site Productivity*. Proceedings, IEA/BE A3 Workshop, Seattle, WA, August 1988. IEA/BE A3 Report No. 8. Forest Research Institute, New Zealand Bulletin 152:125–137.

Andersson, F. & Olsson, B. (eds) 1985. *Lake Gårdsjön – An Acid Forest Lake and its Catchment*. Ecological Bulletins 37. Stockholm: Swedish Natural Science Research Council.

Anonymous 1972. *Air Pollution across National Boundaries. The Impact on the Environment of Sulfur in Air and Precipitation. Sweden´s Case Study for the United Nations Conference on the Human Environment*. Stockholm: Royal Ministry for Foreign Affairs and Royal Ministry of Agriculture.

Anonymous 1982. *Acidification Today and Tomorrow*. Report from the Committee 'Enviroment '82'. Stockholm: Swedish Ministry of Agriculture.

Anten, N.P.R., Schieving, F. & Werger, M.J.A. 1995. Patterns of light and nitrogen distribution in relation to whole canopy carbon gain in C3 and C4 mono- and dicotyledonous species. *Oecologia* 101:504–513.

Aplet, G.H. 1990. Alteration of earthworm community biomass by the alien *Myrica faya* in Hawai'i. *Oecologia* 82:414–416.

Aronsson, A. 1985. Trädens växtnäringstillstånd i områden med skogsskador [kronutglesning] (Nutritional status of trees in areas with forests decline). *Skogsfakta Konferens* 8:51–54.

Arrhenius, S. 1896a. Naturens värmehushållning (Nature's heat usage). *Nordisk tidskrift för vetenskap, konst och industri* 14:121–130.

Arrhenius, S. 1896b. On the influence of carbonic acid in the air upon the temperature of the ground. *The London, Edinburgh and Dublin Philosophical Magazine and Journal of Science* 41:237–276.

Aston. A.R. 1979. Rainfall interception by eight small trees. *Journal of Hydrology* 42:383–396.

Atkin, O.K. & Tjoelker, M.G. 2003. Thermal acclimation and the dynamic response of plant respiration to temperature. *Trends in Plant Science* 8:343–351.

Attiwill, P.M. & Leeper, G.W. 1987. *Forest Soils and Nutrient Cycles*. Melbourne: Independent Publication Group.

Bailey, A.S., Hornbeck, J.W., Campbell, J.L. & Eagar, C. 2003. *Hydrometeorological Database for Hubbard Brook Experimental Forest: 1955–2000*. General Technical Report NE-305. US Department of Agriculture, Forest Service, Northeastern Research Station.

Barnes, B.V., Zak, D.R., Denton, S.R. & Spurr, S.H. 1998. *Forest Ecology*. New York: John Wiley & Sons.

Baumgartner, A. & Reichel, E. 1975. *The World Water Balance: Mean Annual Global, Continental and Maritime Precipitation, Evaporation and Runoff*. Amsterdam: Elsevier.

Benson, M.L., Landsberg, J.J. & Borough, C.J. (eds) 1992. The biology of forest growth experiment – an introduction. *Forest Ecology and Management* 52:1–311.

Berg, B., Müller, M. & Wessén, B. 1987. Decomposition of red clover (*Trifolium pratense*) roots. *Soil Biology & Biochemistry* **19**:589–593.

Berggren Kleja, D., Svensson, M., Majdi, H. *et al.* 2008. Pools and fluxes of carbon in three Norway spruce ecosystems along a climatic gradient in Sweden. *Biogeochemistry* **89**:7–25.

Bergh, J., Linder, S. & Bergström, J. 2005. Potential production for Norway spruce in Sweden. *Forest Ecology and Management* **204**:1–10.

Bergh, J., Linder, S., Lundmark, T. & Elfving, B. 1999. The effect of water and nutrient availability on the productivity of Norway spruce in northern and southern Sweden. *Forest Ecology and Management* **119**:51–62.

Bergholm, J., Jansson, P.E., Johansson, U. *et al.* 1995. Air pollution, tree vitality and forest production – the Skogaby project. General description of a field experiment with Norway spruce in South Sweden. In Nilsson, L.O., Hüttl, R.F., Johansson, U.T. & Pathy, P. (eds) *Nutrient Uptake and Cycling in Forest Ecosystems*. European Commission Research Report 21, 69–88.

Berglund, B.E. 2003. Human impact and climate changes – synchronous events and a causal link? *Quaternary International* **105**:7–12.

Berglund, B.E., Björkman, L., Holmqvist, B.H. & Persson, T. 2007. The history of the vegetation of Skåne – changes during 17 000 years. In Tyler, T., Johansson, H., Olsson. K.A. & Sonesson, M. (eds) *Floran i Skåne. Arterna och Deras Utbredning*. Lund: Lunds Botaniska Förening, 27–38.

Berglund, B.E., Gaillard, M.J., Björkman, L. & Persson, T, 2008. Long-term changes in floristic diversity in southern Sweden: Palynological richness, vegetation dynamics and land-use. *Vegetation History and Archaeobotany* **17**:573–583.

Berglund, B.E., Persson, T. & Björkman, L. 2007. Late Quaternary landscape and vegetation diversity in a North European perspective. *Quaternary International* **184**:187–194.

Binkley, D. & Högberg, P. 1997. Does atmospheric deposition of nitrogen threaten Swedish forests? *Forest Ecology and Management* **92**:119–152.

Birks, H.J.B. 1986. Late-quaternary biotic changes in terrestrial and lacustrine environments, with particular reference to north-west Europe. In Berglund, B.E. (ed.) *Handbook of Holocene Palaeoecology and Palaeohydrology*. Chichester: John Wiley & Sons, 3–65.

Birks, H.J.B. & Birks, H.H. 2004. The rise and fall of forests. *Science* **305**:484–485.

Björkman, O. 1981. Responses to different quantum flux densities. In Lange, O.L., Nobel, P.S., Osmond, C.B. & Ziegler, H. (eds) *Encyclopedia of Plant Physiology*, Vol. **12**A. Berlin: Springer-Verlag, 57–107.

Blennow, K. & Hammarlund, K. 1993. From heath to forest – land-use transformation in Halland, Sweden. *Ambio* **22**:561–567.

Bloom, A.J., Chapin III, T.S. & Mooney, H.A. 1985. Resource limitation in plants – an economic analogy. *Annual Review of Ecology and Systematics* **16**:363–392.

Bonan, G. 2002. *Ecological Climatology – Concepts and Applications*. Cambridge: Cambridge University Press.

Bormann, F.H. & Likens, G.E. 1979. *Pattern and Process in a Forested Ecosystem – Disturbance, Development and the Steady State Based on the Hubbard Brook Ecosystem Study*. New York: Springer.

Bortyatinski, J.M., Hatacher, P.G. & Knicker, H. 1996. NMR techniques (C, N, and H) studies of humic substances. In Gaffney, J.S., Marley, N.A. &

Clark, S.B. (eds) *Humic and Fulvic Acids – Isolation, Structure, and Environmental Role*. Washington, DC: American Chemical Society, 57–77.

Botkin, D.B., Janek, J.F. & Wallis, J.R. 1972. Some ecological consequences of a computer model of forest growth. *Journal of Ecology* 60:849–872.

Bowman, C.T. 1991. Chemistry of gaseous pollutant formation and destruction. In Bartok, W. & Sarofim A.D. (eds) *Fossil Fuel Combustion – A Source Book*. New York: John Wiley & Sons, 215–260.

Bradshaw, R.H.W. & Lindbladh, M. 2005. Regional spread and stand-scale establishment of *Fagus sylvatica* and *Picea abies* in Scandinavia. *Ecology* 86:1679–1686.

Brady, C.B. & Weil, R.R. 2007. *The Nature and Properties of Soils*. 14th edn. Upper Saddle River, NJ: Pearson, Prentice Hall.

Breymeyer, A.I. & Van Dyne, G.M. 1980. *Grasslands, Systems Analysis and Man*. Cambridge: Cambridge University Press.

Buchmann, N., Guehl, J.M., Barigah, T.S. & Ehleringer, J.R. 1997. Interseasonal comparison of CO_2 concentrations, isotopic composition, and carbon dynamics in an Amazonian rainforest (French Guiana). *Oecologia* 110:120–131.

Cajander, A.K. 1909. Über Waldtypen (On forest types). *Acta Forestalia Fennica* 1, 1–176.

Cajander, A.K. 1930. Wesen und Bedeutung der Waldtypen (Nature and importance of forest types). *Silva Fennica* 15: 1–66.

Cannell, M.G.R. & Thornley, J.H.M. 1998. Temperature and CO_2 responses of leaf and canopy photosynthesis: A clarification using the non-rectangular hyperbola model of photosynthesis. *Annals of Botany* 82:883–892.

Cannell, M.G.R. & Thornley, J.H.M. 2000. Modelling the components of plant respiration: Some guiding principles. *Annals of Botany* 85:45–54.

Carpenter, S.R. & Turner, M.G. 1998. At last: A journal devoted to ecosystem science. *Ecosystems* 1:1–5.

Chapin III, F.S., Matson, P.A. & Mooney, H.A. 2002. *Principles of Terrestrial Ecosystem Ecology*. New York: Springer.

Christie, E.K. & Moorby, J. 1975. Physiological responses of semiarid grasses. I. The influence of phosphorous supply on growth and phosphorous absorption. *Australian Journal of Agricultural Research* 26:423–436.

Coleman, K. & Jenkinson, D.S. 1999. *RothC-26.3 – A Model for the Turnover of Carbon in Soil. Model Description and Windows Users Guide*. Harpenden: IARC–Rothamsted.

Conway, T.J., Tans, P., Waterman, L.S. *et al.* 1988. Atmospheric carbon dioxide measurements in the remote global troposphere, 1981–1984. *Tellus* 40B:81–118.

Cornelissen, J.H.C. 1996. An experimental comparison of leaf decomposition rates in a wide range of temperate plant species and types. *Journal of Ecology* 84:573–582.

Cornwell, W.K., Cornelissen, J.H.C., Amatangelo, K. *et al.* 2008. Plant species traits are the predominant control on litter decomposition rates within biomes worldwide. *Ecology Letters* 11:1065–1071.

Cowling, E.B. 1980. A historical resumé of progress in scientific and public understanding of acid precipitation and its biological consequences. In *Research Report 18/80. SNSF-project (Acid Precipitation – Effects on Forest and Fish)*. Oslo-Ås, Norway.

Crews, T.E., Kitiyama, K., Fownes, J.H. *et al.* 1995. Changes in soil phosphorus fractions and ecosystem dynamics across a long chronosequence in Hawaii. *Ecology* 76:1407–1424.

Davidson, E. 1991. Fluxes of nitrous oxide and nitric oxide from terrestrial ecosystems. In Rogers, J.E. & Whitman, W.B. (eds) *Microbial Production and Consumption of Greenhouse Gases: Methane, Nitrogen Oxides, and Halomethanes*. Washington, DC: American Society for Microbiology, 219–235.

de Laplante, K. 2005. Is ecosystem management a postmodern science? In Cuddington, K.E. & Beisner, B.E. (eds) *Ecological Paradigms Lost: Routes of Theory Change*. Burlington, MA: Academic Press, 397–418.

De Lucia, E.H., Drake, J.E., Thomas, R.B. & Gonzalez-Meler, G. 2007. Forest carbon use efficiency: Is respiration a constant fraction of gross primary production? *Global Change Biology* **13**:1157–1167.

de Saussure, N.T. 1804. *Recherches chimiques sur la végétation (Chemical Research on Vegetation)*. Paris: Nyon.

Del Grosso, S., Parton, W., Stohlgren, T. *et al.* 2008. Global potential net primary production predicted from vegetation class, precipitation, and temperature. *Ecology* **89**:2117–2126.

Des Marais, D.J. 2000. When did photosynthesis emerge on Earth. *Science* **289**:1703–1705.

Dewar, R.C., Medlyn, B.E. & McMurtrie, R.E. 1999. Acclimation of the respiration/photosynthesis ratio to temperature: Insights from a model. *Global Change Biology* **5**:615–622.

Duvigneaud, P. 1980. *La Synthèse Ecologique (The Ecological Synthesis)*. Paris: Doin.

Edmonds, R.L. 1982. *Analysis of Forest Ecosystems in the Western United States. US/IBP Synthesis Seeries*. Stroudsburg, PA: Hutchinson Ross Publishing.

Ehrlich, P.R. & Ehrlich, A. 1970. *Population, Resources, Environment: Issues in Human Ecology*. San Fransisco, CA: W.H. Freeman.

Ehrlich, P.R. & Ehrlich, A. 1981. *Extinction: The Causes and Consequences of the Disappearance of Species*. New York: Random House.

Ek, A.S., Löfgren, S., Bergholm, J. & Qvarfort, U. 2001. Environmental effects of one thousand years of copper production at Falun, Central Sweden. *Ambio* **30**:96–103.

Eliasson, P.E., McMurtrie, R.E., Pepper, D.A. *et al.* 2005. The response of heterotrophic CO_2-flux to soil warming. *Global Change Biology* **11**:167–181.

Ellenberg, H., Mayer, R. & Schauermann, J. 1986. *Ökosystemforschung – Ergebnisse des Solling Projekts 1966–1986 (Ecosystem Research – Results of the Solling Project)*. Stuttgart: Ulmer.

Elton, C. 1927. *Animal Ecology*. London: Sigdwick & Jackson.

Emberson, L., Ashmore, M. & Murray, F. 2003. *Air Pollution Impacts on Crops and Forests – A Global Assessment*. Air Pollution Review, Vol. **4**. London: Imperial College Press.

ENFORS 2005. *European Long-Term Research for Sustainable Forestry: A Research Strategy for Sustainable Forest Management in Europe*. Technical Report 5. COST Action E25. Paris: ECOFOR. ISBN 2-914770-08-1.

Ericsson, T. 1994. Nutrient dynamics and requirements of forest crops. *New Zealand Journal of Forestry Science* **24**:133–168.

Eugster, W., Rouse, W.R., Pielke Sr, R.A. *et al.* 2000. Land–atmosphere energy exchange in Arctic tundra and boreal forest: Available data and feedbacks to climate. *Global Change Biology* **6**:84–115.

Falkengren-Grerup, U. 1989. Soil acidification and its impact on ground vegetation. *Ambio* **18**:179–183.

Falkengren-Grerup, U. 1995. Long-term changes in flora and vegetation in deciduous forests of S Sweden. *Ecological Bulletins* **44**:215–236.

FAO 1998. *World Reference Base for Soil Resources. World Soil Resources*, Report 84. Rome: Food and Agriculture Organization of the United Nations.

Farcy, C. & Tabush, P. 2005. Sustainability and forest use: Concepts and prerequisite. In Mårell, A. & Leitgeb, E. (eds) *European Long-Term Research for Sustainable Forestry: Experimental and Monitoring Assets at the Ecosystem and Landscape Level. Part 2: ENFORS Field Facilities*. Technical Report 4, COST Action E25. Paris: ECOFOR, 6–21.

Fargione, J., Hill, J., Tilman, D., Polasky, S. & Hawthorne, P. 2008. Land clearing and the biofuel carbon debt. *Science* **319**:1235–1238.

Firestone, M.K. & Davidson, E.A. 1989. Microbial basis of NO and N_2O production and consumption in soil. In Andreae, M.O. & Schimel, D.S. (eds) *Exchange of Trace Gases between Terrestrial Ecosystems and the Atmosphere*. Chichester: John Wiley & Sons, 7–21.

Florin, R. 1964. Barrträdens utbredning i tid och rum (Conifer distribution in time and space, summary in English). *Svensk Naturvetenskap* **1964**:243–270.

Foley, J.A., Kutzbach, J.E., Coe, M.T. & Levis, S. 1994. Feedbacks between climate and boreal forests during the Holocene epoch. *Nature* **371**:52–54.

Forman, R.T.T. 1995. *Land Mosaics: The Ecology of Landscapes and Regions*. Cambridge: Cambridge University Press.

Franklin, O. & Ågren, G.I. 2002. Leaf senescence and resorption as mechanisms of maximizing photosynthetic production during canopy development at N limitation. *Functional Ecology* **16**:727–733.

Fraústo da Silva, J.J.R. & Williams, R.J.P. 2001. *The Biological Chemistry of the Elements – The Inorganic Chemistry of Life*. Oxford: Oxford University Press.

Fry, B. 2006. *Stable Isotope Ecology*. New York: Springer.

Fung, I.Y., Doney, S.C., Lindsay, K. & John, J. 2005. Evolution of carbon sinks in a changing climate. *Proceedings of the National Academy of Sciences of the United States of America* **102**:11201–11206.

Gaillard, M.J., Sugita, S., Bunting, M.J. *et al.* 2008. The use of modelling and simulation approach in reconstructing past landscapes from fossil pollen data: A review and results from the POLLANDCAL network. *Vegetation History and Archaeobotany* **17**:419–443.

Galloway, J.N., Dentener, F.J., Capone, D.G. *et al.* 2004. Nitrogen cycles: Past, present, and future. *Biogeochemistry* **70**:153–226.

Gillon, D., Joffre, R. & Ibrahima, A. 1999. Can litter decomposabiltiy be predicted by near infrared reflectance spectroscopy? *Ecology* **80**:175–186.

Grünzweig, J.M., Gelfand, I., Fried, Y. & Yakir, D. 2007. Biogeochemical factors contributing to enhanced carbon storage following afforestation of a semi-arid shrubland. *Biogeosciences* **4**:891–904.

Gundersen, P., Schmidt, I.K. & Raulund-Rasmussen, K. 2006. Leaching of nitrate from temperate forests – effects of air pollution and forest management. *Environmental Reviews* **14**:1–57.

Gutschick, V.P. 1981. Evolved strategies in nitrogen acquisition by plants. *American Naturalist* **118**:607–637.

Haeckel, E.H. 1866. *Generelle Morphologie der Organismen (General Morphology of Organisms)*. Berlin: Georg Reimer.

Hallbäcken, L. & Tamm, C.O. 1986. Changes in soil acidity from 1927 to 1982–84 in a forest area of SW Sweden. *Scandinavian Journal of Forest Research* **1**:219–232.

Halldin, S., Grip, H., Jansson, P.E. & Lindgren, Å. 1980. Micrometeorology and hydrology of pine forest ecosystems. II. Theory and model. In Persson, T. (ed.)

Structure and Function of Northern Coniferous Forests. Ecological Bulletins 32:463–503.

Hector, A., Joshi, J., Scherer-Lorenzen, M. *et al.* 2007. Biodiversity and ecosystem functioning: Reconciling the results of experimental and observational studies. *Functional Ecology* 21:998–1002.

Helvey, J.D. & Patric, J.H. 1965. Canopy and litter interception of rainfall by hardwoods of eastern United States. *Water Resources Research* 1:193–206.

Hettelingh, J.P., Posch, M. & Slootweg, J. (eds) 2008. *Critical Load, Dynamic Modelling and Impact Assessment in Europe.* CCE Status Report 2008. Coordination Centre for Effects, Netherlands Environmental Assessment Agency.

Högberg, P., Houbao, F., Quist, M., Binkley, D. & Tamm, C.O. 2006. Tree growth and soil acidification in response to 30 years of experimental nitrogen loading on boreal forest. *Global Change Biology* 12:489–499.

Holling, C.S. 1992. Cross-scale morphology, geometry, and dynamics of ecosystems. *Ecological Monographs* 62:447–502.

Houghton, R.A. & Hackler, J.L. 2002. Carbon flux to the atmosphere from land-use changes. In *Trends: A Compendium of Data on Global Change.* Oak Ridge, TN: Carbon Dioxide Information Analysis Center, Oak Ridge National Laboratory, US Department of Energy.

Hultberg, H. 1985. Changes in fish populations and water chemistry in Lake Gårdsjön and neighbouring lakes last century. *Ecological Bulletins* 37:64–72.

Hultberg, H. & Skeffington, R. 1997. *Experimental Reversal of Acid Rain Effects – The Gårdsjön Roof Project.* New York: John Wiley & Sons.

Hytteborn, H., Maslov, A.A., Nazimova, D.I. & Rysin, L.P. Boreal forests of Eurasia. 2005. In Andersson, F. (ed.) *Ecosystems of the World 6. Coniferous Forests.* Amsterdam: Elsevier, 23–99.

Ingestad, T. 1980. Growth, nutrition, and nitrogen fixation in grey alder at varied rate of nitrogen addition. *Physiologia Plantarum* 50:353–364.

Ingestad, T. & Ågren, G.I. 1988. Nutrient uptake and allocation rates at steady-state nutrition. *Physiologia Plantarum* 72:450–459.

Ingestad, T. & Ågren, G.I. 1992. Theories and methods on plant nutrition and growth. *Physiologia Plantarum* 84:177–184.

Ingestad, T., Aronsson, A. & Ågren, G.I. 1981. Nutrient flux density model of mineral nutrition in conifer ecosystems. *Studia Forestalia Suecica* 161:61–72.

Ingestad, T., Hellgren, O. & Lund Ingestad, A.B. 1994a. *Data base for tomato plants at steady-state. Methods and performance of tomato plants* (Lycopersicon esculentum Mill. *cv. Solentos) under non-limiting conditions and under limitation by nitrogen and light.* Department of Ecology and Environmental Research. Report 74. Uppsala: Swedish University of Agricultural Sciences.

Ingestad, T., Hellgren, O. & Lund Ingestad, A.B. 1994b. *Data base for birch plants at steady-state. Performance of birch plants* (Betula pendula Roth.) *under non-limiting conditions and under limitation by nitrogen and light.* Department of Ecology and Environmental Research. Report 75. Uppsala: Swedish University of Agricultural Sciences.

Ingestad, T. & Lund, A.B. 1986. Theory and techniques for steady state mineral nutrition and growth of plants. *Scandinavian Journal of Forest Research* 1:439–453.

IPCC 2001. *Climate Change 2001: The Scientific Basis. Contribution of Working Group I to the Third Assessment Report of the Intergovernmental Panel on Climate Change.*

Houghton, J.T., Ding, Y., Griggs, D.J. *et al.* (eds). Cambridge: Cambridge University Press.

IPCC 2006. *2006 IPCC Guidelines for National Greenhouse Gas Inventories*. Eggleston, H.S., Buendia, L., Miwa, K., Ngara, T. & Tanabe, K. (eds). Hayama: IGES.

IPCC 2007. *Climate Change 2007: The Physical Science Basis. Contribution of Working Group I to the Fourth Assessment Report of the Intergovernmental Panel on Climate Change*. Solomon, S., Qin, D., Manning, M. *et al.* (eds). Cambridge: Cambridge University Press.

Jackson, R.B., Canadell, J., Ehleringer, J.R. *et al.* 1996. A global analysis of root distributions for terrestrial biomes. *Oecologia* **108**:389–411.

Jansen, D. 1999. The climate system. In Martens P. & Rotmans, J. (eds) *Climate Change: An Integrated Perspective*. Dordrecht: Kluwer Academic Publishers, 11–50.

Jansson, M., Bergström, A.K., Lymer, D., Vrede, K. & Karlsson, J. 2006. Bacterioplankton growth and nutrient use efficiencies under variable organic carbon and inorganic phosphorus ratios. *Microbial Ecology* **52**:358–364.

Jarvis, P.G. & Fowler, D.G. 2001. Forests and the atmosphere. In Evans, J. (ed.) *The Forests Handbook*, Vol. **1**. Oxford: Blackwell Science., 229–281.

Jarvis, P.G., James, G.B. & Landsberg, J.J. 1976. Coniferous forests. In Monteith, J.L. (ed.) *Vegetation and the Atmosphere*, Vol. **2**. London: Academic Press, 171–239.

Jenny, H. 1941. *Factors of Soil Formation: A System of Quantitative Pedology*. New York: Dover.

Joffre, R., Ågren, G.I., Gillon, D. & Bosatta, E. 2001. Organic matter quality in ecological studies: Theory meets experiment. *Oikos* **93**:451–458.

Joffre, R., Gillon, D., Dardenne, P., Agneessens, R. & Biston, R. 1992. The use of near-infrared reflectance spectroscopy in litter decomposition studies. *Annales des Sciences Forestières* **49**:481–488.

Johnson, D.W. & Lindberg, S.E. (eds) 1992. *Atmospheric Deposition and Forest Nutrient Cycling*. Ecological Studies 97. New York: Springer Verlag.

Jones, C., Lowe, J., Liddicoat, S. & Betts, R. 2009. Committed terrestrial ecosystem changes due to climate change. *Nature Geoscience* **2**:484–487.

Jonsson, B. & Sundberg, R. 1972. *Has the acidification by atmospheric pollution caused a growth reduction in Swedish forests?* Department of Forest Production Reports and Essays 20. Stockholm: Department of Forest Production.

Jonsson, B. & Svensson, L.G. 1982. *A study of the effects of air pollution and forest yield*. A follow-up of the report of Jonsson and Sundberg 1972 and a new study based on forest types. Report 9. Section of Forest Mensuration and Management, Swedish University of Agricultural Sciences. Umeå, Sweden: Swedish University of Agricultural Sciences.

Kahle, H.P., Karjalainen, T., Schuck, A. *et al.* (eds) 2008. *Causes and Consequences of Forest Growth Trends in Europe – Results of the RECOGNITION Project*. European Forest Research Report 21. Leiden: Brill.

Karlsson, P.E., Örlander, G., Langvall, O. *et al.* 2006. Negative impact of ozone on the stem basal area increment of mature Norway spruce in S Sweden. *Forest Ecology and Management* **232**:146–151.

Karlsson, P.E., Pleijel, G., Belhaj, M. *et al.* 2005. Economic assessment of the negative impacts of ozone on crop yields and forest production. A case study of the Estate Östads Säteri, SW Sweden. *Ambio* **34**:32–40.

Keeling, R.F., Piper, S.C., Bollenbacher, A.F. & Walker, J.S. 2009. Atmospheric CO_2 records from sites in the SIO air sampling network. In *Trends:*

A Compendium of Data on Global Change. Oak Ridge, TN: Carbon Dioxide Information Analysis Center, Oak Ridge National Laboratory, US Department of Energy, doi: 10.3334/CDIAC/atg.035. §P.

Kiehl, J.T. & Trenberth, K.E. 1997. Earth's annual global mean energy budget. *Bulletin of the American Meteorological Society* **78**:191–197.

Killingbeck, K.T. 1996. Nutrients in senesced leaves: Keys to the search for potential resorption and resorption proficiency. *Ecology* **77**:1716–1727.

Kirschbaum, M.U.F. 2000. Will changes in soil organic carbon act as a positive or negative feedback on global warming. *Biogeochemistry* **48**:21–51.

Kling, G.W., Kipphut, G.W. & Miller, M.C. 1991. Arctic lakes and streams as gas conduits to the atmosphere: Implications for tundra carbon budgets. *Science* **251**:298–301.

Kolasa, J. & Pickett, S.T.A. 1991. *Ecological Heterogeneity*. New York: Springer Verlag.

Kranabetter, J.M., Dawson, C.R. & Dunn, D.E. 2007. Indices of dissolved organic nitrogen, ammonium, and nitrate across productivity gradients of boreal forests. *Soil Biology & Biochemistry* **39**:3147–3158.

Larcher, W. 1995. *Physiological Plant Ecology*. Berlin: Springer-Verlag.

Lewis, S.L., Lopez-Gonzalez, G., Sonké, B. *et al.* 2009. Increasing carbon storage in intact African tropical forests. *Nature* **457**:1003–1007.

Likens, G.E. 1992. The ecosystem approach: Its use and abuse. In Kinne, O. (ed.) *Excellence in Ecology*. Oldendorf/Luhe: Ecology Institute.

Likens, G.E. & Bormann, F.H. 1995. *Biogeochemistry of a Forested Ecosystem*. New York: Springer.

Liljegren, R. 1999. Växternas och djurens invandring (Immigration of plants and animals). In Germundsson, T. & Schlyter, P. (eds) *Atlas över Skåne. Sveriges nationalatlas* (*Atlas of Scania. National Atlas of Sweden*). Uppsala: Almqvist & Wiksell. ISBN 91-87760-46-0.

Lindeman, R.L. 1942. The trophic-dynamic aspects of ecology. *Ecology* **23**:399–418.

Linder, S. 1987. Responses to water and nutrients in coniferous eosystems. In Schulze, E.D. & Zwölfer, H. (eds) *Potentials and Limitations of Ecosystem Analysis*, Vol. **61**, *Ecological Studies*. Berlin-Heidelberg: Springer-Verlag, 180–202.

Linnaeus, C. 1734. Dalaresan. Iter Dalekarlicum. In Swedish and translated into English. In *The Early Works of Carl von Linné 1889*. Stockholm: Royal Swedish Academy of Sciences.

Linnaeus, C. 1751. *Philosophia Botanica*. Stockholm: Kessinger Publishing, LLC.

Lotka, A.J. 1925. *Elements of Physical Biology*. Baltimore, MD: Williams & Wilkens.

Loucks, O.L. 1970. Evolution of diversity, efficiency, and community stability. *American Zoologist* **10**:17–25. §11.

Loucks, O.L. 1986. The Unites States' IBP: An ecosystems perspective after fifteen years. In Poulunin, N. (ed.) *Ecosystem Theory and Application. Environmental Monographs and Symposia*. New York: John Wiley & Sons, 390–405.

Lovelock, J. 1979. *Gaia: A New Look at Life on Earth*. Oxford: Oxford University Press.

Lovelock, J. 1988. *Ages of Gaia*. Oxford: Oxford University Press.

Luyssaert, S., Schulze, E.D., Börner, A. *et al.* 2008. Old-growth forests as global carbon sinks. *Nature* **455**:213–215.

Mackenzie, F.T. & Ver Lerman, L.M. 1998. Coupled biogeochemical cycles of carbon, nitrogen, phosphorus and sulfur in the land-ocean-atmosphere system. In Galloway, J.N. & Melillo, J.M. (eds) *Asian Change in the Context of Global Climate Change*. Cambridge: Cambridge University Press, 42–100.

Malmström, C. 1939. Hallands skogar under de senaste 300 åren (The Forests of the Province Halland during the last 300 Years). *Meddelanden Statens Skogsförsöksanstalt* **31**:171–300.

Marland, G., T.A. Boden & R.J. Andres. 2006. Global, regional, and national CO_2 emissions. In *Trends: A Compendium of Data on Global Change*. Oak Ridge, TN: Carbon Dioxide Information Analysis Center, Oak Ridge National Laboratory, US Department of Energy.

May, R.M. 1973. *Stability and Complexity in Model Ecosystems*, Princeton, NJ: Princeton University Press.

May, R.M. 1999. Unanswered questions in ecology. *Philosophical Transactions of the Royal Society of London Seeries B, Biological Sciences* **354**:1951–1959.

McNaughton, S.J., Oesterheld, M., Frank, D.A. & Williams, K.J. 1989. Ecosystem-level patterns of primary productivity and herbivory in terrestrial habitats. *Nature* **341**:142–144.

McNaughton, S.J., Ruess, R.W. & Seagle, S.W. 1988. Large mammals and process dynamics in African ecosystems. *BioScience* **38**:794–800.

Metherell, A.K., Harding, L.A., Cole, C.V. & Parton, W.J. 1993. *Century Manual*. Great Plains System Research Unit, Technical Report No. 4. Fort Collins, CO: USDA-ARS.

Millennium Ecosystem Assessment (MEA) 2005. *Ecosystems and Human Well-Being: Synthesis*. Washington, DC: Island Press.

Minderman, G. 1968. Addition, decomposition and accumulation of organic matter in forests. *Journal of Ecology* **56**:355–362.

Mitchell, R., Mayer, R.A. & Downhower, J. 1976. An evaluation of three biome programs. *Science* **192**:859–865.

Monteith, J.L. & Unsworth, M.H. 1990. *Principles of Environmental Physics*. London: Edward Arnold.

Naiman, R.J. 1988. Animal influences on ecosystem dynamics. *BioScience* **38**:750–752.

National Atlas of Sweden. The Forests. 1990. *Skogsstyrelsen, Jönköping*. ISBN 91-87760-06-1 (www.sna.se).

Nilsson, J. & Grennfelt, P. 1988. Critical load for sulfur and nitrogen. Report from a workshop at Skokloster, Sweden. Copenhagen: NORD Report.

Nilsson, I., Miller, H.G. & Miller, J.D. 1982. Forest growth a possible cause of soil and water acidification: An examination of the concepts. *Oikos* **39**:40–49.

Nilsson, I. & Nilsson, J. 1981. *Olika källor till markförsurning (Sources to Soil Acidification)*. SNV PM 1411. Solna: Swedish Environmental Protection Agency.

Nilsson, I. & Tyler, G. 1995. Acidification induced chemical changes of forests during recent decades – a review. *Ecological Bulletins* **44**:54–64.

Nilsson, L.O. & Wiklund, K. 1995. Nutrient balance and P, K, Ca, Mg, S and B accumulation in Norway spruce stand following ammonium sulfate application, fertigation, irrigation, drought and N-free-fertilisation. *Plant and Soil* **168–169**:437–446.

Nordin, A., Högberg, P. & Näsholm, T. 2001. Soil nitrogen form and plant nitrogen uptake along a boreal forest productivity gradient. *Oecologia* **129**:125–132.

Odén, S. 1967a. Nederbördens försurning (The acidification of precipitation). *Dagens Nyheter* 24 October 1967.

Odén, S. 1967b. *The acidification of air and precipitation and its consequences on the natural environment* (In Swedish). Ecology Committee, Bulletin 1, National

Science Research Council of Sweden. Translated by Translation Consultants Ltd, Arlington, VA. No. TR-1172.

Odum, E.P. 1953. *Fundamentals of Ecology*. 1st edn. London: Saunders.

Odum, E.P. 1959. *Fundamentals of Ecology*. 2nd edn. London: Saunders.

Odum, E.P. 1971. *Fundamentals of Ecology*. 3rd edn. London: Saunders.

Odum, E.P. 1983. *Basic Ecology (Considered as the 4th edn of Fundamentals of Ecology)*. London: Saunders.

Odum, E.P. & Barrett, G.W. 2005. *Fundamentals of Ecology*. 5th edn. Belmont, CA: Thomson Brooks.

Odum, H.T. 1983. *Systems Ecology: An Introduction*. New York: Wiley & Sons.

Olson, R.K., Binkley, D. & Bohm, M. (eds) 1992. *The Response of Western Forests to Air Pollution*. Ecological Studies 97. New York: Springer-Verlag.

Ovington, J.D. 1962. Quantitative ecology and the woodland ecosystem concept. *Advances in Ecological Research* **1**:103–182.

Pales, J.C. & Keeling, C.D. 1965. The concentration of atmospheric carbon dioxide in Hawaii. *Journal of Geophysical Research* **24**:6053–6076.

Papaik, M.J. & Canham, C.D. 2006. Species resistance and community response to wind disturbance regimes in northern temperate forests. *Journal of Ecology* **94**:1011–1026.

Parker, G.G., Harmon, M.E., Lefsky, M.A. *et al.* 2004. Three-dimensional structure of an old-growth *Pseudotsuga-Tsuga* canopy and its implications for radiation balance, microclimate, and gas exchange. *Ecosystems* **7**:440–453.

Pastor, J. 2008. *Mathematical Ecology of Populations and Ecosystems*. Chichester: Wiley-Blackwell.

Pastor, J., Naiman, R.J., Dewey, B. & McInnes, P. 1988. Moose, microbes, and the boreal forest. *BioScience* **38**:770–777.

Penning de Vries, F.W.T. 1974. Substrate utilization and respiration in relation to growth and maintenance in higher plants. *Netherlands Journal of Agricultural Science* **22**:40–44.

Perakis, S.S. & Hedin, L.O. 2002. Nitrogen loss from unpolluted South American forests mainly via dissolved organic compounds. *Nature* **415**:416–419.

Perring, M.P., Hedin, L.O., Levin, S.A., McGroddy, M. & de Mazancourt, C. 2008. Increased plant growth from nitrogen addition should conserve phosphorus in terrestrial ecosystems. *Proceedings of the National Academy of Science of the United States of America* **105**:1971–1976.

Persson, T. (ed.) 1980. *Structure and Function of Northern Coniferous Forests*. Ecological Bulletins 32. Stockholm: Swedish Natural Science Research Council.

Persson, T. & Nilsson, L.O. (eds) 2001. *Skogabyförsöket – Effekter av Långvarig Kväve- och Svaveltillförsel till Ekosystem (The Skogaby Experiment – Effects of Long-Term Nitrogen and Sulfur Additions to Ecosystems)*. Naturvårdsverket Rapport 5173, Stockholm. ISBN 90-620-5173-3.

Peterson, G., Allen, C.R. & Holling, C.S. 1998. Ecological resilience, biodiversity, and scale. *Ecosystems* **1**:6–18.

Pickett, S.T.A. and Cadenasso, M.I. 2002. The ecosystem as a multidimensional concept: meaning, model, and metaphor. *Ecosystems* **5**: 1–10.

Pickett, S.T.A. & White, P.S. 1985a. Patch dynamics: A synthesis. In Pickett, S.T.A. & White, P.S. (eds) *The Ecology of Natural Disturbances and Patch Dynamics*. Orlando, FL: Academic Press, 371–384.

Pickett, S.T.A. & White, P.S. 1985b. *The Ecology of Natural Disturbance and Patch Dynamics*. New York: Academic Press.

Poorter, H., van der Werf, A., Atkin, O.K. & Lambers, H. 1991. Respiratory energy requirements of roots vary with the potential growth rate of a plant species. *Physiologia Plantarum* **83**:469–475.

Powers, R.F., Adams, M.B., Joslin, J.D. & Fiske, J.N. 2005. Non-boreal forests of North America. In Andersson, F. (ed.) *Ecosystems of the World*, Vol. **6**, *Coniferous Forests*. Amsterdam: Elsevier, 221–292.

Prietzel, J., Kolb, E. & Rehfuss, K.E. 1997. Langzeituntersuchungen ehemals streugenutzter Kiefernökosysteme in der Oberpfalz: Veränderungen von bodenchemischen Eigenschaften und der Nährelementvorsorgung der Bestänts (Long-term study of formerly litter-raked Scots pine ecosystems in NE Bavaria: Recent changes in soil chemical properties and stand nutrition). *Fortwissenschaftliches Centralblatt* **116**:269–290.

Raffaelli, D.G. & Frid, C.L.J. (eds) 2010. *Ecosystem Ecology – A New Synthesis*. Cambridge: Cambridge University Press.

Raison, R.J., Khanna, P.K. & Woods, P.V. 1985. Transfer of elements to the atmosphere during low-intensity prescribed fires in three Australian subalpine eucalypt forests. *Canadian Journal of Forest Research* **15**:657–664.

Raison, R.J. & Myers, B.J. 1992. The biology of forest growth experiment. *Forest Ecology and Management* **52**:1–311.

Rastetter, E.B., McKane, R.B., Shaver, G.R. & Melillo, J.M. 1992. Changes in C storage by terrestrial ecosystems: How C-N interactions restrict responses to CO_2 and temperature. *Water, Air, and Soil Pollution* **64**:327–344.

Rastetter, E.B., Perakis, S.S., Shaver, G.R. & Ågren, G.I. 2005. Terrestrial C sequestration at elevated CO_2 and temperature: The role of dissolved organic N loss. *Ecological Applications* **15**:71–86.

Rastetter, E.B., Vitousek, P.M., Field, C. *et al.* 2001. Resource optimization and symbiotic N fixation. *Ecosystems* **4**:369–388.

Read, D., Beerling, D., Cannell, M. *et al.* 2001. Annex 2 Examples of management activities to maximise carbon sequestration; 2.2 'Carbon Forestry' – the direct role of forest management. In *The Role of Land Carbon Sinks in Mitigating Global Climate Change*. Policy Document 10/01. London: The Royal Society, 25–27.

Reeburgh, W.S. 1997. Figures summarizing the global cycles of biogeochemically important elements. *Bulletin of the Ecological Society of America* **78**:260–267.

Reich, P.B., Walters, M.B. & Ellsworth, D.S. 1997. From tropics to tundra: Global convergence in plant functioning. *Proceedings of the National Academy of Sciences of the United States of America* **94**:13730–13734.

Reichle, D.E. 1981. *Dynamic Properties of Forest Ecosystems*. International Biological Programme 23. Cambridge: Cambridge University Press.

Renberg, I., Bigler, C., Bindler, R. *et al.* 2009. Environmental history: A piece in the puzzle for establishing plans for environmental management. *Journal of Environmental Management* **90**:2794–2800.

Reynolds, J.F. 2001. Non-equilibrium systems. In Mooney, H.A. & Canadell, J. (eds) *The Earth System: Biological and Ecological Dimensions of Global Environment Change*, Vol. **2**, *Encyclopedia of Global Environmental Change*. New York: John Wiley & Sons, 446–450.

Romell, L.G. 1935. Ecological problems of the humus layer in the forest. *Cornell University Agricultural Experimental Station Memoirs* **37**:348–375.

Sala, O.E., Chapin, F.S., Armesto, J.J. *et al.* 2000. Biodiversity – global biodiversity scenarios for the year 2100. *Science* **287**:1770–1774.

Sanderson, J. & Harris, L.D. 2000. *Landscape Ecology: A Top-Down Approach*. Boca Raton, FL: Lewis Publishers.

Saugier, B., Roy, J. & Mooney, H.A. 2001. Estimations of global terrestrial productivity: Converging toward a single number? In Roy, J., Saugier, B. & Mooney, H.A. (eds) *Terrestrial Global Productivity*. San Diego, CA: Academic Press, 543–557.

SCEP 1970. *Man's Impact on the Global Environment. Study of Critical Environmental Problems*. Cambridge, MA: MIT Press.

Schimel, J.P. & Weintraub, M.N. 2003. The implications of exoenzyme activity on microbial carbon and nitrogen limitation in soil: A theoretical model. *Soil Biology & Biochemistry* **35**:549–563.

Schlesinger, W.H. 1997. *Biogeochemistry – Analysis of Global Change*. San Diego, CA: Academic Press.

Schröter, D., Wolters, V. & De Ruiter, P.C. 2003. C and N mineralisation in the decomposer food webs of a European forest transect. *Oikos* **102**:294–308.

Schulze, E.D. (ed.) 2000. *Carbon and Nitrogen Cycling in European Forest Ecosystems*. Ecological Studies 142. Heidelberg: Springer-Verlag.

Schütz, H.P., Schröder, P. & Rennenberg, H. 1991. The role of plants in regulating methane flux to the atmosphere. In Sharkey, T.D., Holland, E.A. & Mooney, H.A. (eds) *Trace Gas Emissions by Plants*. San Diego, CA: Academic Press, 29–63.

Scotese, C.R. 2001. *Atlas of Earth History, Vol.* **1**, *Paleogeography*. Arlington, TX: PALEOMAP Project.

Sears, P.B. 1956. The processes of environmental change by man. In Thomas, W.L. (ed.) *Man's Role in Changing the Face of the Earth*. Chicago, IL: University of Chicago Press, 471–484.

Seyferth, U. 1998. *Effects of soil temperature and moisture on carbon and nitrogen mineralisation in coniferous forest*. Licentiate thesis No. 1. Uppsala: Department of Ecology and Environmental Research, Swedish University of Agricultural Sciences.

Shugart, H. 2002. Forest gap models. In Mooney, H.A. & Canadell, J.G. (eds) *Encyclopedia of Global Environmental Change*. Chichester: John Wiley & Sons, 316–323.

Sjörs, H. 1967. *Nordisk växtgeografi (Nordic Plant Geography)*. Stockholm: Svenska bokförlaget.

Smith, D.H. 1946. *Storm damage in New England forests*. MS thesis. New Haven, CT: Yale University.

Smith, R.A. 1872. *Air and Rain*. London: Longmans Green.

SNV 2000. *Naturens Återhämtning från Försurning: Aktuell Kunskap och Framtidsscenarier* (*Recovery from Acidification in the Natural Environment. Present Knowledge and Future Scenarios*). Report 5034, Swedish Environmental Protection Agency. ISBN 91-620-5028-1.

SNV 2007. *Bara Naturlig Försurning* (*Only Natural Acidification*). Report 5766, Swedish Environmental Protection Agency. ISBN 978-91-620-5766-4.

Söderqvist, T. 1986. *The Ecologists – From Merry Naturalists to Saviours of the Nation. A Sociological Informed Narrative Survey of the Ecologization of Sweden 1895–1975*. Stockholm: Almqvist & Wiksell International.

Sollins, P., Greier, C.C., McCorison, F.M. *et al.* 1980. The internal element cycles of an old-growth Douglas fir ecosystem in W Oregon. *Ecological Monographs* **50**:261–285.

Solomon, E.P. & Berg, L.R. 1995. *World of Biology*. Philadelphia, PA: Saunders College Publishing.

Soussana, J.F. & Lüscher, A. 2007. Temperate grasslands and global atmospheric change: A review. *Grass and Forage Science* **62**:127–134.

Spiecker, H., Mielikäinen, K., Köhl, M. & Skovsgaard, J. (eds) 1996. *Growth Trends in European Forests. Studies from 12 Countries.* European Forest Institute Report 5. Heidelberg: Springer.

Staaf, H. & Tyler, G. (eds) 1995. *Effects of Acid Deposition and Tropospheric Ozone on Forests.* Ecological Bulletins 44. Copenhagen: John Wiley & Sons.

Stearns, F.S. 1949. Ninety years of change in a northern hardwood forest Wisconsin. *Ecology* **30**:350–358.

Stendahl, J. 2007. Delmål 2 Försurad skogsmark (Evaluation of environmental status and trends in forest soils). Appendix 2 in SNV 2007 *Bara naturlig försurning* (*Only Natural Acidification*). Report 5766, Swedish Environmental Protection Agency. ISBN 978-91-620-5766-4.

Stern, D.I. 2006. Reversal of the trend in global anthropogenic sulfur emissions. *Global Environmental Change* **16**:207–220.

Sterner, R.W. & Elser, J.J. 2002. *Ecological Stoichiometry – The Biology of Elements from Molecules to the Biosphere.* Princeton, NJ: Princeton University Press.

Still, C.J., Berry, J.A., Collatz, G.J. & DeFries, R.S. 2003. Global distribution of C3 and C4 vegetation: Carbon cycle implications. *Global Biogeochemical Cycles* **17**:1–14.

Ström, L. & Christensen, T.R. 2007. Below ground carbon turnover and greenhouse gas exchanges in a sub-arctic wetland. *Soil Biology & Biochemistry* **39**:1689–1698.

Sukachev, V.N. 1959. The correlation between the concepts of 'forest ecosystem' and 'forest biogeocoenosis' and their importance for the classification of forests. *Proceedings IX International Botanical Congress. Vol.* **II**. Toronto: University of Toronto Press, 387pp.

Swedish Statistical Yearbook of Forestry. 1995–2008. Jököping: Swedish Forest Agency.

Swift, M.J., Heal, O.W. & Anderson, J.M. 1979. *Decomposition in Terrestrial Ecosystems.* Oxford: Blackwell Scientific Publications.

Switzer, G.L. & Nelson, L.E. 1972. Nutrient accumulation and cycling in loblolly pine (*Pinus taeda* L.) plantation ecosystems: The first twenty years. *Proceedings of the Soil Science Society of America* **36**:143–147.

Tamm, C.O. 1989. Comparative and experimental approaches to the study of acid deposition effects on soils as substrate for forest growth. *Ambio* **18**:184–191.

Tamm, C.O., Aronsson, A., Popovic, B. & Flower-Ellis, J. 1999. *Optimum Nutrition and Nitrogen Saturation in Scots Pine Stands.* Studia Forestalia Suecica 206. Uppsala: Coronet Books.

Tamm, C.O. & Hallbäcken, L. 1988. Change in soil acidity in two forest areas with different acid deposition: 1920s to 1980s. *Ambio* **17**:56–61.

Tamm, C.O. & Popovic, B. 1995. Long-term field experiments simulating increased deposition of sulfur and nitrogen to forest plots. *Ecological Bulletins* **44**:301–321.

Tansley, A.G. 1935. The use and abuse of vegetational concepts and terms. *Ecology* **16**:70–97.

Tarnocai, C., Canadell, J.G., Schuur, A.G. *et al.* 2009. Soil organic carbon pools in the northern circumpolar permafrost region. *Global Biogeochemical Cycles* **23**:1–11.

Teeri, J.A. & Stowe, L.G. 1976. Climatic patterns and the distribution of grasses in North America. *Oecologia* **23**:1–12.

The Royal Society 2008. Ground-level ozone in the 21st century: future trends, impacts and policy implications. Science Policy Report 15/08.

Thornley, J.H.M. & Johnson, I.R. 1990. *Plant and Crop Modelling: A Mathematical Approach to Plant and Crop Physiological Modelling*. Oxford: Clarendon.

Tilman, D. 1999. The ecological consequences of changes in biodiversity: A search for general principles. *Ecology* **80**:1455–1474.

Trass, H. & Malmer, N. 1973. North European approaches to classification. In Whittaker, R.H. (ed.) *Ordination and Classification of Communities*. Handbook of Vegetation Science V. The Hague: Junk, 529–574.

Troeng, E. & Linder, S. 1982. Gas exchange in a 20-year-old stand of Scots pine I. Net photosynthesis of current and one-year-old shoots within and between seasons. *Physiologia Plantarum* **54**:7–14.

Troll, C. 1939. *Luftbildplan und ökologische Bodenforschung* (Aerial Photography and Ecological Studies of Earth). Berlin: Zeitschrift der Gesellschaft für Erdkunde, 241–297.

Turner, M.G. & Gardner, R.H. (eds) 1991. *Quantitative Methods in Landscape Ecology*. New York: Springer Verlag.

Tyler, G. 1987. Probable effects of soil acidification and nitrogen deposition on the floristic composition of oak (*Quecus robur* L.) forests. *Flora (Jena)* 179:170.

Uggla, E. 1957. En studie over bränningseffekten på ett tunt råhumustäcke (Effects of the fire on a thin layer of raw humus). *Sveriges skogsvårdsförbunds Tidskrift* **2**:155–170.

Uggla, E. 1958. Forest fire areas in Muddus National Park, Northern Sweden. *Acta Phytogeografica Suecica* **41**:1–116.

US Soil Taxonomy 1999. *A Basic System of Soil Classification for Making and Interpreting Soil Surveys*. 2nd edn. Soil Survey Staff United States Department of Agriculture Agriculture Handbook. Natural Resources Conservation Service No. 436.

Van Oene, H. & Ågren, G.I. 1995. Complexity versus simplicity in modelling acid deposition effects on forest growth. *Ecological Bulletins* **44**:352–362.

van Oijen, M., Ågren, G.I., Chertov, O. *et al.* 2008. Evaluation of past and future changes in European forest growth by means of four process-based models. In Kahle, H.P., Karjalainen, T., Schuck, A. *et al.* (eds) *Causes and Consequences of Forest Growth Trends in Europe – Results of the RECOGNITION Project*. European Forest Institute Research Report 21. Leiden: Brill, 183–199.

Vik, R. 1975. *International Biological Programme. Final Report of Scandinavian Countries*. Oslo: Scandinavian National Committees of the International Biological Programme.

Viro, P.J. 1952. On the determination of stoniness. *Communicationes Instituti Forestalis Fenniae* **40**:1–19.

Vitousek, P.M. 2004. *Nutrient Cycling and Limitation – Hawai'i as a Model System*. Princeton, NJ: Princeton University Press.

Vitousek, P.M., Walker, L.R., Whiteaker, L.D., Mueller-Dombois, D. & Matson, P.A. 1987. Biological invasion by *Myrica faya* alters ecosystem development in Hawaii. *Science* **238**:802–804.

Volterra, V. 1926. Variazioni e fluttuazioni del numero d'individui in specie animali conviventi (Variations and fluctuations of the number of individuals in animal species living together). *Memorie della Rendiconti dell' Accademia Nazionale dei Lincei* **2**:31–113.

von Liebig, J. 1840. *Die Chemie in der Anwendung auf Agrikultur und Physiologie. 7 Aufl (Chemistry in its Application to Agriculture and Physiology)*. Braunschweig: Friedrich Vieweg und Sohn Publ. Co.

Walker, T.W. & Syers, J.K. 1976. The fate of phosphorus during pedogenesis. *Geoderma* **15**:1–19.

Ward, E.J., Oren, R., Sigurdsson, B.D., Jarvis, P.G. & Linder, S. 2008. Fertilization effects on mean stomatal conductance are mediated through changes in the hydraulic attributes of mature Norway spruce trees. *Tree Physiology* **28**:579–596.

Weber, M.G. & Stocks, B.J. 1998. Forest fires and sustainability in the Boreal forests of Canada. *Ambio* **27**:545–550.

Weber, M.G. & van Cleve, K. 2005. The Boreal forests of North America. In Andersson, F. (ed.) *Ecosystems of the World*, Vol. **6**, *Coniferous Forests*. Amsterdam: Elsevier, 101–130.

Whittaker, R.H. 1975. *Communities and Ecosystems*. New York: Macmillan.

Williams, J., Prebble, R.E., Williams, W.T. & Hignett, C.T. 1983. The influence of texture, structure and clay mineralogy on the soil moisture characteristic. *Australian Journal of Soil Research* **21**:15–32.

WMO 2008. *WMO Greenhouse Gas Bulletin*, November 2008.

Wright, R.F. & Rasmussen, L. (eds) 1998. The whole ecosystem experiments of the NITREX and EXMAN projects. *Forest Ecology and Management* **101**:1–364.

Xu, X., Tian, H. & Hui, D. 2008. Convergence in the relationship of CO_2 and N_2O exchanges between soil and atmosphere within terrestrial ecosystems. *Global Change Biology* **14**:1651–1660.

Index